Substance Abuse Intervention, Prevention, Rehabilitation, and Systems Change Strategies

EMPOWERING THE POWERLESS
Alex Gitterman, Series Editor

Empowering the Powerless: A Social Work Series
Alex Gitterman, Series Editor

The Empowerment Tradition in American Social Work: A History
Barbara Levy Simon

Organizing for Power and Empowerment
Jacqueline B. Mondros and Scott W. Wilson

Empowering Women of Color
Lorraine M. Gutiérrez and Edith A. Lewis

Lesbians, Gays, and the Empowerment Perspective
Carol T. Tully

This series provides perspectives on empowerment strategy in social work, which seeks to help clients draw on personal, interpersonal, and political power to enable them to gain greater control over their environments and attain their aspirations.

Substance Abuse Intervention, Prevention, Rehabilitation, and Systems Change Strategies

Helping Individuals, Families, and Groups to Empower Themselves

Edith M. Freeman

COLUMBIA UNIVERSITY PRESS   NEW YORK

COLUMBIA UNIVERSITY PRESS
Publishers Since 1893
New York, Chichester, West Sussex

Library of Congress Cataloging-in-Publication Data
Freeman, Edith M.
    Substance abuse intervention, prevention, rehabilitation, and systems change
strategies : helping individuals, families, and groups to empower themselves /
Edith M. Freeman.
        p.   cm. — (Empowering the powerless)
    Includes bibliographical references and index.
    ISBN 0–231–10236–4 (cloth)
    1. Substance abuse—Treatment. 2. Substance abuse—Patients—Family
relationships. 3. Family psychotherapy. I. Title. II. Series.
RC564 .F75 2001
616.86—dc21   00–064362

Casebound editions of Columbia University Press books
are printed on permanent and durable acid-free paper.
Printed in the United States of America

c   10 9 8 7 6 5 4 3 2 1

Knowledge is power.

—Anonymous

Contents

Series Editor's Note

Social workers in most fields of practice deal with people suffering from substance abuse addictions and/or with people who suffer because a loved one is addicted. Substance abuse drains individual, familial, and social networks and community resources. In child welfare settings, workers daily witness the association between the abuse of alcohol and drugs and the abuse and neglect of children. In family agencies, workers experience the explosive consequences of alcohol and drugs on intimate partner abuse and the deterioration of family life. In mental health agencies, workers encounter the increasingly common phenomenon of dual diagnoses. Substance abuse further degrades mental functioning and is frequently a trigger for hospitalization. In the health care field, workers observe addiction's deleterious effect on the immune system and vital organs and consequent life stressors. In the world of work, employee assistance counselors help addicted persons hold on to their jobs and spare them and their families the destructive consequences of unemployment. In school systems, social workers develop alcohol and drug prevention programs and help youngsters deal with substance experimentation and abuse. Finally, in communities, workers struggle to deal with the devastation caused by drugs.

Professor Freeman makes an important and distinct contribution to the literature on this subject. She integrates individual and social perspectives and engages the complexity of substance abuse and addiction. Specifically, she links alcohol and drug abuse to personal, interpersonal, and environmental factors and emphasizes interventions at all these levels. She bridges individual, family, and group services; community practice; administration; and policy practice. For example, Professor Freeman effectively explores how policy, funding, and service delivery systems affect delivery of direct services and simultaneously illustrates with case, community, and organizational practice examples how these systems can be influenced. Providing consumers with the opportunity to empower themselves is at the core of her practice framework. Professor Freeman instructs us on how to collaborate with clients along the continuum of care (intervention, prevention, and rehabilitation), using various modalities (individual, family, group, community) and phases of service delivery.

I present this fifth book in the "Empowering the Powerless" series published by Columbia University Press, *Substance Abuse Intervention, Prevention, Rehabilitation, and Systems Change Strategies: Helping Individuals, Families, and Groups to Empower Themselves,* with special pride. Professor Freeman's comprehensive review of the empowerment literature and substance abuse research makes a powerful contribution to our understanding of both substance abuse and related social work practice.

Alex Gitterman

Foreword

Concepts of empowerment have been present within our field for over a century, but it was not until the last third of the twentieth century that we made efforts to develop empowerment as a form of practice. In the first volume of this series, Simon (1994) made a significant contribution by identifying how "the empowerment tradition" has been a consistent theme within the social work profession since its inception over a century ago. She distinguished the empowerment tradition from paternalistic traditions by a focus on themes of self-determination, social justice, and methods that enhance the ability of individuals, families, groups, and communities to act on their own behalf. The empowerment tradition was at the roots of much of the work conducted by settlement house workers, by social group workers, and by radical and other progressive social workers.

Despite this tradition and history, the use of the term "empowerment" to refer to specific methods and processes in social work was not widespread until the late 1960s, when social workers involved with communities of color began developing theories and methods specific to empowerment practice. Since the publication of Barbara Solomon's book, *Black Empowerment*, in 1976 the concept of empowerment has been the focus of an increasing amount of social work literature. For example, prior to 1978, *Social Work Research and Abstracts* listed no articles that had been published on the topic. Currently there are more than 300, the majority of which have been published in the past decade.

The development of empowerment theory and practice in social work is inextricably connected to the development of ethnically sensitive and culturally competent services. Early works on empowerment by Solomon (1976), Gallegos (1982), Pinderhughes (1983), Leigh (1985), and others focused specifically on the experience of people of color. Although we have now moved on to applications to many other populations (Gutiérrez, Parsons, and Cox 1997), the central concepts and methods remain rooted in the experiences of people of color.

Early work on empowerment focused on the significance of power dynamics when understanding and working with communities of color. The authors emphasized the identification and delineation of direct and indirect power blocks in assessment and practice, self-knowledge regarding power dynamics and one's own social location, the use of ethnographic interviewing methods to comprehend the experiences of those who are culturally different, collaboration with natural helping networks, and engaging communities in confronting structures of inequality (Gallegos 1982; Leigh 1985; Pinderhughes 1983; Solomon 1976).

Empowerment is now understood as a multidimensional construct that can refer to both a goal and a process. In our recent book in this series, Edith Lewis and I (1999) identify what we consider to be the building blocks of empowerment—consciousness, confidence, and connection—that are critical to the process. Many in our field are contributing to our understanding of empowerment and how social workers can work toward social justice. This growing body of knowledge can lead to more effective multicultural practice.

It is in this spirit that Freeman's book makes a substantial contribution to our understanding of empowerment and of the different ways we can approach issues of substance abuse. The problem of substance abuse continues to grow in our society, with a significant impact on the problems and issues that concern social workers (Levine and Perkins 1997). Substance abuse is deeply connected to problems of un- and underemployment, family and community violence, personal and property crime, and poor health and mortality. Developing strategies to effectively prevent and treat substance abuse would enhance our ability to improve conditions for our most vulnerable populations.

This book challenges us to transform our thinking about substance abuse and to move beyond our existing focus on individual deficits. Instead, it proposes that we look at how interlocking systems in our society contribute to substance abuse problems and how to develop interventions that effect multiple levels of change. Indeed, Freeman asks us to analyze the language we use in our "war on drugs" to understand how that metaphor predisposes us to focus on changing individual behavior without looking at it in its bio-psycho-social context. In each chapter, she takes a close and careful look at how substance abuse issues can be addressed at each level and type of practice with an empowering and strengths-based approach.

In addition to its substantial contribution to practice literature, this book also advances our understanding of empowerment. Freeman begins with a useful and comprehensive review of the current work on empowerment in social work and related fields. She does a masterful job of integrating different perspectives and theories into one that is directly relevant to substance abuse. This discussion is grounded in current results from research on empowerment methods. However, her greatest contribution is the original research upon which the book is based. Freeman informs her discussions with original qualitative research that looked at substance abuse programs and program participants in depth. The results inform our understanding of empowerment and support the practice model that she presents throughout the book.

Thus this book makes a fine contribution to this series. The intention of the series editor, Alex Gitterman, has been to advance our knowledge of empowerment while exploring its application to different problems or populations. Through Edith Freeman's knowledge of empowerment, her original research, and her application to practice, this volume has much to offer to practitioners and scholars alike.

Lorraine Gutiérrez
University of Michigan

References

Gallegos, J. 1982. The ethnic competence model for social work education. In B. White, ed., *Color in a White Society*, 1–9. Silver Spring, MD: NASW.

Gutiérrez, L. and E. Lewis. 1999. *Empowering Women of Color*. New York: Columbia University Press.

Gutiérrez, L., R. Parsons, and E. Cox. 1997. *Empowerment in Social Work Practice: A Sourcebook*. Pacific Grove, CA: Brooks/Cole.

Leigh, J. 1985. Primary prevention approaches. In S. Grey, A. Hartman, and E. Saalberg, eds., *Empowering the Black Family: A Round Table Discussion*. Ann Arbor: National Child Welfare Training Center.

Levine, M. and D. Perkins. 1997. *Principles of Community Psychology*. New York: Oxford University Press.

Pinderhughes, E. 1983. Empowerment for our clients and for ourselves. *Social Case-work* 64:331–38.

Simon, B. 1994. *The Empowerment Tradition in American Social Work: A History.* New York: Columbia University Press.

Solomon, B. 1976. *Black Empowerment.* New York: Columbia University Press.

Preface and Acknowledgments

It is true that what is personal is political, and what is political is also personal (Davis and Hagen 1995). Therefore, to attempt to address substance abuse prevention and rehabilitation only at the personal and interpersonal level is to perpetuate a trend toward victim blaming. Solomon (1987) reminds us that "practice models that rely heavily on intrapsychic explanations for clients' problems in functioning" have not been effective (79). Therefore, rather than using a traditional clinical focus, this text attempts to connect direct service, community, administration, and policy practice in the substance abuse field. This broad, integrated approach is consistent with social work values and the ecological perspective as well as empowerment practice. An underlying assumption of empowerment practice is that clients' and communities' problems in living, their substance abuse and addiction problems, and therefore, the resolution of those problems are justifiably linked to personal, interpersonal, *and* environmental factors. Conflicting explanations for rehab failures (clients' recidivism and drop-out rates) and the ineffectiveness of community prevention efforts have recently led practitioners and researchers to begin to apply power concepts to substance abuse problems.

Consequently, this book clarifies how important aspects of the larger sociopolitical environment, the community, and service programs themselves influence clients' opportunities for empowerment and the quality of intervention, prevention, and rehabilitation services. The sociopolitical environment includes norms, values, policies, and practices that affect both the supply and the demand sides of this field in terms of funding priorities and mandates. Pathology-focused definitions of substance abuse problems tend to transform people into their problems (Chapin 1994), whereas strengths-focused policies and regulations support empowerment practice to the benefit of clients, programs, communities, and society as a whole. The book addresses how clients' and communities' strengths and needs influence the implementation of empowerment practice as well.

A critical contribution of this book is its discussions about the definition, operationalization, study, and evaluation of empowerment practice from the perspectives of consumers, family members and other significant individuals, staff, administrators, evaluators, and policy makers. Additional contributions include the integration of theory with practical analyses of case, organizational, and community examples. Clear analyses of the research literature on empowerment and substance abuse and the author's recent empowerment research are integrated throughout the book. The research literature is summarized in the epilogue chapter, along with the implications of that research for the future of empowerment practice. Assessment and evaluation tools focused on clients' situations and on organizations encourage the type of collaboration with clients that is consistent with empowerment practice. Tables and figures are used to demonstrate the process and outcomes of empowerment practice and specific strategies for staff *and* clients to use in achieving those outcomes. In this manner, the book demonstrates how helping clients to develop their knowledge, skills, and self-efficacy exemplifies the proverb that "Knowledge is power."

This book is designed for graduate students in social work, psychology, addictions counseling, nursing, human resources, and psychiatry based on the prevalence of substance abuse problems. It may be appropriate for interdisciplinary courses related to community development, policy, health care, and substance abuse practice. Practitioners, administrators, consultants, policy analysts, program evaluators, and researchers, as well as program designers in those fields, should also find it useful.

When I began writing this book, I thought my voice would predominate, following a typical approach to writing about practice perspectives. Instead, as I analyzed my research data, the voices of the individuals I had studied in various programs demanded to be heard, in their own words. Those people included staff members and administrators who were struggling to implement empowerment approaches and to set aside personal biases. The voices of consumers also emerged as they shared their addiction and recovery stories, sometimes during their first days in rehab and recovery or as they completed a program. Most of these clients were extremely honest about the struggles and questions they were experiencing: "Why am I here? What happens if I relapse? How can anyone else accept and care about me—I don't accept myself?" Staff too had doubts, related to their abilities to use empowerment strategies, often commenting that "this is hard work." I hope I have recorded their questions, concerns, and experiences accurately, as they voiced them, and most of all their strengths and incredible courage. I thank them for trusting me and sharing their personal struggles.

I am grateful to Rosella Cox and Marla Sloop, who typed parts of this manuscript. Their support and skills have been invaluable. I am thankful also for Alex Gitterman's review of the manuscript and extremely helpful suggestions for revisions, as editor of the Columbia University Press empowerment series.

Finally, I am most thankful for my family and personal support system's faith in me and my work: Herb, David F., Meredith, Karen, Gloria, Marvin, David L., Theo, Olivia, and Sadye.

Substance Abuse Intervention, Prevention, Rehabilitation, and Systems Change Strategies

Part 1

Foundations of Empowerment Principles and Practice in Substance Abuse Services

This section introduces the reader to the book's purpose and conceptual framework related to empowerment and substance abuse services. Chapter 1 addresses the book's purpose by explaining how various authors have struggled to define, study, and apply concepts of empowerment. In essence, this chapter captures the complexity and richness of social work practice focused on helping consumers to empower themselves. The discussion clarifies how empowerment has become an overused and poorly defined concept. Consequently, the author's analysis of various rubrics for defining empowerment and use of a social work framework for highlighting basic components of an acceptable definition should be beneficial to readers. Similarly, a brief description of this author's research and findings, the basis for many of the following chapters, adds to what is known about empowerment-related theories and their application to the service delivery and recovery process at the personal, interpersonal, and political levels. Substance abuse program factors that have been found to enhance clients' empowerment experiences and outcomes at all three levels are clarified, based on the research literature and on the author's recent empowerment research.

Chapter 2 further develops the book's conceptual framework by applying, for the first time, empowerment and narrative concepts to the development of substance abuse and addiction problems. This discussion identifies a combination of individual, interpersonal, and environmental influences on that process, ranging from clients' attitudes and values to relationship problems and unemployment to the availability of substances and presence of many social, economic, and political barriers to self- and collective sufficiency. An analysis of power issues related to addiction development includes the effects of staff and programmatic responses as well as social work's historical philosophical approaches to those issues. Basically, this chapter, and part 1 as a whole, clarifies how empowerment concepts help to explain the development and maintenance of individuals' substance abuse problems as well as their lifelong recovery. The implications of this perspective on substance abuse for empowerment practice and social work education are also presented.

1 Conceptual, Theoretical, and Research Issues Related to Empowerment Practice

> I am convinced . . . that the nature of . . . (empowerment)
> theory must be ecological.
> —J. Rappaport (1987:134)

The purpose of this practice text is twofold: to identify the components and process of empowerment practice in substance abuse services and to clarify important aspects of the complex multilevel environment outside a program's setting that influences client empowerment and service outcomes. Such an undertaking is fraught with problems, however, due to the tendency of helping professionals and researchers to overuse the concept of empowerment and not to clearly define it. Wasserman (1991) notes that, "Admittedly, it (empowerment) has compelling resonance; but like other catchy slogans, it may go out with the wind, unless we are willing to understand what we actually mean by the term" (235).

Clarifying what is meant by "empowerment" and its theoretical underpinnings may help to provide answers to some important questions: Is it possible to identify and observe an empowerment and/or disempowerment experience? Is what a professional identifies as empowerment consistent with what a client might identify? What effects does the environment or ecology have on whether and how empowerment occurs? Are there primary components that make up an empowerment approach, and if there are, how do they influence each other? And how does empowerment contribute to effective outcomes in substance abuse services—for example, in mandatory rehabilitation and in prevention programs focused on systemic change?

The field's inability to answer these and other key questions has limited effective practice in several ways. First, few components of effective empowerment practice have been documented. Service providers often fail to ask clients what they have learned from their addiction experiences or from prevention of addiction. Clients' undiscovered wisdom, resiliency, and strengths from those experiences could be applied effectively during rehab and prevention services, and then throughout the life span (Miller 1994). For instance, a seventy-two-year-old man was admitted to a rehab program in a large metropolitan area. He had been addicted to alcohol and heroin for fifty years. Staff in the program developed a comprehensive drug and social history, which indicated one failed attempt at recovery many years before and a referral to the current program from a minister. Staff failed to ask other key questions, however, such as how this client had survived fifty years of drug addiction and what factors (strengths and problems) had led to his current decision to enter rehab. Answers to these questions could potentially facilitate his initial commitment to rehab, his maintenance in recovery, his hope for change, and his self-empowerment.

Second, many programs do not give key actors, especially the clients, more active roles in service delivery and in assessing the outcomes of services. Thus, opportunities may be missed for helping clients to develop skills and self- or group efficacy. In one in-service training session, staff from a substance abuse prevention program decided to collaborate in developing criteria for distinguishing among low, moderate, and high-risk middle school youths. The trainer suggested youths currently in the program could be consulted about this issue and about effective prevention strategies. Staff insisted the idea of risk criteria was too complex for these clients, ignoring the contradiction between their conclusion and the program's goals of empowerment and self-development for youths.

A related limitation is the failure of service providers and policy makers to identify and address structural barriers to helping individuals stop abusing, selling, and importing drugs (Rappaport 1981). Instead, the main focus of some policies is on pathology and blaming individuals without also clarifying how their empowerment and disempowerment experiences may be rooted in both their immediate and larger environments (in the family, community, and larger social systems or social policy). Yeich and Levine (1992) state that these roots, the structural causes of problems, must be changed for real empowerment to take place.

As a consequence of these limitations, the addictions field has not been able to apply empowerment concepts to some of the most intractable problems of service delivery, including reducing the high rates of recidivism during and after rehab ends (Freeman 1993). Additional efforts are needed to increase the effectiveness of primary prevention with nonusers and secondary prevention with nonaddicted problem users by addressing the total environment (Chang 1993).

This chapter examines how well the conceptual literature on empowerment addresses the total ecological environment in defining and applying concepts to different populations. An analysis of the research literature on empowerment is included to highlight the process and outcomes of empowerment practice in substance abuse services, along with an analysis of my research findings in this area. These two sources are then used to develop a set of criteria and a conceptual framework for analyzing and understanding empowerment practice in substance abuse prevention, intervention, and rehabilitation from a number of theoretical perspectives.

Empowerment Definitions, Theories, and Concepts

The term "empowerment" has been defined in various ways in the conceptual literature, sometimes very narrowly and at other times more broadly to include different aspects of the ecological environment. A common aspect of the different definitions is the assumption that a person does not achieve empowerment for all time; rather, empowerment is a continuous process of growth and change throughout the life cycle. The definitions differ somewhat in whether they focus on empowerment as a characteristic of a unit or system, a process, a practice or research strategy, an outcome, or a combination of two or more of these elements. The definitions differ too in terms of their implicit or explicit theoretical assumptions.

Empowerment as a Characteristic or Quality of Systems

Some authors and researchers have defined empowerment as a quality related to a system or to a mechanism, structure, context, value, or philosophy of a system. An underlying assumption of this category of definitions is that empowerment is an existing precondition in a system or an opportunity that develops in a given situation for people to gain control over some aspect of their lives. Rappaport (1987), for example, indicates empowerment is a mechanism by which people, organizations, and communities gain mastery over their affairs. Similarly, Zimmerman (1991) notes that an empowering organization is one whose structure encourages participatory decision making and shared rather than centralized power. Yeich and Levine (1992) define an empowered group as one that characteristically exhibits group cohesion. Other authors define empowerment as a value, belief, or philosophy, emphasizing that people should have the power to influence their personal and social lives (Freire 1970; Freire and Macedo 1987; Wallerstein and Bernstein 1988). This definition implies that having such a value or belief in the power to change is a precondition for successfully acting on or altering one's environment.

Health promotion and wellness theories, among others, provide conceptual support for these definitions. A lack of control over one's life and disempowerment experiences are thought to be risk factors (pre-existing conditions) that can lead to physical disease and debilitating psychological conditions (Syme 1986). In comparison, gaining control over a life situation and experiencing empowerment (qualities of certain person-in-environment transactions) can serve as health promotion strategies (Wallerstein and Bernstein 1988). Other theories are also consistent with such definitions of empowerment. For instance, the knowledge is power theory assumes that power is an implicit quality of knowledge and that therefore, one gains power through developing common knowledge (about the connections between personal problems and the social structure) (Freire 1970). Related to this assumption, social conflict theory is based on the belief that forced changes in the structure or in the social, economic, and political context are necessary for oppressed people to gain power (Yeich and Levine 1992).

Empowerment as a Process

A second category of definitions conceptualizes empowerment as a process. Some of these definitions imply a unilevel process while others view it as multilevel. Even authors who define empowerment based on an individually focused analysis of problems assume there are effects at other levels. For instance, Zimmerman (1992) defines psychological empowerment as those intrapsychic, behavioral, and interactional components related to a person's efforts to control decision making that affects their life. While his definition of the psychological level is distinguished from other levels, Zimmerman notes that this process may be influenced by organizational and community empowerment; however, he does not address the environment more directly.

Interpersonal definitions of empowerment have also failed to address the environment adequately in terms of the process. Much of the organizational literature, for example, discusses how leaders can and should delegate power to subordinates and likens empowerment to team building as a process for improving organizational effectiveness (Auerbach and Wallerstein 1987; Farley 1987). Similarly, definitions of empowerment based on concepts of social support are limited. Israel (1985) cautions that some communities have been defined as empowered because they have improved their mutual-helping process. But many of these communities may still not have the power to impact environmental stressors that are controlled by the social structure outside the community.

Multilevel definitions of empowerment are more explicit about interactional and sociopolitical effects related to the environment. Wallerstein and Bernstein (1988) define the concept as "A social action process that promotes participation of people, organizations, and communities in gaining control over their lives in their community and larger society" (380). Yeich and Levine (1992) state that empowerment is a process for mobilizing individuals and groups in order to cause changes in society that give oppressed people more power over their lives. These authors emphasize that the target of change is the existing social structure rather than individuals' ways of coping with that structure.

The focus on empowerment as a multilevel process is based on social change, social influence, systems, and ecological theories. With social change and social influence theories, the emphasis is on group- and society-level power analyses to examine how economic dominance and unequal distribution of resources are creating barriers to the empowerment process (Brown and Tandon 1983). Systems and ecological theories require a similar analysis of larger systems and their social structure to determine who benefits from maintaining existing power disparities and what specific aspects of the system's process block avenues to empowerment. These theories emphasize the importance of examining multiple sources of empowerment and disempowerment in the ecological environment in order to understand these dynamic, interactional processes.

Empowerment as a Practice or Research Strategy

A number of authors have defined empowerment as a strategy in education, community development, and other fields, either as a method of service delivery or as a method for studying the empowerment process. Freire's (1970) seminal definition of empowerment involves the combined strategies of research (investigation of structural sources of problems), education (transfer of knowledge about political and advocacy strategies for addressing those sources), and social action (alleviating oppressive conditions in order to increase economic and political power). Wallerstein and Bernstein (1988) adapt and expand Freire's definition by developing specific ways to structure the problem, posing dialogue about key issues among the participants during the education phase. Their strategy validates and highlights common disempowerment experiences and "moves discussion from the personal to the social analysis and action level" (383).

More comprehensive definitions of empowerment as a practice strategy have been provided by helping professionals, including one by Solomon (1987): "A method by which helping professionals attempt to deal with the power blocks experienced by negatively valued individuals and families" (80). Gutiérrez (1990) defines empowerment as a strategy for increasing self-efficacy, developing group consciousness, reducing self-blame, and assuming personal responsibility. Gitterman's (1994) definition includes helpers in the target of change: "Empowerment practice is viewed as the process and outcome of social work practitioners, supervisors, and administrators helping clients and staff to increase their personal, interpersonal, and political power so that they can gain greater respective control and influence in their personal and professional lives" (personal correspondence 1994).

Other authors have developed comprehensive practical guidelines that help to define and clarify empowerment as a practice strategy (Lee 1994; Mattaini and Kirk 1991; Pinderhughes 1989; Gutiérrez 1990; Geetz 1983). For instance, Simon (1994) identifies nine guidelines for social work practice within an empowerment mode: 1) Shape programs in response to the expressed preferences and demonstrated needs of clients and community members; 2) Make certain that programs and services are maximally convenient for and accessible to one's clients and their communities; 3) Ask as much from one's clients as from oneself; 4) Call and build upon the strengths of clients and communities; 5) Devise and redevise interventions in response to the unique configuration of requests, issues, and needs that a client or client group presents. Resist becoming wedded to a favored intervention method; 8) Make leadership development a constant priority of practice and policy development; 7) Be patient, since empowerment takes substantial amounts of time and continuity of effort; 8) Take ongoing stock of social workers' own powerlessness and power at work; and 9) Use "local knowledge" to contribute to the general good (30). These definitions of empowerment as a practice strategy, including social justice issues, are consistent with the process definitions in the previous section because they focus on multilevel environmental factors that affect people's power (Lee 1994; Simon 1995).

Another set of interesting definitions are focused on empowerment as a research strategy or method. For instance, Yeich and Levine (1992) define participatory research as a strategy for involving oppressed people in the study of and solutions to social problems in order to empower them. This method is assumed to result in empowerment because it recognizes and supports the ordinary knowledge of people as valid and useful, in contrast to other research methods, which lead to the monopolization of knowledge by experts (the powerful few) (Brown and Tandon 1983). Rapp, Shera, and Kisthardt (1993) define empowerment research as that which amplifies "the voice of the consumer by attending to the context of research, the vantage point, the process of formulating research questions, the selection of interventions to be tested, the selection of outcomes and measures, and the dissemination of research results" (727).

Other definitions emphasize the building of partnerships in which community members work directly with researchers throughout the research and community action process. Consumer participation, rather than simple involvement, begins during the initial planning and conceptualization phase and continues through data collection, analysis, and interpretation and dissemination and application of results (Minkler and Roe 1993; Minkler 1994; Woodhouse and Livingood 1991; Turnbull and Friesen 1998). Finally, Yeich and Levine (1992) note that an empowerment research strategy is one that provides an examination and understanding of empowerment in action.

Conceptually, what Dunst et al. (1992) call promotion theories are most consistent with definitions of empowerment as a practice or research strategy. These theories have a mastery and optimization orientation that supports capacity building, self-sufficiency, resiliency, strengths, proactive rather than reactive coping patterns by individuals and groups, and social action and systems change. Although authors such as Dunst et al. (1992) and Cowen (1985) distinguish between promotion and paternalistic theories in terms of empowerment, they have not identified the former theories more specifically.

Empowerment as an Outcome

Definitions of empowerment as an outcome focus on various knowledge areas and skills that are strengthened as a result of enabling opportunities. For instance, Bandura (1986) refers to empowerment as an array of observable behavioral abilities that lead to a sense of control. Many authors have identified some of these abilities and qualities in their definitions: a sense of efficacy, a sense of community, flexibility, critical awareness, collective action and responsibility, initiation of network resource exchanges, knowledge about and skills in conducting power analyses, an enhanced cultural/ethnic identity, and competence (Dunst, Trivette, Gordon, and Pletcher 1989; Gutiérrez 1990; Lewis and Ford 1991; Simon 1995; Thomas and Velthouse 1990; Whitmore and Kerans 1988; Yeich and Levine 1992).

In spite of the range of empowerment outcomes that has been identified, the literature in this area lacks specificity in describing or operationalizing behaviors that indicate empowerment. For example, many authors fail to define what they mean by "competence," "mastery," and "social action skills." Some authors have concluded that this gap is not surprising since manifestation of empowerment outcomes varies across different people and different social contexts as well as in the same person over time (Dunst et al. 1992; Rappaport 1984; Zimmerman 1990).

Social learning, group, and social support theories provide a conceptual basis for definitions of empowerment as an outcome. Social learning theory explains how environmental stimuli help individuals to gain control over situations and develop observable behaviors and skills that are evidence of empowerment outcomes (Bandura 1986). Group and social support theories assume that group process can encourage the group consciousness raising and cohesion that lead to collective empowerment (Freeman, Logan, and Gowdy 1992) and that mutual help activities and a sense of community are indicators of empowered social support networks (Germain and Gitterman 1996; Lewis and Ford 1991).

Summary of Efforts to Define Empowerment

What can be concluded from this analysis of empowerment definitions and theory? First, very little of the literature addresses addiction problems or service delivery in that area. The substance abuse field has traditionally used encounter and confrontational practice approaches and cognitively oriented prevention approaches. This emphasis on deficit models and education may have delayed exploration of more consumer-oriented, empowerment approaches. Miller (1994) believes that many authors mistakenly assume these newer approaches might reinforce the denial and resistance that substance abusers typically exhibit before and during early phases of rehabilitation and prevention.

What then is the focus of this empowerment literature? Most of it addresses the fields of public education, health education, community development, health care and allied health professions, family and child welfare, mental health, and action or stakeholder research. Many different vulnerable populations have been discussed, including women, the aged, the poor, people of color, children and youths, those with chronic or acute health problems, and those with disabilities (e.g., chronic mental illness).

There is much disagreement in the literature about how empowerment should be defined and conceptualized. Some of the definitions conflict by focusing only on personal aspects of empowerment rather than multiple factors, including the environment. Other conflicts seem to result from authors emphasizing one part of the empowerment paradigm, such as outcomes, rather than viewing the construct more holistically. Recently, some authors have taken a more integrated perspective, making it possible to combine key factors from the different definitions in the previous section (Zimmerman 1990; Rappaport and Hess 1984). For example, Dunst, Trivette, and LaPointe (1992) define empowerment in terms of six interrelated aspects: philosophy, paradigm, process, partnership, performance, and perception.

With this type of integrated approach, empowerment can be defined as a lifelong, dynamic process that involves certain power-sharing qualities of systems, practice or research strategies, beliefs and values, and outcomes that provide opportunities for individual or collective control over personal, interpersonal, and political aspects of life situations (Freeman 1995). Such a definition focuses simultaneously on process, conditions or strategies that influence the process, beliefs about the process, collaborative relationships and collective action, and the outcomes or observable indicators of empowerment or disempowerment.

Theoretically, more integrated approaches to the concept can provide "a unified framework for defining the meaning and key elements of empowerment" (Dunst et al. 1992:111), including developmental, systems, organizational, community development, and cross-cultural theories. However, developing more clarity and consensus about the definition of empowerment and some of its theoretical implications is only one step in the right direction. Equally important is researchers' documentation of individual empowerment and disempowerment experiences under empirical conditions, along with factors that influence those events.

Empowerment and Disempowerment Research

Overview of Current Research

The discussion in the previous section helped to clarify what "empowerment" means theoretically and conceptually (how it is defined), while the discussion in this section describes how the concept has been operationalized in research (how it works under certain empirical conditions). A combination of interacting factors is assumed to influence empowerment and disempowerment experiences in service delivery. Some factors are related to the individual (previous mastery experiences), interpersonal relationships or systems (availability of recovering or abstinent social support networks), and social systems (policies that support community self-sufficiency or program factors that require active consumer involvement).

Research is beginning to document program factors in substance abuse services that can influence empowerment processes and outcomes, although such information is still very sparse at this time. Toubouron and Hamilton (1993) define program factors as any aspects of treatment that can be manipulated or readily altered by a program. Some examples, as documented by the research literature, are summarized across various types of programs in table 1.1. This table also contains aspects of intrapersonal, interpersonal, and social systems that may either influence empowerment or disempowerment experiences and/or be changed by these processes.

Gaps and Limitations in This Research

Most of the literature on empowerment practice documents only a few of the program factors included in table 1.1. Some factors, such as the planning and implementation of social action strategies, use of mutual support activities, opportunities to link personal problems with community/societal conditions, and the validation of common knowledge were frequently identified across the different studies. Other studies, however, clarified unique factors that were population-specific in terms of clients' ages and stages of development, ethnicity and life circumstances, or gender, and the longevity or severity of their substance abuse problems. Overall, although the focus of research on empowerment practice with different populations includes substance abuse prevention and rehab services, most research addresses rehabilitation services and recovery. (For a more detailed, in-depth discussion of research on empowerment practice with specific population groups, see the epilogue, which summarizes that information in relation to future empowerment practice).

A Systemic Study of Empowerment Practice

Considering the limitations and gaps identified in the previous discussion of research on empowerment practice, I conducted a four-component study of substance abuse services between 1994 and 1997 focused on multiple systems that affect service delivery. The perspectives of clients and staff at different system levels were the central focus of this research since, as documented by current and past literature, their voices have been largely ignored by researchers, policy makers, and program developers in exploring empowerment practice. Their ordinary knowledge (Freire 1983) and "lived experiences" (Gulati and Guest 1990) related to abstinence or nonproblem use, problem use, and addiction and recovery are essential for operationalizing an empowerment paradigm and for validating their wisdom and strengths. Qualitative research seemed the most appropriate method for focusing on these key actors because of its attention to the unique perspectives and meanings people derive from their experiences (Jacob 1988).

This qualitative study included the following research components, each of which focused on one of four interrelated systems: 1) rehabilitation and prevention programs across the country that use empowerment methods and approaches; 2) the immediate communities in which these programs are located and the impact of their strengths, barriers, and other factors on the programs' empowerment approaches; 3) state policy and organizational variables relevant to empowerment practice in the identified programs; and 4) federal agencies' policy and funding patterns for substance abuse services

TABLE 1.1 Examples of Program Factors Related to Effective Empowerment Practice in Substance Abuse Services in the Literature
(T = treatment program; P = prevention program)

| | Major Themes | | |
Focus	Professional Services	Peer-Led Services	Professional/Client Collaboration
Personal (individual clients)	(T) Groups for youths are focused on ethnic and age-related issues regarding addiction and recovery (Freeman 1990) (T) Individualized treatment and teaching skills of daily living are provided to homeless dually diagnosed clients and perinatal women (Blankertz and Cnaan 1994; Galanter et al. 1993)	(P) Older peer leaders are reinforced and empowered by conducting drug abuse prevention activities with younger students (Porter et al. 1986)	(P) Youth participants provide feedback/help revise alcohol and drug programs and policies regularly (Wallerstein and Bernstein 1988) (T) Clients and staff determine treatment plan (initial and ongoing) (Toumbouron and Hamilton 1993)
Interpersonal (peers, family members, social networks, co-workers)	(T) Reentry phase involves client preparation for assuming social roles without drugs (Toumbouron and Hamilton 1993) (P) Older Hispanic youths develop critical consciousness and knowledge of common powerlessness, and plan for social action to change university structure (Gutiérrez and Ortega 1991)	(T) Peer-led orientation, counseling, and twelve-step groups are used to counter powerlessness in homeless dually diagnosed clients (Galanter et al. 1993) (T) Results from clients' analyzing mental health research literature presented to peers in regular group meetings (Pratt and Gill 1990)	(T) Clients and staff participate in research study group to increase mental health knowledge and in program evaluation committee to revise service and evaluation strategies (Pratt and Gill 1990)

	(T) Social supports (family members or friends) used to help addicted women seek and continue treatment (Robinson 1984)	(P) Teens use information from their interviews of adults in drug treatment and jails to design and conduct education sessions with younger peers (Malekoff 1994)	(P) Youth research and leadership skill development are the main focus of drug policy changes in a youth/social workers collaborative social action program (personal influence and program planning) (Malekoff 1994)
Political (service program, community, social systems, public policy)	(P) Focus on changing community norms through citizen participation in community action program targeting multiple indicators of social disorder, including drug abuse (Perkins et al. 1990)	(P) Peer-led social action activities to reduce drug abuse/trafficking and powerlessness (drug hotlines, crime stoppers, neighborhood watch projects) (Rosenbaum et al. 1989) (P) Youths are taught media and policy analysis and dissemination skills that they apply in drug and alcohol town campaigns to reduce consumption/availability (policy impact) (Wallerstein and Bernstein 1988) (P) Action research and political action to change or transfer power involving community members and professionals (Yeich and Levine 1992)	(T) A percentage of program graduates serves on governing board to make and revise policy (Gulati and Guest 1990) (P) Community members develop and conduct multiple political action strategies re drugs (mobile citizen patrols, police reports, legislative lobbying to change policies/ community disorder) (Lurgio and Davis 1992) (P) Community members are involved in solution-focused needs assessments and program development to increase their ownership of process and reduce alcohol consumption by youths (Wheeler 1992)

that can influence empowerment practice. Table 1.2 illustrates these four components of the research and the types of substance abuse programs that were included in the study.

Research Methodology

The program, community, state, and national phases of this ethnographic qualitative study overlapped, with the initial work focused on the selected programs and their surrounding community and state environments. In this chapter, however, only the methodology and some of the findings related to the identified service programs are reported. The methodology and findings for the other three research components are included in chapters 3–5 on the general multisystem empowerment process and in chapters 13–16 on specific empowerment programs in the sample and the effects of the multi-level system on those programs. This discussion of methodology includes the research questions, the subjects and settings, the study design, research protocols and data collection, and the data analysis.

The Research Questions.   A set of questions was developed to guide phases 1–3 of the study and then modified as needed to be consistent with the population/type of program under study at a given time. The questions helped to identify individuals and organizations that should be included because of their unique knowledge and perspectives about the multiple systems under study.

The common generic questions were as follows:

1. What is the typical process of rehab and prevention service delivery in the identified program, and what criteria are used for program decisions (e.g., for deciding what services are provided to clients, during what phases of helping, and consisting of what particular components)?
2. Which conditions and services (including empowerment experiences) in each program and within the surrounding community are identified by clients and staff as most important for effective recovery and prevention, and what is the basis for their identifications?
3. How are successful program outcomes defined by clients and staff

TABLE 1.2 Research on Substance Abuse Empowerment Programs

Organizational Sample (N = 17)	Organizational Subsample (N = 6)
Research Design: prospective/retrospective, qualitative, time series, organizational	*New Alternatives:* serves ethnically diverse population of adolescents from 12 to 19 years of age, residential services; period of service from 9 to 18 months; uses positive peer culture approach, peer mentors, and clients as part of the treatment team (chapter 13)
Sampling Strategy: reputational convenience sample, key informant snowball strategy	*Restore and Repair:* serves women of color primarily along with white clients, 18 to 45 years of age, day treatment; services range from 18 to 24 months; provides gender-specific rehab services for the clients and their infants and children (chapter 14)
The Sample: 12 rehabilitation and 5 prevention programs (rehab programs: 8 coed and 4 women-only; 9 adult and 3 adolescent)	*Recovery Works:* serves dually diagnosed homeless adults (mentally ill substance abusers) from 18 to 65 years of age, integrated day treatment and outpatient services; range from 6 months to 2 years; emphasis on client-driven rehab services for this ethnically diverse client population (chapter 15)
Research Focus (relevant interrelated systems): federal agencies' policy and funding patterns; state organizational and policy variables; community context of the programs; substance abuse rehabilitation and prevention programs	*Dareisa:* serves African American adults primarily, using an Africentric approach with clients from 18 to 75 years of age; includes cultural healing, recovery, social advocacy, and residential services ranging from 18 to 24 months (chapter 16)
Research Procedures and Protocols: participant observation (observation data collection form); focus groups: planning and member checking (focus group topic guide); ethnographic interviews: staff and clients (semistructured interview guide); narrative inquiry (narrative sections: interview guide); review of key documents (document data collection form); stakeholder surveys (client/staff survey instruments)	*Better Life:* serves ethnically diverse group of adults; traditional rehab services include short-term residential and outpatient components (14 to 28 days) and a one-year aftercare phase
	Grassroots: serves middle and high school youths and their families; community-centered prevention approach; parent and youth peers facilitate the eight-session program, including policy and systems change components

based on the client group's special needs (e.g., gender-oriented needs), and what is the rationale for their definitions?

4. In what ways are clients involved actively in the services provided, and what are their conclusions about these experiences? What are the effects of their involvement on how they view themselves, the services provided, and their nonuse or recovery?

5. How do clients who complete programs successfully differ in their backgrounds and other characteristics from those who drop out prior to program completion?

6. To what extent are the values, philosophies, and conceptual frameworks of key actors in national and state substance abuse funding agencies, community leadership roles, and in-service programs consistent with an empowerment approach?

7. How do the values, philosophies, and conceptual frameworks of these key actors influence empowerment practice and other important service aspects in the study programs?

The Subjects and Settings.   A key informant, snowball strategy was used to develop a reputational sample of programs engaged in empowerment practice (Gutiérrez et al. 1995). I used a comprehensive literature review and contacts at national, state, and local levels to identify potential key informants, then contacted those individuals to identify examples of programs that were using empowerment approaches. Using data from the key informants, I compiled a list of thirty programs to be contacted for possible inclusion in the sample. The list was reduced to seventeen based on organizational and conceptual issues identified through telephone contacts (e.g., a program was in a financial crisis and did not want to participate in the study or defined itself in terms of a conflicting paradigm). Among the seventeen remaining programs, six were identified as target programs whose clients represented certain special populations or the general population of people needing services. (Information obtained from all seventeen programs is included in some of the general discussions about empowerment practice in other sections of the book.)

Subjects were included in each of the six client samples based on convenience sampling; that is, each sample included from 50 to 100 percent of the clients being served by the identified programs at the time of the study. Clients were excluded due to absence, failure to volunteer to participate in the study, redundant themes and patterns showing in the study (indicating that a sufficient number of clients had been sampled in a particular treatment phase), or time limitations that dictated only a certain number could be interviewed.

Table 1.2 summarizes information about the subjects and settings: the population groups served by each of the six programs and the types of programs included in the study. The treatment programs included one primarily for women of color and their drug-involved infants and children; a dual diagnosis program for an ethnically diverse group of chemically addicted, homeless, mentally ill adults; an adolescent program for an ethnically diverse population; a culturally specific program for African American adult males and females; and a traditional mainstream program serving an ethnically diverse group of adults. A community-centered, multicultural prevention program that serves youths, families, and individuals was also included in the subsample. As can be seen from this table, the age range across the samples was from thirteen to seventy-five years; participants included males and females with one exception (the women's perinatal program); participants tended to be ethnically diverse except in the womens' and culturally specific programs; participants were primarily poor but also included some middle-income clients; and geographically they represented the East Coast, West Coast, South, and Midwest areas of the country. More detailed information about each sample and setting can be found in chapters 13–16, each of which is focused on one of the four programs.

The Study Design.   This research involved the use of a combined retrospective and prospective time series design. Some retrospective data were collected, for example, information about how clients no longer in a program responded to treatment, experiences of current clients that influenced them to seek out and remain in treatment, and the sources of individual and collective power drawn upon by community residents to cope with or change conditions related to drug abuse and other problems. Current or prospective data were also collected, including clients' and community members' current empowerment and disempowerment experiences. The research period for each program varied from one to three weeks, with the research on the women's program also including a secondary, more in-depth substudy over several months.

Research Protocols and Data Collection Procedures.   Table 1.2 includes the research protocols that were developed for the program component of the research, as well as for the other three components: individual client interview guides and focus group guides; a critical incident direct observation form for treatment sessions, staffings, twelve-step sessions, and other meetings; and various document coding forms for analyzing the programs' written policy and procedures manuals. The fifty-item client and forty-item staff interview guides were organized into a semistructured format and included items about factors that influence treatment and prevention effectiveness, clients' and community members' involvement in the service process, and detailed information about clients' empowerment and disempowerment experiences related to alcohol/drug use or nonuse and addiction/recovery.

Therefore, a combination of data collection procedures was utilized in each setting, including: relevant written treatment or prevention policy, procedures, and program description materials; selected closed records for the past year representing each program's successful and unsuccessful cases/ experiences; direct observation of client treatment/prevention sessions and other key events; and ethnographic interviews and focus groups with clients and staff. The interviews and focus groups were audiotaped. Directly observed sessions and events were recorded on the observation forms as soon as possible afterward. The written program materials were coded onto forms developed for that purpose during the actual process of reviewing each document.

Data Analysis Procedures.   Written transcriptions of the taped interviews and focus groups as well as the forms for direct observations and written program materials were reviewed informally to identify common and unique themes and patterns for each data set. This information was used to develop separate data coding forms for each of the four data sets (interviews, focus groups, observed events, and written materials). The forms were pilot tested by using them to code several items for each data set (e.g., five written transcripts of individual interviews were coded by the researcher and a research assistant independently). Each of the four forms was revised based on feedback from the pilot testing process.

Then the information from each data set was coded onto the forms and was subsequently analyzed in terms of major themes/patterns unique to each data set and program and those common to all. Inter-rater reliability was achieved by randomly selecting items from each data set (e.g., four written transcriptions of focus groups) and having a third person who was not involved in the research code those items. Comparisons were made between the interviews coded by the researcher or the research assistant and the same ones coded by the third person. The discussions and eventual agreement among the three coders on items used for reliability helped to improve the overall consistency and clarity of the coding process. The themes and patterns across data sets and programs are reported in the next section, highlighting program factors that were identified as key influences on the process and outcomes of substance abuse empowerment practice in the six programs.

Study Findings and Discussion

As noted previously, although this study focused on the seven research questions listed on page 00, the findings reported in this section focus more narrowly on program factors relevant to empowerment practice (questions 1–4). Data related to these four questions are reported utilizing Gutiérrez and Ortega's (1990) tri-level empowerment paradigm consisting of personal, interpersonal, and political aspects of power.

Personal Power in Rehab and Prevention Services. The findings are consistent with Gutiérrez and Ortega's (1990) assumption that having power at this level is a foundation for the availability and use of power at the other two levels. The focus of the present research on substance abuse treatment and prevention has, however, helped to clarify more of the complexities involved in attaining personal power. The sources of personal power for the clients in this study were strongly integrated into the structure of the programs, allowing staff to serve as the arteries through which empowerment opportunities flowed and were implemented. Table 1.3 illustrates examples of empowerment-related program structures or factors that can be compared with the examples of similar factors identified in the literature and summarized in table 1.1.

The main themes or sources of personal power across the six study programs were professional, peer-led, and staff-client collaborative supports. These same three sources of power were used to organize data from the literature summarized in table 1.1. This common organization method enhances a comparison of the literature findings and findings from my research. The examples in table 1.3 suggest that program factors for helping

TABLE 1.3 Examples of Program Factors Related to Effective Empowerment Practice in Substance Abuse Services from Freeman (1997) (T = treatment program; P = prevention program)

Focus	Professional Services	Peer-Led Services	Professional/Client Collaboration
Personal (individual clients)	(T) Clients set own recovery goals (personal goal contract)	(T) Client expediters or escorts help orient new clients to routines and remind old clients of appointments/treatment sessions	(T) Any discharge from treatment (client- or staff-initiated) requires mutual chart review of progress and a reentry plan
	(T) Client-centered, culture-specific groups re gender, age, dual diagnosis, ethnicity		(T) Clients and staff collaborate and agree on recovery treatment plan development/revisions in case staffing where staff are not viewed as the only experts
	(T) Engagement phase of several weeks allows client to "try out" program and assess commitment to treatment		(P) Initial planning contacts allow community members to "test" their power to disagree with professional staff or consultants in a program
	(T) Clients develop and present a Heritage Book on their background/identity, sources of power by interviewing key informants		
Interpersonal (peers, family members, social networks, co-workers)	(T) Family groups can involve anyone the client identifies as in a "family" relationship	(T) Client buddy system, positive telephone-calling network, graduates mentor current clients, current clients write/call recent graduates to support their recovery	(T) Clients give feedback to other clients about their progress/lack of progress ("pull-ups") in collaboration with staff to shift those who are stuck at certain points in recovery
	(T) Client amnesty meeting can be called by staff to allow clients to reveal their mistakes and negative risks and discuss the impact on peers' recovery without censure	(T) Daily peer counseling groups, periodic peer-led phase meetings to determine if individual clients have met criteria for next phase	

Political (service programs, community, social systems, public policy)	(T) Clients are involved in supported work outside the program during later phases of treatment or on in-program work crews involving collaboration/cooperation	(P) Community members develop informal self-help groups relevant to drug abuse prevention, e.g., parents of children killed by gang violence, Tough Love	(T) Family members and staff collaborate in confronting clients who deny treatment is needed, is working, or requires more effort on their part
	(T) Individual/family/group treatment revised every four months to accommodate clients' phases of recovery/special needs/interests (client-accepted treatment)	(P) Peer-directed coalitions are formed among community residents to reduce alcohol and drug availability and accessibility (liquor stores, drug houses, billboards)	(P) Clients and community members are represented on program advisory board
	(T) Regular community meetings are held to ask clients what is working or not and address new issues, unresolved issues, needed changes	(T) Clients participate in peer-determined social action/environmental impact activities related to drug abuse and other social risk indicators while in treatment (housing inadequacies, violence, transportation problems)	(P) Youths help plan and implement prevention activities: conferences, education sessions, program evaluation, task forces on demand reduction
	(T) Clients are expected to do volunteer work to improve some aspect of the community in later phases of treatment (step work)	(P) Trained community leaders teach substance abuse social action/ prevention skills to other community members (proposal writing, program evaluation, policy analysis and reform, systems change, community mobilization)	
	(T) Staff complete a specific reunification plan, including client tasks and advocacy strategies for impacting the court and protective service systems, when client's children have been removed prior to/during drug treatment		
	(P) Alcohol and drug seminars are provided for community members in various stages of recovery to prevent relapse		

an individual to "become a client" can often lead to initial empowerment experiences in treatment (e.g., "Professional Services/ Personal Focus": "Engagement phase of several weeks allows client to 'try out' program and assess commitment to treatment."). These types of events are empowering because, as noted by many respondents, they mark a discernible transition in the individual's status from observer to client in a treatment program, or the point at which some of the initial game-playing ends. A similar transition sometimes occurs in prevention programs that require consensus between community residents and staff or consultants as part of an initial commitment to the work (see table 1.3, "Professional/Client Collaboration: Personal Focus").

Other themes helped to identify additional professional or staff services that influence empowerment and recovery at the personal level. Those themes included clients' input being solicited and considered (having clients develop personal goal contracts), and being regarded as unique and special (providing client-centered treatment or prevention services or having clients interview significant others about their unique cultural/ethnic backgrounds). The focus on uniqueness emphasizes that the individual is of value and thus brings something valuable to the service process. The process of discovering the uniqueness is empowering because it is acknowledged by the client and contributes to a staff-client bond when both integrate the discovery/ empowerment process as a shared experience. Chandler (1992) notes that these activities convey trust, respect, and recognition of the individual's value through interaction.

Themes related to peer-led services and staff-client collaboration at the personal level were also evident in the findings. Being viewed as responsible (escorting other clients or doing program maintenance tasks) and collaborating in decision making (mutually developing and revising the treatment plan in an open meeting involving all staff) are also consistent with Chandler's (1992) findings about empowerment in the health field. The theme of collaborative tasks was identified as more important to empowerment because these tasks provide a "public" venue for recognizing the value of the client. In contrast, respondents indicated professional service themes relate more to "private" acts of empowerment, for example, developing a personal goal contract at the direction of the primary counselor.

In addition, collaborative tasks demonstrate the staff's commitment to support mutual decisions about each client's treatment or the use of a certain prevention strategy, even if they do not fully agree with those decisions.

Another example of this theme is when discharge is not an automatic consequence if a client relapses. In some programs, a meeting is held with the client to mutually determine the reasons or conditions that led to the relapse, the consequences, and what should be done about it. Some programs require clients who want to leave against medical advice to petition for a meeting where they present their request to leave and the reasons, negotiating/collaborating with staff on whether and the conditions under which they should leave. Other programs require the client and his or her primary counselor to complete a mutual chart review of the client's progress and develop a reentry plan for when and under what circumstances the client will be ready to return for services (See table 1.3, "Professional/Client Collaboration: Personal Focus.") The common aspect of these themes is the client's active involvement in decision making as an empowerment strategy. This involvement counteracts his or her previous denial and/or avoidance of issues needing to be addressed during the addiction or the inability of community members to control drug activities in their communities. Those denial and avoidance reactions were identified by respondents as a major source of their feelings of shame and guilt (their disempowerment).

Interpersonal Power and Substance Abuse Services. As noted by Gutiérrez and Ortega (1990), sources for this level of power are related to clients' abilities to influence others. My findings regarding this theme indicate that empowerment during treatment and prevention develops from opportunities for discovering and using that power. With professional support, the focus is on helping clients to develop a family or community. Empowerment occurs from defining who the family consists of, who should participate in treatment or prevention, and the interdependence between self and other community members or other clients in recovery (for example, see table 1.3, "Professional Services: Interpersonal Focus," i.e., amnesty meetings). The peer-led theme of interpersonal power includes program factors that allow clients to assume leadership roles in facilitating the recovery of other clients (leading peer counseling groups) or conducting prevention activities with other community members (developing and leading a self-help or mutual-support group).

In contrast, the professional/client collaborative theme refers to clients and staff working together to provide needed feedback to other clients. Respondents noted that a type of reciprocal empowerment occurs for the targets of the feedback, during an intervention, for example. Those in denial about the need for treatment or those who are "stuck" in a certain phase of recovery, as well as family members or other clients who provide the feedback, may experience empowerment during interventions. Again, study participants concluded that it is the public venue made possible by the collaboration that leads to a greater sense of group efficacy and empowerment.

Substance Abuse Services and Political Power.   The most recurring and important overall theme related to this level of power was the respondents' ability to change the service delivery system. This common theme was evident for prevention *and* treatment services, as seen in examples included in table 1.3, for instance, keeping flexible and modifying client-determined treatment and clients/community members' service on prevention program policy boards. In comparison, the examples of political power from the literature primarily focused on prevention programs (see table 1.1). Themes related to political sources of power in the current research, however, involved other large systems as well as the respondents' substance abuse programs.

For instance, the professional support theme tended to emphasize the efficacy of impacting particular systems such as protective services or the courts when addiction has led to out-of-home placements for a client's children. Another source of power is integrating formal treatment with twelve-step work, i.e., helping to improve some aspect of community life by doing community service (the atonement or giving back step) (see table 1.3, "Professional Services: Political Focus"). On the other hand, the peer-led and professional-client collaboration themes identified multiple sources of political power and collective empowerment, including more dramatic and radical transfers of power than the professional support theme, according to study respondents (see table 1.3, "Peer-Led Services and Professional/Client Collaboration: Political Focus"). Overall, the findings from this research provide a useful set of implications, or a framework, for analyzing empowerment practice across various substance abuse programs.

An Empowerment-Oriented Conceptual Framework

Table 1.4 illustrates some of the implications of empowerment practice that have been inferred from the previous literature review and from the author's research findings in the preceding section. These implications have been organized into a framework for analyzing and understanding practice with different populations of nondrug users, nonproblem users, and addicted individuals. The discussion includes the sources or levels of empowerment and the types of theories that are consistent with these levels, and three categories of empowerment programs that apply to different aspects of this paradigm.

Empowerment Levels and Relevant Theories

The levels of empowerment listed in table 1.4 indicate how power at each level is interrelated with the other levels, consistent with Gutiérrez and Ortega's (1990) assumptions and my research findings. Conceptually, those findings showed that within each power level, the degree of reciprocity and public observation of empowerment experiences increases in the shift from professional to peer-led to professional/client collaborative supports. This finding implies that a balance may be needed at each empowerment level based on the stage of treatment/prevention involved, a client's past power-related strengths or deficits, and current issues.

Gutiérrez and Ortega (1990) imply that at the personal level, the client develops an understanding of his or her disempowerment experiences in terms of social conditions without necessarily taking any action. But my findings indicated that across all three empowerment levels, empowerment of the study participants required lesser to greater degrees of action (from the personal to the political levels) leading to change from the individual to the collective level. Possibly, addicted individuals and community members who have lost control of their communities to drugs have become so disempowered that some form of direct action is necessary for them to become empowered, even at the personal level (see table 1.3).

The types of theories that support this view of empowerment, therefore, are those that assume a close interdependence between the individual and the environment. This is important, conceptually and in practice, because consumers who are served by substance abuse programs need multiple sources of power from various parts of the ecological system (Germain and Gitterman 1980; Freeman and O'Dell 1993). At the same time, these different parts of the system may involve barriers to empowerment and recovery or prevention that need to be addressed at the personal, interpersonal, and political levels. Examples of relevant theories in table 1.4 include cognitive

TABLE 1.4 Conceptual Framework: Empowerment Practice in Substance Abuse Programs

Empowerment Levels	Definition of Empowerment	Relevant Theories/Domains	Three Types of Empowerment Programs		
			Empowering	Microcosm	Empowered
Personal Level (foundation for other levels)	Development of individual feelings of personal power and self-efficacy	Psychological or personal change (critical consciousness) Ego psychology and cognitive-behavioral theory	Program factors help to construct new social reality of self as powerful and capable recovering person through individualized treatment, resocialization, accepting/giving feedback from/to peers, personal inventory activities, step work, obtaining basic resources and a social network	Program factors exist for clients selecting own work assignments, engagement phase, culture-specific treatment with client input	Program factors exist for involvement within program and community by individual clients (e.g., feedback to staff about program barriers and supports and involvement in self-selected community service projects)

Interpersonal Level (*simultaneous development of interpersonal and political skills*)	Development of skills for influencing others (e.g., problem solving, assertiveness, power analysis, social action, education) resulting in competence and a sense of group efficacy	*Interpersonal/ intragroup change* (increasing resources for self and others) Family systems and mutual aid theories	Program factors help to construct new social reality of self as powerful and capable recovering person through individualized treatment, resocialization, accepting/giving feedback from/to peers, personal inventory activities, step work, obtaining basic resources and a social network	Program factors exist that require self-defined family involvement, peer mentoring and counseling, staff and client collaborative treatment planning, collective and structured feedback to staff	Program factors exist for within-program and peer-led environmental impact activities related to common issues (e.g., impacting protective services by women with children in out-of-home placements)
Political Level (*based on achieving personal and interpersonal empowerment*)	Transfer of power between groups in society leading to a sense of collective and self-efficacy, and effective systems/structural change	*Social action and social change* (structural and institutional change) General systems, social influence, organizational, and community development theories	Program factors help to construct new social reality of self as powerful and capable recovering person through individualized treatment, resocialization, accepting/giving feedback from/to peers, personal inventory activities, step work, obtaining basic resources and a social network	Program factors exist for transferring power from the program system to clients (e.g., for changing client-directed treatment regularly; service on program policy-making committees)	Program factors exist that impact or redistribute power from multiple social institutions to the clients and other community members (e.g., service by staff and clients on community planning boards, ad hoc task forces, public hearings re policies, antiviolence campaigns, public school drug prevention sessions, community action programs)

behavioral theory (personal power), mutual aid theory (interpersonal power), and systems change theory (political power), which are explored more fully in chapter 2 (Barth 1994; Freeman 1992; Freeman 1996; Hawkins and Catalano 1992).

Types of Empowerment Programs

In addition to illustrating the empowerment process using the three levels of power (and the necessary theory base), this framework helps to conceptualize the empowerment themes summarized in table 1.3 in different program categories. The substance abuse field is just beginning to explore the use of empowerment paradigms, so this framework is an initial effort to specify how they are being applied. Programs are applying empowerment concepts in at least three ways currently, and often not very explicitly, according to the literature and my research findings.

The first category includes programs that are applying the empowerment paradigm to the general process of recovery or prevention, but very narrowly. Their focus includes some aspects of the personal and interpersonal levels of empowerment, but only in terms of the professional theme area (see table 1.3). Clients are encouraged to develop a positive self-identity, to take a personal inventory and improve certain personal and interpersonal qualities important for successfully completing the program, and to give feedback to peers in these same areas based on what they have learned themselves.

Program factors such as a requirement for journaling and the use of "the hot seat" for confronting a peer about unacknowledged barriers to recovery support this process of self-reflection and growth. But there is no focus on the environment except in helping clients to procure basic tangible resources such as housing, health care, and employment or intangible resources such as a recovery support network. These programs enhance the confidence, personal competence, and empowerment of individual clients. They are what Florin and Wandersman (1990) describe as empowering organizations.

A second category of programs within this framework includes those with mechanisms that require clients to affect the service program structure and its political dynamics as part of the process of recovery or prevention. These microcosm programs tend to focus, therefore, on many aspects of the personal, interpersonal, and political levels of power within the program as well

as professional, peer-led, and collaborative supports for impacting the program (Freeman 1994). The active and respected involvement of clients
makes these programs a microcosm of "the real world"; power is transferred
from the system to clients (Gutiérrez and Ortega 1990) in a process of consciousness raising and collective empowerment.

Microcosm programs go beyond the individual growth and limited self-
empowerment focus of empowering programs, which strengthen clients' personal power or internal lives. Microcosm programs focus on personal empowerment as well as on collective empowerment via a systems change
process within the programs, strengthening clients' internal and external
lives (Freeman 1994). By doing so, these programs fit between Florin and
Wandersman's (1990) definitions of empowering organizations and empowered organizations. Those authors define the latter as programs that influence the environment or community by helping to redistribute power and
decision making ability within the community.

Thus, empowered organizations, the third category of programs within
this framework, contain factors that help clients to change social systems in
the larger environment external to the service program *and* the personal,
interpersonal, and political environment within it. These more ecologically
focused programs have a stronger concentration of politically oriented factors, social action, and environmental impact activities for changing external
structural barriers. Table 1.4 has examples of these factors under "Empowered Programs: Political Level," such as a requirement to do volunteer community service, participate in antiviolence campaigns, or help to plan and
implement prevention programs (also see table 1.3 under "Political Focus").
Empowered organizations involve the same themes of professional, peer-led,
and collaborative supports found in the other two types of organizations, in
order to achieve the required transfer of political and social power.

Conclusion

This discussion on the strengths of empowered organizations points out
the unique contribution the empowerment paradigm can make to services
for special populations. The poor, women, and ethnic groups of color often
experience strong barriers to their empowerment and recovery in the immediate and larger environments (Freeman 1992). Therefore, prevention
and rehab programs that include an empowerment orientation can better

facilitate effective outcomes with those population groups as well as with other consumers and community members. Additional research is needed to illuminate what these individuals understand and can contribute to knowledge about what works or does not work from an empowerment perspective. Qualitative research and the use of ethnographic and narrative approaches can facilitate a collaborative and respectful client/researcher exploration of these issues (Yeich and Levine 1992).

There may be a danger, however, in assuming that an empowerment perspective is what's needed to create effective substance abuse programs. Empowerment paradigms should be only part of the response for achieving improved effectiveness, since there cannot be one answer or approach to addressing any problem. A more fruitful strategy is to explore what empowerment can add to a more holistic and ecological approach that considers multiple issues and methods with regard to program effectiveness. At best, an empowerment framework can only help to organize our thinking about the role of power issues in substance abuse rehab and prevention. And this framework can inform our attitudes about multiple sources of disempowerment as well, as a new way of thinking about how addictions develop: the focus of chapter 2 in this book.

2 Understanding the Substance Abuse and Addiction Process from an Empowerment Perspective

It is necessary to take into account the dynamics of such negative transactional outcomes as oppression and other injustices derived from the misuse of power.
— B. Solomon (1987:80)

Empowerment concepts can help to clarify how substance abuse problems, including addictions, develop. Addictions may represent extremely self-destructive efforts to achieve personal power over seemingly unmanageable problems such as parental or peer rejection, low self-esteem, or job loss, or addictions may precede or occur simultaneously with these other problems. The result can be a cumulative loss of power despite efforts to control the loss. Ironically, these efforts often diminish rather than extend personal power. Moreover, the environment's role cannot be ignored. Resource deficits and non-nurturing environments can block appropriate avenues to personal, interpersonal, or political power while exposing people to risks such as easy access to substances and addicted role models (Hawkins and Catalano 1994).

These risks may reinforce an individual's or community's sense of powerlessness. For example, research interviews with a group of children and youths four to seventeen years old who were receiving services from a mental health center for psychological problems revealed that most of them witnessed several episodes of drug use, drug sales, and acts of family and community violence daily. Their case records in the center did not include information about these environmental factors or their impact on the children's own drug use, depression, attempted suicides, powerlessness, or lack of hope about the future (Freeman and Dyer 1993).

Even though there are obvious links between substance abuse and power-lessness, many people in the substance abuse rehabilitation and prevention field discourage power analyses of individual and environmental conditions. Individual clients' or communities' questions about the role of these factors in substance abuse are often viewed as excuse making and labeled as part of their denial of and projections about the problem (Freeman and Landes-man 1992). Power analyses may be troubling to service providers not only because they believe such analyses avoid the question of personal respon-sibility but also because providers feel inadequate: they do not understand policy or macro issues and/or they have personal conflicts about power in-equities.

Some policy makers and other leaders are uncomfortable about these issues as well. For them, "blaming victims" helps to maintain the status quo between the powerful few (Freire 1989) and the powerless. Policy makers' pathology-focused analyses of social programs are the basis for current na-tional reform proposals that will undoubtedly reduce the availability of sub-stance abuse prevention and rehab programs, as well as health care, mental health, housing, and other social supports (Freeman 1996). Power-focused analyses can reveal the negative influence of structural factors, including punitive social policies and lack of viable employment options, on individ-uals' disempowerment experiences and substance abuse (Poole 1995).

In spite of these barriers to addressing environmental factors, the field should encourage researchers to explore the role of power inequities in sub-stance abuse problems. The results could explain the effects of power-reducing transactions between individuals and their environments from a systems perspective and reveal power-related conditions that influence a per-son's progression from problem use to addiction. The exploration might clarify also how some individuals resist becoming addicted in spite of cu-mulative disempowerment experiences and other risk factors. The identifi-cation of certain types of empowerment experiences and methods necessary for preventing and resolving substance abuse problems may be another im-portant outcome.

Accordingly, chapter 2 summarizes the effects of disempowerment on problem use and on addiction development and resistance, and vice versa. Service programs' responses to power issues are discussed in terms of how programs can facilitate or hinder the service delivery process. A summary is included about social work's traditional struggle to address powerlessness and vulnerable populations, using the substance abuse field as an exemplar and explaining how the application of power concepts to this field is somewhat unique compared to other fields of practice and problem areas. Finally, the implications of this discussion for specific changes in social work education are outlined.

Problem Development and Disempowerment

Analyzing the relationship between disempowerment and substance abuse problems includes examining the power concepts in table 2.1. In that table and this discussion, Gutiérrez and Ortega's (1991) empowerment framework is applied to disempowerment at the personal, interpersonal, and political levels. Also, disempowerment is related more specifically to the development of substance abuse problems. Although the primary focus of this discussion is on power concepts, it is clear from research that multiple factors precipitate, reinforce, and are influenced in turn by substance abuse problems (Freeman 1992).

Power Concepts and Disempowerment

Powerlessness and disempowerment are the common base for the concepts in table 2.1. Pinderhughes (1988) defines powerlessness as the absence of power. Disempowerment, on the other hand, is the mechanism that leads to an individual's, family's, group's, or community's powerlessness: an act that denies, mitigates, or eliminates a person's or unit's power (Chandler 1992). The concepts in this section reflect the different ways people are disempowered at each of the three levels.

The Personal Level. Power impairment and paralysis are examples of powerlessness at the personal level. Pinderhughes (1983) indicates, for example, that individuals can develop a personal identity as chronically impaired and vulnerable due to lack of power. The impairment may stem from an eagerness for environmental supports and influence. The individual's boundaries can become too open, admitting all influences, positive and negative. An inability to control the impact of negative influences then leads to a perception of chronic powerlessness. Power impairment can also result from fatalism about gaining control over the life situation, which causes an

TABLE 2.1 Disempowerment and Substance Abuse Problems

Empowerment Levels	Power Concepts	Relevant Theories	Application to Substance Abuse Problems
Personal Level	Power impairment: chronic powerlessness	narrative approaches (postmodern and social construction theories)	Construction of narratives that organize people's lives around their power impairments and substance abuse or their denial of powerlessness and addictions
	Power paralysis: immobilization and isolation from personal sources of power (self-efficacy)	learned helplessness theory	Individuals are taught through reinforcement that their efforts do not affect outcomes; they become habituated to costimuli: power paralysis and self-medication
		cognitive-behavioral theory	Belief systems about situations cause powerlessness and substance abuse rather than the situations themselves, along with people's self-talk about power impairment and paralysis
Interpersonal Level	Power cutoffs: negative transactions block relationships and influence over situations and other people	mutual aid theory	Disempowered co-enabling systems are formed that perpetuate power cutoffs and sabotages and strongly reinforce substance abuse and enabling as collective mutual support strategies
	Power sabotages: seizing power by disempowering others	social deviance theory	Shared deviance provides intragroup acceptance and sanctions the focus of deviance: common power cutoffs and substance abuse

	narrative approaches	Mutual storytelling (mutual construction of narratives) about common disempowerment experiences and war stories involving substance abuse escapades encourage power sabotage or continued disempowerment
	community development theory	Community norms conducive to substance abuse develop in response to power inequities and inconsistencies based on a collective sense of inadequacy in coping with those deficits and other social indicators
	labeling theory	Punitive substance abuse policies transform people into problems and hold them accountable for their own powerlessness and substance abuse or other maladaptive coping patterns
	narrative approaches	Pathologizing media myths (a form of narratives) reinforce denials that power inequities and inconsistencies exist and false beliefs that substance abuse glamorizes or improves the life situation (increases personal, social, and political power)
Political Level		Power inequities: socially sanctioned, politically maintained power gaps lead to social disorder, which discriminates against certain groups more severely (e.g., ethnics of color)
		Power inconsistencies: maintain social injustices related to certain vulnerable groups (e.g., women) through denial and discounting (invalidating and scapegoating)
	systems theory	Social institutions are operated to maintain social injustices through power inequities and inconsistencies; a dynamic tension between those with power and those without power exists. Substance abuse supply and demand reduction strategies help to maintain power inequities and substance abuse problems, especially for certain devalued groups: women, ethnic groups of color, elderly people, and gay males and lesbians

individual's boundaries to become too rigid. This rigidity closes off both positive and negative sources of power and results in an inability to exercise personal power through positive influences.

Either boundary problem can lead to power paralysis, which involves depression about the lack of control over life events and immobilization (Pinderhughes 1983). A profound sense of personal impotence (Chantang 1976), rather than personal efficacy, is usually associated with the paralysis. For instance, even when addicted individuals' attempts to obtain treatment are reframed as evidence of personal power, their sense of impotence can prevent them from actively participating in treatment (Schilit and Gomberg 1987).

The Interpersonal Level.   Power cutoffs result when, during interactions with others, an individual is ignored, not responded to, or verbally or physically abused (see table 2.1). These events create interpersonal barriers that essentially cut off the relationship and the individual's ability to control the situation (Chandler 1992). The person who is cut off experiences disempowerment.

When cutoffs occur, the disempowerment can have a ripple effect, leading to instances of power sabotage (see table 2.1). The person who has experienced cutoffs may disempower or sabotage either the person who did the cutting off or someone else in another situation. In Woodhouse's (1990) study, addicted women's family members, partners, or peers sometimes encouraged them to drink or sabotaged them in order to gain power or a secondary payoff for themselves. The payoffs included an opportunity to feel needed and freedom for leisure time activities. In some addicted family units and drinking or drugging networks, a system of reciprocal power sabotage may develop and be maintained over time.

The Political Level.   Power inequities exist for certain groups of devalued status, such as women and ethnic groups of color, as noted in table 2.1. These disparities are so institutionalized that their existence is denied by those in power. The denial makes it more difficult to address or redress the inequitable distribution of power and therefore helps to maintain it (Freeman 1996). Individual or collective efforts to call attention to the inequities often are met with what family systems theorists describe as a scapegoating response. Such responses label those who raise the issue as either "bad or mad" in order to divert attention from the structural problems (Papp 1990).

In addition, scapegoating often invalidates and silences both the message and the messengers. Thus, it results in their collective political disempowerment.

Power inconsistencies are institutionalized discrepancies between the words (legal rights) and deeds (practices) of societal representatives (Chastang 1976). Although individuals and communities may have a legal right to certain resources and social supports, there may be inconsistencies between what they are entitled to and what they actually receive. Impoverished communities often develop a collective sense of inadequacy and disempowerment when they are not provided with the same essential resources as more affluent communities (Hawkins and Catalano 1992). Impoverished communities have higher proportions of unemployed residents, female heads of households, ethnic groups of color, and elderly individuals with few resources than affluent communities. These groups are at high risk for powerlessness.

Freeman and O'Dell (1993) identify examples of resources that are less available in poor communities, ranging from police protection, business incentives, supported work and job training, and social programs to leadership development and community education about how business and political systems work. These resources can prevent a loss of control over drugs and violence or help overcome economic and political barriers that impede a community's self-sufficiency. Power inconsistencies not only affect the present, they can inhibit a community's belief in its ability to change the future (Freeman and Pennekamp 1993; Luturgio and Davis 1992).

Applying Power Concepts to Substance Abuse Problems

This general discussion about power concepts has implications for how they are related specifically to substance abuse, from nonproblem use to addiction. Table 2.1 gives examples of theories that help to explain the transactional, reciprocal relationship between disempowerment and substance abuse. It is possible that neither condition causes the other but that as each develops, it influences and is influenced by the other. In addition to the interactional effects of power issues, the complex processes of substance abuse and addiction are affected by many other individual and environmental factors (Freeman 1992). This discussion addresses the application of multiple-level power concepts to substance abuse problems, the use of power concepts for understanding resistance to substance abuse, and unique inter-personal aspects of power issues and substance abuse.

Multiple-Level Applications.   Some theories, such as those involved in narrative approaches, help to clarify the relationship between substance abuse and powerlessness at the personal, interpersonal, *and* political levels. Narrative approaches are based on postmodern and social construction the-ories, which emphasize strengths and empowerment (White and Epston 1991). "The aim is to help clients find alternative stories of their lives and to mobilize their strengths to fight the problem and its effects" (Kelly 1995:349). This is accomplished through the use of alternative stories and meanings that help people to transform or to reconstitute their situations and themselves.

But narrative approaches facilitate understanding of disempowerment as well. In disempowerment situations, some people may construct narratives that afflict them rather than help them to reconstitute themselves as capable and empowered individuals (Wynne, Shields, and Sirkin 1992). Possibly, they internalize the substance abuse problem, its symptoms, and even en-vironmental risk factors by retelling their disempowerment narratives over time. One meaning they may derive from their special type of narrative is that they are incompetent, chronically powerless, and a hopeless substance abuser (Borden 1992; Imber-Black 1988).

For other substance abusers, narratives may be used to perpetuate their *denial* about eventually becoming addicted and chronically powerless. For instance, Kelly (1995) describes narratives as the stories around which people have organized their lives. Perhaps the carefully constructed narratives of some substance abusers reinforce a false view of themselves as being in control, causing them to ignore or discount indicators of their power losses (Freeman 1992). The construction and retelling of these narratives over time and the interaction of multiple other bio-psycho-social factors then influence the progression from substance abuse to addiction. The individual reframes his or her problem-saturated stories as evidence of survival or control over ordinary power-reducing experiences. For example, a middle-aged addicted social worker interpreted her numerous stories about job losses as evidence of her ability to cope with economic stress rather than as evidence of the increasing consequences of drug addiction.

Problem-saturated stories reinforce power concepts and substance abuse connections beyond the personal level. Table 2.1 shows how this connection can be initiated and maintained at the interpersonal level through mutual storytelling within a co-enabling, disempowered network. Mutual story-telling can be a form of power sabotage or "one-upmanship" in which one person seems to win (the person whose war story tops all others). But the storytelling actually reinforces the powerlessness of all the members. Environmental factors that precipitate and reinforce their powerlessness and substance abuse may be ignored. Some of those factors, such as the availability of drugs within a community, also may be characterized as neutral rather than negative influences, according to community norms or media myths.

At the political level, the media's pathologizing myths either deny existing power inequities and inconsistencies and/or blame certain devalued groups for their lack of power (Poole 1995). Community norms conducive to substance abuse may be a collective effort to cope with the negative messages, may be precipitated and reinforced by those messages, or both. In addition, some socially and politically inspired policies can transform people into problems (Chapin 1995), particularly in regard to substance abuse. For instance, political and media narratives tend to focus on the substance abuse problem primarily in terms of individuals who abuse and become addicted to substances and their communities, thus blaming individuals for their problems and their powerlessness.

But these narratives ignore the supply side of the problem: individuals and legitimate industries that provide advice about illegal drugs or launder, transfer, or invest money from drugs as well as transport them into this country and help to distribute them (Taylor 1994). Overwhelmingly the policy and institutional focus is on the demand component, and from a punishment rather than a treatment perspective. By ignoring the structural factors in their politically constructed narratives, policy makers neutralize those factors and reinforce assumptions that people rather than power and resource inequities are the problem (Chapin 1995).

Application to Substance Abuse Resistance. In spite of these personal, interpersonal, and political power barriers, some people are able to resist becoming addicted. They may be confronted with the same multiple risk factors for substance abuse as addicted people. However, they either do not use substances at all or use them (alcohol, for example) without becoming addicted. One assumption is that resisters create different narratives about their situations than individuals who become addicted. The former's (empowerment) narratives may be focused on personal or other sources of power around which they can organize their lives. Another possibility is that resisters develop the same (disempowerment) narratives as addicts, but that they extract different themes and meanings from those narratives (Freeman 1992). For example, by concluding that a disempowerment experience has made them stronger, their narratives about a negative experience may empower rather than disempower them. In one family where both parents were addicted, six out of seven children also developed addictions from early adolescence. The son who did not develop addictions described the same disempowerment experiences as his siblings, including physical, verbal, and emotional family abuse. His conclusion about the family narratives was that he was special because his parents treated him worse than his siblings.

Other theories included in table 2.1 offer alternative views about how some individuals resist addiction. Cognitive-behavioral theory implies that people can resist addiction by establishing a belief system about power and addiction similar to that of abstinent, empowered role models. The theory involves teaching people that they have personal power over life situations and over peer pressures to use substances based on how they view those situations. Helping them to develop resistance skills reinforces this belief (Shorkey 1994).

Some resisters join prosocial networks, such as organized sports groups, that are considered "deviant" according to community norms that encourage substance abuse. Deviance theory assumes that belonging to an "appropriate" outgroup gives the members a sense of collective power that helps them to resist substance abuse and achieve educational and social goals. Other resisters learn to externalize and deconstruct pathologizing media myths that, according to labeling theory, could otherwise be disempowering to them (Freeman 1994; Kelly 1995). The externalization process can be an important tool because it prevents resisters from blaming themselves for potentially disempowering experiences. At the same time, it encourages reframing and relabeling those experiences as opportunities for personal and interpersonal development, which is an adaptive coping mechanism (Freeman 1994). Interpersonal development, however, involves some additional complex issues related to power and substance abuse.

Unique Interpersonal Dynamics.   Table 2.1 indicates that unique bonding and attachment factors can make the disempowerment and substance abuse connection more complex at the interpersonal level. For example, mutual aid theory helps to explain how members of disempowered interpersonal systems can develop a bond due to common power impairments, whether they are a family or a social network (Shorkey and Rosen 1993). The provision of mutual support begins to focus on centralizing and maintaining the members' substance abuse problems through power cutoffs and sabotages.

Eventually, these networks become co-enabling units that exacerbate individuals' interpersonal power issues as their substance abuse problems become worse and develop into addictions (Shorkey and Rosen 1993). Interpersonal supports may influence this progression to addiction more strongly than personal factors alone, validating both the common powerlessness of the members and the co-enabling and addictive behaviors that they develop (Hanson 1988).

Schilit and Gomberg (1987) found that this type of mutual aid can also decrease individuals' personal power because the co-enabling relationships often involve requests for support that the members believe they cannot refuse. For instance, individuals are expected to lie about other members' addictions and about the consequences of their addictions for the unit. Shorkey and Rosen (1993) indicate individuals also may be asked to overfunction by taking over addicted members' various roles either periodically or permanently. Although overfunctioning places great strain on all members of the unit, it is a form of power sabotage that develops first as a type of adaptive coping, which then becomes maladaptive. Overfunctioning also maintains the denial that the substance abuse and addictions within the unit are a problem by masking the negative consequences (Shorkey and Rosen 1994). In one situation, a farmer's two adult sons moved back to the family farm at the father's request. The rational was that they could help save the farm from the effects of the country's farm crisis and alleviate the financial problems experienced by the sons, who had moved previously to a nearby city. In reality, the father's alcoholism had progressed to a point where he could no longer take a major role in farming. Very subtly the family was colluding to mask his addiction by sabotaging the sons' independence and sources of personal power.

These power issues are pertinent to programs that serve high-risk, substance-abusing, and addicted individuals. Consumers' pre-existing power issues can affect their responses to services; similar issues embedded in a service program's structure can also influence outcomes. A service program can conceivably do harm by exacerbating consumers' power and substance abuse issues through its structural problems, or it can facilitate an effective resolution of those issues. Thus, it is helpful for social workers to clarify to what extent programs address these issues and how effective they are at it.

Programmatic Responses to Power Issues

As noted previously, many service providers have been reluctant to address power issues because they lack knowledge about policy and macro-level factors. Most of them have been trained to fulfill clinical or direct service roles, which emphasize a different knowledge base than administrative, planning, and policy roles. Like many people, they may have unresolved personal issues about power that can affect their ability to help clients. Providers also may be experiencing disempowerment in their own personal relationships, the service program, or their communities. In essence, they may suffer periodically from the same power cutoffs or power inconsistencies that their clients struggle with. For these reasons, and according to what type of empowerment organization a program is, providers' and service programs' responses to power issues may be adaptive or maladaptive.

Adaptive and Maladaptive Responses by Programs

Because of staff-related factors discussed in the previous section, even when programs address power issues, the focus is sometimes implicit rather than explicit and is often contradictory and/or inconsistent. Some examples of programs' responses from the literature and from my research described in chapter 1 are summarized in table 2.2. These responses range from adaptive to maladaptive coping on the part of staff and organizations; for example, from facilitating and supporting political power (#1) to perpetuating the same power inequities in the treatment setting that clients have experienced in their environments (#11). The empowerment-oriented program factors shown in tables 1.2 and 1.3 in chapter 1 can enhance an organization's and staff's ability to respond adaptively to power issues. Conversely, the absence of these factors or barriers to their implementation can cause programs to respond maladaptively.

Some programmatic responses to power issues are more maladaptive for particular clients, such as women, because they affect their role expectations. These responses tend to oppress or revictimize women and other client

TABLE 2.2 Programmatic Responses to Power Issues in the Substance Abuse Field

	General Responses	Specific Strategies
More Adaptive Responses	1. Facilitating and supporting political power	1. Political action opportunities within and outside the program
	2. Helping to network power or to form power alliances	2. Coalition building and structured interventions to enhance collaboration
	3. Trading off interpersonal power	3. Resource pooling, mentoring, or service opportunities
	4. Acknowledging and supporting personal power/ teaching about power	4. Education, normalization, and support of power
	5. Disputing the lack of power/providing practice opportunities	5. Cognitive restructuring, role rehearsal, and power analyses
	6. Spiritualizing power	6. Twelve-step work
	7. Acknowledging power issues exist, but assuming clients cannot change their powerlessness	7. Colluding in maintaining addictive behaviors and enabling powerlessness
	8. Acknowledging power issues exist, but discounting their impact on substance abuse and the effects of other structural barriers	8. Negative reframing, blaming, or pathologizing clients
	9. Insisting that power issues are not a factor in substance abuse or addiction problems	9. Denial and confrontation, emphasizing personal responsibility only for substance abuse
	10. Invalidating personal power	10. Giving double-bind messages (don't think, don't feel, don't be, but get healthy)
Maladaptive Responses	11. Perpetuating environmental power inequities and inconsistencies and disempowerment experiences	11. Negative modeling, power cutoffs, power sabotages, and scapegoating

groups in unique ways, for example, by invalidating the individual's personal power (see item #10). In one residential treatment program for women and children, a mother with a history of inadequate parenting was told by a staff member to leave her five-month-old infant in their room alone while she participated in a required activity. The mother said she could not leave her child alone, then asked why the infant could not stay in the program's day care center while she was involved in the activity. She was told that if she wanted to stay in the program she should follow orders.

Without understanding that she had other alternatives, this woman decided to leave the program. She felt disrespected and unable to trust the staff to not misuse their power in the future. Essentially, her struggle to become a better mother, her attempt to use personal power, was invalidated by the staff. As a result of leaving the program, this client had to wait three weeks to get into another treatment program. But she believed that risking not returning to treatment in the interim was more important than risking further disempowerment in the first program.

Other maladaptive responses tend to have more common effects across different population groups. For instance, some programs readily acknowledge that power issues exist but insist that they are not a factor in substance abuse or addictions (see #9). These programs emphasize the disease model of addiction, which uses a linear cause-and-effect perspective: "A," the disease, causes "B," the addiction. Therefore, addressing disempowerment as a factor in the individual's substance abuse is seen as encouraging denial about his or her disease. Denial is viewed as a natural but undesirable part of the disease syndrome (Freeman 1992). Ironically, staff in these programs often respond to clients' attempts to address disempowerment with denial and confrontation. This response is maladaptive because it ignores factors that have and will continue to influence consumers' nonuse of, abuse of, and addiction to substances.

The disease model conflicts with a multiple-factor system or ecological perspective, which assumes that multiple bio-psycho-social factors, including genetic predisposition or "disease" factors, interact to influence the substance abuse and addiction process. The relationship among factors is viewed as circular rather than linear, so that all are both precipitators and consequences of substance abuse problems (Freeman 1992; Hanson 1991). Power issues are assumed to be among the multiple interacting factors that influence substance abuse problems, and therefore, addressing them should be part of the prevention and treatment of those problems.

This assumption is consistent with many of the adaptive programmatic responses included in table 2.2. For instance, facilitating and supporting political power (#1) includes helping to remove barriers to empowerment within the service program as well as in the larger environment outside it. Examples include formal opportunities to provide peer and staff feedback, change service program policies that are punitive, or influence community norms/local policies that make substances more available. Helping consumers to increase their political power is adaptive because it can eliminate risk factors or strengthen their resistance to those factors during prevention or treatment services (Freeman 1992).

Spiritualizing power is also an adaptive response because it aligns consumers with a higher power and interpersonal networks that support recovery and prevention goals (Kurtz and Powell 1987). This response to power issues requires involving clients in a structured process of twelve-step work based on the philosophy of "one day at a time" and in a mutual help process in which peers support and challenge each other's goals (Kurtz 1992). Although it is primarily a treatment program response, spiritualizing power could be generalized to prevention programs. Mutual help groups similar to Alateen could be organized and integrated with prevention services for high-risk youths who would continue in these groups after completing the prevention program.

Responses Influenced by the Type of Empowerment Program

There are other influences on how adaptively or maladaptively a program responds to power issues. Responses are often influenced by the type of organization, i.e., empowering, microcosm, or empowered (see table 1.4 in chapter 1). Sometimes programs' descriptions of their orientations conflict with the programs' actual implementation and structure. For example, some treatment programs in the literature that claim to have an empowerment orientation do not offer individualized treatment. Many empowerment-oriented prevention programs targeted for high-risk youths do not involve them in planning, service delivery, or evaluation activities. Such programs either perpetuate power inequities and/or invalidate clients' efforts toward empowerment.

Some of these programs fit into Florin and Wandersman's (1990) conceptualization of empowering organizations because they include other program factors consistent with some of the adaptive responses shown in table 2.2. For example, some programs have clients journal or do personal inventory work to enhance their personal power and development. These programs provide group sessions for consciousness raising to help clients identify their common strengths and problems by trading off their interpersonal power and/or pooling their resources (see #3). Others have few or none of the empowerment program factors in Florin and Wandersman's (1990) lowest-priority category of empowering organizations.

Programs that fit within the microcosm and empowered categories seem to utilize more of the adaptive responses to power issues included in table 2.2. Many do not automatically discharge clients who relapse. As noted in item #4 of this table, these programs acknowledge and support personal power by focusing on what individuals have learned from the relapse. They then help clients to use these experiences to understand factors that can lead to and prevent their unique pattern of relapses.

In one program, when clients relapse, their primary counselor goes into detox to spend time with them, using the experience to help them transition back into treatment. One dually diagnosed client who had been poly-addicted for twenty-two years and who had been in treatment eight times unsuccessfully said that having staff support during his last relapse was a turning point. He said the experience proved staff really believed "he was worth something and that he could actually recover."

An example of an empowered prevention program (Florin and Wandersman 1990) involved youths in planning a conference designed to increase their political action and power. The conference included youth and adult speakers. A number of task forces were created to implement the goals identified during the conference in order to change the prevention infrastructure in the city. These included youth task forces to work with the mayor, school superintendent, police, chamber of commerce, and the prevention program itself. The program's sponsorship of the conference and its support of these community task forces, including the one designed to change its own operations, indicates it is an empowered organization (Florin and Wandersman 1990). It facilitated the participants' political power by helping them to change larger social systems and its own service delivery structure (see #1 and #2 on table 2.2). In contrast, a microcosm program would have focused only on the use of political power within the program itself.

An advantage of microcosm and empowered programs is the ripple effect they often produce from clients' empowerment experiences. Staff experience a sense of collective and self-efficacy indirectly from facilitating client empowerment. Moreover, these programs are more likely to include program factors and adaptive responses to power issues directly designed to enhance staff empowerment. Such resources include regular retreats or meetings that encourage their input into planning, allow discussions about the difficulties they encounter in using an empowerment approach, and highlight methods that work in empowerment practice through staff training and staff development opportunities (Chandler 1992; Guiterrez, GlenMaye, and DeLois 1995).

Social Work and Power Issues

The previous discussion on programmatic responses to power issues can be generalized to the profession of social work, which is immersed in power issues because its consumers are often personally and politically powerless. Social work's mission to serve vulnerable groups in particular has placed it at the crossroads where clients' personal issues become political issues (Davis and Hagen 1992).

As a result, social work provides direct services to both referred clients and those who may be at risk for problems in the future. It also provides indirect services to address social justice issues on behalf of groups whose power has been delimited by structural problems. Therefore, the profession's simultaneous focus on the individual and the environment concentrates on power issues. This ecological systems focus implies that all people should have minimal levels of power to control their lives and to gain access to resources necessary for exercising that control.

Structural problems can limit people's opportunities for possessing and exercising even minimum amounts of power. This section is focused on social work's traditional role in addressing such problems. It also highlights common and unique power issues in substance abuse problems compared to other problems, an emerging role for social work based on those issues, and the implications for related changes that are needed in social work education.

Traditional Social Work: Structural and Power Issues

Structural problems include public policies and the policies, regulations, and practices of large institutions (Chapin 1995) that inhibit people's survival and growth, including funding patterns, coverage, eligibility and access, and client service options (Kunnes et al. 1993). Generalized structural problems affect the majority of the population. Targeted structural problems affect mostly special populations on whom they are designed to have detrimental effects or on whom they have a differential effect for other reasons. Negative effects can include power impairments in the familial, social, political, economic, health and mental health, or legal domains or in a combination of these areas. The nature of structural problems, their impact, and their resolution are discussed in more detail in chapter 3.

Generalized structural problems affect the lives of most people, causing them to seek formal services or informal supports at various points. This process of help seeking throughout the individual or family life cycle has been normalized in social work, based on a life span developmental perspective and systems theory (Germain and Gitterman 1980; Hartman 1983). One example of a generalized structural problem is a prolonged economic recession involving under- and unemployment. People's ability to cope with this more universal problem depends in part on their current resources and on their past empowerment experiences, which can affect their hope about controlling or resolving the situation and their motivation to work toward change (Chestang 1976).

Social work services are designed to help people normalize and manage reactions to such economic problems. Those reactions might include situational depression and role and power conflicts over a family's reduced or changing resources (Turner 1988; Reid 1988). Services are provided also to eliminate or reduce power inequities and inconsistencies in the environment. They may focus on influencing business and industry to increase the availability of jobs or on influencing decision makers to develop policies that support increased opportunities for employment retraining (Akabas 1995).

People's use of these formal services *and* their informal supports can decrease their disempowerment experiences while helping them to manage economic problems and related stressors. Helping to decrease individuals' disempowerment experiences has been an important social work goal (Solomon 1987) that helps prevent clients from blaming themselves and eventually suffering from power impairments and paralysis.

In addition to generalized structural problems, social work is particularly concerned about targeted problems that impact oppressed groups more strongly than other groups. Oppressed groups include women, ethnic groups of color, gay males and lesbians, the elderly, and individuals with physical and mental disabilities. Formal and informal policies that decrease educational and work opportunities for these groups are examples of this type of targeted structural problem. Services such as resource pooling and group consciousness raising may be needed to support and reinforce group strengths and help members to cope adaptively with oppression (Devore 1983; Hardy-Fanta 1986; Lewis and Jordan 1983; Schilit and Gomberg 1987). In addition, services for these groups often include the elimination of structural barriers to the ordinary power that members of other groups have for exercising control over their lives. Thus advocacy, legislative influence, and policy analysis are a few of the strategies that social work has emphasized traditionally for addressing the social justice issues of oppressed groups (Freeman 1990). Wright, Kail, and Creecy (1990) suggest that helping to resolve individual problems that some people develop in response to those barriers, including self-hate, maladaptive problem solving, or addictions, is equally important. Whether such groups' need for empowerment experiences is unique compared to other clients is an issue still to be addressed by the profession.

Common and Unique Power Issues in Substance Abuse Services

Common Issues.   The need for an emphasis on substance abuse and empowerment is just beginning to be raised and debated in the literature. Few definitive answers have been provided to date as scholars and researchers in social work and in the substance abuse field struggle to address this issue. Therefore, it is useful to summarize available information and perspectives.

Several authors assume that many of the empowerment needs presented by substance abuse clients are similar to those presented by clients with other problems (Cochran 1985; Eng, Solomon, and Mullan 1992; Gutiérrez 1990). Low self-esteem and depression related to powerlessness are common in substance abuse clients as well as in clients with mental health, child abuse, family divorce, chronic health, and community violence problems (Pinderhughes and Pittman 1985; Segal, Silverman, and Temkin 1992; Urbancic 1992; Wallenstein 1992). These authors emphasize that in many ways, powerlessness, power impairments, and the need for empowerment experiences are common across all problems and clients who use social work services. The sources of personal, interpersonal, and political power may be similar across all problem areas as well (Gutiérrez et al. 1995).

Moreover, many of the program factors discussed in this chapter for facilitating empowerment have been generalized to programs that serve the broad range of client and community problems encountered by social workers in all fields of practice (Lee 1995; Solomon 1987). Freeman (1996) indicates that the ecological perspective and systems theory can help social workers to maintain a common bio-psycho-social focus on the person *and* the social context in which many different types of problems develop and are resolved.

Issues Unique to Substance Abuse.   Given these commonalities, are substance abuse problems unique in terms of empowerment? Some authors assume that substance abuse problems are different because of their high incidence and pervasiveness across all ethnic, racial, religious, socioeconomic, age, and gender groups. For example, alcohol abuse affects approximately 22 million people in this country directly (Mellville 1989), while 13 million individuals 12 years and older identified themselves as current users of other drugs in the 1990 National Household Survey (NIDA 1991). As many as 4 million people in this country are reported to be drug addicts (Malcolm 1989). Many are polyaddicted, which tends to increase the serious consequences for them, their significant others, and society.

It has been estimated that from 10 to 12 percent of substance abusers' family members, friends, employers, and co-workers are affected indirectly (Wallace 1990; Favazza and Thompson 1984). Knowledge about power concepts indicates that addiction is a systemic problem in which severe power cutoffs and sabotages occur among all members of the system (Steinglass 1989; Freeman and Palmer 1989). Therefore, it is understandable that disempowerment affects not only the substance abuser but also family members, peers, co-workers, and others. The ripple effects of substance abuse and disempowerment on healthy relationships, growth and development, and effective problem solving within units make substance abuse a more intractable and complex problem to address.

Moreover, substance abuse is often interrelated with other problems experienced by clients who request social work services. It has been identified as a factor in the following areas: lost wages and unemployment, industrial and home accidents, chronic health problems such as high blood pressure and heart disease, family and community violence, mental health disorders, child abuse and neglect, automobile accidents involving injuries and fatalities, sexual and other types of assaults, robbery, property crimes, homelessness, prostitution, and other coaddictions such as compulsive gambling

(Agras 1987; Guadia 1992; Freeman 1992). The coexistence of substance abuse and these other problems poses at the least dual risks for dis-empowerment experiences and multiple other losses that can render people powerless. The complex dynamic relationships among these coexisting prob-lems makes it impossible to address each alone and difficult to address them in combination (Freeman and Landesman 1992; Leukefeld and Battjes 1992; Turnbull 1988).

Some authors and researchers assume substance abuse problems are unique in their influence on power issues in another way. Members of op-pressed groups have a greater susceptibility to substance abuse in combi-nation with the effects of other individual and environmental risk factors. For example, Luekefeld and Battjes (1992) indicate that "The AIDS epi-demic associated with intravenous drug abuse has especially impacted Af-rican Americans and Hispanics. African Americans comprise 50 percent of these cases among heterosexual intravenous drug abusers, and Hispanics comprise 30 percent of these cases. Among homosexual-bisexual intravenous drug abusers with AIDS, African Americans comprise 25 percent and His-panics 15 percent" (124). In general, ethnic groups of color are assumed to be at higher risk for substance abuse problems than other groups.

In summary, clients who experience the broad range of problems that are presented to social workers have similar empowerment needs. In many in-stances, the clients' problems involve resource gaps, power cutoffs, sabotages, inequities, and inconsistencies that have rendered them powerless. Thus the service process may be similar, including helping clients to cope with and resolve individual aspects of problems and to advocate for structural changes regarding environmental factors. There are also differences in the power issues related to substance abuse problems versus other problems. The high incidence of substance abuse in the general population, the serious conse-quences for abusers and their significant others, and the coexistence of these problems with complex other problems increases the risks and effects of powerlessness. Increased risks are especially likely for ethnic groups of color, women, and other special populations due to multiple structural problems that reinforce their oppression.

Social Work's Role in Substance Abuse Services

What is required of social work beyond fulfilling its traditional dual role with oppressed groups and other clients, as discussed in a previous section?

The common and unique empowerment needs of substance abuse clients indicate more comprehensive approaches are necessary for working with the general population of abusers and with substance abusers from oppressed groups. This emphasis is consistent with the profession's special mission toward vulnerable populations. Until the 1980s, however, relatively small numbers of social work practitioners, researchers, educators, and policy analysts were involved in this field of practice (Wright, Kail, and Creecy 1990). With the increasing prevalence and serious consequences of these problems, there is a need to greatly increase the involvement of the profession.

Social work's important contribution to the substance abuse field involves its emphasis on the bio-psycho-social and ecological perspectives. This chapter has focused on powerlessness and disempowerment as factors in how substance abuse problems or resistances to those problems develop. The role of structural problems in that process has been highlighted as well. Much of the substance abuse field's attention has been devoted to treatment and prevention issues at the individual, family, organizational, and community levels. Social workers are just beginning to explore the impact of power issues at those various levels.

Less attention has been devoted to policy and other types of structural problems. Social work, along with other fields such as public health, community psychology, and community health, can provide the theory and methods necessary for addressing substance abuse and empowerment at the policy and large systems levels (Blume 1987; Mbanuso 1991; Moreau 1990; O'Dell and Freeman 1996; Rappaport 1981). Social work will need to generalize some existing systems change skills, including the use of policy analysis techniques, advocacy strategies, coalition building, legislative influence, and social network interventions (Chavkin and Brown 1992; Figueira-McDonough 1993; Israel 1985; O'Donnell 1993). Freeman (1996) recommends analyzing policy makers' definitions and value frameworks related to self-sufficiency in order to affect punitive policies based on those definitions. These strategies can be generalized to reforming substance abuse policies that are barriers to client empowerment and self-sufficiency.

Other skills may need to be developed specifically for this area. Examples include substance abuse policy-impact dissemination strategies, community planning and consensus building around prevention goals, citizen-involved research strategies, and empowerment education and training strategies that can impact organizational and staff barriers to empowerment (Freeman 1996). Wallerstein and Bernstein's (1988) study provides a creative example of how empowerment education strategies can be taught to youths. That study involved teaching young people how to analyze media messages and policies that increase their consumption of substances. The youths then collaborated with helping professionals to develop and disseminate empowerment-oriented educational materials to decrease the impact of those messages and policies. These and other changes in substance abuse empowerment practice will require corresponding changes in social work education.

Related Implications for Social Work Education

A number of complementary changes in social work education are needed to support the changes in social work roles suggested in the previous section: social work specializations, more integrated policy-practice curriculum, and increased content on client-involved and multidisciplinary teams.

Social Work Specializations

Two types of specializations can be either introduced or enhanced in graduate schools of social work. Substance abuse specializations should be increased, given the serious incidence and consequences of the problem, especially related to power issues and oppressed groups (Freeman, McRoy, and Logan 1987). Accordingly, these specializations should include an empowerment perspective to teach social workers how to address power issues and the sociopolitical environment's impact on individuals' substance abuse problems. The emphasis should be on client-centered practice, and on policy development and reform activities along with direct services (Strom and Gingerich 1993). Other specializations, including family, health, child welfare, school, and mental health, need to integrate a similar empowerment and environmental focus. These changes are consistent with social work's mission regarding vulnerable populations and social justice issues.

More Integrated Policy-Practice Curriculum

A related change is for schools of social work to develop a more integrated policy-practice, clinical-community curriculum. Social workers need more substantive knowledge about policy development and reform at a practical level in order to impact organizational and local policy. Clinicians can be taught to work with people who are skilled in administration, planning, and social policy to influence state and national policies. Knowledge about policy development and policy roles should be taught from a strengths and empowerment perspective (Chapin 1995) and can be integrated with knowledge about the community as a system and its influence on individuals' substance abuse problems, recovery, and resistance to risk factors. Social work instruction should emphasize coalition building with clients to help change community risk factors and to empower clients in the process (Freeman 1996).

Client-Involved and Multidisciplinary Service Teams

This emphasis on facilitating client involvement is related to another necessary change in social work education. The importance of having clients as part of the service team was emphasized in the literature and confirmed by my research. This view of the client as an expert team member is an important component of strengths-oriented policy development (Chapin 1995) and an empowerment approach that builds in opportunities for empowerment experiences within the service program *and* the community, consistent with Florin and Wandersman's (1990) concept of empowered programs. Therefore, more should be included in social work programs about the multidisciplinary approach, with teams potentially including substance abuse counselors, psychiatrists, psychologists, nurses, and occupational and physical therapists. This content is different from the traditional focus in two ways. First, it includes the client as an expert team member. For example, content on client involvement can include how to develop teams for treatment planning, analysis and dissemination of research from the literature, and evaluation planning and implementation (see related discussion in chapter 1). Second, the team-development content should be related to power issues and the complex interrelationships between substance abuse and other problems. Thus social workers can learn to use more comprehensive approaches to interrelated problems, both for the empowerment of team members and for the consumers they are serving.

Conclusion

This discussion has clarified the nature of power issues and their connection with the development of substance abuse and other interrelated problems. What is even more clear is the important role that service programs and social workers, as well as other helping professionals, have in treatment. Programs and helpers must understand how their approach can complicate or help to resolve clients' power-related substance abuse problems and extend their efforts into clients' environments, where many of their individual problems, and certainly their structural problems, are maintained. Social work's mission requires this social justice emphasis and attention to the needs of special populations.

Part 2

The Multilevel Substance Abuse Service System: A Context for Power, Policy, and Funding Decisions

This section introduces the reader to the larger context of empowerment practice and its influence on the nature and quality of substance abuse services, a topic seldom addressed by most practice texts. Three subsystems within this context, the substance abuse service system, are analyzed: the policy and funding subsystem, the community development subsystem, and the program subsystem. The goal is to highlight how factors within this multilevel environment affect direct practice at the staff and consumer level and in turn, how consumers, staff, administrators, community residents and leaders, policy analysts, researchers, and consultants can influence that larger environment. Case, organizational, and community examples illustrate how this dynamic, reciprocal process unfolds and how the empowerment concepts discussed in part 1 can be applied to enhance our understanding of this process.

Chapter 3 clarifies how aspects of the sociopolitical environment have led to substance abuse policy and funding reforms, both currently and historically, and the underlying value biases and priorities that are driving some of those reforms. Many of the consequences for clients and service providers are included in this analysis, particularly significant limitations in service accessibility imposed by managed care policies and the politicization of substance abuse issues by policy makers and the media. The consequences have been worse for consumers dependent on the inequitable public system of health care: the poor, women and children, those with physical and mental disabilities, and people of color. This chapter also summarizes emerging

funding trends that are more consistent with a humanistic and empowerment perspective, and then proposes an integrated services model with related strengths-based policy and funding supports that involve consumers
actively in the planning and implementation of services.

In chapter 4, the focus is on the community's role as a second component
of the substance abuse service system. Three empowerment-based roles for
communities are emphasized: 1) mediation of antidrug norms; 2) broad-
based community, economic, and political development; and 3) health promotion and resource development or systems change. Factors that influence
those roles and community practice implications are summarized, including
daily struggles that practitioners and preventionists encounter in defining
and helping to mobilize communities. The specific knowledge areas and
skills required for using community-oriented social work models are discussed and then applied to a community example to illustrate the underlying
implications for empowerment.

In contrast, chapter 5 addresses the program subsystem, the third component of the substance abuse service system. Tools and procedures for helping consumers, staff, administrators, and communities to understand and
assess the influence of both internal and external factors on empowerment
and program outcomes are included. Internal factors involve structure, philosophy, and other program factors identified in chapter 1. External factors
include a program's organizational auspices and the surrounding community. Chapter 5 also focuses on the process of organizational change and
self-empowerment when various assessment tools are used, and includes
organizational examples that clarify staff and consumer power-sharing roles
and strategies for enhancing this process. Finally, addiction concepts are
used to draw out the implications for organizational change based on a
program's health or openness to change versus an addictive-enabling approach to managing/resisting change.

3   The Substance Abuse Policy and Funding Subsystem: Sociopolitical and Power Issues

Inclusion means public policy is more likely to reflect consumers'
realities because they are on the policy making team.
—R. K. Chapin (1995:509)

This country's current approaches to policy development and
funding for substance abuse services are extremely fragmented. Kleber
(1992) highlights the many overlapping demand reduction activities conducted by nineteen federal agencies alone and states that fragmentation has
significantly diminished the effectiveness of their efforts. A number of factors
have contributed to this fragmentation, including the recent politicalization
of the problem.

For example, a nineteen-year-old mother was arrested in a midwestern
city for trying to sell her three-month-old baby for drugs in a neighborhood
bar. Lydia M., the mother, was a crack addict who had just been released
from a twenty-eight-day inpatient treatment program the week before. Newspaper accounts of the incident stated the bartender overheard the mother
negotiating the sale of her baby with a drug dealer. The bartender took the
child from the mother and called the police. An investigation revealed that
the mother was homeless, unemployed, and a high school dropout.

The newspaper article reported political leaders' questioning why the
bartender had allowed the mother to bring an underage child into the bar.
Their other concerns included why the treatment center had released Lydia
without "curing" her drug addiction and why child protective services had
not taken custody of the baby at birth. These questions evade the main issue:
an addicted mother attempting to sell her baby for drugs, a serious crime
and a tragic circumstance. The questions do highlight, however, both the

fragmentation of services between the different systems in this example and the politicalization of substance abuse problems.

Politicalization occurs when decision makers' considerations are more heavily influenced by political issues than by issues directly related to a problem (Taylor 1994). Officials' desire to be perceived as "hard on drugs" may be a stronger influence on their funding decisions than the need to provide adequate resources for identifying and implementing effective services. Some political leaders have competed to develop the most punitive and stringent social service and criminal justice policies (NASW 1996). Their rhetoric obscures the real policy dilemma in the case of Lydia M. and in other examples: how to protect children *and* respond effectively to the treatment needs of addicted parents (Freeman 1992; Watson 1992).

Political rhetoric about the war on drugs reflects a war-on-people perspective, contrary to the stated intent, that encourages decision makers to remain detached from these problems. Detachment supports a punishment-only funding philosophy rather than a combined treatment and punishment-as-necessary philosophy, which is more consistent with an empowerment perspective. Detachment and a war-on-people philosophy may prevent policy makers from considering substance abusers' empowerment needs in their funding decisions.

This chapter analyzes the current political environment's impact on the organization and financing of substance abuse services. It highlights conditions and values in the sociopolitical context that are driving reform proposals and decreasing client and community empowerment opportunities. Traditional ways of financing and organizing those services at federal, state, and local levels are described and a different approach outlined. This recommended approach is more consistent with empowerment concepts and a systems-change orientation involving policy-impact research and dissemination activities.

The Current Sociopolitical Environment

It has been said that this country lacks real commitment to resolving its substance abuse problems. It has solved equally complex problems, such as the 1929 depression and the 1950s polio epidemic, by mobilizing and coordinating major technological, economic, political, legal, public health, and human resources (Hale 1989). Why has the United States not yet marshaled its many resources as effectively against substance abuse? Strategies have not been adequate in quantity, comprehensiveness, or coordination, given the severity of the problem. Primm (1992) applied Hippocrates' dictum from 2,400 years ago to today's substance abuse: "Extreme remedies are most appropriate for extreme diseases" (625). This implies a need for large systems and environmental change to resolve the problem.

Perhaps a closer examination of the environment in which the problem and its fragmented responses developed can offer important insights. This environment has been called the sociopolitical or cultural context. It is defined as the combined norms, values, policies, and practices that influence the supply and demand sides of substance abuse (Freeman 1994). It is important for service providers and administrators to understand the nature of this larger environment and the values underlying its operation. Only then can the implications for substance abuse problems and opportunities for influencing empowerment-oriented policy development be clarified.

Nature of the Current Sociopolitical Environment

The current environment operates in such a way that its social and political dimensions are dynamically intertwined. Often it is difficult to separate them or analyze where one dimension ends and the other begins. Focusing on them separately in relation to problems such as substance abuse provides only a partial view of the situation. Therefore, the following section on the social component is presented only as a foundation for illustrating how the two components interact.

The Social Component.   Examples of social factors in the sociopolitical environment include changes in drug lifestyles, patterns of use and abuse, availability of basic resources, and consequences of use and abuse. Changes in these areas have shifted the context in which people become involved in and maintain substance abuse. In the past, many people who used substances as a social experience had separate lifestyles apart from their substance use. However, the normalization of drug use during the 1960s and 1970s has been associated with a major increase in the use of illegal drugs in this country (Kleber 1992). The advent of highly addictive crack, the inexpensive, smokable form of cocaine, and other social factors also have influenced the current drug epidemic (Nunes-Dinis and Barth 1993).

This epidemic has made it more difficult for larger numbers of people to keep their drug abuse separate from other parts of their lives. Many have become immersed in drug lifestyles. Drug use pervades their family, peer, social, work, financial, legal, and housing situations and has resulted in an unfortunate cycle: the immersion of more people into highly visible drug lifestyles has further increased the social acceptance of drug abuse, in what Kleber (1992) calls the normalization process.

A related change in the social context of substance abuse has been in patterns of use and abuse. The increased availability of drugs, especially crack, has led to an increase in polydrug use by a broader range of the population, including all age, racial/ethnic, and socioeconomic groups. For example, some elderly chronic alcohol abusers are now also using crack cocaine and other illegal drugs (Gfroerer 1987; Schonfeld and Dupree 1991; Smart and Adlaf 1988). Many drug dealers use young children and elderly individuals to sell drugs or to move drugs from one part of a city to another because they are less noticeable to law enforcement officers. Many of these "foot soldiers" are already or will soon become polydrug users themselves. Although the pattern of "casual drug use" has decreased in recent years among some youths and young adults, the incidence of heavy and problem use has increased in the general population (NIDA 1988, 1990; Nunes-Dinis and Barth 1993).

Another factor that has changed the social environment and quality of life for some groups is a decreased availability of basic resources. People living in poverty, single female heads of household, and some members of ethnic groups of color are over-represented among the homeless and the under- and unemployed. These high-risk groups are less likely to have access to health care and an adequate food supply compared to the general population (Coulton and Chow 1990; Mulroy 1995; Wilson 1987).

Economic recessions in the last twenty years have affected basic resources for everyone in this country, but already disadvantaged groups have suffered more (Poole 1995). They have experienced increased vulnerability to disempowerment and other environmental stressors associated with health and substance abuse problems. However, substance abuse treatment and prevention resources have become more limited as part of the current national trend toward nondeficit funding (Kunnes et al. 1993).

Equally important in analyzing the social context of substance abuse problems is attention to the changing consequences of abuse. Increased risks for HIV/AIDS, tuberculosis, hepatitis, and congenital syphilis are now associated with the use of certain types of drugs, for example, intravenous heroin and crack cocaine. Primm (1992) indicates there is a higher risk for African American and Latino substance abusers in this regard, "part of a triad of poverty, disease, and unemployment" (616). With these changing consequences, the term "dual diagnosis" is being reconceptualized as poly-diagnosis (e.g., individuals with substance abuse problems, HIV/AIDS, and mental illness).

Another new consequence is the masking and integration of drug profits into legitimate professions and industry in this country. Banking and invest-ment companies, law, real estate, other large and small businesses, and the national and international transportation industry are a few examples (Taylor 1994). This pattern has blurred the line between legitimate business and illegal activities and between white collar and street crime. It is more difficult to trace drug profits and therefore to prosecute these more profitable white collar drug crimes compared to street crimes (Taylor 1994).

The Influence of the Political Component on Social Conditions.   The political component of the environment, or the politicalization process, is both a stimulus and a reaction to the social component. It can distract policy makers from creative and comprehensive problem solving by leading them to focus on symptoms rather than underlying problems and complex social conditions. For instance, politicalization encourages a search for the quick fix or strategy of the week, which often requires little commitment by policy makers and the smallest amount of change. Kleber (1992) likens this search to addicted people's search for the ultimate high, their quick fix for resolving complex life situations. Examples of factors from the political component include the influence of media stereotypes; the drug criminalization move-ment; a fragmented and inequitable system of care; and the conservative movement in government, which supports present cost containment policy reforms.

Media stories have shaped people's perceptions about who substance abusers are and how the country should respond to them. For instance, stereotypes reinforce the idea that most drug abuse, related violence, and other crimes are committed by people in poverty and ethnic groups of color. These stereotypes persist in spite of research findings that most substance abusers and addicted people are white, most people who use substances are not poor, and most of the poor do not use drugs (Kleber 1992; Primm 1992). However, such stereotypes serve a political purpose. Some policy makers use them to blame individual substance abusers and ethnic groups of color. Primm (1992) indicates that "Harsh federal laws against narcotics usually have run parallel with criticism or blame of a foreign nation or ethnic minority" (612). Blaming means the problem does not have to be addressed at a large systems level and conveys an impression that appropriate problem-solving efforts are taking place in the prosecution of individual substance abusers and dealers (Freeman 1996). Consequently, criminal justice policy has failed to address the increasing integration of drug profits into legal industries until recently. Now policy development has shifted its focus to banking practices, for example, to making the use of wire transfers for hiding drug profits illegal (Taylor 1994).

This de-emphasis of drug-related white collar crime is associated with an increased emphasis on criminalizing related street crimes. The criminalization movement has been influenced by data on the changing consequences of substance abuse noted in the social component section, and a get-tough-on-crime political philosophy. For example, epidemiological data have documented the increased availability of drugs, greater involvement in drug lifestyles, polydrug use, and increasingly severe consequences, including higher risks for communicable diseases such as HIV/AIDS. The war on drugs, including increased surveillance and arrests of substance abusers (Lurigio and Davis 1992) and passage of the 1987 Federal Mandatory Sentencing Guidelines (BJS 1992), is a response to those data.

One goal of those guidelines is to increase incarceration rates for people who commit crimes habitually, including substance abusers who commit crimes to pay for drugs. Another goal is to resolve social class, race, and other biases within the justice system's structure (BJS 1992). But inadvertently, political and institutionalized biases may have been built into the guidelines. People in poverty, people of color, and women still have higher incarceration rates compared to more affluent, white, and male populations with the same drug possession charges (Raeder 1993; BJS 1992).

A third political factor is the fragmented and inequitable system of care that has developed for addressing substance abuse problems. Some policy makers have constructed a political reality that assumes the current system is adequate in spite of its gaps and the fragmentation within it. Their narrow perspective keeps them from understanding how the need for services is changing based on new patterns of use and the changes in drug lifestyles discussed under the social component. Moreover, many policy makers do not understand how substance abuse problems and the adequacy of the system of care are affected by other power blocks (Solomon 1987) involving economic and social conditions. Consequently, they believe "tinkering" with the present system is sufficient. Overhauling it may be considered too difficult because of the conservative political and economic trend in the U.S. Congress and among some political constituencies (Poole 1995; Keigher 1994).

Although efforts are being made to coordinate the multiple organizations involved in the present system (Kleber 1992; Primm 1992), the fragmentation, and consequently the negative impact on service outcomes, persists. Levin et. al. (1993) indicate that "specialized alcohol, drug abuse and HIV/AIDS treatment services . . . are often fragmented, isolated from each other and from the primary care system" (2). Other authors suggest, "medicine, mental health, public health, and alcohol and drug treatment represent separate cultures, with different languages and values" (Kunnes et al. 1993:26).

Fragmentation and other financing issues have led to an unequal, two-tier system of care. One part is mostly for people who have insurance or who self-pay and the other is for people who have Medicaid coverage or whose care is reimbursable from other public funds. Publicly funded payment per client is less than 50 percent of that in private programs, and there are long waiting lists for public beds (Kunnes et al. 1993). The failure to reconcile differences in the two systems is at least in part political. Primm (1992) states that health care financing experts have recommended to government that one system, highly coordinated, comprehensive, and equitable, be developed for resolving substance abuse problems. However, this recommendation has not been acted upon to date.

Finally, the present policy reforms in many health and social programs are part of the conservative leadership's efforts toward cost containment. These reforms can lower the national deficit because they restrict the amount of resources and services available and people's access to them (NASW 1996). Economic conditions discussed in the section on the social component have already contributed to a decrease in basic resources. Proposed reforms, such as welfare to work and managed care policies for health and social programs (Personal Responsibility and Work Opportunity Act and the repeal of Title XIX of the Social Security Act), will further reduce the availability of these resources (Freeman 1996). There is competition among policy makers to see who can propose the most restrictive policies. Even liberals have made proposals that are only slightly less restrictive than conservatives' proposals (Freeman 1996; Poole 1995).

For instance, six different proposals were made during 1995 for reforming the Medicaid program. The proposals were from the following sources: 1) the White House, 2) the House Republicans, 3) a group of moderate House Republicans, 4) a conservative coalition of House Democrats, 5) the Senate's Chafee-Breaux bipartisan coalition, and 6) the National Governors' Association (NASW 1996). The proposals differ in how much money they recommend cutting from the program and whose coverage should be eliminated. Common restrictions across the proposals have diminished hope that additional coverage will be included for substance abuse problems. Other proposed reforms that will affect substance abuse services include Block Grants to the states for mental health, Aid to Families of Dependent Children, community revitalization, and maternal and child health. Ryan White funding for HIV/AIDS programs has been cut as well (NASW 1996; Freeman 1996).

It is clear that this intertwined sociopolitical environment influences not only the context in which substance abuse problems develop but also perspectives on those problems and available resources for addressing them. People have more opportunities for empowerment and self-efficacy when their basic needs are being met and when they have some control over key areas of their lives. On the other hand, an inequitable allocation of basic resources, being blamed for individual *and* systemic aspects of the substance abuse problem, having restricted access to a quality system of care when problems develop, and an inequitable criminal justice system related to punishment can increase people's disempowerment experiences and powerlessness. Therefore, this environment, by institutionalizing these power blocks (Solomon 1987), exerts a strong influence on those experiences and on substance abuse policy development.

Value Dimensions Underlying the Sociopolitical Environment

To understand this policy-development process more fully, it is important to analyze the underlying values of the sociopolitical environment. Political judgments and values have been paramount in the establishment of national drug policies (Musto 1987; Primm 1992). Values shape the world views of policy makers—how they seek out and interpret information about substance abuse problems—and then serve as guidelines for developing and reforming policies based on those interpretations. The sources of those values may be personal but also may be part of the accepted culture. Table 3.1 shows that some of these values are pathology-focused

TABLE 3.1 Substance Abuse Policy Formulation Process: Value Dimensions

Pathology-Focused Values (Disempowerment)	Strengths-Focused Values (Empowerment)
Individual Self-Sufficiency emphasis on economic independence and self-control	Collectivism/Family and Community Self-Sufficiency emphasis on mutual interdependence in all domains
Problem-Focused and Blaming Assessment symptom reduction/us-and-them focus	Strengths-Focused Neutral Assessment individual and systems change/personal is political as a unifying mechanism
People Are the Same/Mistrust Diversity categorize people and problems/ depersonalize	People Are Unique/Diversity Is an Opportunity build on and celebrate differences/ personalize and individualize
Privilege Should Be Reserved for the Few some people deserve more than others and are in a protected class	Equity Is Required for All the playing field is uneven for some people and some groups and social supports should be used to achieve equity
Exclusion/Professionals Are the Experts power hoarding/emphasis on authority and scientific knowledge for decision making	Inclusion/Clients and Communities as Experts power sharing/emphasis on collaboration and many ways of knowing for decision making
Competition Is the Best Measure of Value community isolation/"creaming"	Everyone Is of Value community partnerships/rebuilding
People Are Not Responsible/People Are Fragile lack of trust or belief in human potential	People Are Capable of Good and Bad/ People Are Resilient belief in human potential and self-healing/transformation process
Narrow World View/Cause-and-Effect Thinking people are the problem focus/problem definition and the perspective is hopeless	Broad World View/Systems Thinking multiple systems and factors are considered/solution-focused and hopeful perspective

and therefore their impact on policy is to limit empowerment opportunities through funding restrictions. Other values are more strengths-focused because their impact on policy is designed to provide more access to services and to increase consumer and community empowerment (Chapin 1995; Chambers 1993).

The values in Table 3.1 span a broad range within both the pathology and strengths categories, from views about cultural diversity to those about human potential in general. Each set of values also varies across the two categories, for instance, in defining expert knowledge as either the sole knowledge of professionals (pathology focused) or as including the knowledge of clients and the community (strengths focused). Other contrasts between pathology- and strengths-focused values include issues of responsibility (individualism versus collectivism), the sources of problems (people seen as problems versus separation of people and the multiple sources of their problems), and the focus of change (symptom reduction versus individual and systems change).

Two examples are useful for clarifying how these values shape social policy related to substance abuse problems. First, the value of privilege in table 3.1 encourages policies that support the existing two-tier system of care and fragmented public funding patterns. This value implies that affluent people are often more responsible than poor people, so they should be able to have more choices, including engaging in casual drug use. If they develop problems, they deserve a higher quality of care. Economic resources and self-sufficiency are viewed as evidence of privilege and of the right to be one of society's protected classes (Freeman 1996).

In contrast, lack of self-sufficiency (see table 3.1) and adequate resources for obtaining substance abuse services is viewed as evidence of a lack of motivation or will, and of value and cultural deficits (Poole 1995). Based on this attitude, policy reforms were developed by the 104th Congress to restrict services within the public system of care, even though the need for such services is expanding. In contrast, the strengths-focused value of equity encourages policies that provide social supports to augment individual and environmental strengths (Chapin 1995). Community Revitalization Block Grants are an example of an equity-focused policy and funding source that can increase empowerment opportunities and community rebuilding efforts (Freeman 1996).

Privilege implies also that white collar drug-related crimes are negligible compared to street crimes, requiring fewer criminal justice resources. Too, the nature of these crimes (unobserved property and financial crimes) and the perpetrators (businessmen and women) are assumed to be less objectionable than violent street crimes involving drug dealers and users. The result has been policies that provide inequitable penalties for the two types of crimes, such as the Federal Mandatory Sentencing Guidelines and drug property seizure laws (Taylor 1994; BJS 1992).

The value of exclusion provides a second example of how values influence the policy development process (see table 3.1). Proposed reforms such as Block Grants for Mental Health (including substance abuse funding) are consistent with a top-down decision-making paradigm that excludes consumer participation and empowerment. Freeman (1996) indicates that in going from federal entitlement programs to block grants to the states, the "funding system may simply shift from what Freire (1983) calls a monopoly by the 'powerful few' (at the federal level) to a similar hoarding of power at the state and local level" (523).

To decrease the effects of power hoarding and exclusion, strong safeguards should be included in block grant policies that require community involvement in various decision-making boards at the local level (Freeman 1996). Consumers and other community members should be part of the policy-making team based on the value of inclusion or power sharing (see table 3.1). As noted in the epigraph to this chapter, consumer and community involvement allow for inclusion of the diverse voices "and realities of oppressed groups and others experiencing the brunt of social problems" (Chapin 1995:508). Inclusion emphasizes the expert knowledge of consumers and the community rather than professional knowledge alone and top-down decision making. Exclusion, on the other hand, maintains people's powerlessness (Chapin 1995) and the social and political conditions that are risk factors for substance abuse.

Traditional Funding and Service Organizational Patterns

The social and political conditions discussed in the previous section, as well as value dimensions, have impacted traditional ways of funding and organizing substance abuse services from the public and private sectors. However, these two sectors do not operate separately. Public policy has influenced both public and private systems of care, as have policy and funding patterns from the private sector.

Policy Development and Funding Patterns

Key Public Policies.   Table 3.2 illustrates the connections between the development of key substance abuse public policies and related social/political
conditions, and their impact on substance abuse services. For instance, the
1963 Presidential Commission on Narcotic and Drug Abuse effected the
relaxation of mandatory incarceration policies. Similarly, conditions in the
early 1960s led to an increase in society's positive attitudes about drug use
(normalization). About the same time, during the late 1960s, alcohol and
drug abuse treatment became a major part of the public health care system.
Other examples are the rapid increase in drug addiction rates when crack
cocaine became available in large quantities in 1985 and the passage of the
1986 Anti-Drug Abuse Act, which emphasized the war on drugs, law enforcement strategies, and prevention (Kleber 1992).

Table 3.2 is useful also in identifying milestones in substance abuse public policy development prior to and after the 1980s. The 1914 Harrison
Narcotic Act and the 1970 Hughes Bill, which authorized the creation of
the Division of Alcoholism and Alcohol Abuse (NIAAA) within the National
Institute of Mental Health (NIMH), are examples of early milestones. More
recently, a number of special short-term commissions and other initiatives
have addressed and recommended policy for specific areas related to substance abuse problems. See, for example, the 1988 Presidential Commission
on the HIV Epidemic and the 1991 Primary Care-Substance Abuse Linkage
Initiative. While these milestone events have provided special opportunities
to address the problems, the chosen venues have made the development of
consistent and coordinated efforts more difficult.

Prior to the 1980s, nineteen different federal agencies, often with overlapping responsibilities, received funding for substance abuse demand reduction services. Kleber (1992) indicates that this lack of coordination in
fighting the cocaine epidemic led to another milestone, causing Congress
to create the Office of National Drug Control Policy (ONDCP) through the
1988 Anti-Drug Abuse Act. This act also created the Alcohol, Drug Abuse,
and Mental Health Administration (ADAMHA) and made NIDA, NIAAA,
and NIMH research institutes within ADAMHA (see table 3.2). ONDCP's
major goal is demand reduction (reduction of illegal drug use) and supply
reduction through its Offices of Demand and Supply Reduction. The demand reduction goal implies the need to denormalize drug use, which requires decreasing permissive views or "working with the American people

to change attitudes about illicit drugs that prevailed in the last few decades" (Kleber 1992:32). It was assumed that this policy goal, coordination at the federal level, would model and reinforce a similar coordination at state and local levels.

Since the 1980s and this landmark policy, the nineteen federal agencies have been organized into the demand reduction working group shown in figure 3.1. As can be seen from this figure, the policy's demand reduction component includes treatment, education and prevention, the workplace, and international subcommittees. Some agencies are responsible for activities under more than one of the four components. For example, Health and Human Services (HHS) has responsibilities within all four components through its various agencies. The Office of Treatment Improvement (OTI) from HHS sits on the treatment subcommittee, while the Office of Substance Abuse Prevention (OSAP) sits on the education and prevention subcommittee.

Funding Patterns. The complexity of this organization of national agencies and their funding priorities is difficult to illustrate with table 3.2 and figure 3.1 alone. The case of Lydia M. discussed in the introduction of this chapter is useful for demonstrating this complexity in terms of funding for programs for women and infants. Figure 3.2 illustrates the organizational funding and policy structure at the federal, state, county, and local levels for a program in the same midwestern community where Lydia attempted to sell her baby. The 1989 Abandoned Infant Assistance Act at the federal level provided the major funding for this program, Team for Infants Endangered by Substance Abuse (TIES), for two years in 1990 and again for four years in 1992. The focus is on pregnant and postpartum women with substance abuse problems. In spite of the impact of structural factors on these problems, the funders' lowest priority for environmental change is public policy and large systems, while its highest priority is family intervention (McCann 1995).

The objectives for TIES include the following:

1. To strengthen interagency collaboration for families in the program.
2. To prevent child abandonment with crisis intervention and linkage to services.

TABLE 3.2 Social Policy and the Sociopolitical Environment

	Social Policy Developments		Social-Political Conditions/Events
1914	Harrison Narcotic Act and the Narcotic Import and Export Act	1880s and 1920s	first and second national cocaine epidemics
1937	Marijuana Tax Act	1929–35	Great Economic Depression
1938	National Council on Alcoholism (NCA) established	1935	Alcoholics Anonymous (AA) founded
1963	Presidential Comission on Narcotic and Drug Abuse (relaxed mandatory incarceration policies)	1960s–early 1980s	normalization of drug use nationwide (increased positive attitudes toward drug use and abuse among general population)
1970	Hughes Bill established the Division of Alcoholism and Alcohol Abuse (NIAAA) within the National Institute of Mental Health (NIMH)	1967	disease theory of alcoholism endorsed by the American Medical Association (AMA)
1971	Special Action Office for Drug Abuse Prevention established	late 1960s–early 1970s	community-based alcohol and drug abuse treatment became major part of the public health care system (rise of inpatient programs based on Minnesota model)
1974	Uniform Alcoholism and Intoxication Treatment Act		
1975	Title XX of the Social Security Act mandated 75/25 state matching for personal social services	1970s	comprehensive systemwide antismoking campaign launched by federal government

1981	amendment of Title XX of the Social Security Act—block grants for social services, including mental health and substance abuse services	1980	criteria for alcohol dependence first established in the *Diagnostic and Statistical Manual of Mental Disorders (DSM-III)* by the American Psychiatric Association (APA)
		1980s	dramatic increase in percent of general population living below poverty line, homeless, and unemployed due to economic downturns
1986	Anti-Drug Abuse Act (emphasis on war against drugs/law enforcement demand reduction strategies)	1980s	rapid increase in proportion of privately funded alcohol treatment programs and organizations
1987	federal mandatory sentencing guidelines	1985	crack, an inexpensive, smokable form of cocaine, became readily available (third national cocaine epidemic)
1988	Presidential Commission on the HIV Epidemic	mid-1980s	HIV/AIDS epidemic among IV drug users acknowledged as additional risk category
1988	White House Conference for a Drug-Free America	late 1980s	paradigm shift in alcohol and drug abuse prevention programs from education only to resistance training and systems approaches
1988	Anti-Drug Abuse Act created Alcohol, Drug Abuse, and Mental Health Administration (ADAMHA) in the Department of Health and Human Services (HHS) with subdivisions of Office of Substance Abuse Prevention (OSAP), National Institute of Alcoholism and Alcohol Abuse (NIAAA), and Office of National Drug Control Policy (ONDCP)	1989	smokable form of methamphetamine (ICE) introduced to this country in Hawaii

continued

TABLE 3.2 Social Policy and the Sociopolitical Environment *continued*

	Social Policy Developments		Social-Political Conditions/Events
1990	Office of Treatment Improvement (OTI) established as the service delivery agency for ADAMHA	1990s	smokable form of heroin use/abuse increases
1990	Community Partnership Initiative developed by ONDCP in collaboration with HHS for substance abuse prevention and treatment		
1990s	Community Partnership Grants for substance abuse prevention became new initiative using integrated funding (HUD, OSAP, NIDA)	1990s	gradual increase in treatment programs for special populations (women, ethnic groups of color/culture specific; youths, gay males, and lesbians)
1991	Primary Care-Substance Abuse Linkage Initiative of OTI (HIV, substance abuse, and mental health: for polydiagnosis clients)		decrease in the proportion of individuals with private insurance coverage for treatment of mental health and/or substance abuse problems

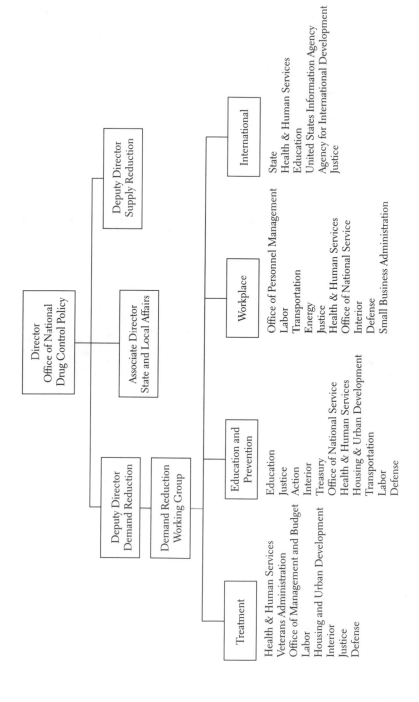

FIGURE 3.1 Federal Organization/Structure: Substance Abuse Policy Development and Reform (Demand Reduction Component)

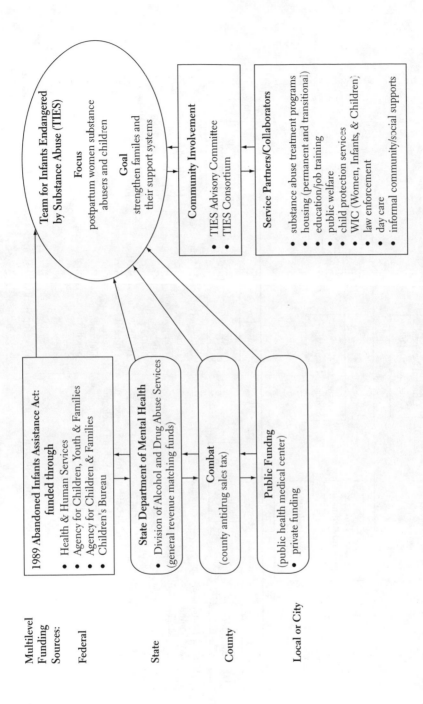

FIGURE 3.2 Multilevel Organizational, Policy, and Funding Dimensions: Perinatal Substance Abuse Services (The Case of Lydia M.)

3. To build problem-solving and daily living skills with participating families.
4. To enhance family functioning and child development with participating families.
5. To assist grandparents and other relative caregivers of drug-exposed children.
6. To provide training to professionals and paraprofessionals working with substance-abusing families.

Services to meet the above objectives involve:

1. Support, substance abuse referral, parent education, and in-home counseling services.
2. Developmental services for each child.
3. Child care and day treatment for drug-exposed children and their siblings.
4. Relative caregiver services.
5. Community training services for formal and informal helpers (TIES 1994).

For the most part, funding from the various federal substance abuse agencies is provided through general revenue appropriations by Congress, some of which match state or local funds (Chapin 1994). Most of these funds are dispersed through targeted service and research grants from the various federal agencies based on proposal applications solicited through requests for proposals (RFPs). These RFPs can support or inhibit empowerment opportunities by the manner in which they organize and mandate service delivery. For example, RFPs based on strengths-focused values typically mandate that services be organized to include community partnerships and consumer-run components. There is often an emphasis on empowerment as well as individual and systems change outcomes.

Another source of public funding for substance abuse services is block grants. These restricted grants represent taxes collected at the federal level that are then transferred from the general treasury to the states and local taxpayers from whom they were collected. Block grants not only target particular problems such as substance abuse but may also target particular high-risk groups (Chapin 1994) among the general population of abusers. Although the money must be spent for the specified function or problem area, states and local communities can decide how to use it within that area. This allows opportunities for input from various local constituency groups on funding for all locations.

Within each state, designated agencies have responsibility for decision making about how those funds are used. A typical agency is a division of alcohol and drug abuse within a department of mental health, which in addition may have separate divisions of mental health and mental retardation (Surls 1994). Other states have a different organizational structure in which there is a *department* of alcohol and drug abuse, along with separate departments of mental health and mental retardation. Even when a state's department of alcohol and drug abuse is separate from its department of mental health, some services for dually diagnosed consumers (those with substance abuse and mental illness) may be housed within the department of mental health (Surls 1994).

The amount of coordination among agencies at the state level is therefore dependent on how administrative departments and their divisions are organized. When the lines of authority are clear and role overlapping and conflicts are low, coordination is often less difficult. High coordination among departments and divisions is extremely important for effective policy development. But coordination of policy and funding by states is affected also by the amount of resources available at the federal level. When funding for alcohol, drugs, and mental health was collapsed into the Alcohol, Drug Abuse, and Mental Health Block Grants through the 1988 Anti-Drug Abuse Act, the amount of money available to various states was greatly reduced (Chapin 1994). Thus, the value of competition (see table 3.1) among state departments may currently be emphasized more because this federal policy has decreased their resources.

In addition, recent public policy development has influenced the growth of the privatization funding movement involving managed care providers who contract with public agencies for funds in order to provide substance abuse services. Both private for-profit and nonprofit providers bid on these contracts. Managed care policies often contain hidden incentives that discourage providers from extending services to meet needs once the preset fees per client have been reached (Freeman 1996). Moreover, policies may restrict what services are provided and how they are organized through cost containment incentives and reimbursement restrictions. Time spent by primary care providers in alcohol and other drug abuse screening or in counseling or making referrals for related services is not usually covered (Levin et al. 1993). Services such as peer-led treatment and practitioners' family-focused in-home prevention activities may not be reimbursed because they are not provided by professionals or they involve home visits outside the required service setting (Chamberlain 1995).

A third source of funding for substance abuse services can be special local or state taxes (Chapin 1994), such as community mill levies, local initiatives, and state or local alcohol user taxes. These funds may be designated for particular services during the period of taxation or for general use for those services. Either type of funding pattern can affect how services are conceptualized and organized. Some user taxes are designated to fund and expand traditional substance abuse services that may encourage a more pathology-focused framework, emphasizing individual change only. Other tax funding policies have taken a more innovative empowerment approach by mandating consumer-involved outcome-based evaluation or the use of peer technicians for outreach activities (Freeman 1994; Surls 1994).

Private Funding of Substance Abuse Services and Related Policy

In addition to public policy, some private sources of funding are also shaping the funding and organization of substance abuse services. Many of these growing private sources emphasize empowerment and community re-building from a much more comprehensive and holistic perspective. Some include foundations that are now generalizing what they have learned about best practices from their international initiatives in developing countries to urban and rural communities in the United States. Two examples of this type of designated private funding are The Robert Wood Johnson Fighting Back Initiative and the W. K. Kellogg Foundation's Urban Community Initiatives. Both foundations emphasize influencing public policy, prevention, and outcome-based and ethnographic evaluation.

The Robert Wood Johnson Foundation funded 15 community planning grants in 1987 from a pool of 300 applications. In 1992, the Foundation provided $26 million to fund five-year implementation grants for the same sites for up to $3 million each (Kleber 1992). The goal of these grants is community, public policy, and systems change in regard to substance abuse problems, using an empowerment and strengths framework. In order to qualify for implementation funding, the projects had to develop community partnerships that included formal and informal leaders and other community residents.

The W. K. Kellogg Foundation's African American Men and Boys Initiative (AAMB) provided grants to 32 sites nationally to strengthen services to African American males in 1993 and again in 1995. The emphasis was on leadership development and violence and substance abuse prevention, not only with African American males but also with males from other ethnic groups and females who are served by the programs. Public policy impact, academic achievement, and focus on social and educational goals were the means for achieving the identified outcomes. Although many of the core components across programs were similar, the programs were organized into clusters based on their emphasis: personal growth and leadership, entrepreneurial leadership, and family and community improvement. In addition to supporting the programs' various direct services to men and boys and females, the Foundation has helped the programs organize themselves into a collaborative that will seek out funding for their collective public policy and large systems change initiatives (Gordon 1996).

A Proposed Funding and Service–Integrated Organizational Paradigm

This discussion on funding and policy patterns has highlighted the strengths and barriers inherent in the current public/private system. Other approaches to funding and policy development are needed to overcome those barriers to empowerment and effective service delivery. A proposed approach is briefly summarized in this section, as a step toward exploring alternative policy and funding paradigms. The discussion includes a different conceptual framework and related policy, the organization of integrated services, the required funding, and the field's role in policy/research activities for influencing the necessary policy and funding changes.

The Conceptual Framework and Related Policy

The proposed conceptual framework is based upon Chapin's (1995) assumptions that "the integration of the strengths perspective into the social policy making process can provide policy practitioners with new tools for conceptualizing social needs or problems, a more inclusive approach to policy formulation, and an expanded array of empowering policy options" (507). Systems theory and an ecological perspective are other important aspects of this framework. As noted by Hanson (1991), substance abuse and addiction are socially acquired and maintained by multiple consequences and impinging systems. Policy needs to consider all social conditions that precipitate, reinforce, and affect substance abuse problems and resistance.

The framework draws upon the strengths-focused values included in table 3.1, which apply specifically to substance abuse and related problems/needs. For instance, the value of collectivism and mutual interdependence normalizes "each family's need for social supports at various points in its life cycle due to a changing and dynamic goodness of fit between needs and resources" (Freeman 1996:525). This value and others in table 3.1 provide a rationale for social policies that offer such supports at different critical stages of the life cycle.

The need for supports may occur at a particular stage when existing strengths and resiliency in the individual and environment are insufficient (Freeman and Pennekamp 1988), or a combination of individual and environmental factors may lead to substance abuse at critical points in reaction to certain environmental stressors or inadequate problem solving. Public policy is needed not only to normalize and provide formal social supports according to strengths-focused values but also to encourage the use of informal social supports for helping to resolve substance abuse and other problems.

Organization of the Proposed Services and Policy

An equitable and integrated, wrap-around system of care is needed to effectively achieve individual and environmental change. Integrated services models concentrate a broad array of comprehensive services in one site for "one-stop shopping" (Aguirre 1995). For example, in the case of Lydia M. discussed in the introduction to this chapter, some of the ten different systems implicated in her situation—housing, education, public assistance, work and employment, child protective services, substance abuse treatment, criminal justice, local policy, health care, and the family and community—could have been concentrated into an integrated services model for more effective coordination.

An integrated model like that in figure 3.3 involving some or all of these systems would have assessed and addressed Lydia M.'s needs at several important points: during prenatal care if she came for services; at the point of delivery; or during substance abuse treatment related to gender, education, work, and systems change issues. Aftercare planning related to transitional housing, relapse prevention, family and other social supports, and community service by Lydia might have presented other empowerment and coordination opportunities. In figure 3.3, it is clear that substance abuse services are the "hub" for the array of related services in the model's "wheel."

Integrated models increase opportunities for coordination of services and therefore for greater efficiency and creativity in addressing needs. Coordination is achieved by community advisory or executive boards, which represent diverse constituencies within a community, and by a director, liaison staff, and a coordinative committee who are organizational representatives of the services being provided. Moreover, the proposed integrated services model can be enhanced by making it community-centered to offer multiple opportunities for empowerment and self-efficacy. Community-centered approaches "require structural components that make programs accountable to community members by involving them in advisory, executive, and citizen review boards for planning, implementing, and monitoring programs." These approaches include the use of peer-led services "by youth, family members, and other community residents" (Freeman 1996b:4). The details of the proposed integrated services model, in terms of organizational and power issues and in-service delivery involving consumer and community participation, are discussed more fully in chapter 5.

Strengths-focused policies are needed to support these models, including mandates for both peer and community involvement as well as individual and environmental changes. In addition, policy reforms are needed to link the primary health care and substance abuse systems and their private and public tiers. These reforms can address the present gaps and lack of coordination that make it difficult for individuals with polydiagnoses to receive integrated services and treatment for mental health, HIV/AIDS, and substance abuse in the same program.

Some existing public and private policy supports the use of integrated service models. Kunnes et al. (1993) indicates that co-location of services, or "one-stop shopping," is supported by OTI's Office of Primary Care and Substance Abuse Linkage. In addition, the Robert Wood Johnson Foundation's Fighting Back project is one of several private sector initiatives for

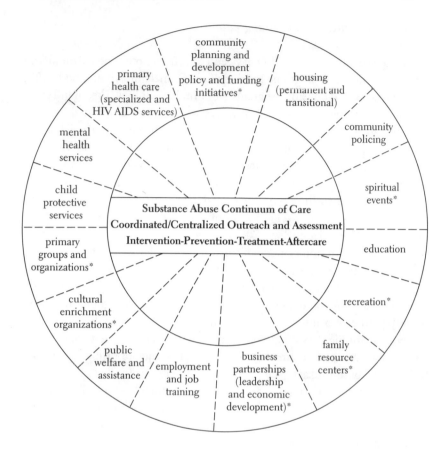

*Sources of informal community supports for addressing substance abuse and other problems that collaborate with formal and partnership supports.

FIGURE 3.3 Community-Centered Integrated Service System (Integrated Policy, Funding, and Service Streams)

coordinating substance abuse treatment services from prevention and early intervention to treatment and aftercare, instead of traditionally separating treatment and prevention (Kunnes et al. 1993). The proposed integrated services model in figure 3.3 requires a similar concentration of services that cover the entire continuum of care in one setting. Such services and related policy require changes in the current funding patterns and priorities.

Supportive Integrated Funding Patterns

Merged or integrated funding has been effective in other fields, including academic and social programs in education (Pennekamp 1980) and health, mental health, and housing programs for homeless families (Freeman 1996); therefore, it is not a new idea. It involves well-planned combined funding from two or more federal or private sources, which provides a mechanism for state and local authorities to serve their various populations with substance abuse problems in an integrated fashion. "This (approach) requires careful monitoring and bookkeeping so that each funding component can be clearly linked to the service it provides to the target population. The advantages, however, outweigh the administrative complexities, which exist in any case" (Pennekamp 1980:70).

Although this funding mechanism has been used successfully in other fields, its use in substance abuse prevention and treatment is relatively new. Examples of first efforts do exist, including funding for co-location of services, primary care, and substance abuse collaborative programs and community partnership initiatives. Co-location of services is perhaps the least invasive beginning step; it has been provided through some federal agencies such as the Office of Treatment Improvement's Office of Primary Care and Substance Abuse Linkage (see 1990 entries in table 3.2).

The latter agency supports a co-location treatment philosophy through targeted funding for comprehensive health care in traditional primary health care settings that includes assessment and treatment for alcohol and other drugs and progressive managed mental health programs with alcohol and drug treatment providers, including psychiatrists with various subspecialties, psychologists, social workers, and nurses (Kunnes et al. 1993). An underlying assumption for such funding is that service accessibility will increase substance abuse referral networks and improve case management services. A disadvantage of this type of funding is that it provides only minimal support for the more comprehensive integrated services model proposed in figure 3.3.

Funding designed to directly improve or strengthen collaboration among service providers presents a second type of opportunity for integrated funding. For example, an Office of Treatment Improvement–sponsored effort through the same Primary Care and Substance Abuse Linkage Initiative is designed to strengthen collaboration between primary care providers and HIV/AIDS, substance abuse, and mental health treatment systems (Kunnes et al. 1993). To ensure that services are integrated and coordinated once funding is available, treatment programs must complement their care with case management, vocational rehabilitation, social services, transportation, child care, and other supportive services and involve consumers in developing the service guidelines.

Currently, separate reimbursement and funding patterns are inadequate to support the proposed linkages. Policy, treatment, and financing experts are attempting to develop payment mechanism reforms to increase the coverage and merged funding streams necessary to strengthen these linkages. This funding strategy for improved collaboration, while promising, is still in the planning stages and is more narrow than the funding required for the proposed integrated services model in figure 3.3.

Funding initiatives for community partnerships and coalition building are closest to the type of integrated funding that is needed. The Office of Substance Abuse Prevention (OSAP) in HHS provided $50 million in 1990 and more than $100 million in 1991 for these types of efforts (Kleber 1992). The ONDCP and HHS cooperated to develop the Community Partnership Initiative for comprehensive community-involved prevention services (Kleber 1992). It is not clear whether such funding can be sustained in the current period of social program and cost containment reforms, especially with present cuts in OASP funding (NASW 1996). However, an implication of these beginning efforts toward integrated funding is the need for treatment and prevention professionals to collaborate in advocating for more supportive policy reforms.

Conclusion

The "war on drugs" is an unfortunate, although well-intentioned, metaphor for this country's goal of solving its complex substance abuse problems. This metaphor has encouraged a pattern of leaders' excluding stakeholders from policy making and therefore excluding them from the implementation of programs funded by these policies. It has also heightened competition among policy makers to develop the most punitive pathology-focused reforms rather than individually and collectively to overhaul the current inequitable and inadequate system of care.

The resulting policy war has diverted attention away from other structural problems in the sociopolitical environment toward various symptoms and quick-fix solutions. An example is the increased criminalization of drug-related street crimes, which may be appropriate, but only as part of a broad array of comprehensive approaches developed from a systematic study of the problems and underlying conditions. The inclusion of consumers and community members in the study and development process is critical and less likely than traditional, exclusionary decision making to result in fragmented approaches such as that applied in the tragic case of Lydia M. Such casualties of this war are unacceptable.

4 The Community Development and Primary Group Subsystem: Sources of Power, Resiliency, and Substance Abuse Prevention

> In (community) mobilizing, people who have been disempowered and dispossessed begin to find their voices, to discover confidence, to feel that they actually have a chance of changing the conditions of their lives and communities.
> —S. Kahn (1995:571)

The discussion in chapter 3 on integrated substance abuse policy, funding, and service delivery raises questions about the community's role in supporting such systems. Communities should not only advocate for empowerment-oriented policy and services in this field but also should strengthen their members' general self-sufficiency and quality of life. These supports enable individuals and families to resist substance abuse by serving as protective factors (Hawkins and Catalano 1992). Communities with an array of protective factors are more likely to be empowered. Often they can avoid some of the problems experienced by disempowered communities.

Empowered communities are able to mobilize members in direct response to specific problems (Kahn 1995). One substance abuse treatment program reported that some of its graduates were having difficulty reintegrating themselves into their communities. Program graduates felt either stigmatized or invisible, each of which made them feel disempowered. Members of an antidrug campaign in one community responded by developing several reintegration opportunities for recovering residents. For example, they recruited some graduates to be mentors for youths participating in a prevention program and scheduled AA and NA meetings as part of an annual community picnic held to celebrate the campaign's successes.

Community mobilization can involve the use of existing resources, as in the antidrug campaign in the previous example, or new resources that may be developed. Each experience of consciousness raising and social action that addresses a problem situation effectively increases a community's empowerment capacity. Communities can become empowered also by mobilizing residents in response to more long-term needs for social or economic development (Martinez-Brawley 1995). The focus may be on conditions that increase the impact of risk factors associated with substance abuse. Risk factors include community norms favorable to drugs, availability of drugs, lack of economic growth and prosperity, inadequate leadership, community disorganization, and low community attachment and bonding (Hawkins and Catalano 1992).

In one community a two-year social planning process was initiated in response to a series of newspaper articles and new census data indicating the presence of many of these risk factors. The planning process resulted in a number of community development initiatives and partnerships for implementing them. One partnership between law enforcement and a coalition of social action organizations focused on eliminating drug sales and related violence.

Thus, communities are an important component of the multilevel service system charged with helping to prevent and treat substance abuse problems. For effective empowerment practice, social workers and other helping professionals must understand this component and its role, which are analyzed in this chapter. Factors that influence how well communities respond to their role demands are discussed; then models of practice for involving communities in prevention and treatment, with emphasis on those consistent with integrated services and empowerment approaches, are described.

Roles of the Community Subsystem

Definitions of Community and Role Expectations

Defining communities and identifying their expected roles is a difficult task. Pelly-Effrat (1974) notes that "the elusive concept of community is like Jello: It is slippery and hard to hold" (quoted in Martinez-Brawley 1995:539). Never has this metaphor been more true than today. The increasing mobility and transitions experienced by members of this society have changed both the nature of communities and our attitudes about them. There is more reliance on communities to meet basic needs as extended family networks have grown smaller (Harrison 1995) and social relationships have been disrupted significantly by the drug epidemic (Etzioni 1993).

Current definitions reflect this expansion of roles but also point out some of the enduring characteristics of communities. A community has been defined as "a network, or informal relationships between people connected with each other by kinship, common interest, geographical proximity, friendship, occupation, or the giving and receiving of services—or various combinations of these" (National Institute for Social Work 1982:199). People defining themselves as a community, based on one or more perceived commonalities, is another characteristic (Darvill and Smale 1990), regardless of the community's structure or functions.

General Community Roles

Definitions such as the one above emphasize the traditions of social care and mutual interdependence among residents that are addressed currently in different ways by various types of communities (for example, urban, rural, small, large, affluent, poor) (Hawkins and Catalano 1992; Martinez-Brawley 1995; Poole 1995). These caring community roles lead to empowerment because they focus on either enhancing the functioning of communities (improving citizen participation) or reforming major social structures (shifting power from institutions to people when power inequities and inconsistencies exist) (Darvill and Smale 1990; Florin and Wandersman 1990). The roles illustrate what communities do for their members—the various functions they perform.

Examples of these general community roles include advocacy, social and economic development, political action, social justice, social support, services integration, attachment and bonding, socialization, and leadership development (Harrison 1995; Rubin and Rubin 1986). Empowered communities fulfill more of these roles consistently over time due to protective factors such as opportunities for residents to become involved in decision making. A combination of factors may hinder disempowered communities from developing and maintaining such roles, including institutionalized power blocks and serious risk versus protective factors (Hawkins and Catalano 1992). Lerner (1979) indicates that surplus powerlessness, or perceptions in some disempowered communities that the members cannot change their situations, is another factor.

Special Community Roles: The Multilevel Service System

Some community roles serve particular functions in the multilevel substance abuse treatment system. These roles develop within communities according to the severity of existing substance abuse problems and how well the environment supports or discourages their development and maintenance. Three examples are the mediation, community development, and health promotion roles. The mediation role is the most basic, needed within all communities. The community development and health promotion roles provide additional supports for the substance abuse service system and strengthen communities in other ways that can lead to empowerment.

The Mediation Role.   It is critical for communities to assume a mediation role regarding substance abuse among their members, policy conflicts between internal organizations, and funding/policy decisions by external systems that affect them. The mediation role is necessary in all communities for strengthening the substance abuse service system, but especially in disempowered communities with fewer protective versus risk factors. Communities must provide a consistent and strong set of norms that are unfavorable to drug use. It is equally important to reinforce primary groups (youth associations) and other organizations (civic groups) that help to support and apply the norms (figure 4.1).

These consistent standards help the community to arbitrate disagreements and different perspectives about substance abuse treatment and prevention priorities and needs. Power issues also help determine how those differences are mediated, and therefore who and what criteria determine the problem's severity, the most at-risk populations, the needed resources, and allocation of those resources. This specialized role involves mediating the following issues:

1. the community's norms about substance abuse (how strongly individuals and families should be discouraged from using substances through natural consequences and community-service provider partnerships, e.g., cosponsoring a youth curfew policy to impact drug use and violence)

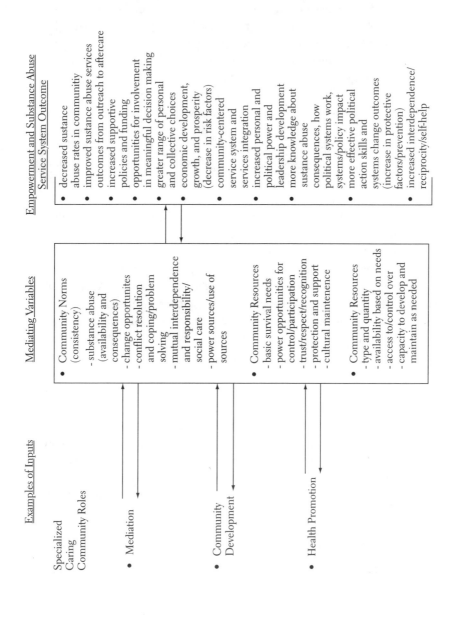

Examples of Inputs

Specialized
Caring
Community Roles

• Mediation

• Community
  Development

• Health Promotion

Mediating Variables

• Community Norms
  (consistency)
  - substance abuse
    (availability and
    consequences)
  - change opportunites
  - conflict resolution
    and coping/problem
    solving
  - mutual interdependence
    and responsibility/
    social care
  - power sources/use of
    sources

• Community Resources
  - basic survival needs
  - power opportunities for
    control/participation
  - trust/respect/recognition
  - protection and support
  - cultural maintenence

• Community Resources
  - type and quantity
  - availability based on needs
  - access to/control over
  - capacity to develop and
    maintain as needed

Empowerment and Substance Abuse
Service System Outcome

• decreased sustance
  abuse rates in community
• improved sustance abuse services
  outcomes from outreach to aftercare
• increased supportive
  policies and funding
• opportunities for involvement
  in meaningful decision making
• greater range of personal
  and collective choices
• economic development,
  growth, and prosperity
  (decrease in risk factors)
• community-centered
  service system and
  services integration
• increased personal and
  political power and
  leadership development
• more knowledge about
  sustance abuse
  consequences, how
  political systems work,
  systems/policy impact
• more effective political
  action skills and
  systems change outcomes
  (increase in protective
  factors/prevention)
• increased interdependence/
  reciprocity/self-help

FIGURE 4.1 Impact of Community Roles on the Multilevel Substance Abuse Service System

2. substance abuse service outcomes (mediating between internal organizations to encourage resource development, resource prioritizing and management, and services integration: community-sponsored How to Cope Groups for families, community-centered reintegration services for recovering people, integrated service models involving the substance abuse continuum of care and other social programs)
3. public policy and funding decisions (resolving conflicts between community needs and external systems' funding priorities: influencing block grant allocations, supporting grant development, conducting policy impact analyses, advocating for policy reforms, disseminating substance abuse developments and research findings).

When they mediate or arbitrate their own anti–drug use norms consistently, some communities are perceived as self-sufficient and empowering by their members and by external systems (Lurigio and Davis 1992). In communities where disempowerment experiences are frequent, the community norms may be inconsistent with practices that occur. A community may give antidrug messages but fail to eliminate street drug sales and the sale of drug paraphernalia in convenience stores, or law enforcement may focus on preventing street drug sales but ignore stores that sell tobacco and alcohol to minors. In those situations, the community's failure to consistently promote and mediate its own norms may indicate to residents that they are powerless to resolve the problems. This failure also undermines the effectiveness of the community's substance abuse service system.

Consistent norms make it easier for more resourceful communities to arbitrate between internal systems, including networks of treatment and prevention providers that often serve the same families but have different priorities. Primary groups and other community organizations sometimes have different goals and ideas about resolving substance abuse problems. Providers' priorities may differ from those of community members, especially regarding members' input into program development and implementation decisions. Fitzpatrick and Gerard (1993) indicate, "To assume that residents share the same knowledge, perceptions, and feelings regarding alcohol and drug use as program developers or even community leaders can be a grave mistake"(953–54). Therefore, consistent norms help communities give voice to and mediate conflicting perspectives more effectively, thus enhancing the work of integrated service systems.

Similarly, consistent norms are important when a community mediates different policy and funding priorities between internal and external systems. A community may be required to represent diverse needs to local, county, state, and national decision makers whose resource priorities and concerns about empowerment conflict with those of the community. Through community mediation, primary groups, service providers, informal leaders, and other residents can influence external systems' decisions about substance abuse resources. The mediation process can help them to gain "personal and collective efficacy related to concepts of empowerment" (Florin and Wandersman 1990:43).

The Community Development Role.   This role involves efforts to create conditions that lead to social and economic progress (Martinez-Brawley 1995), along with a shift of power from external leaders to local constituencies (Harrison 1995). It may become necessary when a community's members cannot be mobilized initially to resolve a specific problem such as substance abuse. In other situations, a series of unsatisfactory events or conditions (police brutality, community violence, deteriorated housing, drug sales, inadequate political representation, lack of economic development) may reveal a common root problem, which is often labeled either surplus powerlessness (Learner 1979) or a lack of real autonomy and self-determination (Rubin and Rubin 1986) (figure 4.1).

The solution involves "mobilizing and enabling people to make choices about whether and how they want to work to enhance community functioning" leading to their "empowerment" (Harrison 1995:561). The common goal is improved community self-sufficiency and an infrastructure that supports strong indigenous leadership. Consequently, the community development role includes the following types of activities:

1. economic development (changes that help the community and members to prosper and eliminate substance abuse risk factors, resulting in job training and work, cooperatives, microenterprises, local investments, enterprise zones, and other capacity-building opportunities)
2. citizen participation (involvement of primary groups, self- and mutual-help groups, community organizations, and individuals who model norms unfavorable to drug use in mobilization and decision-making processes)

3. community-centered service systems (shifting control of the overall service system to internal actors: community-run schools, community governing boards for social service organizations, community-led integrated services models for substance abuse treatment and prevention, community-run antidrug campaigns)
4. political power (creating shared internal leadership infrastructure, leadership development and mentoring of youths/adults; shifting power from external to internal control: winning elections, participating in policy decisions, social action, educating constituencies about large systems' operations).

Because the long-term goal of community development is self-sufficiency, these types of activities can also strengthen the work of the substance abuse service system. The political aspects of the role help to build or rebuild a community leadership infrastructure (Freeman 1996a) that can collaborate with the service system in influencing policy reforms. The goal of economic development is not only to provide work opportunities (e.g., to eliminate risk factors) but also to develop local enterprises that contribute to the community's overall economy and stability. The rebuilding process can help resolve the initial problems that required the community development role and the root problem of powerlessness. Thus, through this role communities can build their capacities for autonomy and empowerment while resolving their substance abuse problems.

The Health Promotion Role. This community role is important in substance abuse prevention and empowerment because it teaches self-regulation or control over one's behavior and the environment (Leukefeld and Battjes 1992). It may be more possible in communities that have experienced some success in mediation, community development, and other basic roles. Those experiences can often lead to the development or enhancement of protective factors and a sense of community empowerment. Health promotion is based on wellness principles that emphasize a broad, more proactive approach to reducing risk factors in many areas. Risk factors often are associated with more than one problem: for example, poverty is a risk factor for teenage pregnancy, substance abuse, and school dropouts (Chilman 1980). This assumption indicates that more comprehensive health promotion approaches are potentially more effective in protecting against substance abuse and other problems (figure 4.1).

This role can encompass promoting good physical health, physical fitness, mental health, stress management, nutrition, family life development, racial/ethnic relations, communication and conflict resolution, alcohol and drug-free lifestyles, and consumerism (Caplan and Weissberg 1989; Hawkins and Catalano 1992). The following types of activities and examples are related to it (Hawkins and Catalano 1992; Moore 1994):

1. awareness activities (public service announcements and dissemination of written materials about healthy lifestyles, substance abuse and other risk assessments, power analyses)
2. information and knowledge for increasing personal choices and alternatives (community education including alcohol-drug education, consciousness raising, and lifelong learning curricula)
3. life skill development based on life cycle transitions (increases in individual/family behaviors or competencies that support healthy lifestyles and effective coping: preventive health care, communication, problem solving, money management)
4. resource development (changes in large systems' policies, procedures, and practices that are favorable to substance use/abuse and unfavorable to healthy development, empowerment, and social supports).

Thus, the health promotion role protects residents against factors associated with substance abuse and other problems by strengthening and broadening the community's total prevention infrastructure. The underlying wellness principles provide norms about healthy lifestyles consistent with prevention programs' anti–drug use norms. This role can support substance abuse interventions staged by the nuclear or extended family, co-workers, church members, or peers in social organizations (pretreatment activities), through community education about wellness principles, or it may involve a community utilizing recovering people in substance abuse resource development or awareness activities as part of their treatment or post-treatment twelve-step work.

Factors That Influence Community Roles

A number of factors influence whether communities assume the roles discussed in the previous section and how they involve themselves in the service system of care. Communities whose members feel bonded with and in control of their environments often mediate substance abuse service outcomes by encouraging residents to support reintegration activities for recovering people. Those whose members are unattached and chronically powerless are not as likely to promote development activities such as residents' involvement in political action. Public policy, communities' frameworks about inclusion, and their service organizations' power structure are examples of factors that influence these roles.

Public Policy Influences

The foundation for community involvement in the substance abuse service system is public policy, which can either support or hinder the necessary roles. Policies that require or encourage community partnerships for substance abuse prevention and treatment are one example. Some require substance abuse treatment programs for prenatal women and their children to collaborate with homeless shelters that serve the same population (Galanter, Egelko, De Leon, and Tohrs 1992). Others fund joint training projects and similar partnerships between child welfare and substance abuse practitioners serving families at risk for child abuse and substance abuse (Bays 1990).

The Community Service and Economic Revitalization Block Grants proposed by the 104th Congress in 1996 are another type of policy that supports caring community roles. These and other block grants were designed to decentralize funding, returning decision making and power to local and state control (Freeman 1996a). The grants can help residents and community organizations to rebuild disorganized and economically disadvantaged communities troubled by drugs, crime, powerlessness, and other problems.

The underlying philosophy of such funding is commitment to the community service ethic and long-term community development and capacity building (Byron 1992; Freeman 1996a). This philosophy encourages communities to adopt the caring community roles of mediation, community development, and health promotion by providing the formal social supports for such roles. Policies that ignore structural barriers and encourage competition rather than partnerships among organizations in the substance abuse service system reduce opportunities for communities to take on such roles, making it more difficult for them to be self-sufficient in addressing these and other problems and exacerbating existing power blocks.

Community Frameworks

The degree to which a community embraces an inclusion or empower-ment framework is another influence on its assumption of caring roles. The empowerment framework requires service systems to shift from a community-based to a community-centered approach. Communities that have more community-based systems have a number of advantages in spite of their limitations. These systems often are located in physically accessible sites such as public schools or community centers. Services are school- or health-linked, involving a range of comprehensive, integrated, and wrap-around programs (Aquirre 1995). They depend on the community's support for continuance, for example, for substance abuse referrals and co-sponsorship of awareness activities. However, a lack of more active involve-ment of community members limits the systems' accountability as well as their commitment to the community (Freeman 1996b).

In comparison, some communities require service systems to be community-centered, which increases their accountability. Community-centered systems have the same broad range of services as community-based systems, but their accountability includes required community involvement in planning, implementing, and monitoring the whole range of integrated services, including substance abuse programs (see figure 3.3 in chapter 3). Freeman (1966b) indicates that certain factors in community-centered sys-tems enhance accountability, such as service by community members on programs' executive and advisory boards and peer-led services by consumers, community residents, and informal leaders from all age groups. These sys-tems increase empowerment opportunities "by focusing also on consumer-determined, long-term family and community capacity-building" (Freeman 1996a:529). This focus complements the community development and me-diation roles discussed earlier.

The capacity-building focus of community-centered systems is similar to Moore's (1994) description of the Community Empowerment Paradigm, shown in table 4.1, which "requires inclusion at every level and at each step of the process" (13). In contrast, because community-based systems utilize community support in more limited ways, their residents' empowerment experiences are limited as well. Table 4.1 reinforces the assumption that those systems hinder caring community roles because they emphasize "do-ing for the community" (paternalism) and "maintaining external leadership" (power hoarding).

TABLE 4.1 Community Empowerment System:
A Contrast in Paradigms (Lee 1994)

Delivery of Service Paradigm	*Community Empowerment Paradigm*
professionals are responsible	shared responsibility
doing for the community	doing with the community
power vested in agencies	power residing with the community
professionals seen as experts	community is the expert
planning and services responsive to each agency's mission	services planned/implemented based on community's needs
fragmentation of planning and services delivery	planning and services integrated, interdependent
external leadership based on authority, position, and title	internal leadership based on shared vision, broad support, community problem solving
denial of ethnic and cultural differences	ethnic diversity is valued
external linkages limited to networking and coordination	emphasis on cooperation and collaboration
decision-making process is closed	decision-making process is inclusive
accountability is to the agency	accountability is to the community
primary purpose of evaluation is to determine funding	evaluation is used to check program implementtaion and decision making
categorical funding issues predominate	funding based on critical health or need
community participation limited to providing input and feedback	community maximally involved at all levels

The Power Structure of Service Organizations

Three types of empowerment organizations identified in chapter 1 are a third potential influence on the roles that communities fulfill. Table 1.4's conceptualization implies that some organizations' power structures are so closed that they are not at all empowerment-oriented. Other organizations range from empowering to microcosm to empowered according to the opportunities they provide for participants to influence personal/interpersonal, organizational, and political or large systems change. For example, substance abuse programs in the empowered category offer the greatest support for many caring community roles. One source of support is required community service by program participants as part of treatment or prevention services (e.g., mentoring youths or volunteering in a soup kitchen). Other examples include opportunities for social and political action by participants that contributes to community development and rebuilding (e.g., service on community planning boards).

Community Roles and Self-Sufficiency: Practice Implications

Having identified caring community roles and factors that influence them, it is important to clarify practitioner skills and approaches that can facilitate community self-sufficiency. This is often the underlying goal, whether a community's immediate focus is resolving substance abuse issues or changing more long-term conditions that contribute to a range of problems, including substance abuse. Weil and Gamble (1995) summarize eight specific models of community practice for social workers, two of which are very consistent with this chapter's focus on empowerment practice and integrated service systems. Martinez-Brawley's (1995) conceptualization of community-oriented social work as an overarching framework for all community models is also relevant to this discussion. Although these authors focus on general practice rather than on particular problems, many of their ideas can be applied readily to substance abuse and power issues.

Models of Community Practice

Weiland and Gamble (1995) assume that "Community practice uses multiple methods of empowerment-based interventions to strengthen participation in democratic processes, assist groups and communities in advocating for their needs and organizing for social justice, and improve the effectiveness and responsiveness of human services systems" (577). They include under the umbrella of community practice models neighborhood and community organizing, organizing functional communities, community social and economic development, social planning, program development and community liaison, political and social action, coalitions, and social

THE MULTILEVEL SERVICE SYSTEM

movements. Although all of these models grew out of this country's social work traditions (Weil and Gamble 1995), the community social and economic development and political and social action models are most consistent with the resources needed for an effective substance abuse service system.

The Community Social and Economic Development Model.   This model is particularly relevant to effective practice in low-income and oppressed communities in which social and economic conditions interact as risk factors that limit self-sufficiency. To eliminate those risk factors, the model emphasizes a community reinvestment philosophy that targets external systems to provide resources, leading to economic profits that are expected to remain in the community. Resources may come from government, banks, foundations, corporations and other businesses, and external developers (Weil and Gamble 1995). The model also involves the establishment of basic services, such as housing and job training, as part of the community's infrastructure development (National Congress for Community Economic Development 1991).

This grassroots approach is designed to strengthen the empowerment capacity of both residents and the community by developing people's leadership, technical, management, political, and process skills. These skills may be absent in some urban and rural communities with large numbers of low-income, marginalized, or oppressed groups. The lack of education about systems and skill development in problem solving and decision making often contributes to loss of hope and surplus powerlessness, which in turn contribute to the development of substance abuse problems and other social and economic conditions that are the basis for community decay and disorganization. Thus, the model's focus on these conditions and power issues makes it particularly useful for strengthening community development and health promotion roles and enhancing the substance abuse service system's effectiveness.

Social workers and other helping professionals may be hired by a grassroots economic development corporation within a community, a substance abuse treatment and/or prevention coalition, a local prevention initiative focused on multiple problems, or funders of the community development process (the government or a foundation). To use this model effectively, the selected practitioner skills and roles should be considered in terms of community and power dynamics. For example, needs assessment skills include the ability to assess and emphasize a community's strengths and other resources as well as its problems. Assessments should include and value input from all racial/ethnic, gender, sexual orientation, age, income, and political constituencies based on an empowerment perspective (Freeman 1994; Hawkins and Catalano 1992). Table 4.2 is an example of a community assessment from designed for youths' feedback on community conditions. Since these assessments are the basis of subsequent action leading to social and economic development, conducting them is both a technical skill and a political act (Tropman 1995). Other skills relevant to this model include planning, goal setting, organization, training, leadership development, group process, management, and conflict negotiation skills. It is critical for social workers and other practitioners who use this model to understand power issues as well as substance abuse and the treatment and prevention process.

The Political and Social Action Model. This model targets specific power inequities and inconsistencies of larger systems, contributors to community substance abuse and disorganization, for change. Weil and Gamble (1995:587) assume such efforts "empower people through strengthening their belief in their own efficacy and developing their skills to change unjust conditions." The goal is to shift power for future policy decisions to community residents, because their exclusion from previous decisions has limited their opportunities. Therefore, social justice is both a short- and long-term outcome of the model.

This model's process of investigative research followed by social and political action is similar to Freire's (1970) empowerment approach involving research, education, and social action. The emphasis of Freire's research phase is on identifying the structural sources of personal problems and common disempowerment experiences. Community social action groups are involved in recruiting, educating, mobilizing, and leading other residents in the action phases. These groups may represent certain segments of the population such as labor, people of color, a geographical area, or children and youths at risk for problems such as substance abuse or large-scale unemployment (Weil and Gamble 1995). The model is consistent with the community development and mediation roles because it focuses on power inequities and inconsistencies. Its emphasis on local control makes it useful for developing community-centered service systems designed to enhance empowerment opportunities.

This model is appropriate for social workers in administrative and direct service positions within empowered substance abuse treatment and preven-

TABLE 4.2 Youth Community Environment Assessment Form

Date: _____
Age: _____
Grade: _____
Community: _____

1	2	3	4	5
Strongly Disagree	Disagree	Neither Disagree nor Agree	Agree	Strongly Agree

Neighborhood/Community Environment (Make an X below the number that corresponds to your opinion.)

1. In my community, there are adults who have the type of successful job or career I am interested in.

2. When faced with an important problem, the members of my community can usually join together and decide what action to take.

3. It is fairly easy for teenagers to get alcohol, tobacco, and other drugs in my community.

4. Teenagers in my community are provided with a variety of organized recreational activities.

5. My community sponsors cultural activities that encourage members to feel positive about their own racial/ethnic group.

6. Usually, I do not feel safe in my community.

7. Families are encouraged to participate in community organizations and activities.

8. People in my community have taken action to discourage drug dealers and liquor store owners from doing business in our community.

9. There are many adults in my community who are involved in illegal activities (e.g., drugs, stealing, community violence).

10. Resources such as good housing, employment, and health care are difficult to find in my community.

11. The values of my community discourage youths from becoming teenage parents.

12. Teenagers in my neighborhood do not feel they are important members of the community.

13. Overall, the environment in my community encourages children and youths to develop positive values and attitudes.

14. People in my neighborhood often discourage youths from using alcohol and other drugs.

15. Frequently, people in my neighborhood do not get along with each other.

16. My neighbors are caring and helpful to each other most of the time.

17. There are good opportunities for teenagers in my community to find work.

18. Youths are encouraged to participate in and give feedback to organizations that provide services in my community.

19. People in my community are hopeless about solving the area's problems.

20. When I look at my neighborhood, I can see that the area is not kept clean and orderly.

Please add below any other comments you have about your community's Strengths and Problems.

tion organizations. Such organizations focus on political power and change within their programs *and* in the community. Social workers who are consultants for community organizations or who do community action research may find the model useful. Important skills include advocacy, education, investigative research, organization, collaboration, communication, fund raising, media relations, and management. Because the focus is on capacity building and leadership development, these skills should be taught to community residents while being applied and used by practitioners. For example, Weil and Gamble (1995:588) caution that "Although the organizer may serve directly as an advocate in some instances, it is much more important that the organizer assist group members in becoming their own advocates." Moreover, practitioners' use of these skills for capacity building can encourage residents to require community-centered rather than community-based systems of care for addressing substance abuse problems.

Community-Oriented Social Work

Community-oriented social work is useful as an overarching framework for applying the two practice models discussed in the previous section as well as other models. It is not a technique or specific model but more an attitude that community members are partners in the provision of care and services. Therefore, it reduces the boundaries between formal services (public, voluntary, or private organizations) and informal networks of family and friends. This interweaving of the formal and informal systems is the essence of the proposed integrated substance abuse system of care shown in figure 3.3.

The community is viewed as the glue that binds the individual substance abuser, family members, social network, or primary group to larger systems and policy (Martinez-Brawley 1995). The goal is to make the environment egalitarian so that residents are encouraged to become active participants in the social care of their community members (Martinez-Brawley 1995). The social planning example from this chapter's introduction illustrates community-oriented social work. A private foundation was asked to fund the two-year planning process that followed the identification of multiple community risk factors related to substance abuse, school dropouts, gang violence, unemployment, and inadequate parenting. The foundation hired several consultants, including two social workers, to facilitate the needs assessment and planning process. The purpose was to identify the community's definition of self-sufficiency and the resources and barriers to that goal.

The foundation was primarily interested in funding a parenting program in the future but agreed to the social workers' broader focus on the community as a whole and on a range of risk and protective factors. The social workers obtained input not only from formal service providers but also from natural helpers and informal networks. Community residents reviewed and gave feedback on all procedures used in the assessment and participated actively in interpreting the results and in designing and implementing the two-year planning process. Community-oriented social work resulted in recommendations made to the foundation for a more expansive community development process to address the area's root problem of powerlessness. The initiatives implemented later, with the foundation's continuing support, included a youth-directed antidrug campaign, large-scale school reforms (community-run public and Catholic schools), and an economic reinvestment project involving leadership development and entrepreneurial supports.

Conclusion

This discussion has focused on the important roles that communities can assume in helping to resolve complex substance abuse problems. The complexity arises from interrelationships between substance abuse and other social, economic, and political conditions that may hinder communities in their struggle toward self-sufficiency. Those interrelationships imply that a narrow focus on substance abuse in isolation is likely to exacerbate rather than resolve the problems. An additional aspect of this complexity is the substance abuse service system, which includes policy, community, and service organization components. Again, a narrow focus, on the service program component and its resources alone, is insufficient. It is clear from this discussion that operations of the three components are intertwined, requiring practitioners and administrators to understand the system as a whole as well as its components individually.

It is important also to understand the reciprocal and circular influences of the components on each other. Analyzing the community's roles and functions is enlightening, because that component provides the opportunities and means for including and helping to empower community members. The community is also the venue for helping individuals to influence the policy and program components, leading to the ultimate goal of power sharing.

5   The Substance Abuse Program
Subsystem: Organizational,
Administrative, and Direct Service Issues

New (alternative) programs are deeply committed to social
change. They are concerned not only with changing the larger external systems,
but with altering internal procedures and structures to ensure a democratic and
egalitarian operation.
—F. D. Perlmutter (1995:204)

The program subsystem is almost an invisible component of
the substance abuse service system. Most authors acknowledge its importance, for as Taber (1988:115) notes, "the program is the environment in
which helping transpires." But the program's impact on the nature of services
is seldom explored under research conditions; rather, it is taken for granted
and therefore remains somewhat unobtrusive. With few exceptions, even
authors and researchers who apply systems theory to organizational dynamics
are just beginning to explore this topic in more depth (Hannan and Freeman
1989; Holland 1995; Weick 1981). Existing literature analyzes complex organizations such as hospitals, public child welfare agencies, and public
schools (Kunnes 1994; Gibson 1993; Freeman 1985), but very little addresses organizational and power dynamics in substance abuse treatment
programs (Kerr 1994).

However, the growing interest in empowerment practice has shifted attention to power issues in substance abuse organizations and to their impact
on empowerment outcomes for staff and consumers (Galanter, France, Kim,
Metzger, and DeLeon 1993; Pratt and Gill 1990). It is assumed that empowerment outcomes are also affected by an organization's purpose, structure, life cycle, culture, ecology, and staff and consumer relationships, and
by other components of the service system (the policy and community

subsystems) (Czarniawska-Joerges 1992; Hannan and Freeman 1989; Ilgen and Klein 1988; Kimberly 1980).

The community subsystem includes part of each organization's external structure: other organizations and providers with whom it needs to coordinate services. Therefore, its organizational set may involve programs that provide complementary services and/or the same services to different populations (Prager and Holloway 1978). These may include both traditional and alternative programs; the latter are designed to resolve societal inequities not addressed sufficiently by traditional programs. In either circumstance, coordination may be difficult because organizations often have different philosophies and values related to empowerment (see table 3.1 in chapter 3).

One example involves an outpatient treatment center that admitted a forty-year-old white man because of his alcohol and crack addictions. His wife, who was Latino, became involved in family groups for codependency issues, but clearly she too was addicted to alcohol. The wife then entered treatment, where later their fifteen-year-old daughter's marijuana and crack abuse surfaced. This information led to a referral for inpatient treatment for the daughter in a nearby program for adolescents.

The daughter's program required the parents, and especially the daughter as the consumer, to become active participants in treatment team staffings and in other aspects. The parents' positive experiences with organizational empowerment in the daughter's program highlighted the more limited empowerment focus of their own program. Their overzealousness in trying to influence treatment decisions there caused the staff to assume the couple was attempting to manipulate the program, as part of their "addictive" and maladaptive coping styles.

A case staffing was held without the couple in which staff decided to discharge the wife. They concluded, based on the conflicts, that their initial decision to admit the couple to the same program was not a good one. Unfortunately, this conclusion did not encourage the staff to assess the program's responsibility for handling power issues more effectively; nor did it allow them to question the program's policy of limiting consumer involvement in treatment decisions. Effective coordination might have revealed major differences in the two programs' policies earlier and allowed the staff to prevent or manage the treatment conflicts more successfully.

This chapter begins with a description of how to assess the impact of internal factors, such as a program's structure, on its functions. The chapter then continues the discussion on the service system (from chapters 3 and 4) by analyzing external influences on substance abuse programs, such as their parent organizations, their service partners and other parts of the community, and policy. Strategies are included for helping to change such systems by increasing supports for and eliminating barriers to empowerment practice. Since organizational change is difficult, the implications of these changes for staff and consumers, particularly in programs that function as addicted systems, are described.

Assessing the Impact of Internal Program Factors

Distinguishing Between Internal and External Factors

Assessing the impact of organizational and other factors on empowerment practice with substance abusers requires making distinctions between internal and external influences. Internal factors provide supports or barriers to empowerment practice. Many of these were analyzed and discussed extensively in chapter 1. Here I extend that discussion by clarifying how organizational structure (e.g., decentralized leadership) influences the development of empowerment-oriented program factors (e.g., consumers as participants on the treatment team). (See tables 1.1 and 1.3 in chapter 1 for additional examples of program factors.)

Externally, the larger organizational setting in which a program operates influences its functions, and vice versa. Other factors to be assessed include interactional effects between policy or large institutions and programs, and between programs and the surrounding community. Wallerstein (1992:202) encourages this type of multilevel assessment: "In addition to psychological empowerment variables, a comprehensive measurement would analyze the organizational and community settings where the intervention is taking place." Although this discussion is about assessing organizational, community, and policy influences, intra- and interpersonal variables should be analyzed simultaneously.

The Focus of Internal Assessments

Periodic assessments of how a substance abuse program's structure affects and is affected by empowerment practice are necessary for understanding and improving such practice. Essentially, assessment is a measure of a program's organizational competence in empowerment practice; it should include analysis of both supports for and barriers to empowerment practice. These are equally relevant to substance abuse treatment and prevention programs.

Supports for Empowerment Practice.   A number of authors have identified and assessed factors in the internal structure of programs that support empowerment practice (Gruber and Trickett 1987; Gutiérrez, GlenMaye, and DeLois 1995; Segal, Silverman, and Temkin 1993; Wallerstein 1992). For instance, Gunde and Crissman (1992) conclude that decentralized leadership structures promote power sharing and more creative and autonomous decision making among staff. Assessment should identify examples of institutionalized power sharing, including when administrators delegate meaningful decisions in which they do not need to be involved and solicit respectfully others' input about nondelegated decisions (Gunden and Crissman 1992). Assessment can measure also how well administrative power sharing and decentralized leadership model a similar, parallel process between staff and clients (Friedland, Siegel, and Grenock 1989; Gowdy and Freeman 1993).

Surls (1994) identifies five components of decentralized, participatory decision making by client-centered substance abuse organizations that support empowerment opportunities for staff and clients. At the state, local, or program level, staff and clients are requested to

1. give input or share their ideas about key issues
2. review or respond to a summary of ideas or positions from other expert sources (based on Freire's [1989] values about the expert knowledge of "ordinary people")
3. consult and advise about a specific policy
4. recommend specific policy and implementation developments or reforms
5. vote on specific policy and implementation developments or reforms.

In this inclusive empowerment approach, organizational structure can involve a fixed plan that delineates which clients and staff are to take part in each component. Or the plan can be flexible in terms of whom to involve, depending on the issue or policy of concern. As Surls (194) indicates, an organization can be assessed on how well it applies a "clients first" (decentralized) model versus an expert (centralized) model. The former promotes client and staff empowerment because the organizational structure places clients and direct service staff at the decision-making table in different phases of the process (Surls 1994).

Similarly, Gutiérrez et al. (1995) recommend that organizational leadership should model, advocate for, and directly encourage the staff's use of an empowerment approach. Administrators are responsible for helping to develop the program's vision, including its empowerment orientation, and to coordinate the vision with program implementation. Therefore, assessment should clarify to what extent the program mission, administrative advocacy for implementing an empowerment approach, and staff incentives for using the approach are congruent.

Gutiérrez et al. (1995) identifies other important structural supports for empowerment practice, including systemwide collaboration and institutionalized staff development. To facilitate empowerment, structured opportunities for collaboration between the executive board and staff/administrators, line staff and administrators, and clients and line staff are needed. Systemwide collaboration diffuses knowledge about the program among all stakeholders and demystifies the different roles and sources of power. Assessing who collaborates with whom and who is accountable to whom at all levels helps to clarify important supports for empowerment practice (Gutiérrez et al. 1995).

Institutionalized staff development includes advanced training and in-service training, encouragement to develop innovative programs and services, promotions for achieving self-defined learning goals, and flexible hours and other incentives for self-care (Gutiérrez et al. 1995). Often overlooked as "perks" rather than incentives to staff and client empowerment, these supports for maintaining a capacity-building approach should be assessed along with other supports.

Barriers to Empowerment Practice.   In contrast to these internal supports, internal barriers have been identified and assessed for their interactional effects on practice. For example, Gunden and Crissman (1992) indicate that controlling and domineering leadership is a barrier to empowerment. Centralized leadership encourages administrators and staff to involve themselves in power sabotages and cutoffs to maintain the feeling of being in charge

(Gunden and Crissman 1992). More specifically, it encourages them to hoard power and to continue behaviors that are self-protective but disempowering to others. Assessment can identify when such behaviors exist and how they affect program functions and empowerment. Internal barriers include a lack of congruence between a program's empowerment philosophy and disempowering interactions among key actors, a failure to follow through on decisions, a failure to delineate or encourage shared decision making with staff and clients, or an undermining of staff and clients' input and decision making (Surls 1994; Gunden and Crissman 1992).

Other internal barriers to an empowerment approach can involve interpersonal and intrapersonal manifestations of organizational structure. For example, Gutiérrez et al. (1995) identify an organization's unclear or unrealistic standards for success as one barrier. Often programs do not anticipate that empowered or disempowered clients may make decisions that staff do not agree with. Staff may not be clear about their role in these situations, or they may assume or be told they should pressure clients to make "the right" decisions. For example, a female client may decide to return to an abusive relationship, another client may leave treatment against medical advice, or a youth may refuse to become a peer facilitator in a prevention program for fear of being ostracized by gang members.

Empowerment practice requires more time than traditional approaches. Clients and staff members may become frustrated when clients' progress is more incremental then expected (Gutiérrez et al. 1995) or requires involvement in several programs before recovery or prevention is effective. Double-bind situations can be disempowering for staff and clients. Assessment should clarify examples of such conflicts and how they are resolved. The results can identify lessons learned about empowerment practice and some of the frustrations inherent in such practice.

Tools for Program Assessment

Not only should assessment focus on how organizational structure supports or impedes empowerment practice; the assessment process itself and the selected procedures or tools should involve empowerment opportunities. Gowdy and Freeman (1993) assert that staff and clients should have input into program review and change efforts, because this collaboration "creates a process in which power is shared and people are involved in the programs affecting them" (62). Thus, collaboration and capacity building should be a major purpose of the tools selected for internal program assessments.

Program Design and Systems Change Tools. Although only a few tools exist for assessing organizational empowerment, many of the factors discussed previously are included among them. Logan and Freeman (1988) adapted Taber's (1988) client-centered program review or assessment framework into a program supervision tool that can be used to assess and critique a program's competence in encouraging input from clients and staff in its design, implementation, and subsequent modification (systemic changes). The design components include personal and societal aspects of the problem definition, program goals based on this ecological definition, the most at-risk group within the target population, mutually developed objectives, the program hypotheses linking objectives and interventions, and the service plan, which includes the implementation variables (Gowdy and Freeman 1993).

This plan involves ten implementation areas, including accessibility of the services to potential clients, incorporating their input into the needs and strengths assessment; client-staff expectations; well-defined, client-involved and -accountable interventions; empowerment-oriented staff training; and client-driven evaluation. In this type of empowerment evaluation, consumers are taught to conduct their own evaluations and thus to become more self-sufficient and skilled (Fetterman 1994).

The design components in Logan and Freeman's (1987) assessment tool are reviewed and rated by staff and clients and analyzed by an elected subcommittee; then results are reported to the participants for their feedback. Consensus about empowerment supports and barriers leads to program or systems changes for improving empowerment practice. An advantage of this tool is that it can be used to assess a broad range of service programs and organizations.

Another example of program design and systems change tools is Freeman's (1995) Multicultural and Empowerment Organizational Assessment Form (table 5.1). This tool is useful for assessing substance abuse programs that serve ethnically diverse populations, but it is adaptable to other types of programs and to all aspects of diversity (age, gender, sexual

TABLE 5.1 Multicultural and Empowerment Organizational Assessment Form (Freeman 1995)

Name: _____
Date: _____
Organization: _____

This form should be completed by each individual staff member of an organization. It was designed to encourage open discussion and sharing of different assessments of the organization, along with opportunities to brainstorm ways to improve or enhance the multicultural and empowerment climate. Please circle the number for each item below that most closely reflects your opinion and experience.

	Not at All	Very Little	Somewhat	Very Much	Completely
1. The program's mission statement highlights a commitment to services for a multicultural population.	0	1	2	3	4
2. The program goals focus on the unique strengths, values, and cultural perspectives of the ethnic group(s) being served.	0	1	2	3	4
3. The organization's physical surroundings reflect a positive attitude about diversity: the decorations, reading materials, and posted announcements show people of different ethnic groups in positive interactions.	0	1	2	3	4
4. The organization sponsors ethnic food fairs, traditions, and holiday celebrations of the group(s) being served.	0	1	2	3	4
5. The organization is physically and emotionally accessible through the use of outreach workers from the ethnic backgrounds of the community members, community-based satellite offices, and ethnically oriented public relations brochures.	0	1	2	3	4

	0	1	2	3	4
6. Cases are assigned to line staff fairly and without racial/ethnic/gender/age discrimination toward clients/staff.	0	1	2	3	4
7. Administrators request staff input into important decisions, reflecting sensitivity toward staff's diverse ethnic backgrounds, experiences, skills, ideas, and empowerment needs.	0	1	2	3	4
8. Administrators and staff request and use clients' input into important treatment decisions to help them become empowered.	0	1	2	3	4
9. The organization provides special or reduced-fee arrangements for people of color, poor clients, and clients with other special needs.	0	1	2	3	4
10. Staff have opportunities to develop cultural sensitivity through training on clients' ethnic values, traditions, holiday celebrations, lifestyles, and substance abuse patterns.	0	1	2	3	4
11. The informal policies and practices of the organization discourage the use of stereotypes about different ethnic groups, labeling, racist or sexist language, and biases about addicted people.	0	1	2	3	4
12. The ethnic backgrounds of line staff reflect the ethnic and gender composition of the population being served.	0	1	2	3	4
13. The ethnic backgrounds of the administrative staff reflect the ethnic and gender composition of the population being served.	0	1	2	3	4

continued

TABLE 5.1 Multicultural and Empowerment Organizational Assessment Form (Freeman 1995) *continued*

	Not at All	Very Little	Somewhat	Very Much	Completely
14. An effort is made to match clients who need help with ethnic, gender, sexual orientation, and developmental issues with staff who have expertise in those areas.	0	1	2	3	4
15. The organization's treatment procedures, videotapes, films, and exercises are culturally relevant to the ethnic groups being served and to issues of oppression and powerlessness (i.e., they are culturally specific).	0	1	2	3	4
16. The organization makes culturally relevant training available to all staff without discriminating on the basis of ethnic group, staff position, or recovering versus nonaddicted status.	0	1	2	3	4
17. Clients are encouraged to informally offer suggestions to the organization about how to make the program more culturally relevant and empowerment oriented.	0	1	2	3	4
18. The organization has made changes in its formal policies and practices in order to improve the multicultural climate in important ways.	0	1	2	3	4
19. The organization has made changes in its formal policies and practices in order to improve power imbalances among staff and clients.	0	1	2	3	4

	0	1	2	3	4
20. Staff and administrators from different ethnic backgrounds use informal contacts with each other to enhance their working relationships.	0	1	2	3	4
21. Staff and administrators model cultural competence by not using ethnic stereotypes and racist language during staff meetings and client treatment sessions.	0	1	2	3	4
22. Staff and administrators demonstrate cultural competence by pointing out the ethnic strengths and resources of clients during meetings and client sessions.	0	1	2	3	4
23. Administrators and other informal leaders give positive feedback to empower staff who use culturally competent skills effectively in client or staff contacts.	0	1	2	3	4
24. The organization uses formal procedures to get input from staff and clients about the program's level of cultural competence.	0	1	2	3	4
25. Administrators encourage staff to avoid making generalizations about members of particular ethnic groups based on experiences with clients from the same group.	0	1	2	3	4
26. Line staff and administrators are encouraged to improve their cultural competence skills through ongoing professional development and informal learning.	0	1	2	3	4
27. Other (write in):	0	1	2	3	4

orientation, disability, and socioeconomic status). It emphasizes empowerment needs and substance abuse issues across five major cultural groups (African Americans, Asian Americans, European Americans, Native Americans, and Latino Americans). Similar to Logan and Freeman's (1987) program supervision tool, this form encourages collaboration in assessing an organization's competence in empowerment practice. The process of responding to the form also leads to modifications in programs' empowerment practice based on assessment results.

Informal Team-Building Assessment Procedures.   A number of informal brainstorming and experiential exercises can be used to assess a program's level of empowerment practice. Most of these involve a six- to eight-stage process that results in a collective assessment of organizational supports and barriers to empowerment. Consensus is then used to develop a plan, and subcommittees or task groups help to implement changes that have been prioritized in the planning process. Self- and group efficacy results from collective action and effective systems change, as well as staff and consumer skill development.

This type of procedure is especially useful in substance abuse programs where, because the work is often difficult and stressful, periodic team building is important. Consumer advisory boards and community volunteers can be involved as well by sharing their unique perspectives. The process involves the following steps, which can vary across programs and participants due to unique dynamics in each situation (Linney and Wandersman 1991; Schofield 1980). The first seven steps can be completed over several sessions or during an extended retreat; step eight requires more involved work over time.

1. orientation to the purpose, outcomes, and ground rules of the procedure, and an ice-breaker exercise that allows participants to get acquainted on a new basis
2. participation in collaborative and physically risk-taking exercises such as ropes courses (for trust and team building), followed by discussions of participants' reactions and insights about the experience
3. definition of concepts (empowerment practice, supports, barriers) and instructions about brainstorming (all ideas are valuable

and no retaliation or later censure should occur in reaction to
participants' ideas/inputs)
4. brainstorming exercise in which each person writes at least two
   organizational supports and barriers to empowerment on large
   newsprint sheets, creating two separate lists that are attached to
   the walls (psychological risk taking/collaborative process)
5. debriefing: explanations of unclear entries, identification of patterns, gaps, and implications of entries for quality empowerment
   practice
6. consensus building: clustering related entries and prioritizing the
   lists of supports and barriers based on criteria selected by the
   participants
7. planning for systems change in order to improve empowerment
   practice (based on previous steps), assigning participants to task
   groups, and deciding how work will be monitored: with what
   tools, by whom, and how often
8. implementation: incremental implementation of plan; monitoring and revising it as needed; periodic organizational reassess-
   ment as planned.

Research-Based Assessment Methods.   Other methods of program and
organizational assessment are research-based, yielding comparison data on
empowerment practice across groups of programs. The methods have
been used to assess single programs as well (Boswich 1987; Gibson 1993;
Indyk, Belvelle, Lachapell, Gordon, and Dewart 1993; Patton 1986). Gutiérrez et al. (1995) used a multiple case study method to assess seventeen
human service organizations engaged in empowerment practice (for example, mental health centers, family and child services, and educational
and employment programs). The researchers used qualitative interviews
with a staff person and an administrator from each organization in their
sample. Responses to the telephone interview protocol helped them assess
the organizations' competence in empowerment practice.

The results clarified how the agencies and practitioners defined, carried
out, and evaluated empowerment practice. Programs using these assessment methods can identify supports, and thus how the organization han-
dles barriers to empowerment and should change to improve practice.
Changes can include having clients participate in the process along with
staff and administrators.

Analyzing External Influences on Programs

Along with the internal factors and assessment tools discussed in the previous section, the impact of external factors on programs should be considered. Often barriers and supports from external and internal environments influence each other in a circular, interactive process. Factors in the external environment, including the larger organization in which a program operates and the community and policy subsystems, also interact with and influence each other.

A Program's Organizational Auspices

The agency or larger organization within which a substance abuse program operates may influence the quality of its empowerment practice. A first step in clarifying such influence is to identify the range of organizational auspices in which program operates. Figure 5.1 demonstrates that programs range from freestanding entities to units that function within larger systems, sometimes with multiple organizational layers.

The Nature of the Organizational Continuum.   The organizational auspices along the continuum in figure 5.1 do not completely represent reality, because most programs are a combination of one or more of the arrangements shown. There are also variations or alternative programs, which have developed due to major social and political changes discussed in chapter 3, that are not shown on the continuum. For example, the growing homelessness problem, which has economic and political roots, has led to the development of detached units providing substance abuse, medical, and mental health services. A specialized, self-contained team may provide services from a mobile van parked in key areas of a community at predetermined times. Another example is the deployment of teams that specialize in providing in-home, family-centered substance abuse prevention and treatment services. Often these services are designed for multiproblem and isolated families, but some prevention programs offer in-home health promotion services to the general population, provided by one substance abuse program or by two or more of them in partnership.

O'Connor and McCord (1991) indicate that whether a situation involves these alternative programs or more traditional services, the organizational arrangements in figure 5.1 are seldom static and complete. Instead, they are a fluid, ever-changing process. True collaboration and integration are seldom achieved completely or maintained consistently over time.

Some of the organizational arrangements shown in figure 5.1 are more applicable to prevention programs than others. For example, organizational settings for prevention programs are often within the range of secondary to integrated auspices, while freestanding or primary-setting prevention services are more rare. In contrast, treatment programs cover the entire continuum, although fewer freestanding programs are surviving the current political (cost containment) climate because they lack a diversified funding base (Saunders 1995).

Assessing the Effects of Organizational Auspices. Informal assessments of a program's organizational auspices can help to clarify their effects on empowerment practice. Informal interviews with key staff and administrators, direct observations of significant events and interactions, and an analysis of selected written documents (e.g., the organizations' mission statements and program curricula) can be used. A collective investigative research process involving consultants, staff, consumers, and board members can explore a number of important areas (Fetterman 1994; Freire 1989).

Using the advantages and disadvantages listed in figure 5.1, assessment can clarify a number of issues relevant to empowerment. Multiple organizational layers often encourage centralized leadership and inequitable resource allocations (e.g., in secondary, umbrella, and integrated model settings). Assessment results may imply a need for improved collaboration and stronger administrative advocacy and incentives for shared decision making (Gutiérrez et al. 1995; Surls 1994). Or the process may reveal the effects of conflicts over specialized versus general programming in organizations whose structure reinforces those conflicts (e.g., freestanding and primary settings). Such results can support specialized training for staff in culture- and gender-specific addiction services and more flexibility in general programming (Wright, Kail, and Creecy 1990; McRoy, Shorkey, and Garcia 1985; Van Den Bergh 1991).

Overall, assessment can help to determine the impact of larger organizations' policies and practices on a program in the following areas (Freeman 1985; Gummer and Edwards 1995; Gutiérrez et al. 1995; Lee 1992; Perlmutter 1995):

1. program philosophy, vision/mission, empowerment orientation
2. program methods, services, and implementation process

FIGURE 5.1 Continuum of Larger Organizational Auspices: Substance Abuse Prevention and Treatment Programs

	Lesser Comprehensiveness					Greater Comprehensiveness
Types of Organizational Auspices	Freestanding substance abuse service programs	Multiple substance abuse services in a primary setting (e.g., homeless, perinatal)	Substance abuse services in a secondary setting (e.g., school, mental health, medical, criminal justice)	Parallel services arrangements with substance abuse and other services in the same community site (e.g., a youth service organization)	Comprehensive umbrella organizations with range of services including substance abuse (with community-centered focus)	Integrated community-centered services with substance abuse as the hub and community development as the main spoke, and an array of other essential services
Advantages	specialized components; few organizational layers	specialized programs; common methods and resources	interagency collaboration; integrated funding	reciprocal referrals; service accessibility	centralized referrals; high intraagency accountability	high accountability/resource pooling; high services integration/power sharing
Disadvantages	off-site referrals; lack diverse funding	specialized training required; diversified funding required	low priority for resources; value/method conflicts	low accountability; lack coordination/planning	resource competition; low interagency accountability	high conflict potential; loss of organizational autonomy and control (highest number of organizational layers)

3. leadership-administrative-collaborative structure (level of power sharing and collegial roles/tasks)
4. diversity of funding
5. accountability and inclusion standards (across programs, formal service partners, and consumers)
6. equity of resource availability, priorities, and allocations
7. sources of support and sanctions (organizational sources, funders, and the surrounding community, i.e., whether community-based or community-centered programs are required).

Impact of the Surrounding Community

Community Members and Organizations. Factors in the surrounding community can affect empowerment practice in substance abuse programs and interact with factors related to organizational auspices. Some of these elements of the community's informal structure were discussed in chapter 4, for example, caring community roles such as mediation and health promotion (Hawkins and Catalano 1994). Those roles support an effective substance abuse service system and programs by reintegrating recovering community members into nonusing social networks and providing community education about health promotion and prevention.

In addition, substance abuse treatment organizations can develop integrated, comprehensive models that reduce boundaries between informal and formal services, as illustrated in figure 3.3 in chapter 3. This community-centered model highlights community organizations and networks that provide informal services, such as cultural enrichment organizations and family resource centers (Hutchinson and Nelsan 1985; Smith and Breathwick 1986). A combination of informal and formal services within programs is emphasized as well. Peer counselors provide social supports in mental health services and informal leaders augment mentoring in community policing services (Brown 1996; Daniels 1992; Segal et al. 1993). Further, the model requires a community advisory or executive board that sets and monitors policy for the integrated services and exchanges information with administrators of organizations and informal helpers. An executive director and an appropriate number of other staff members implement the policies and conduct liaison activities with the board.

Periodic assessment of the impact of informal community partners on substance abuse programs should focus on the ratio of formal and informal services provided by the model and community members' evaluation of that ratio and service effectiveness, and on the process and outcomes of inclusive decision-making and interorganizational communication activities. When a substance abuse program operates within another organization or model of service delivery (see figure 5.1), the same assessment areas pertain. These areas highlight standards relevant to empowerment practice and community involvement (Lee 1994) and can guide organizations and programs in developing goals to enhance their services.

The model also can reduce discrepancies between a community's efforts to resolve specific problems, such as substance abuse and unemployment, and efforts to address more long-term capacity-building needs. Each spoke of the wheel depicted in figure 3.3 identifies domains for community growth, such as housing and primary health care. The main spoke (the bolder area at the top of the wheel) is community planning and policy and funding initiatives. This domain and the others shown in figure 3.3 are closely interrelated (Harrison 1995), as they provide mutual guidance. Wherever programs are on the continuum of organizational auspices in figure 5.1, assessment should focus on how much they emphasize capacity building and skill development for consumers and community members, and on the level of integration within programs that focus on two or more domains and across programs that focus on different domains.

Organizational Set/Formal Service Partners.   Each program's formal service partners also can influence empowerment practice. The introduction illustrates how receiving services from two programs with conflicting empowerment orientations impacts practice. In that example, the couple's disparate experiences regarding empowerment in the two organizations and the mother's subsequent relapse when dismissed from the adult program point out the seriousness of these conflicts.

Interorganizational assessments (among service partners) should focus on the seven areas identified earlier in this chapter, including empowerment orientations. The integrated services model in figure 3.3 facilitates this type of interorganizational assessment. A liaison/coordinating committee involving representatives of formal and informal service providers and the staff (the executive director and others) could be responsible for interaction and ongoing assessments. O'Connor and McCord (1991) call this arrangement a community empowerment network. In other situations (see figure 5.1), providers within an organizational set can develop a case management or social action network, depending on need, periodically assessing the network's empowerment and integration outcomes (O'Connor and McCord 1991). These types of networks also should include informal community helpers.

The Influence of Policy on Programs

Chapter 3 presents an extensive analysis of policy influences on substance abuse programs' use of empowerment approaches. The focus is on methods of funding and policy development and the need for integrated funding streams, along with policies that consider the impact of systemic factors on people's substance abuse and disempowerment experiences. With regard to this chapter's topic, there are two other important areas where policy can influence programs. One is decision makers' commitment to funding empowerment programs and the other is their understanding of the nature of empowerment practice.

Commitment to funding services that lead to community capacity-building and systems change is often low among decision makers. A participant in Gutiérrez et al.'s (1995:252) study said unequivocally, "I don't know that . . . funding sources and the government are all that interested in people having that kind of power." Funders may be more interested in programs that reduce social indicators such as incarceration, school dropout, homelessness, and substance abuse rates. A focus on recidivism implies that only minimal growth is expected and that any underlying problems will be resolved through individual changes (Chapin 1995).

Decision makers' low commitment to empowerment outcomes is related to a lack of knowledge about the nature of empowerment practice, the incremental nature of capacity building and systems change. And they may be unsympathetic about the difficulties service providers encounter when attempting to measure and document empowerment outcomes (Fetterman 1994). Their assumption may be that these outcomes are too intangible to be measured or are not sufficiently important. Even if they fund empowerment programs initially, funders and policy makers may be reluctant to continue support without measurable outcomes related to known social indicators.

Policy and funding influences on programs can be assessed in an ongoing manner before crises happen by conducting policy impact analyses. Programs can request such analyses as part of their program evaluators' tasks or have the analysis/assessment done on a more informal basis by staff and community members who receive training and technical assistance. A number of authors have described detailed frameworks for guiding the process, suggesting a combination of structured and unstructured individual interviews, written surveys, focus groups, observations, and analysis of written documents (Chapin 1995; Zellman et al. 1993; Kleben 1991).

The following areas should be included in the assessment:

1. policies that support a program's empowerment practice and the effects of that support
2. policies that hinder a program's empowerment practice and the specific effects on practice (on consumers, staff, and the community)
3. specific policy reforms needed to resolve the barriers to empowerment practice
4. political and social action needed to initiate the identified policy reforms (program evaluation, dissemination of evaluation findings and other reports, coalition building, community mobilization, and education and advocacy with decision makers).

The Process of Organizational Change

Various influences on a program's use of empowerment approaches can be illustrated with an example of organizational change. Freeman's (1995) Multicultural and Empowerment Organizational Assessment (table 5.1) was used in one substance abuse agency that provided both specialized and general substance abuse treatment programs. Thus, the agency was a primary setting in terms of its organizational auspices (see figure 5.1). This section discusses the experience of assessing this organization and describes the organization's change process.

The Organizational Assessment

Purpose of the Assessment of Organizational Climate.   Two issues frame this example of organizational assessment, and indeed, are critical to every instance of assessment. Gowdy and Freeman (1993) address one of these issues, indicating "less-than-successful performance is likely to be taken personally" (61). Therefore, organizational assessment must shift staff attention away from this narrow perspective of helping to a view that clients benefit from a total program environment that provides the context for staff-client relationships.

The second issue is that organizational assessments, like community needs assessments, have a political aspect that needs to be acknowledged (Tropman 1995). The stated reasons for requesting an assessment are seldom the only or most important reasons. Power issues or conflicts may undergird the request or the process of assessment as well as staff reactions to and use of the results. Thus another purpose of the assessment is to address power issues and people's reactions to change, related to the identified problem and the general political climate in the organization.

In this example, the identified problem was ethnic and racial conflicts among the agency's multicultural staff and their lack of cultural sensitivity to the clients. The agency's executive director requested that this author help address these problems by serving as a consultant and trainer. The director had only been in her position for nine months, having been hired to reorganize the agency after the previous, very controlling director's termination. The new director wanted the agency to be more structured but decentralized in its leadership, which led to the firing of several long-term staff members (raising political and power issues). Consequently, many of the staff believed the training represented a personal criticism of their work (a narrow view of helping) rather than an organizational problem.

Training Participants and Program. The agency's staff is 60 percent Caucasian and 40 percent African American, while 90 percent of the clients are African American, 6 percent are Caucasian, and 4 percent are Latino. The agency has two substance abuse programs, one for women and one coed. Fifty-five staff members (administrators, supervisors, direct service practitioners, and support staff), with from one week to ten years' longevity, were involved in the following training project based on Freire's (1989) empowerment process.

1. consciousness raising/critical awareness: introductory discussion of cultural frameworks related to addiction; trust-building and awareness exercises (e.g., writing about and sharing the most significant multicultural experience/feelings about being different)

2. education and skill development: effective cross-cultural communication, conflict negotiation, multicultural team building,
   connecting "color blind" and "power is not an issue" perspectives
   with the addiction denial syndrome (see #9 on table 2.2 in chapter
   2) (cognitive and experiential methods)
3. collective investigative research: staff conducted the organizational
   assessment using Freeman's (1995) Multicultural Empowerment
   and Organizational Assessment (table 5.1), with instructions and
   technical assistance from the author, who helped to debrief, analyze, and draw conclusions about the results
4. planning/political action: prioritizing problem areas identified in
   the assessment, developing task groups and activities to resolve the
   problems, taking action to change the organization politically (systems change).

Outcomes of the Change Process

This organizational assessment, training, and systems change process produced several important outcomes. First, task groups were developed to address organizational leadership, programming, interagency collaboration,
and funding issues based on the priorities identified by the staff. The organizational leadership group identified and implemented a decision-making
process that shifted some decisions from administrators to supervisors and
from supervisors to line staff (items #7 and #13 in table 5.1). This change
was consistent with the director's previous efforts to shift some decisions (and
power) from her position to the administrators, who, until the training, had
been hoarding the new power. The task group's goal was to have the agency
leadership at all levels model the type of power sharing and empowerment
that was needed in the individual helping encounters with clients (items
#19–20).

The programming group focused on two areas. They developed, implemented, and later evaluated a specialized multicultural client group similar
to existing specialized groups (e.g., a women's group) and developed a multicultural staff/client team. The multicultural group helped to make the program's services more culturally appropriate and specific (item #14 in table
5.1). Clients were able to identify connections between their oppression
experiences, their addiction, and an empowered recovery process (discussed

in detail in chapter 2). The multicultural team was designed to identify personal and professional opportunities to celebrate cultural diversity and prevent/manage cultural conflicts (items #3, 4, 6, 15, 17, and 18). The team's empowerment focus expanded later when a lesbian staff member, who had not acknowledged her orientation previously, advocated for more culturally sensitive programming for lesbian, gay, and bisexual clients.

The interagency collaboration and funding groups developed individual political action plans and then combined their efforts to design and get funding for an innovative program for high-risk families with children not currently in treatment (item #25 on table 5.1). Current funding and policy did not allow the program to extend its services to individuals not in treatment. This proposal for integrated services aimed at reducing intergenerational abuse involved a stronger collaborative arrangement with day care, prenatal substance abuse programs, transitional housing, and education services (the agency's organizational set) (item #26).

While these outcomes from the assessment process resulted in a more empowerment-oriented and culturally sensitive total program environment, some important areas were not addressed. Clients were not involved in the assessment process except later, when they were encouraged to become part of the multicultural team. Community residents are not a part of the decision-making process in the agency; however, staff ignored this deficit even though it was identified in the assessment. Thus the agency continues to be a community-based organization. Finally, more action could have been taken to address policy issues beyond developing the grant proposal, because there continues to be a lack of support for family-centered prevention programs (Hawkins and Catalano 1994).

The Implications of Organizational Change

Organizational change is difficult because it places systems (programs) in a state of disequilibrium, disrupting a predictable though sometimes problematic status quo. People's reactions to change, whether they are administrators, line staff, or consumers, tend to reflect their personal beliefs and experiences. Some of them may associate such disruptions with disempowerment and a loss of control. For clients and recovering staff, in particular, organizational change may cause flashbacks to periods of chaos and addiction. The health of an organization is determined by how well it promotes individuals' healthy reactions to change and provides opportunities for their growth and empowerment in the process.

Open and Healthy Organizations

Healthy organizations establish and reinforce staff and consumer roles that keep the system open and capable of accepting change. Therefore, these organizations are more likely to support the visionary and innovator roles shown in table 5.2 (Freeman 1994). Healthy organizations also contain the more dysfunctional roles, such as the organizational restrainer, but challenge them instead of reinforcing them. They use individuals' historical knowledge of what has worked or not worked in the agency to anticipate barriers to change and allow them to dispense rewards for other key actors' positive responses to change. Roles tend to be more fluid in healthy organizations, assumed by different people depending on the situation. Consequently, role shifts and role sharing occur often. Healthy organizations are identified not

TABLE 5.2 Substance Abuse Prevention and Treatment Programs Healthy and Addicted System Roles

Organization System Roles	Addicted (Family) System Roles	
Restrainers: Good Soldiers system historians block change dispense rewards and sanctions	*Primary Enablers* super-responsible members martyrs	
Visionaries: Organization Pets system dreamers plan change create paradigm shifts	*Mascots* hyperactive members eccentrics	
Risk Takers: Organization Jesters/ Irritants system stressors stimulate change disorient system/absorb blame	*Lost Children* marginalized members retreaters	*Scapegoats* acting-out members delinquent
Innovators: Organization Heroes system motivators/facilitators implement change provide growth opportunities	*Family Heroes* hope-bearing members overachievers	

by a complete absence of problems but by an ability to adapt positively to change and to prevent the escalation of unavoidable problems (Tebbitt 1993).

Unhealthy/Addicted Organizations

In contrast, addicted organizations are characterized by an inability to tolerate change, even positive transitions. These organizations tend to have more rigid role expectations and related behaviors, much like chronically addicted families and peer networks (Kerr 1991). System sanctions occur when individuals attempt to call attention to the co-enabling network's dysfunctions. For example, staff members or clients who engage in whistle blowing may be fired or dismissed from treatment. They may be positive or negative risk takers who become scapegoated by the system or innovators who lose their hero status by ceasing to be team players (see table 5.2), whereas the organizational restrainers are always rewarded for their efforts to maintain the addicted system's status quo.

The organizational assessment example in this chapter ("The Process of Organizational Change") involved an addicted system that was founded by a charismatic visionary (see table 5.2). As the organization grew over the years, however, the director shifted into the chronic role of restrainer. Other staff assumed chronic dysfunctional family roles such as addict, mascot, lost child, and scapegoat, which were enabled and supported by the director. The conflicts and stress from the roles provided a rationale for the director's centralized and controlling decision-making process.

The new director's organizational changes, including the training and assessment process, put the system in disequilibrium and challenged the staff's dysfunctional roles. More important, the changes allowed some staff to move into more functional roles (visionary, innovator, and positive risk taker) and others to leave voluntarily or be fired. These organizational and staff changes provided clients with a healthier environment in which to work toward recovery and empowerment.

Conclusion

This chapter provides more of the missing pieces of the substance abuse service system puzzle, making the picture clearer and highlighting how the pieces fit together. Understandably, if one or more pieces are absent, it is not possible to see the whole picture or to grasp these close connections. The risk of engaging in empowerment practice without clarity about connections is readily apparent. Factors from the policy-funding, community, and program subsystems affect empowerment practice whether or not attention is focused on those areas.

Since the program subsystem is where the primary helping process takes place, it is also the level where problems throughout the service system are likely to manifest themselves. Therefore, programs are obligated to assess the entire system's impact on services and to provide feedback to other parts of the system about barriers to empowerment outcomes. In addition, programs are responsible for proposing service innovations that have not yet been considered at other levels of the system. Healthy organizations effectively collaborate with consumers, staff, service partners, and community members in this process of systems change and empowerment practice.

Part 3

An Empowered Substance Abuse Service Delivery Process: Expanding the Client-Centered Continuum of Care

This section contains the largest number of chapters in the book and illustrates, at a very practical level, the nature and quality of empowerment practice in the substance abuse field. The manner in which the three components of the substance abuse service system influence practice across different types of programs is integrated into each chapter. Various chapters address the collaborative work of practitioners and clients along the continuum of care, including intervention, prevention, and rehabilitation, as well as the different modalities (e.g., group work), targets of change (e.g., political or systems changes), and phases of service delivery (e.g., aftercare).

Chapter 6 conceptualizes intervention as a dynamic, ongoing transition that may be influenced by many unique personal and social contingencies. Intervention is often linked with rehabilitation; however, this chapter illustrates how intervention provides a foundation for people's acceptance of either prevention or rehabilitation. Specific strategies and case-community examples demonstrate how intervention can also create a psychological readiness for services that people may not accept until later, after several other interventions have occurred. Chapter 7 addresses community prevention, based on discussions about the intervening function of needs and assets assessments in chapter 6, and community roles, related to the substance abuse service systems discussed in chapter 4. The effects of historical and current theoretical paradigms on substance abuse prevention are highlighted. Two fully detailed community prevention examples illustrate how goals for program development-capacity building and political, policy, and large systems change can be accomplished and then documented with consumer-driven evaluation and dissemination tools.

Chapter 8 clarifies how service providers can use the wisdom and resiliency of consumers to mutually assess their substance abuse problems. Very practical assessment-evaluation procedures are presented to illustrate the nature of staff-client partnerships during this service phase, leading to power sharing and self-efficacy. The dynamic process of using client-centered tools such as solution-focused questions and clients' inoculation narratives to strengthen early recovery is highlighted through case examples of the application of these tools.

In chapters 9, 10, and 11, issues related to empowerment practice with groups, families, and individuals are addressed respectively, along with case examples and illustrations that clarify how these different modalities can be combined for effective outcomes. The chapter on group work provides theoretical underpinnings and practical strategies for groups in rehab, self-help, and prevention programs. It demonstrates how the application of those strategies should vary due to unique factors within the three types of programs. In twelve-step programs, for example, group members struggle to balance preserving anonymity with encouraging the use of political action strategies. Similar to the groups chapter, the family chapter is presented within the context of theoretical approaches to family work. It illustrates the application of those approaches and related strategies during sessions with nuclear and intergenerational families. Cultural influences on how families define and seek to resolve substance abuse problems are reflected in case and family examples, along with client-driven evaluation tasks and outcomes.

Cultural diversity is highlighted also in the chapter on individual work, which emphasizes using individual sessions to address important within-group differences, build upon clients' strengths, and support the work in the other modalities. The focus is on using empowerment-oriented strategies and evaluation tools to address issues of ethnicity and race, gender, age, sexual orientation, disabling conditions, socioeconomic status, and location. Case examples clarify how these factors of diversity interact and that they should be addressed together, as they affect people's drugs of choice, motivations for entering rehab, struggles in early and ongoing recovery, and power issues.

Chapter 12 focuses on aftercare and termination of services, documenting how these phases may reawaken power and loss and grief issues that clients identified during intake and assessment, and therefore the importance of relapse prevention supports during early recovery and termination. A process of phased services is proposed to provide an opportunity for transition work related to personal, family, programmatic, and policy barriers and supports. Research findings on the aftercare phase are presented to concretize the lessons learned about clients' effective reintegration and management of their recovery-relapse cycles.

6 Intervention: An Empowerment-Based Preservice Foundation for Prevention and Rehabilitation

The current division between prevention, intervention, and treatment in preservice education, practice, and program administration is a barrier to a comprehensive analysis of the continuum (of care).
— E. M. Freeman (1993:18)

Intervention, a process for influencing substance abusers' receptivity to and entry into rehabilitation, is more critical today than at any other time. New drugs such as ecstasy are more available, and new forms of known drugs have been developed, such as crank (methamphetamine), specialty or flavored beers, and smokable heroin and cocaine (Lurigio and Davis 1992; *New York Times* 1989; Schwartz 1992). Substance abuse rates have increased across all age, racial, ethnic, and socioeconomic groups at varying rates and in regard to different drugs. Even the consequences of substance abuse have changed, with more people being affected directly and indirectly by related automobile and train wrecks, violence in the workplace, and gang violence (Kleber 1991).

Now, when the need for intervention is so critical, current practitioner perspectives may hinder it. Intervention is generally viewed as static, and its success is evaluated informally, according to one standard: whether the substance abuser enters rehab following the event. But this view does not focus on what happens from the different perspectives of interveners and substance abusers, and it ignores the possibility that intervention may be a continuous process or transition. In one situation, Connie, a forty-year-old African American woman attempting to cope with depression resulting from her husband's death, abused Valium and alcohol for eight years. The Valium was prescribed by a psychiatrist who grew concerned that she might become addicted and later stopped the prescriptions. Connie then began to obtain her Valium illegally. Co-workers, family members, and three members of her church choir intervened unsuccessfully at different times during a two-year period after her addiction became apparent.

A hospitalization due to a fall at home led to her primary care physician confronting her about substance abuse. The experience left her feeling very vulnerable and also angry because he was a member of her social group. Three months later, Connie decided to check herself into rehab when an anxiety attack prevented her from driving home from work one evening. She said not being able to drive made her realize she had lost control of her life.

This example illustrates the need to reconceptualize intervention as a continuous process rather than a static event that is influenced by many of the individual and social contingencies that affect the addiction development process (Hanson 1991). Such a view is consistent with the ecological perspective and systems theory. The example also highlights how power issues may influence people's responses to intervention and their motivation and hope for change. This chapter explores intervention as a continuous preservice process that sets the stage for both treatment and prevention and out of which important power issues may emerge. It suggests how knowing this can improve empowerment outcomes in the social networks and communities where intervention occurs. The impact of a reconceptualized and more effective intervention process on the service phase and provider roles is addressed as well.

Reconceptualizing Intervention and the Continuum of Care

The reconceptualization of intervention as shown in figure 6.1 transforms substance abuse problems into network and community problems that often involve large institutions. The process encourages a disempowered network or community, previously unable to manage the substance abuse or to cope with structural barriers, to gain power by collaborating on how to address the problem. The process is similar whether rehabilitation or prevention is the ultimate goal, that is, whether intervention involves a social network that is readying itself to confront an addicted member or an informal coalition that has just become aware of high substance abuse rates in the community. Reconceptualization can provide numerous empowerment opportunities for interveners as well as substance abusers or those at risk for the problem.

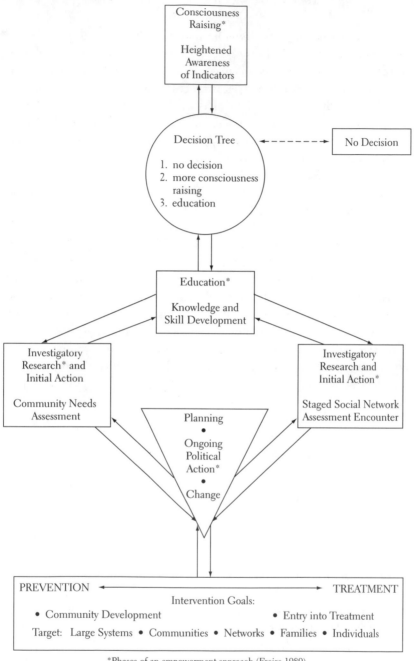

FIGURE 6.1 Intervention as the Foundation for Prevention and Treatment

Empowerment Opportunities During Intervention

Reconceptualizing intervention as continuous, as in the example of Connie's situation, means assuming this process may occur in many forms or phases before the impact is observable. Each effort to intervene may affect the person's decision to enter rehabilitation to varying degrees depending on a combination of circumstances, including his or her interpretation of the intervention and the effects of previous efforts. Similarly, in communities experiencing substance abuse problems, various factors may influence whether residents initiate prevention efforts, including their attitudes about new and existing risk factors (Lurigio and Davis 1992; Davis, Smith, Lurigio, and Skogan 1991).

The literature has not yet clarified whether these assumptions about intervention can be documented, or if the process is continuous and composed of discernible stages or patterns. Research is needed to explore natural patterns, explanatory theories, and factors that influence what works and does not work with different individuals or communities and different levels of problem severity. Freire's (1989) empowerment approach offers one way of reconceptualizing and explaining aspects of the intervention process, using continuous cycles of consciousness raising, education, investigatory research, and political action.

The Critical Awareness or Consciousness-Raising Phase.   In this phase, individuals become aware of the existence and severity of substance abuse problems and their powerlessness over the situation. Initially, consciousness raising may occur with a member of the network or with residents in one area of a community. Support networks can include immediate or extended family, peers, a social or work group, a self- or mutual help group, a religious or spiritual advisor, a helping professional, and informal leaders or community groups (Fine, Akabas, and Bellinger 1982; McNkman 1991; Schilit and Gomberg 1987; Westermeyer and Neider 1988).

Of course, for the purposes of intervention, only networks with norms against drug use should be involved. Indicators that can no longer be denied may contribute to the heightened awareness noted in figure 6.1. Examples include the increasing presence of drug dealers and houses in a community, community violence related to drug use (e.g., children's deaths from drive-by shootings), and a peer or family member becoming dysfunctional in work or family areas due to substance abuse (Fitzpatrick and Gerard 1993; Freeman 1992; Lurigio and Davis 1992).

Indicators point out the need for initial decision making: acknowledging the problem and deciding what to do about it. One possibility is to ignore and continue to deny the problem, which may exacerbate the network's or community's original disempowerment. An alternative is to identify others in the social network or community who may be concerned and to do more collective consciousness raising about the problem. The result may be the identification of knowledgeable people who can help, such as informal leaders who can identify resources for mobilizing the community or a facilitator who can help the social network understand the need for confronting the issues.

The Education Phase.   Education is another component of Freire's (1989) approach that helps individuals to learn about the connections between individual substance abuse problems and the structural roots of those problems (in the network, community, or larger institutions). Efforts can focus on conveying information about the consequences of substance abuse that are affecting network or community members and the reasons they are feeling chronically powerless and immobilized (Pinderhughes 1983). The members receive and discuss information about initial roles to be assumed and tasks that must be completed at different points during intervention.

In the network, education also includes skill building or coaching by a professional or informal leader on specific roles for each member. Effective communication skills are developed for confronting the addicted person about the severity of the problem and the consequences experienced by each member (Freeman 1993). In the community, skill building may focus on how to conduct the needs assessment, assume flexible roles for accomplishing this, and involve all stakeholders in the process (Delgado 1996; Tropman 1995). The skill-building aspects of intervention lead to empowerment because network and community members experience group efficacy and develop competence (Solomon 1987; Gutiérrez and Ortega 1990).

The Investigatory Research Phase.   This phase of Freire's (1989) approach is empowering because it encourages network and community members (rather than traditional experts) to identify the questions to be asked, how they are to be explored, and how the answers can be established. Yeich and Levine (1992) explain that "Participatory research is a theory and intervention approach for involving oppressed people in the study and solutions to social problems" (1894–1895). Thus, conducting a community needs assessment or other research and searching for and locating treatment resources for an addicted member of the network can lead to empowerment by offering opportunities for participation. Another source of empowerment is the mobilization of stakeholders to identify solutions that can change the structure of their networks, communities, and in some instances, large institutions and policy (Freeman 1992; Yeich and Levine 1992).

The Political and Social Action Phase. As part of Freire's (1989) approach, this phase involves initial and ongoing action. Initial action in the network consists of the staged confrontation and support provided to addicted members for entering rehabilitation. Ongoing action during service provision includes emotional and tangible support, participation in specialized groups (e.g., groups for family members or significant others), and additional interventions if the substance-abusing members later regress or plateau (Freeman 1992).

In communities, initial action involves the social planning process, while ongoing action includes community mobilization, community development, advocacy, policy reform, and other systems change activities (Lurigio and Davis 1992; Yeich and Levine 1992). As can be seen from this analysis, the ongoing political/social action aspect of intervention provides the bridge between the preservice phase and the service phase depicted in figure 6.1 (prevention and rehabilitation). This perspective on intervention clarifies its role in the substance abuse continuum of care but raises questions about the theoretical underpinnings of this process related to empowerment.

Underlying Theories

Theories that unify the network and individual substance abuser and the community coalition and community substance abuse problems in a common intervention process can be found in table 1.4 in chapter 1. Theories of psychological or personal change, interpersonal and group change, and social action and social change help to conceptualize the empowerment process experienced during intervention, regardless of the level of analysis (i.e., whether the individual social network or the community coalition). Moreover, Gutiérrez and Ortega's (1990) assumptions about empowerment levels clarify how a network's intervention with a member can involve personal and interpersonal empowerment, while a community's intervention process can extend beyond those to the political level.

Table 1.4 provides examples of theories that explain the empowerment opportunities involved in intervention at each level. For example, cognitive-behavioral theory explains the connection between self-control and self-efficacy, mutual aid theory clarifies the impact on people from supporting and influencing others, and community development theory identifies how changing social structures within and outside the community transfers power from institutions to people (Barth 1994; Florin and Wandersman 1990; Shulman 1992).

The Network Intervention Change Process

An advantage of viewing intervention as continuous is that it shifts the theoretical and interactional emphasis away from powerlessness (a problem focus) to empowerment (a solution focus). This view also emphasizes that network members who are experiencing different levels of problem severity may require different solutions. Thus, a differential assessment of the entire network is required so that all members' needs will be addressed eventually, with addicted members being the highest priority.

Intervention with Addicted Network Members

Problem-Focused Communication.   Often, although well intentioned, a network can develop a process of negative communication with the addicted individual because members feel powerless to change the situation. Baker and Steiner's (1995) concept of metamessages is useful for understanding the initial circular communication between addicted members—"you can't make me change"—and the network—"we'll force you to change." Metamessages are relationship messages, verbal or nonverbal, conscious or unconscious, that pass between people when they interact (Baker and Steiner 1995).

The metamessages within a network may change over time, becoming progressively more negative and painful. They both reflect and reinforce the members' disempowerment and helplessness. For example, the metamessages from addicted members may eventually convey, "You made me the way I am, you're responsible, you're hopeless, you're mean and rejecting, I'll make you as miserable as I am!" Metamessages from the network often

Variations occur also in the focus of the intervention, based on the type of support network: family, peers, or work group. For example, in the spontaneous intervention by Connie's work group (see the introduction to this chapter), her colleagues focused on how her dysfunctions at work affected them and the whole department. They pointed out how the consequences included reduced bonuses for the department and less teamwork. The group's focus was primarily on work and peer relations, whereas a family network might focus on several other areas of functioning.

Connie's situation points out two other intervention challenges. Serendipitous events, such as Connie's anxiety attack that prevented her from driving her car, may act as pseudo-interventions. Further, a series of interventions can have a cumulative effect in which the last, seemingly less powerful one becomes the "proverbial straw" (Golan 1986), leading to the person's subsequent movement into recovery.

Interventions with Substance-Using Members or Problem Users

Since a secondary goal of intervention is to differentially assess the entire network, this process should help identify network members who have less severe substance abuse problems. A systems approach indicates that a network contemplating intervention is already in disequilibrium and therefore is more open to change (Kauffman 1985; Shorkey and Rosen 1993). Intervention coaches should encourage each substance user or abuser to acknowledge his or her problem and its probable role in the network dynamics. Examples include a spouse or sibling who gets high with the addict or members of a drinking or drugging network who also work together (Fine et al. 1982). Acknowledging how their denial or overemphasis of the addicted member's problem helps to rationalize their own use is an important consequence for the network to be aware of.

Substance-abusing members need to be referred for services in their own right. Otherwise they can become triggers for an addicted member's relapse either during or after rehab, or their own substance abuse can escalate into addiction. Efforts should be made to coordinate recovery services to addicted and substance-abusing members so that potential individual and network recovery barriers can be addressed effectively (Flanzer and Delany 1993). Involvement in twelve-step groups can provide alternative nonusing networks that facilitate recovery and replace drug networks such as an addicted social or work group (Fine et al. 1982). Nowinski (1995) has demonstrated the efficacy of empirically validated cognitive-behavioral strategies that help clients and family members to make use of AA, NA, and other self-help groups essential for their recovery.

Intervention with High-Risk Nonusing Members

Even when network members do not use drugs or are just initiating drug use (e.g., tobacco, marijuana, or alcohol), they are at high risk for becoming substance abusers (Hawkins and Catalanc 1992). Often these members may be exhibiting gradually more tolerant attitudes toward drugs, which can be a precursor to drug use (Kleber 1992). They may have adopted some of the lifestyles of addicted and substance-abusing members, including stuffing their feelings, self-medicating with food or behaviors such as compulsive shopping or gambling, lying in order to appear more responsible, or participating in crimes (Freeman and Landesman 1992).

The education phase of intervention should help high-risk members to acknowledge their adoption of such behaviors as one consequence of the substance abuse problems in the network. Taking responsibility for their own actions requires agreeing to participate in a substance abuse prevention program to reduce the level of risk. It also requires participation in the addicted member's rehabilitation program as a significant other who has influenced and been affected by the network's substance abuse problems. If prevention is not sufficiently effective, counseling may be indicated, along with participation in a twelve-step group such as Alanon or Alafam (McCrady and Irvine 1989).

Intervention with Low- or Moderate-Risk Nonusing Members

Although low- or moderate-risk network members are not substance users and do not exhibit related high-risk behaviors discussed in the previous section, it is dangerous to assume they have not been affected by the network's problems. Symptoms of or reactions to the addict's problem may be unobservable but can manifest themselves later (Flanzer and Delany 1992). Therefore, these network members should be encouraged to participate in the addicted member's substance abuse rehab as a significant other. They should also become involved in a twelve-step group such as Alateen, Alanon, or Alafam, depending on their age and coping abilities. Those groups can enhance adaptive coping (McCrady and Irvine 1989) and help low-risk members to support others' recovery. Young network members who are at low to moderate risk may benefit from involvement in a substance abuse prevention program provided to all students in a school or to all participants in a community program (Hawkins and Catalano 1992).

The Community Intervention Change Process

Just as interventions by a network transform it and its addicted member(s), interventions by a community transform its structure and capacity for collective sufficiency. Two aspects of assets assessments help to transform (empower) communities during the intervention process: the assessments can be the foundation for planning and implementing a community development process that often includes prevention programs, and they provide the baseline and consumer orientation necessary for client-centered evaluation of those programs (Innes and Heflinger 1989; Siegel, Attkisson, and Carson 1995; Tropman 1995). During an intervention change process, it is important to clarify the methods used and who is involved and transformed as a result.

Methods That Facilitate the Transformation Process

Planned Collaborative Stages and Stakeholders' Roles. The emphasis on collaborative planning and conducting of intervention tasks points out how the process is as important as the outcomes. The process encourages stakeholders to become involved and provides empowerment opportunities such as knowledge and skill development (see figure 6.1). For instance, the consciousness-raising process described in "Reconceptualizing Intervention" above helps the initial planners, perhaps an informal coalition, to begin understanding substance abuse and other problems confronting the community. The members may be empowered from having their concerns and impressions validated by others and feeling less vulnerable because their individual concerns have become collective concerns.

The education phase helps to identify key informants who are knowledgeable about the community and its residents and can collaborate in designing the assessment procedures and methods of data collection and analysis. This phase is useful also for identifying the specific tasks necessary to accomplish the assessment, other roles that will be needed, specific people to fill the roles, and the knowledge and skills they must have. Education can be empowering because it clarifies for the participants what will happen during intervention, giving them more control over the process. Knowledge about the nature and pervasiveness of substance abuse locally and nationally, its consequences, and what strategies have worked or not worked in similar communities provided during this phase is often another source of empowerment.

The investigatory research phase, in which the assets assessment takes place, builds on the two empowerment phases discussed above. This phase involves several planned collaborative steps that help to facilitate empowerment and capacity building. In spite of differences in conditions across communities, most assessments address two main questions: Does the community have substance abuse and related problems? and What are the strengths and necessary growth areas related to such problems on which the community should focus? (Cunningham 1993).

A research protocol can be developed to identify more detailed questions in these two general areas. Decisions about what to ask, how, and in what format are part of the consensus-building process necessary for effective planning (Johnson 1987). Various community members will have different perspectives and will need to be heard in order to ensure the broadest range of diverse input into decisions. Often, being heard and respected encourages members to explore and negotiate potential areas for compromise. They can become empowered through collaborating or sharing power rather than through individual competition.

It is equally important to involve coalition members and other residents in the data collection and analysis stages of assets assessments. The education phase may have helped them to understand data collection and how it is to be accomplished, but often they need technical assistance to apply the knowledge and skills (Hawkins and Catalano 1992). If the participants understand how this process has empowered them, they can use their knowledge and skills during data collection to help respondents experience a similar empowerment.

Facilitators or consultants should help coalition members identify their strengths and the roles they can best fulfill (Gilmore 1987; Yeich and Levine 1992). Some people may be skilled in identifying previously ignored but important types of data and data sources, which can vary across different geographic and ethnic areas within a community (Freeman 1994). Others may be more effective as mediators and facilitators, introducing data collectors to community members who will provide data for the assessment. Still others may be good at establishing rapport and trust, getting people to share their perspectives and opinions openly, and therefore will be more useful as interviewers, focus group facilitators, or community forum chairs.

Community participation in the data analysis phase can be accomplished in two ways. First, complex procedures such as statistical and content analysis may be required. Skilled consultants and indigenous leaders can help to conduct these objective analyses. Later, other community members can be asked to react to the results and to the analysts' interpretations of them. Participants can question results that conflict with their knowledge of the community and provide alternative conclusions about other results they may agree with. This member checking process can improve research validity and increase participants' empowerment experiences (Yeich and Levine 1992).

A second way of involving participants is to have them actually conduct data analysis from their more subjective perspective, using their understanding of the cultural context, language, meanings, nuances, and world views that undergird study participants' lives and responses to the assessment (McCracken 1988). This process helps to ensure that subsequent planning based on these results is culturally relevant to the community. The process also builds on the collaboration and power sharing that have characterized previous stages rather than encouraging a monopoly by the powerful few (Freire 1989), those with professionally based, expert knowledge.

Therefore, data analysis is the bridge to prioritizing needs and planning the political and social action necessary to address them. Tropman (1995) points out that planning must lead to "the establishment of priorities among needs because not all needs can be met in a given situation" (563). If the previous steps have been sufficiently collaborative and members have experienced self- and group-efficacy, it is easier for them to reach a consensus about priorities at this point. Figure 6.1 indicates that prior to political action, the process can move from planning back to education, if necessary. Returning to the education phase can improve community members' knowledge and skills in consensus building and planning, and thus their later effectiveness as political activists (Mondros and Wilson 1994; Zimmer and Rappaport 1988).

Effective Tools and Procedures.   A number of procedures have been developed for conducting assets assessments that increase the collaborative and empowerment aspects of this phase. Although some are more culturally sensitive than others, a common goal is to include all areas and constituencies within a community (i.e., members of all racial/ethnic, age, religious, political, gender, sexual orientation, family structure, and socioeconomic groups). Tropman (1995) recommends that a combination of indicator, social survey, and community group approaches/procedures be used as a triangulation strategy.

Indicator approaches include the use of data from public records, such as the U.S. Census, that are indirect indices of a community's quality of life and basic resources as well as its service utilization rates (Tropman 1995). These approaches also document the availability of alcohol and other drugs, use and abuse rates among community members, and direct versus indirect consequences of those rates (e.g., the amount of alcohol sold versus the

TABLE 6.1 Community Needs Assessment Tools and Procedures

Indicator Approaches
(availability/consequences of community substance abuse and other issues)
census records
emergency room drug-related data
crime statistics
treatment utilization rates for substance abuse

Social Survey Approaches
(community members'/providers' knowledge, attitudes, and opinions about problem severity/resources/needs related to substance abuse)
written questionnaires
telephone surveys

Community Group Approaches
(sample representative populations within a community about common and unique experiences/knowledge about substance abuse issues and community development needs)
community forums
focus groups
individual interviews
participant observation

---

number of hospital emergency room admissions for drug overdoses) (Freeman 1994). Social survey approaches involve the use of written questionnaires with service providers and community members. Questionnaires for the latter require careful review and adaptation to address potential barriers related to language, reading level, and cultural biases (Freeman 1994). Community group approaches include community forums, town meetings, focus groups, individual interviews, and participant observations (Tropman 1995).

Decisions about the combination of methods to be used depend on the type of change or intervention process a community determines is needed (McKillip 1987; Siegel, Attkisson, and Carson 1995). For example, qualitative methods such as in-depth interviews and focus groups with key informants and other community members provide more active roles and a sense of empowerment for them as more than sources of data. Further, such methods can provide richer, more in-depth information about a community than written surveys. These consumer-centered methods may be more useful in communities whose members have little hope for change, where small, cumulative experiences in self- and group efficacy are needed to rekindle motivation (Hawkins and Catalano 1992).

Tropman (1995) indicates that community education about the advantages and disadvantages of various methods is extremely important. For instance, some methods involve more time and measurement expertise than others (e.g., social indicators and surveys versus interviews with community members). Quantitative methods are useful when more objective data are desired or when a combination of objective and subjective data is the goal (Tropman 1995). Another factor to consider is the ethnic diversity within a community, as some methods are likely to be more relevant to different groups' learning and communication styles than others. For example, face-to-face data collection methods such as community forums, participant observation, interviews, and focus groups may be more effective with some groups of color because they allow opportunities for trust building and individual expression (Lee 1994).

Stakeholders' Changes and Transformations During Intervention

This discussion about the process of community intervention and change has identified methods and specialized roles for various stakeholders in each phase. The long-term goal of this process is community planning and de-

velopment, as well as prevention programming. The short-term goal, however, is the transformation of the community from powerless to empowered
through its efforts to acknowledge and assess the area's substance abuse and
related problems. Potential changes in the different stakeholders include the
following (Cunningham 1993; Innes and Helflinger 1989; Hawkings and
Catalano 1992; Tropman 1995):

1. informal leaders and coalitions: expansion of existing leaders'
   groups (in numbers and expertise) and reformulation of their identities as more trusted, accountable, inclusive groups that facilitate
   power sharing and community rebuilding
2. community constituency groups: decentralization of power to
   include previously marginalized and voiceless groups in the
   decision-making process, resulting in a new sense of belonging,
   efficacy, and competence (empowerment of different ethnic, age,
   gender, political orientation, and socioeconomic status groups)
3. substance abusers, users, and high-risk members of the community
   and their significant others: opportunity to voice their unique experiences and needs and to develop an advocacy group for artic-
   ulating their strengths, needs, and solutions that addresses environmental risk factors and supports from their perspective
4. policy makers: new joint ownership of the problem by the community and readiness to become partners in changing community
   and structural factors that affect the problem and effective
   development/use of resources
5. facilitators-consultants-coaches: increased openness and ability to
   integrate divergent ideas, more power sharing and joint ownership
   of the process, and opportunity to test commitment to community
   empowerment and rebuilding.

Impact of Intervention on the Service Phase
and Provider Roles

That substance abuse intervention can test professionals' commitment to
social network and community empowerment is one of the dilemmas inherent in this change process. By investing in change, professionals often
commit themselves to certain predetermined outcomes and standards for

judging their success, and to ensuring, through the best professional efforts, that those desired outcomes occur. Efforts that are effective in traditional practice situations, however, do not always work in empowerment practice. Three role shifts are necessary for service providers to accommodate empowerment practice during intervention and the subsequent service phase (rehabilitation and prevention services).

The Environmental Coach and Facilitator

In contrast to traditional practice, an empowerment-based definition of intervention is grounded in the assumption that people who share a common experience have something to offer each other that is complementary to but should not be replaced by services from helping professionals (Segal et al. 1993). Members of intervention networks and community coalitions are stakeholders in the problems and their resolution at a much more intimate and personal cost level than professionals. Substance abuse and other disabling conditions that impede a person's ability to function in certain areas can be mediated if "the appropriate social and environmental accommodations are provided" (707).

Social network and community interventions are designed to provide such accommodations in order to influence individuals to acknowledge, assess, and accept help with substance abuse problems. The main role of professionals is to help informal leaders develop these environmental accommodations and to facilitate, but not subvert, the network's or community's decision making and self-empowerment. The specific coaching and environmental influence aspects of this role were discussed in detail in the previous two sections. Its overall purpose is to initiate a strong collaborative process between formal and informal helpers, leading to a similar pattern of power sharing between these stakeholders during the service phase.

The Services Integration Role

Another provider role implicit in empowerment-oriented interventions also helps to link that phase with the service phase of prevention and rehabilitation. A major cause of disempowerment for clients entering a rehab program or a coalition working toward community development is a fragmented service system. Intervention is designed to identify such potential barriers to recovery and prevention as well as to empowerment. The facilitator or consultant's role is to work toward improved services integration with other formal and informal helpers.

An example of the services integration role resulted in the development of a centralized outreach, assessment, and referral system that serves all rehab programs in one city. The system developed through advocacy by a group of practitioners concerned about clients who responded positively to intervention but were hindered by a fragmented service system. Now potential clients are sent for centralized assessment through several avenues: their calls to individual rehab programs and referrals from detox programs, intervention coaches, community outreach staff, and informal community leaders. The goal is to match clients with appropriate programs after an initial screening and brief assessment of their needs, such as the severity of addiction; family, legal, or employment problems; age; gender; and availability of social supports (Freeman and Landesman 1992; McLellan and Alterman 1991; Smyth 1995).

Another example of the services integration role is related to prevention. Often when the services integration models discussed in chapters 3 and 5 are developed (see figures 3.3 and 5.1), substance abuse prevention programs are not included. Practitioners and administrators should work toward including prevention, to improve services integration not only between substance abuse programs and other providers but also between substance abuse prevention and rehab services.

The previous discussions about social network and community intervention change processes illustrate the range of substance abuse that exists within networks and communities, from addicted to substance-abusing to high- and low-risk nonusing individuals. The variety of potential service needs within one family or peer group, as well as within communities, is equally wide. Thus the services integration role is critical for effective intervention and for subsequent rehab and prevention services (O'Connor and McCord 1990–91).

The Mutual Support/Self-Care Role

Reconceptualizing intervention as a continuous process has advantages and disadvantages. It helps networks and communities to empower themselves by clarifying their roles and the resources necessary for effective intervention, while providing hope for change. However, the outcomes are not within the control of interveners and facilitators, and thus the process may lead to increased frustration and burnout. Therefore, empowerment approaches to intervention require an emphasis on mutual support and self-care among intervention facilitators, coaches, and other service providers.

O'Connor and McCord's (1990–91) study of networking among service providers identified seven types of networks that benefit clients and workers, directly and indirectly. One of the identified networks benefited workers only: the mutual support network for close partners in which there is an exchange of socioemotional supports for personal and professional self-care. There is a clear rationale for the development of this type of network: "The rigors, frustrations, and emotional drain of direct service work could take its toll" (15). Strengthening mutual support roles can address this type of practice drain while helping to empower providers.

Conclusion

The perspective on intervention discussed in this chapter is gradually gaining acceptance because it is consistent with the renewed emphasis on consumer empowerment and strengths-based approaches. Since intervention sets the stage for prevention and recovery, clarity about the role of these approaches is essential. Waiting until the service phase to introduce these concepts and procedures overlooks an important and early opportunity to influence empowerment outcomes.

To reconceptualize the intervention process, it is necessary to redesign the roles that practitioners assume to facilitate it, either direct service workers or consultants and coaches within communities. This discussion points out an equally important issue: that network and community empowerment cannot occur in isolation of staff who facilitate the process. Staff empowerment and mutual support are essential self-care strategies. Moreover, they model a healthy and functional coping style for substance abusers and other stakeholders within consumers' social networks and community coalitions.

7   Community Prevention:
Empowerment, Systems Change,
and Culturally Sensitive Evaluation

Although more recent preventive approaches have not abandoned
the role and responsibility of individuals in changing their lifestyles, they have
emphasized local empowerment and policy changes as opposed to solely
behavioral or education approaches.
— N. Bracht (1995:1879)

The substance abuse prevention field has been criticized
for its many schisms, including the emerging trend toward systems change
noted by Bracht above. Conflicts have existed also among previous trends:
emphasizing personal responsibility versus the role of cultural and other
environmental factors in prevention, prioritizing resource allocations for
primary versus secondary and tertiary prevention, and promoting proactive
versus reactive primary prevention (Bloom 1995; Catalano and Dooley
1980; DeJong and Winsten 1990; Orlando 1986). Moreover, the field has
been characterized by some as a movement without a credible theory
base (Lee 1994). Bloom (1995) asserts, however, that three clearly iden-
tifiable theoretical paradigms have guided the development of primary
prevention.

These conflicts may have inhibited efforts to organize the prevention field
and to address some basic issues more constructively in both theoretical and
applied areas. They also may have obscured the role of policy and other
large system barriers to effective prevention. Only recently have efforts to
organize preventionists been successful: for instance, the National Prevention Coalition and the National Association of Prevention Professionals and
Advocates were formed in 1986 and 1987, respectively (Bloom 1995;
Mowrer and Strader 1992). Until that time, many practitioners in substance

abuse and other specialized prevention areas assumed they must remain apolitical in order to be effective.

Bloom (1995) states that rather than ignoring political and power issues, the prevention expert's role is to be extremely political by advocating for social and systems change. In fact, "Prevention science exists in a political-economic matrix" (1897). Besides taking political action, practitioners in the field need to integrate and disseminate the multidisciplinary knowledge and other resources being developed nationally and internationally. Further, substance abuse prevention and prevention in general need to respond to criticisms identified above, which can influence important policy and funding decisions related to the field's survival.

Thus, in the current political environment, substance abuse prevention has two major, interrelated goals: developing and implementing prevention programs that lead to community capacity building and creating collaborative consumer and professional networks to impact policy and other structural barriers. Often, however, preventionists' efforts have fallen short of these goals. They may develop and implement prevention programs, but not in a manner that leads to empowerment and skill development for consumers. For example, some programs conduct program evaluations and share the findings with consumers without involving them more actively in the process. Or they build networks and coalitions with other professionals but exclude consumers or do not encourage them to participate in the related political action activities (Orlandi 1986; Price and Smith 1985).

In one prevention program for adolescents, two social workers who conducted family groups used a combination of verbal and written feedback to evaluate their program at the end of each six-week cycle. The family groups were scheduled during the six-week period before the youths were scheduled to complete a four-month juvenile diversion program for first offenders of property crimes, including stealing cars, shoplifting, tagging, and vandalism. The groups focused extensively on preventing substance abuse; some of the participants were experimenting with drugs, while others were at risk for the problem because family members or peers were using. Other goals included preventing the youths from returning to criminal behavior and subsequent involvement in the criminal justice system and teaching them stress management and family communication skills. The feedback at the end of the six weeks was usually very brief and nonspecific, such as, "Good group," "Our family learned a lot," or "I didn't like the role playing, but it helped."

As a consultant for the groups, I helped the facilitators to identify some of the control and power issues inherent in work with juvenile substance abusers within a social control agency. To address these issues, the facilitators first decided to invite the youths to help redesign the evaluation form but then agreed to have them also redesign the group format, focus, and evaluation. The latter task included having youths help to pretest and analyze data collected with the new evaluation form.

These programmatic (or mezzo) changes highlighted yet another area of the facilitators' work at the macro level from which youths and their families had been excluded. An advisory committee had been developed recently for the diversion program, consisting of professionals who represented various community agencies. One goal was to advocate for more clarity, flexibility, and equity in the court's admission and dismissal policies for the program because of recent punitive decisions involving some of the participants. However, prior to the work with the consultant, neither the youths nor their parents had been considered as potential committee members. Fortunately, very little of the organizing and planning for the advisory committee's work had been done before youth and parental representatives were included.

This chapter summarizes approaches to substance abuse prevention that have shaped perspectives about consumer involvement in both prevention and evaluation, including both historical and current paradigms such as the empowerment approach. Two goals related to the community prevention process are discussed: the implementation of prevention programs through individual and community capacity building and the policy impact/systems change process. Because evaluation can facilitate programs' efforts toward capacity building, strategies that communities have used to achieve a parallel empowerment and evaluation process are included, along with two fully developed community examples. The chapter ends with a discussion of new directions for the substance abuse prevention field based on issues identified in the examples and in the literature.

Historical and Current Prevention Paradigms

Historical Paradigms and Consumer Involvement

Bloom (1995) identifies three major paradigms in the general field of prevention and their underlying assumptions about causal conditions. Those paradigms not only shape perspectives about causality but also influence ideas about the role of consumers in prevention in terms of physical and mental health, family life education, early childhood interventions, and other areas. The paradigms are shown in table 7.1, along with specific sub-stance abuse prevention approaches that have been used during different time periods. Two of these paradigms developed out of specific historical conditions related to professional disciplines such as medicine.

During the period when the disease-pathology paradigm (or the medical model) developed, the focus of treatment was individual areas of weakness, including knowledge gaps, genetic factors, unhealthy behaviors or lifestyle patterns, and attitudes that lead to the development of certain problems such as heart disease or substance abuse. Bloom (1995) points out that this para-digm took a very simplistic view of complex, chronic social problems and ignored many individual and environmental factors that influence under-lying conditions and prevention outcomes. Very few organized and well-conceptualized approaches to substance abuse prevention existed prior to this period, although approaches to the general field of prevention are much older. Specific models that developed at this time are shown under the disease-pathology paradigm in table 7.1. Those approaches were primarily short term and unidimensional. They viewed consumers as passive recipients

TABLE 7.1 Historical Overview of Prevention Paradigms and Approaches

Historical Paradigms in the Field of Prevention (Bloom 1995)	Time Periods	Related Substance Abuse Prevention Approaches (Freeman and Gordon 1995)
Disease-Pathology Paradigm	1960s	"one shot" scare tactics
	early 1970s	education or information approaches
	late 1970s	affective and activities model
Public Health Paradigm	1980s to present	public health model
	late 1980s	impactors model
Competency Paradigm	late 1980s	competence, life skills, pychosocial, and resiliency models
	early 1990s	risk and protective factors model
		multicultural outcome-based model
	currently	community-rebuilding/capacity-building/systems change model

of services, often generalizing from knowledge about acute physical illnesses without adequate social research to document transferability outside the medical field (Albee 1983).

In comparison, the public health paradigm uses a more complex lens to view underlying conditions and important lifestyle factors that influence problem development (Coates 1990). Nevertheless, it focuses on those conditions in a linear manner. The host or the individual, who is the target of prevention efforts, is viewed as dependent and limited in his or her ability to act without support. This view of consumers as primarily reactors to the environment rather than as proactive made it less likely that the related approaches to prevention would emphasize active consumer involvement.

In addition, the paradigm ignores complex interaction and mutual influence among the host, the agent (or drugs), and the environment or structural factors. For instance, this paradigm may identify failed interdiction policies that have led to increased accessibility of alcohol and drugs for people living in poverty. But its focus is seldom on clarifying aspects of the environment beyond accessibility to drugs that should be changed, or how they should be changed. More specifically, the related public health and impactors models do not teach community residents how to change negative media messages, public policy, inequitable resource allocations to poor communities, high unemployment and underemployment rates, and culturally insensitive prevention strategies that influence substance abuse rates and/or prevention outcomes (Caplan, Vinokur, Price, and van Ryn 1989; DeJong and Winsten 1990; Orlandi 1986).

Current Paradigms and Consumer Involvement

Table 7.1 also includes Bloom's (1995) most recent theoretical perspective on prevention, the competency paradigm, which de-emphasizes specific causes of underlying conditions. This paradigm recognizes that people's strengths and limitations, their multiple resources and risk factors at various systems levels, must be considered in planning, implementing, and evaluating prevention and health promotion programs in order to involve them actively in all phases (Gullota 1987). This implies the need for coordinated and integrated prevention activities at each level, including the physical and cultural environments, involved. Stress and coping, or strengths, are an integral part of the paradigm, with stress being defined as any excess of environmental demands over the individual's capacity to respond effectively. In comparison, strengths are growth-producing experiences that increase people's capacities to respond to or cope with such demands (Bloom 1995).

Four examples of substance abuse approaches consistent with the competency paradigm are shown in table 7.1. Some emphasize teaching and building on people's existing life skills and resilience to prevent substance abuse (Botvin and Tortu 1988) or to prevent problems in general (Libassi and Maluccio 1986; Rutter 1987). Other approaches using this paradigm focus on strengthening protective factors and eliminating risk factors to substance abuse (Hawkins and Catalano 1993), and addressing cultural aspects that influence substance abuse (Albee, Joffee, and Dusenbury 1988) through active consumer involvement. Thus, the competency paradigm offers the greatest support for expanding the use of empowerment and client-driven approaches in the substance abuse field, as illustrated by the four models.

Summary of Prevention Paradigms

A number of authors have identified problems with both historical and current approaches to substance abuse prevention. These problems help to clarify why paradigm shifts were necessary in the past and what challenges exist in using current paradigms and approaches (Bloom 1995; Lee 1994; Manger, Hawkins, Haggerty, and Catalano 1992; Spaulding and Balch 1983; Wallach 1984):

1. Earlier models focus mostly on demand reduction. The current political and economic reform climate may encourage preventionists to continue that trend in spite of the ecological focus on both demand *and* supply reduction required by current models.
2. In the demand reduction area, older models were too narrow in addressing the complexity of people's real lives, whereas current models may overwhelm preventionists with their much broader scope and the effort they require to address factors at multiple levels.
3. Previous models required rigid boundaries between prevention, intervention, and treatment along the continuum of care. Current efforts to link these three areas in integrated or combined services

models and to conceptualize intervention as the foundation for prevention and treatment (see chapter 5) could increase competition and turf issues within the field.

4. Historical and current models emphasize providing prevention to impoverished and resource-deficient communities. With the incidence and prevalence of substance abuse increasing in all communities and the new block grant funding process, equity issues and competition for prevention resources may increase across communities in the future.

5. Current paradigms and approaches to substance abuse prevention are potentially more effective than previous approaches in addressing structural problems, including policy reforms and systems change. The country's conservative political leaders and policy makers, however, may increase pressures to de-emphasize the empowerment and systems change strategies required by the new models through funding limitations.

6. Past paradigms mostly focused on the expert model, which greatly limits active consumer involvement in prevention efforts. Current approaches, on the other hand, emphasize consumers as the experts and professional-consumer partnerships. This implies a need for more sophisticated grant development and research dissemination in support of empowerment and partnership prevention projects (systems change strategies).

These issues indicate that perhaps using any one of the current approaches described in this section is insufficient. More than at any other period in this field, combining parallel approaches—that is, competence-centered and multicultural models or multicultural and community rebuilding–systems change models, depending on the situation—may be more useful. In addition, there is a need to develop coalitions for social planning and action, not only among substance abuse preventionists but also with consumers and professionals along the whole continuum of care, including intervention and treatment. Social planning and action emphasize the importance of consumer involvement and empowerment, which are supported most effectively in models related to the competence paradigm. That paradigm also emphasizes skill development and capacity building within communities, and thus the importance of long-term prevention goals.

Goal 1: Prevention Program Development and Capacity Building

This discussion of consumer involvement and community rebuilding expands ideas introduced in chapter 6, in which intervention is addressed as a foundation for treatment as well as prevention. That discussion illustrates how community residents can be involved in conducting, analyzing, and drawing conclusions from needs assessments and in long-term program development, planning and implementation, and systems change. This chapter illustrates how that process actually unfolds in communities, that is, how the consciousness-raising, education, investigatory research, and political action phases are operationalized with consumers, along with the associated nontraditional and empowerment-oriented professional roles.

The following community example primarily illustrates goal 1, although efforts to achieve goal 2 (political, policy, and large systems change) at the community level are closely related. This example represents the first comprehensive effort by an eastern state to target families in the prevention of substance abuse. The state consists of four large urban, industrialized cities along with a combination of small farming communities and rural towns mostly dominated by small, local industries.

Project Philosophy and Service Components

The prevention approach used by this statewide project was the risk and protective model (Hawkins and Catalano 1993), included under the competency paradigm in table 7.1. This model requires consumer involvement in the form of communitywide mobilization, planning, and implementation. It is based on a philosophy and conceptual framework that drug abuse risks are decreased and protective factors are increased substantially when children are strongly bonded to their social institutions, communities, and families. Families are viewed especially as guides and nurturers of their children's development while assuming a variety of special roles in helping children to lead drug-free lives (Hawkins and Catalano 1993).

As the project proceeded, four core components and a plan for their coordination were developed. These components made the project unique in terms of programming and capacity building: they involved families *and* professionals, and they emphasized early intervention by targeting the families of elementary and middle school children across the state. Also, the components addressed micro, mezzo, and macro system changes, thus involving many of the stakeholder roles and strategies discussed in chapter 6 and illustrated in figure 7.1.

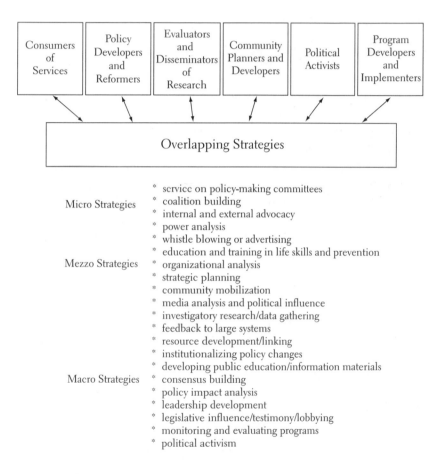

FIGURE 7.1 Systems Change and Community Rebuilding: Stakeholder Roles and Strategies

The four components were (Freeman 1992):

1. mass media and public information/education strategies
2. a training-of-trainers program that included preventionists and parents
3. a plan to institutionalize the risk-focused prevention model in the operations of various state agencies that received substance abuse funding
4. mobilization of families in a statewide prevention network to reduce drug abuse among children and youths

The Planning and Implementation Process

The above integrated set of multilevel prevention components was planned, developed, and evaluated by a coalition selected and convened by the Governor's Office on Substance Abuse. In addition to staff from that office, the coalition included families and representatives of the State Board of Education, the State School Administrators' Association, Drug-Free Schools, Child Protective Services, Alcohol and Drug Abuse Services, public health officials, mental health professionals, and law enforcement. The State Association of Broadcasters, Partnership for a Drug-Free America, State Extension and Agricultural Services, State 4-H Units, Boy and Girl Scouts, Parents as Teachers, National Federation of Parents, and the Parents and Teachers Association also were involved (Freeman 1992).

The coalition met several times, and then, as the initial planning proceeded, organized into five task forces to continue the planning and implementation of the project's components over a three-year period. There were separate task forces for each of the four project components and an additional one for evaluating the project. Families served on all five. A private consulting firm was hired to help design the initial process of convening and facilitating the coalition and to coordinate the work of the project and its task forces. Staff from the Governor's Office provided some of the administrative oversight. Some of the work of these task forces (Freeman 1992) was consistent with Freire's (1989) empowerment process as follows (other aspects of the work inconsistent with an empowerment framework are discussed in the next section on evaluation of the project):

1. *Consciousness-Raising and Education*: The goal of the mass media task force was to raise the public's awareness of the important role

of families in preventing substance abuse (de-emphasizing the professional expert model and emphasizing family and community empowerment).

2. *Education and Investigatory Research*: The training task force planned and coordinated the training-of-trainers program, which targeted 500 professionals and 5,000 parents. The focus was on skill and capacity building among "hard to reach" parents through three alternative programs: a traditional school–community based prevention program, a culture-specific program for African American families, and a culture-specific program for Hispanic families with English and Spanish versions. Each community could select one or a combination of these programs for its training workshops. All three included a community assets/needs assessment process conducted by parents who had been trained in the project.

3. *Political Action at the Mezzo Level*: The family mobilization task force ensured that the assets/needs assessment process led directly to efforts to organize families in a statewide network to support ongoing substance abuse prevention among youth across different types of communities. The network included existing family/parent organizations and informal coalitions as well as previously unrepresented individual families.

4. *Political Action at the Macro Level*: The state agency task force's main goal was to institutionalize the risk-focused model of substance abuse prevention within twenty-three state agencies that received substance abuse funding. The focus was on grafting the model onto each agency's long-range strategic plan, policies, training process, and service delivery systems.

5. *Evaluation*: The evaluation task force was charged with designing and implementing the statewide evaluation plan: developing the Request for Proposals for Evaluation of Projects (RFP) statewide; reviewing and approving proposals; coordinating the evaluation process across the state; and reviewing, approving, and disseminating information from interim and final evaluation reports.

Evaluation of Project Results

Evaluation Overview. This author served as a consultant to the projects' evaluation task force, helping to design the RFP for evaluation. Initially, the

RFP required that the evaluation gradually include an increasing number of process, impact, and short- and long-term outcome evaluation procedures over a three-year period. The task forces decided, however, only to require applicants to propose a combination of process, impact, and very modest short-term outcome evaluation procedures including, for example, pre- and post-training questionnaires for measuring participants' (preventionists', parents', and children's) increased knowledge and skills at the beginning and end of the workshops, forms for participants to evaluate the training workshops and the instructional materials, a survey of substance abuse prevalence and use patterns among targeted youths, and an analysis of the project's implementation process in reaching the target families (Freeman 1992).

Thus, the overall evaluation had the following limitations in measuring prevention program development and capacity-building and empowerment opportunities for families:

1. It did not include any long-term outcome data for any of the four components (mass media, training workshops for families and professionals, family/community mobilization for conducting on-going prevention programs, and state agency or systems changes).
2. It only included short-term outcome measures for evaluating the training workshops immediately after participants completed them.
3. There was no evaluation of the extent to which families were actually involved at all levels of planning and implementation of the project or of their skill and empowerment outcomes, as recommended for comprehensive, empowerment-oriented program evaluations (Cunningham 1993; Fetterman 1994; Freeman 1995; Jacobs 1984; Walker and Crocker 1988).

The Process Evaluation Results.   Related to this last drawback, although the intent was to involve a broader range of stakeholders in the project, the process evaluation documented that the planning and implementation consisted of a "top-down" process that automatically excluded some important unrepresented voices (Weiss 1983). More specifically, both the process evaluation and participants' responses on workshop evaluation forms documented that the elderly, members of self-help recovery groups, informal community leaders, some non-English-speaking groups, the undocumented, uninvolved youths (e.g., school dropouts and gang members), and the homeless population within various communities were not included.

The process evaluation indicated also how and in what areas the program was effective. For instance, the project reached approximately 80 percent (4,000) of the targeted families and involved them in training workshops during the 3-year period. Data identified both positive and negative attitudes toward cultural issues by targeted families in various communities. In some instances, evaluation identified resistance to using the two culture-specific prevention programs to train families and professionals, even though the population included people of color. Negative attitudes about the need for culture-specific prevention were observed directly in some participants' statements during training workshops as part of the process evaluation.

The Outcome Evaluation Results.   Similar negative attitudes were identified in the analysis of some participants' responses on pre-/post-training questionnaires, while other participants' responses indicated a shift toward increasingly positive attitudes. It is assumed that negative attitudes decreased opportunities for empowerment among families and professionals of color in various communities (Cunningham 1993; Solomon 1987), although unfortunately, such short- and long-term outcomes were not measured.

Other short-term outcomes in two major areas of the project were documented and are relevant to capacity building. First, data showed that efforts to mobilize families across the different communities within the state and to involve them in ongoing prevention programming were successful in some instances but understandably failed in other, more diverse communities (Slaughter 1988). The state's emphasis on consistency in mobilization and prevention program strategies failed to recognize the special needs and assets of such communities (urban, suburban, or rural; multicthnic versus homogenous; impoverished versus affluent; or low risk versus high risk for substance abuse and other community problems) (Freeman 1992). Thus, some communities mobilized their members and implemented prevention programs that met their needs in an ongoing manner, while other communities could not develop consensus about programming based on state guidelines or could not mobilize their members effectively.

Second, the short-term outcome evaluation of the training workshops documented that they were effective in developing the identified knowledge and skills in a majority of the participants. Key knowledge areas in which participants showed significant gains included information about risk and protective factors and strategies families can use to reduce the former and increase the latter. However, skill development outcomes were only measured by the extent to which participants carried out between-session homework assignments or increased communication, policy impact, or resource development skills shown in figure 7.1. As noted previously, no efforts were made to document long-term outcomes in these areas or the connection between such outcomes and the prevention or reduction of particular risk factors, including substance abuse rates among youths and family members.

The Impact Evaluation Results.   Finally, because the mass media and agency policy change components were not evaluated directly or formally, it was difficult to document their impact. An improved impact evaluation could have measured changes in families' and communities' attitudes or a denormalization of drug use, DUI arrests or other crime statistics for youths, or emergency room drug overdose rates as a result of mass media/public education efforts. Similarly, impact evaluation for systems change could have measured changes in state agencies' strategic plans and training programs to include key elements of the risk and protective factor model (Freeman 1995; Cunningham 1993). Anecdotal feedback indicated that while a few agencies integrated the model into their operations, others did not or did so for only a brief period. The "top-down" process from the Governor's Office mobilized rather than decreased resistance to policy or systems change and eliminated opportunities for families to develop the macro-level political action skills shown in figure 7.1.

Goal 2: Building Networks for Political, Policy, and Large Systems Change

The second community example included in this discussion is focused primarily on goal 2, although again, elements of the other goal are illustrated also because they are so closely interrelated. The focus of a community research project in a medium-sized midwestern city was on the social support needs of families with young children and their ability to impact large systems that were barriers to their self-sufficiency. The project was sponsored by a private foundation to explore how it could serve those families more effectively. The foundation contracted with a graduate school of social work to conduct an ethnographic study of the community to clarify the residents' assessment of their assets and needs; I was the principal investigator.

In terms of empowerment, the study was guided by an ecological perspective. It focused on self-sufficiency not only for families but also in regard to the organizational, community, and larger environments that affect them (Freeman and O'Dell 1993). It was assumed that when families are self-sufficient in those different environments, when they experience more control over their lives, they have increased opportunities for empowerment (Chang 1993; Dunst, Trivette, and Deal 1989; Gutiérrez, GlenMaye, and DeLois 1995; Solomon 1987).

The Community and Its Residents

This community of 4,126 people is located in a midwestern metropolitan area of approximately 500,000 residents. The community was settled by European immigrants in the early 1880s; Latinos began to move in during the early 1900s and African Americans during the 1960s. There are a number of strong community organizations and both Latino and multicultural social programs that were established from 17 to over 100 years ago. The area is known as the cultural center for the city's Latinos because of its ethnic celebrations, businesses, and organizations. The celebrations often attract people of various ethnic backgrounds from throughout the city.

Demographically, 77 percent of employed residents in this community earn less than $19,999 per year, and the unemployment rate is 9.5 percent. The majority of families consist of married couples with children (50 percent), with 16 percent consisting of single female householders with children. Most families (71 percent) live in single-family housing, while others live in one of three low-income housing developments or in other multiple-family dwellings.

One hundred ninety members of this multicultural community participated in individual and focus group interviews designed to help them mutually assess their assets and needs. Of these, 50 were interviewed as individuals (34) or as couples (16), and the remainder (140) in 14 separate focus groups. Participants in the individual and couple interviews included community residents who were pregnant or who had infants up to 18 months of age, their spouses or partners, and extended family members in the same household. These criteria were chosen in order to include as many young families with children in the study as possible. From 3 to 15 people participated in each of the focus groups, representing 12 community organizations and 6 areas of special interest (including cultural or ethnic, health, education, political, social service, business, civic, voluntary, and legal organizations or interest groups).

A key informant, snowball sampling technique was used to develop the convenience sample. A cross section of residents, formal leaders, and informal helpers was included. The ethnic composition of the sample was approximately the same as of the community: 75 percent Latino, 15 percent white, and 10 percent African American. The total number of participants was determined at the point when interview themes and response patterns across the participants became redundant.

Study Design and Procedures

The project's qualitative study was conducted over a four-month period in 1992–93 and consisted of a time series ethnographic survey design. Separate 25-item, semistructured interview guides were developed specifically for the project, pretested, and then revised as needed for the individual interviews and focus groups. The guides consisted of open-ended questions for gathering the following information: participants' views about how the private foundation could serve the community's families with young children, definitions of self-sufficiency, families' and community's resources and other strengths and their needs, and demographic information about the individual families and the community.

The 50 individual interviews and 14 focus group meetings were audiotaped and then transcribed into verbatim written reports for a content analysis. A coding form was developed by informally reviewing a subsample of the written reports to identify the main content and theme categories. Then all written reports were coded so that they could be analyzed individually and as a group. Reliability was addressed by having a second person code 10 percent of the written reports to achieve an interrater reliability of 90 percent. The 3 interviewers and a second focus group facilitator were graduate social work students with research experience who were specially trained by the principal investigator to conduct the data collection and analysis procedures.

Findings and Discussion

Self-Sufficiency/Empowerment Themes.   The content analysis on the study data indicated that the participants' various definitions of self-sufficiency were related to themselves individually or to barriers or supports in their families, community, or the larger environment outside the community. Their responses were therefore organized into these four categories; that is, examples of their definitions were paraphrased and included in the category each seemed to fit. As can be seen in table 7.2, these definitions identified both barriers and supports to self-sufficiency that are tangible and intangible, formal and informal, and internal as well as external to the community.

The Member Checking Results Related to Empowerment. After these themes and other data had been organized and analyzed, the research team met with study participants to conduct the member-checking process. The importance of this consumer involvement phase of participatory research (Bowman 1989; Luirgio and Davis 1992) was discussed in chapter 6 on community intervention and illustrated in figure 6.1. The goal of this collaborative process is twofold: to encourage community members to react to the preliminary results that they might not agree with (Are those results consistent with their knowledge of the community?), and to have them brainstorm alternative interpretations of results they might agree with (What do the results mean based on their expert knowledge?) (Gilmore 1987; Yeich and Levine 1992). This process also provides community members with environmental supports for empowerment, with the researchers serving as coaches and facilitators, two of the new service provider roles discussed in chapter 6 (Segal et al. 1993).

The participants first clarified results they did not agree with. For example, their highest-priority needs from their perspective included deficits in educational and employment opportunities rather than other barriers to self-sufficiency shown in table 7.2. Their conclusions about these priority areas were based on a 60 percent high school dropout rate, high substance abuse rates among youths and adults, gang violence in the community and violence within families, and a history of inadequate and inequitable resource allocations to the community by the city (leading to a sense of collective powerlessness among the members). The participants indicated that people outside their community viewed them as either self-contained or inadequate. Those views were seen as barriers because both helped to maintain the status quo.

Second, the participants disagreed with a preliminary interpretation of some of the results: that resource deficits identified by the research meant a family-centered early childhood program should be developed. Instead, the

TABLE 7.2 A Community's Definitions of Self-Sufficiency and Necessary Social Supports

	Self-Sufficiency Means	Examples of Necessary Supports for Achieving Self-Sufficiency
Regarding the Individual:	a greater range of personal choices	culturally relevant consumer education
	an increased number of things that the individual can do without needing help from others	opportunities for skill development in work, household maintenance, parenting, problem solving
	an understanding of the problems encountered	intergenerational mentoring/natural helper networks
Regarding the Family:	less dependence on parents (ability to live independently or interdependently)	reciprocal and mutual helping community networks
	ability to solve conflicts in beliefs among children, parents, and grandparents (intergenerational value and cultural conflicts)	education related to values clarification, family mediation, cultural enrichment, and cultural history and traditions; and bilingual education
Regarding the Community:	a desire to make life better for others in the community (teenage parents, youths—especially dropouts, non-English-speaking neighbors, undocumented persons)	*formal and informal youth services (*school dropout and pregnancy prevention, employment*), amnesty and relocation services for undocumented persons, parenting classes, leisure time activities for families and youths, drug and alcohol abuse prevention services

changes that make the community a better place to live overall	*nondiscriminatory police protection and enforcement (drugs, violence), community-controlled safety programs, community partnerships for comprehensive and integrated services, *community-run schools*, community membership on social service agency boards
changes that help the community grow and prosper	*supported work and job training*, day care, safe housing, consumer services, health care, entrepreneurial and business development resources
Regarding the Larger Environment:	
increased knowledge about how "The System" works (business and politics)	community education about "The System," leadership development for youths and adults to build and maintain communities economically and politically
changes that increase the political power and opportunities for residents to influence external system	*collective community and political action (winning elections, changing local policies, eliminating system barriers to self-sufficiency, influencing funding decisions related to jobs, substance abuse services, housing, and education)

*the community's highest priority needs

participants and other community members requested the foundation's support in developing their political power to influence education and employment policies developed by larger systems (the city, the county, and local school boards).

Community Planning, Policy, and Systems Change Outcomes.   With the foundation's financial and technical assistance, the community undertook a two-year mobilization, planning, and political action process to gain control over its parochial and public schools. The target was policy making for and coordination of the area's Catholic elementary school and its public elementary, middle, and high schools. Strategies were developed, therefore, to influence the Catholic Diocese, the local board of (public) education, and the city-county government systems. The community's strategies included some of those shown in figure 7.1, such as power and organizational analyses, investigatory research, coalition building, advocacy, consensus building, and leadership development. This approach was most consistent with the community-rebuilding/capacity-building/systems change model shown in table 7.1 under the Competency Paradigm.

Evaluation of Systems Change Outcomes.   All of these strategies, but especially leadership development, were important in achieving and maintaining the community's goal of systems and political change. Prior to this change process, youths had to be bussed to a high school outside the community. As a result of the community's political action strategies, the board of education established a new public high school in the area. A community advisory board was created as well to help prevent the 60 percent dropout rate from continuing after the new school was opened, utilizing community members' newly acquired or enhanced leadership skills.

The community applied for and received a Drug-Free Schools Grant for the new high school and its feeder schools, the public elementary and middle schools. That project helped to lower the high substance abuse and community violence rates in the area. For the Catholic elementary school, the community was able to establish a community advisory board, along with a Drug-Free Schools Project and a new multicultural curriculum. The well-documented evaluation of this community planning and systems change process highlighted the members' skills and continuing empowerment experiences, encoding the latter in their collective memories as important "lessons learned."

Although this change strategy could have resulted in a top-down process, it was flexible enough to allow a bottom-up or consumer-driven process. It was more culturally sensitive than the first example in this chapter because the qualitative research procedures accounted for previously marginalized, disempowered voices and perspectives. As a result, consumers' expertise, rather than professionally based expertise only, was emphasized. The community's assets were stressed in the research report (Freeman 1993) and again when the foundation responded positively to the residents' request for help with their political change efforts.

However, those strengths could have been encouraged and built upon even more effectively if the foundation had not developed preconceived ideas about the community's needs and limitations. Moreover, the foundation's initial approach was to counsel the community to "go slow" and not to anger the city and school boards involved. The evaluation/research team was able to point out contrasts between more traditional professional roles in community development and newly emerging roles that support community empowerment. This collaborative educational process among the foundation, the research team, and the community shifted to an emphasis on the community's decision-making and leadership development process, but important time, momentum, and community trust were lost. Nevertheless, the process helped to identify community substance abuse, violence, and collective disempowerment as problems and placed them within the context of the community's lived experiences and their other concerns.

New Directions in Substance Abuse Prevention

This discussion indicates that systems change and community capacity building are critical goals for effective substance abuse prevention in the long term. These goals can help communities to utilize existing resources and to create and mobilize additional resources. However, an important quality of the systems change approach or of any paradigm is its ability to adapt as needed over time while retaining essential components that contribute to its effectiveness. Some of the challenges in maintaining this type of healthy tension were included in this chapter's summary of historical and current approaches to prevention. For substance abuse prevention in particular, maintaining such a balance requires additional paradigm shifts, more inclusive ideas about consumer involvement, and increased community skills in policy impact analysis.

Emphasis on Future Paradigm Shifts

The paradigm changes illustrated in table 7.1 will need to be supported by preventionists and policy makers in order to encourage a continuing trend in the field toward increased use of resilience and empowerment approaches. Kaplan, Turner, Norman, and Stillson (1996:158) note that, when used alone, "Risk factor interventions target pathology, injury, and deficits, whereas resilience-factor interventions emphasize coping skills and protective environmental agents." These protective agents keep the "focus on strengths and opportunities and attempt to reinforce the ability to cope and bounce back in the face of adversity."

This trend toward self-efficacy and empowerment approaches highlights the importance of long-term, comprehensive prevention strategies. The type of community-centered, integrated services models discussed in chapter 3 and illustrated in figure 3.3 are consistent with the movement toward more comprehensive approaches to prevention (Aguirre 1995; Kunnes et al. 1993). Integrated services models require a merging of substance abuse prevention, intervention, and treatment services, along with services for education, employment and job development, mental health, child protection, health, public welfare, housing, recreation, business and economic development, mentoring and leadership development, and community planning/development (Freeman 1996).

Another new direction related to paradigm shifts involves organizing prevention to include the aftercare services that are an essential component of treatment. Traditional Alanon and Alateen services could be used as part of the aftercare phase for adolescents once they complete prevention programs, especially for those at high to moderate risk for substance abuse problems. Or more specialized community aftercare services could be developed by preventionists, providing transitional services to help maintain resistance to substance abuse and other problems that have been identified in vulnerable children, adolescents, and young adults (Berlin and Davis 1989; Hawkins, Catalano, and Miller 1992).

More Inclusive Consumer Involvement

The community examples both in this chapter and in other literature have highlighted the exclusion of certain vulnerable populations from traditional prevention efforts. With the problem of substance abuse increasing across the entire population, it is important for practitioners and policy makers to collaborate in identifying under- and unrepresented groups and creative methods for reaching them. For example, the elderly, uninvolved youths (school dropouts and gang members), adults in high-stress jobs (law enforcement and teaching), and people in stressful developmental transitions (the sandwich generation) are often overlooked. Only by including a broader range of unrepresented voices in planning, implementing, evaluating, and consuming prevention services can we make those services more community-centered in the future.

Fetterman (1994) identifies three roles professionals can assume to strengthen community-centered research and programming, and thus residents' involvement in program evaluations. These roles build on assumptions about community residents as the experts and include teaching people to conduct their own evaluations based on the goal of self-sufficiency, serving as coaches and facilitators of this process, and conducting evaluations for people after collaborating with them on the goals and evaluation design. Therefore, effective consumer involvement in future prevention programs and systems change efforts should include the area of evaluation.

Policy Impact Analysis and Dissemination

Broader consumer involvement will require more nontraditional sites for implementing and disseminating the results of prevention services. For example, including more elderly in planning and using services to prevent late-onset substance abuse requires elderly meal sites, pre-retirement training seminars, community centers, churches, and medical clinics to reach this group for their input and to provide convenient, relevant services. Strategies for disseminating research findings from prevention programs will need to be equally creative and innovative to reach key policy makers. The Internet, interactive computer games and videos, executive summaries of position papers, and eye-catching overhead transparencies with bullet points of legislative testimony can reach policy makers in their language and in the usually brief time segments they have available.

Policy impact analyses and dissemination of those findings also can be useful for influencing policy makers. Residents can be involved in documenting how policy affects their community (Chapin 1995) and prevention efforts. For instance, they can videotape attempts to eliminate ongoing community risk factors such as liquor stores that sell to minors and drug sales near schools. They can interview residents and preventionists about their opportunities for meaningful involvement in the block grant funding process as mandated by substance abuse prevention policies.

Conclusion

Substance abuse prevention may be one of the most difficult areas in which to integrate and evaluate an empowerment orientation. It is clear from this chapter's discussion and from the literature in general, for example, that early prevention efforts did not include an empowerment orientation because of underlying, rather narrow, paradigms about causation. Current paradigms are more compatible with self-efficacy and empowerment, at least conceptually. Operationally, however, more research is needed on how to build prevention programs with mechanisms for enhancing empowerment opportunities that are implied by program goals. Examples of community prevention programs illustrate the struggles and challenges that such programs encounter when planning and implementing consumer-involved, empowerment-focused components.

The greatest challenge beyond programming and capacity building is the second goal of substance abuse prevention: large systems change. In this process, empowerment is the key to helping residents demand more say in decisions that affect their communities. What strategies and ideas are essential to convince policy makers to agree to shift power from institutions to people? To convince residents that such a shift is possible and that they are the necessary means for influencing it? Research and the case examples in this chapter indicate that these parallel activities are a process that begins with consciousness-raising and a growing belief in the human potential for change.

8 Assessment: Clients as Experts on Their Experiences, Recovery Motivation, and Power Resources

During assessment and thereafter, focusing only on minority clients' addiction without attempting to help them become empowered is usually viewed by them as irrelevant and useless. Empowerment helps all clients learn specialized problem-solving skills during recovery to alleviate the powerlessness that has resulted from negative self- and environmental valuations.
—E. M. Freeman and T. Landesman (1992:31)

Substance abuse rehab, like other helping fields, has accepted two practice models that automatically place consumers in a subordinate position. The medical model (and its offspring, the disease concept) is pathology focused and thus encourages practitioners to overemphasize clients' problems and ignore their strengths (Weick, Rapp, Sullivan, and Kisthardt 1989) from the initial assessment process throughout rehab and aftercare. This model assumes that problems such as substance abuse are caused by the individual, and therefore does not address family, community, and structural influences sufficiently, if at all. Chiauzzi and Liljegren (1993:304) suggest that "the near-religious acceptance of the disease concept in the United States, as opposed to more flexible, psychosocial models of treatment" and assessment can hinder efforts to resolve the environmental power barriers noted in this chapter's epigraph.

Similarly, the expert model encourages the use of hierarchical approaches, or what Brown and Tandon (1983) characterize as power monopoly appoaches. This model considers expert knowledge to be solely professionally based, whereas Freire's (1989) empowerment approach emphasizes the parallel expert knowledge of ordinary people. The expert model discourages practitioners from collaborating with clients during assessment or pairing their knowledge with what clients have learned about their substance abuse. The model can encourage staff to replicate the power cutoffs and inequities that clients have often experienced in their environments (see table 2.2 in chapter 2 for ways programs address clients' power issues).

Disempowerment experiences, particularly during intake and assessment, tend to reinforce clients' negative thinking and communication patterns. Their denial about being addicted may be prolonged and their resistance to rehab increased. Some authors believe such reactions are a substance abusive personality trait (Smyth 1995). Miller (1983), however, assumes resistance and denial are often a consequence of the dynamics between clients and practitioners who use confrontation too frequently and indiscriminately (based on the expert model) prior to providing alcohol and drug education. Empowerment means helping clients to identify treatment choices in their situations and analyze potential consequences, which can decrease clients' initial denial and resistance while increasing their motivation for change (Miller 1983).

One rehab program approach is similar to Miller's (1983). Rather than conducting a traditional intake process, the center schedules preassessment meetings in which staff ask clients to present their current life situations to preassessment staff, based on the following questions: "What led you to rehab at this time in your life?" "What changes do you want to make in your life and for what reasons?" and "What factors could undermine or support your recovery?" Staff can prompt clients to include information that they have learned about consequences by asking questions such as, "And what happened then?" "What did you learn from that experience?" or "How were you changed by what happened?" This program utilizes an empowerment-oriented approach from the initial contact to illustrate the obvious: that only clients can be experts on their experiences and on their motivation for recovery.

This chapter describes empowerment approaches that emphasize clients as experts during initial contacts, based on a program's humanistic philosophy and goals. It also analyzes staff's common practice dilemmas in exploring clients' needs and strengths, the level of flexibility and resources programs have for meeting those needs, and the effects of staff dilemmas on assessment. The assessment-evaluation process is described as a vehicle for facilitating staff-client partnerships, and a case study illustrates how this dynamic empowerment process unfolds. While the primary focus of the chapter is on assessment, this process is viewed as dynamic and ongoing; therefore, the discussion clarifies how assessment continues throughout later phases of service delivery and recovery.

Providing a Humanistic Environment for Assessment: Setting the Stage

Empowerment, Humanism, and Assessment

Effective assessments provide a strong foundation for empowerment practice when they are focused on helping clients identify power and disempowerment sources related to their recovery. Effective assessments are also a collaborative process between clients and practitioners. According to Anderson and Brown (1980), "An observer might describe this activity [assessment] as two people trying to solve an intriguing puzzle together. . . . It helps the client to survey the events of his or her life and interpret their significance" (321, 323). A program's environment can either set the stage for this intriguing collaborative process or impede it, albeit unintentionally.

Barriers to mutual assessments include denial that power differentials between clients and staff can influence this process, thus invalidating clients' perceptions about power inequities and dehumanizing the service organization. Rehab programs are clearly political environments, like other organizations, the community, and larger policy-making institutions. For example, new managed care policies require programs to justify requests for keeping clients in rehab beyond fourteen, twenty-eight, or forty-five days. In one program that emphasizes client advocacy, the assessment process is used to identify strengths as well as factors that indicate the severity of clients' problems, and hence, whether there is a need to appeal those policy limitations. Some of the program's staff are more skilled at and/or committed to appealing these limitations as needed than others. Under those circumstances, the choice of a staff member to whom a client is assigned for intake/assessment could be considered a political act. To deny this assumption is to deny that programs can shape clients' perceptions and use of power in a manner that enhances or blocks an effective assessment and recovery process.

Gummer and Edwards (1995) have identified one source of this denial, that "Americans tend to focus on the negative aspects of power, seeing it primarily as an instrument for destructive purposes" (62), whereas a positive attitude toward power supports the need to teach clients how to use it constructively as part of collaborative assessments. In data gathering and analysis, clients need to be asked evocative questions to help them assess their motivation for coming to rehab and the strengths required to acknowledge their decision-making power. As one client, twenty-three-year-old Olivia, remarked to a counselor during the assessment process, "Learning to read myself, as you said, and my motivation for bein' here, can help me ride out the low points, stop me from makin' bad decisions, like when I wanta get outta here before I'm ready!"

Clients need opportunities to practice using power adaptively rather than manipulatively during assessment. They can help encourage significant others to provide important data about their reactions to the substance abuse and their own roles in the family. Clients should be taught how to negotiate supportive relationships with staff and peers in order to continue the often stressful assessment of their life stories and explorations of previously ignored self-healing experiences. These activities can lead to clients' personal and interpersonal empowerment during assessment. Moreover, managing organizational politics and having their input into program decision-making valued and utilized by administrators and staff provides clients an arena and model for handling political power. Thus, empowerment approaches can humanize rehab programs based on their organizational philosophies, client-staff-peer roles, and the operationalization of their goals from the point of intake and assessment through the aftercare phase.

Program Philosophy

As indicated in chapter 1, empowerment programs vary in terms of focus of change and level of client empowerment. Such programs range from those that help clients to increase their personal and interpersonal power (empowering programs) to those that include changing the program's structure (microcosm programs) to those that also change the community, social policy, and large systems (empowered programs). Although the philosophies of the three types are different, some common characteristics have been identified across empowerment programs related to assessment.

One common characteristic is a belief that each client is a unique and valuable part of society. Understanding the individual's qualities and his or her culture during assessment is considered indispensable for determining appropriate strategies to reduce power inequities (race or ethnicity, social class, gender, family structure, age, religion, disability, or sexual orientation biases) that affect not only the substance abuse but also other problems such as family relationships and motivation for change. Another philosophical tenet is that the individual can be viewed separately from his or her condition (the substance abuse problems or addiction) and that rehab programs should mobilize clients' inner resources and the social supports necessary for their growth and development. To achieve this type of humanistic assessment, clients and practitioners need to collaboratively identify and explore factors that can impede clients' movement toward a more adaptive lifestyle and improved problem-solving and coping skills (Prochaska, DiClement, and Norcross 1992).

An empowerment philosophy involves supportive assumptions about clients' potential for relapsing. Relapse is viewed as a natural part of recovery, beginning with a thought or craving to use drugs, that can be survived if it is managed effectively (Annis 1986; Daley 1987). The empowerment philosophy holds clients responsible for their relapses but does not blame them by automatically dismissing them from rehab. Empowerment programs teach this philosophy early, beginning with assessment, rather than during aftercare, when relapse prevention is traditionally taught (Williams 1995). Thirty-two-year-old Bill smoked crack the second day into his forty-five-day rehab program after visiting his critically ill father in the hospital. The visit interrupted the assessment process in which he and the counselor were engaged. Instead of discharging him from rehab, his counselor, Reggie, used Bill's experience to explore what triggered his slip (shame about his drug abuse contributing to his father's illness), and what tools prevented him from having a full-blown relapse (a close relationship with a brother who talked him into returning to rehab). Reggie assigned Bill exercises to apply relapse prevention information about triggers and tools. Reviewing this philosophy with clients during assessment, as Bill's counselor did, helps to identify what they already know about their triggers and tools related to relapse, or their strengths (Surls 1994). Moreover, concretizing this self-knowledge is often an important source of power for clients who may be feeling particularly vulnerable and unsafe during intake and assessment.

Finally, most empowerment-oriented philosophies assume alcohol and other drug abuse is treatable but indicate that effective rehab requires attention to a broad range of emotional, physical, psychological, spiritual, social, and political areas (Hanson 1991; Smyth 1995). Thus, assessment needs to be broad based and ecological in nature. Such tenets help to humanize programs by emphasizing their mission to facilitate rather than take charge of clients' assessments and identification of important goals in their lifestyles, substance abuse problems, and environmental conditions.

Client, Staff, and Peer Power-Sharing Roles

Certain client-staff roles are necessary for implementing an empowerment philosophy. Tables 1.1 and 1.3 in chapter 1 include examples of empowerment practice roles from the literature and from my national study on empowerment practice that can be applied specifically to assessments. Three themes or categories of roles were identified, involving the use of personal, interpersonal, and political power sharing between clients and staff. The professional and client collaborative roles involve activities that require joint planning and implementation. One example is the practitioner and client developing a joint treatment plan based on a collaborative assessment, and their conjoint participation in staffings to monitor the client's progress in implementing the plan. Another example involves clients serving on a program's needs assessment-evaluation committee with staff to identify trends in clients' needs and analyze how well program strategies and resources are used to meet them (Gulati and Guess 1990; Toumbouron and Hamilton 1993).

The peer power-sharing role refers to services that are provided by peers or that require collaboration among peers, with staff involved only as consultants when necessary (Galanter 1993; Pratt and Gill 1990). Senior peers can be assigned to help orient clients to a rehab program during intake and assessment, or they can serve as ongoing mentors, similar to the twelve-step practice of encouraging clients to select a supportive sponsor. One rehab program for women has developed the special peer role of expediter to assist clients during the orientation and assessment phase. The expediters help new and potential clients move from one group session to another; introduce them to other clients; answer their questions about the program and the assessment process; help them to select components of the program to observe; and accompany them to off-site medical, legal, and other appointments. The expediter's role can be critical during early recovery. One expediter in this program, Evelyn, accompanied a new client, Lori, to court for a preliminary hearing in which her boyfriend was being arraigned. He was accused of causing a fire in their apartment, while under the influence of heroin and alcohol, that killed two of their neighbors. Evelyn's support was crucial for helping Lori keep her court appointment and to manage emotional stress that could have triggered a relapse. Moreover, her feedback on Lori's reactions to the court hearing provided vital information to staff involved in Lori's assessment.

Professional service roles include staff requesting, supporting, and monitoring a clients' completion of certain tasks. Examples during assessment include having clients directly observe particular aspects of a program, such as weekend process groups or alcohol and drug education groups, as part of their orientation to rehab prior to their acceptance. Clients are then asked to prepare a list of questions about the program to help them explore the match between their needs and the program's resources. In one dual diagnosis program, twenty-eight-year-old David was observing various aspects of the program during his orientation. One of the questions he listed was whether he was required to be on his medication in order to be admitted. He told the intake worker, "I'm not interested in a program that won't listen to how I feel about my medications; I know I feel better without them." The worker commented that she wanted to know more about David's experiences with his medications, especially about situations in which he felt better without them, and whether he ever felt worse without them. Her response conveyed a message that David's knowledge, experiences, and perceptions were valuable in their mutual assessment of his needs and strengths, and that her role was to encourage his sharing and his parallel assessment of the program's approach.

Program Goals

The above client-staff roles imply that the development of collaborative, power-sharing relationships between clients and staff is an important goal for empowerment programs. This goal helps to increase clients' interpersonal power with peers and staff during assessment and ongoing recovery. The power sharing helps to address the typical interpersonal dysfunctions and disempowerment experiences associated with substance abuse in clients' lives (Shorkey and Rosen 1993). A second goal related to collaborative relationships is to plan, during assessment, how to increase clients' power to resolve the substance abuse and change or prevent other individual or environmental problems (Bricker-Jenkins and Hooyman 1991; Gutiérrez, GlenMaye, and DeLois 1995). While these goals are critical for helping clients to plan real environmental change and effective recovery, they often lead to significant practice dilemmas for staff in empowerment programs.

Common Dilemmas During Assessment and Ongoing Services

A Balance in Program Flexibility and Structure

Empowerment approaches require substance abuse programs to increase their flexibility in conducting mutual assessments and in revising their services to meet various client needs identified during such assessments. The process involves not only analyses of individual clients' needs but also periodic analysis of collective needs to identify new trends or patterns. To consider both types of data, programs need flexible mechanisms for integrating assessment feedback and for undertaking major and minor program modifications.

Modifying Assessment Procedures.   Changes may be needed in the assessment tools or procedures used by empowerment programs. Therefore, it is important for programs to solicit clients' feedback about the process during the initial assessment, as they move through the middle recovery period, complete or leave rehab, and after they complete long-term aftercare. Programs' responses to such feedback can hinder or support clients' motivations for recovery and sense of empowerment (Smyth 1995). Therefore, clients should have opportunities to provide anonymous as well as direct feedback. Responses should be solicited about how user-friendly and culturally sensitive a program's assessment procedures are, the length and format of the assessment process, clients' opportunities to be actively and collaboratively involved, whether their strengths were identified and affirmed, to what extent they felt accepted and supported by staff and peers, what aspects of assessment should be changed or maintained, and other reactions they would like to share (Freeman and Landesman 1992).

Feedback from Ann, a thirty-seven-year-old white lesbian client in one program, helped staff identify culturally insensitive items on their assessment form. The form asked for the name of the client's husband or wife, omitted a category for biracial clients to indicate their racial/ethnic backgrounds, and ignored or failed to ask about clients' strengths. Ann later commented that the wording or omission of those items on the form made her assume the staff would not accept or be sensitive in handling cultural diversity issues. For that reason, she seriously considered not completing the assessment process at the time, and even though she decided to stay in the program, the shame and humiliation she experienced impeded her early recovery. Such practices and policies often contribute to the marginality and invisibility of diverse clients (Greene 1994; Symth 1995).

The counselor Ann later shared her reactions with was an "out of the closet" lesbian in this program. Consequently, she willingly risked joining Ann in advocating for administration to modify the form, without concerns about hiding her own sexual orientation. Their joint effort was successful in changing the form and in encouraging administration to look more closely at the program's intake/assessment process. The program eventually established a new written client feedback procedure for monitoring the assessment process. This example of systems change and client political empowerment should be generalizable to similar assessments involving diverse clients and staff members.

Modifying General Program Services.   Feedback from clients during the assessment may be important for helping a program to modify its services beyond intake and assessment. Some programs respond to the need for flexibility by instituting formal change mechanisms. For instance, when the results of collective assessments are analyzed or tabulated periodically, some programs change the array of counseling and education groups offered (Freeman 1994). If a program is part of an integrated services model, suggested changes might involve modifying conjoint or related services (Aquirre 1995). Changes might be made in a peer orientation program offered by a rehab program or in an employment mentoring program offered by business leaders (see figure 3.3 in chapter 3 on integrated services models).

Other programs elicit feedback in an ongoing, informal manner, modifying their services in small ways as needed. Because clients' needs often change as they progress through rehab, the assessment must be dynamic and constant in order to continuously address their changing needs. Furthermore, changes may occur in the patterns of needs presented by clients at intake and assessment, with implications for how a program's array of services should be changed. New patterns may emerge in clients' drugs of choice,

prior rehab histories, education and reading levels, and access to basic resources and support networks (Joseph 1992; Miller and Hester 1989; Smyth
1995; Wallace 1991). The strategy of monitoring trends and patterns in the
needs of clients to determine programmatic changes is consistent with an
empowerment philosophy. However, it may pose difficulties for programs in
terms of resource management and power dynamics.

Clients' assessments may reveal a need for services that require different
staffing patterns than a program is currently using, such as more staff resources for individual counseling or family groups. For example, one program began to experience an increase in referrals of suicidal clients and
those with other legal, housing, or medical crises. These collective results
indicated a need for more crisis counseling sessions with individual clients
during assessment and early rehab. In another example, a homeless program
found through unexpected assessment results that it was experiencing an
increase in the number of clients who had maintained connections with
their family members. This change created a need for family groups and for
staff who were skilled in family assessments and interventions. It also challenged the staff's stereotypes about homeless substance abusers and their
family resources and other strengths, which had been negatively affecting
previous assessments. Subsequent family sessions were facilitated by a consultant and staff members; the former pointed out examples of useful assessment data often overlooked by staff.

Administrators and practitioners may not be willing or able to address
needed changes related to staff-client ratios, staff skills, or staff philosophical
orientations (Anderson and Wiemer 1992). Smyth (1995) indicates that staff
orientations, theoretical approaches, and training determine whether practitioners are more comfortable with hierarchical approaches or empowerment and client-centered models. Programs can attempt to influence staff
attitudes about empowerment practice with professional development opportunities, as the homeless program did in the previous example. However,
changes may be very gradual and in some instances impossible to achieve
(Gutiérrez, GlenMaye, and DeLois 1995).

Meeting Specialized Program Needs Related to Cultural Diversity.
Many programs are becoming more aware of cultural diversity issues among
clients, through the use of more comprehensive and culturally sensitive
assessment procedures. With this increased awareness, however, comes a
need for greater flexibility in responding to those needs identified initially

during assessment. According to research, chemically dependent women are more likely than men to use drugs in isolation, have fewer friends, and lack access to social networks due to societal gender biases (Gomberg 1988; Nelson-Zlupo, Kauffman, and Dore 1995). Therefore, programs serving women are often required to employ a more sensitive lens for assessment and for an equitable allocation of staff and basic resources. Flexibility may be necessary in providing specialized staff training on gender differences and in selecting gender-sensitive audio-visual and written assessment and counseling materials.

Programs should also seek out new interagency partnerships for resource development in order to meet assessed needs in special areas. For example, a women's program developed a joint project with a housing agency to provide specialized transitional housing for women and their infants and children. A third agency, a specialized medical center for women, was included when reassessments completed with the women at the beginning of aftercare revealed an acute need for specialized maternal and child health services. While such specialized programs are critical for meeting womens' assessed needs, they may strain programs' already diminishing resources (Burman and Allen-Meares 1991; Finkelstein 1994) (see figure 5.1 regarding advantages and disadvantages of freestanding and multiple-service substance abuse organizations).

Similarly, assessment may indicate a need for specialized services to meet the empowerment needs of other culturally diverse groups. For example, an increase in the number of African American and Latino clients in one predominantly white program required more flexible policies about who was included in family group sessions. Many of the new African American and Latino clients had large extended family networks, godparents or a *compadrazgo* system, and fictive kin who fulfilled key roles. While these family resources have much to offer in the collaborative problem-solving process, working with them in a culturally sensitive and relevant manner required specialized training and skills (Smyth 1995) for this particular program's mostly white staff. The need for specialized programming and staff training may be revealed through a program's assessment data related to many diverse groups, including youths, the elderly, gays and lesbians, dual diagnosis clients, and those with HIV/AIDS, as well as clients of color and women (Ochen and Levy 1992; Kaminer 1991; Lawson 1989; Lewis and Jordan 1989; McRoy, Shorkey, and Garcia 1985; Schleifer, Delaney, Tross, and Keller 1991; Wright, Kail, and Creecy 1990).

There are other emerging demands for specialized assessments and programming that require more refined staff skills and greater flexibility in programming. Therapeutic community programs in prisons, drug diversion programs for first offenders, and home-based rehab programs for families are a few examples (Saunders 1995; Smyth 1995). Conducting specialized assessments and counseling at nontraditional sites involves complex organizational dynamics that can affect clients' recovery and empowerment. Policy changes such as managed care and mandated rehab referrals for prisons, the workplace, housing developments, and schools, along with block grants, will increase funding opportunities and sources. But programs will be required to address new philosophical, organizational, assessment, intervention, and power conflicts that can impede their effective use of empowerment approaches (Creager 1991; Jackson 1996; NASW 1996; Saunders 1995).

Linking Assessment with Client-Centered Evaluation

Just as programming should be guided by clients' assessment results, so should the process and outcomes of program evaluations. Programming for diverse client groups requires the use of culturally sensitive assessment and evaluation methods, whether differences in age, gender, socioeconomic status, ethnicity, sexual orientation, or physical or mental disabilities are involved. Moreover, for effective monitoring, the same methods used to help clients to mutually assess their needs must also be used to evaluate outcomes.

This requirement and the standard for more precise and scientific methods may make programs reluctant to use empowerment approaches (Clinton 1991). Empowerment approaches focus clients' and practitioners' attention on the meaning of clients' experiences for recovery, implying a value of subjective data in addition to more objective scientific data (Fetterman 1994). However, these approaches also increase programs' accountability; thus they can be a disincentive for linking their assessments (what is revealed about clients' needs and their involvement in the assessment-evaluation process) with evaluation of outcomes (how effectively those needs are addressed through staff-client collaboration).

Fetterman (1994) suggests three alternatives through which consultants can involve consumers in client- and empowerment-centered evaluations, and by extension in mutual assessments. The alternatives imply that consumers are experts; hence, they can be applied to program administrators and staff members as well.

1. Teach people to conduct their own evaluations, starting with a collaborative assessment or assets mapping process, so they can become self-sufficient in these areas.
2. Facilitate and coach the assessment and evaluation activities of community groups, other organizations, or rehab program staff and clients.
3. Conduct assessments and evaluations that have been designed and shaped by these stakeholders and then help them to advocate for related programmatic and social/political changes.

An Empowered Assessment-Evaluation Process

The assessment and evaluation procedures included in figure 8.1 and the preceding discussion can help to shape a program's collaborative assessments with clients, along with its process and outcome evaluations. This critical linkage between dynamic, client-centered assessments and evaluations is demonstrated in the following discussion on traditional versus client-centered procedures, such as analysis of recovery supports, solution-focused questions, and motivational interviewing. A case example illustrates how this client-centered mutual process unfolds as part of an interrelated assessment and evaluation.

A Case Example: Background Information

Thirty-five-year-old Stephanie, a white client who worked as a banker, entered rehab shortly after her fourteen-year-old son, Duane, was suspended from school for smoking marijuana. The school was in an upper middle-income neighborhood where school personnel and parents were just becoming aware that there was a drug problem among the community's youths. During a conference with the principal, he commented to Stephanie that in some situations like Duane's, he often asked if the parents also used drugs, but he was certain that was not a problem for Stephanie. Her business attire and concerned manner, her banking and education background, and her involvement in the school did not fit his stereotypes about drug abusers.

In fact, Stephanie abused cocaine and alcohol on a regular basis, and her husband was a recovering alcoholic who was currently in relapse. The principal's comment, although it was intended to reassure Stephanie of his posi-

FIGURE 8.1 Empowerment-Oriented Assessment and Evaluation Procedures

Less Empowerment-Focused (focus on worker expertise and accountability)	Analysis of:	More Empowerment-Focused (focus on client skill development and self-efficacy)
Direct Observations spontaneous interactions and unstructured exercises structured and planned exercises		*Mutual Mapping Procedures* ecomaps genograms time lines/life history grids
Written Procedures and Exercises progress notes checklists and behavioral inventories sentence completion forms behavioral rating scales rapid assessment instruments (RAIs) standardized questionnaires and surveys, and interview procedures global trait instruments (e.g., measure depression, self-esteem) specific trait instruments (e.g., measure assertiveness skills, addiction severity) diagnostic criteria and standards (e.g., DSM-IV) structured diagnostic interviews exit interviews		*Mutual Assessment/Evaluation Procedures* solution-focused questions recovery supports analysis motivational interviewing clinical measurement packages client focus or critical dialogue groups videotaped client narratives/life histories *Client/Peer Self-Evaluation Procedures* client journals client treatment session summaries client pull-up forms client self-monitoring forms self-anchored behavioral forms risk/protective factor assessments/evaluations

tive regard for her, had the opposite effect. It provided the sharpest possible contrast for Stephanie between the drug-addicted lifestyle she lived within her family and the highly functional façade she presented to the rest of the world. His comment was, in essence, a powerful intervention with Stephanie, following closely after her husband's relapse, Duane's school suspension, her eight-year-old daughter's asking to stay with her grandparents, and a reprimand about sloppy work and unexcused absences at the bank (see chapter 6, which describes intervention as a continuous process in which the outcomes are influenced by a unique combination of individual and social contingencies).

Traditional Assessment Tools

Interventions such as Stephanie's set the stage for client-centered assessments; however, an effective exploration requires a strong emphasis on clients' expertise and strengths. This emphasis counteracts the effects of traditional, organizationally centered assessment tools, which often skew the focus to emphasize pathology. Examples of such tools, which some programs are mandated to use, include the *Diagnostic and Statistical Manual of Mental Disorders (DSM-IV)*, the Alcohol Dependence Scale, the Addiction Severity Index (ASI), the Inventory of Drinking Situations, the Inventory of Drug-Taking Situations, the Michigan Alcohol Screening Test (MAST), and the McMaster's Scale of the Minnesota Multiphasic Inventory (the MMPI) (American Psychiatric Association 1994; Annis 1993 1986; Blackmon 1985; Horn, Skinner, Wanberg, and Foster 1984; McLellen, Luborsky, and O'Brien 1985).

These instruments can inply to staff that "clients may deny the extent and severity of their alcohol and drug use" (Symth 1995:2329), and therefore should be viewed as unreliable informants rather than as partners in this process. Moreover, because these traditional instruments generally do not focus on the context of clients' lives or their environments, they are not as useful in the dynamic pre- and post-analyses that programs require for their outcome evaluations. To overcome these limitations, empowerment programs such as Stephanie's often modify how they use traditional instruments by combining traditional tools with more client-centered procedures. Combining tools can enable staff to build upon clients' expertise and wisdom by:

1. beginning the assessment with more open-ended, client-centered, and collaborative assessment procedures
2. expanding aspects of traditional assessment tools that emphasize strengths, for example, gathering detailed data for Axis V of the *DSM-IV* about clients' highest current levels of occupational, social, and psychological functioning to identify individual and environmental strengths for recovery
3. decreasing the number of organizationally centered procedures used along with client-centered tools during the assessment.

In Stephanie's assessment, her counselor, Don, used the ASI and the *DSM-IV* in conjunction with the client-centered tools described in the next section. These traditional tools confirmed certain data obtained with the client-centered procedures, while clarifying important data in other areas. For example, the *DSM-IV* and the ASI documented the severity of Stephanie's addiction (see figure 8.1 under less empowerment-focused procedures). It was particularly useful in clarifying the interactional effects between Stephanie's medical problems, a tentative diagnosis of hypoglycemia, which Don listed on Axis III; and her addiction problems, which caused her to eat infrequently and non-nutritionally. Information that Don gathered for Axis V indicated Stephanie was not involved in any social activities except her work-related interactions at the bank. Although she had maintained her employment for eight years, she was beginning to experience negative feedback as the effects of her addiction on her work quality and habits escalated. Currently, she was in crisis due to the principal's unintended intervention and her marital problems (she and her husband had separated right before she entered rehab). Thus, her highest level of functioning, or the Global Assessment of Functioning (GAS) for Axis V, was rated 55 (current functioning) out of a possible 100:

Stephanie's DSM IV Multiaxial Assessment

Axis I 305.00 Alcohol Abuse

305.60 Cocaine Abuse

Axis II V61.1 Partner Relational Problem

Axis III No diagnosis, Rule out Hypoglycemia

Axis IV Marital Separation, Occupational Problems, Son's Substance Abuse/ Educational Problems

Axis V GAF = 55 (current)

Open-Ended, Client-Centered Procedures

Assessment of Recovery Supports.   Helping clients like Stephanie to assess recovery supports includes encouraging them to discuss experiences and resources that can enhance their recovery, emphasizing their role as experts and active partners. Clients may have learned unacknowledged lessons from both adverse and positive experiences that improved their coping and problem-solving. Those experiences can serve as inoculation stories that they can retell periodically, when they are under stress, to support and enhance their continued recovery (Freeman 1998; Freedman and Combs 1996). Assessment is a critical stage for identifying and helping clients practice how to use such stories to empower themselves and to prevent relapse during early recovery.

For example, when Don asked Stephanie about past experiences that she had been able to cope with, involving handling painful feelings, she told him the following story:

> I was raised by my grandparents after my mother became an alcoholic and gradually lost contact with our family. My father was a businessman who traveled a lot. He deserted my mother when I was very young. My grandmother was very stern, she was Scots-Irish and believed you could live through anything if you committed yourself to it. But she was also very wise and loving. When I made mistakes, like most young people did, she would just say try not to make the same mistake twice. As I got into my teenage years, I changed from an obedient child to a rebellious one: I talked back, to my grandmother of all people; my grades went down; I stopped taking care of myself. My grandmother tried everything, from being stern to grounding me to trying to reason with me; nothing worked. One day she asked me what I thought was wrong. It surprised me, because no one else had asked what I thought. After thinking about her question, I told her no one loved me, both my parents left me when I was still young. My grandmother said she was an ol' women, that she'd lived a long time and learned a thing or two about life. When you lose someone, she said, God puts a big block of ice 'round your heart, to protect you from the hurt and pain. The wall's not there permanently. If you keep it there too long, it gets harder, ice expands don't you know, takes up more and more room. She said at some point, when you least expect it, the ice wall'll break into a thousand pieces, and you with it. You

don't want your life broken in a thousand pieces, you might never get it back together again. But if you warm up the wall of ice slowly, instead of letting it get too hard, the ice can take its own time melting. She said a person can even feel it happening slowly, maybe get used to it that way. Then things wouldn't be so scary. Other people can see it happening and help out, if they need to.

When Don asked Stephanie how this experience with her grandmother had affected her, Stephanie said it caused her to express her feelings gradually and made her less angry and lonely. She became more calm and slowly got herself back on track at home and at school. But now, the experience reminded Stephanie that she had started hiding her feelings and fears again, that she had built another solid wall of ice around her heart. Don wondered if retelling this experience to herself and others could remind Stephanie of when it helped her to cope with painful feelings more openly. He pointed out how the experience could support her work during early recovery based on her own wisdom, on the lessons she had learned from it.

A second type of recovery support that should be identified during assessment is resources that can prevent relapse, particularly during early recovery. In this case, Don, Stephanie's counselor, helped her analyze resources that could enhance her recovery through the use of an ecomap they constructed together (see this mutual assessment procedure in figure 8.1 under empowerment-focused assessment-evaluation tools). The ecomap, Axis V of the *DSM-IV*, and their discussion about recovery supports revealed that Stephanie was socially isolated like many addicted women, although she had a number of supports that she could use appropriately for recovery. One resource included her stable employment of eight years, which had an EAP program whose policies they could explore. Another resource included Stephanie's grandfather, who was extremely loyal in spite of not understanding her addiction and the consequences for her functioning (her grandmother was now deceased). Other resources were stable housing— Stephanie and her husband agreed that she would keep their house; her involvement in her children's schools; a supportive neighbor and friend, Carole, who did not use substances but from whom Stephanie was cut off; Stephanie's insistance that Duane enter rehab for help with his own substance abuse; and her past, assertive style of communication before she became addicted.

In addition to using the ecomap during assessment with Stephanie, Don could have used this procedure throughout rehab to monitor changes that were occurring in her recovery resources and social skills as a result of their work together. Each new entry could have been written by Stephanie in a different color pen and dated to help them distinguish and monitor what changed in those areas, when, and how, as well as what strategies and other factors influenced the changes. This feedback could have increased Stephanie's self-efficacy as they monitored her effectiveness in learning and practicing new social and relationship skills; developing new environmental resources, including gender-sensitive social networks; and assuming new power-sharing roles with Don or her peers. Further recovery supports and skill development might have occurred from Stephanie's feedback to Don and the program about what facilitated or hindered her changes, and how the program's services to women might be modified accordingly. Don and Stephanie could have used her journal entries to monitor how often she used her inoculation story and other lessons learned to cope with stress and prevent relapse, and under what circumstances she did so successfully.

Using Solution-Focused Questions in Assessments

The strategy of using solution-focused questions during assessment can complement the exploration of recovery supports discussed above (see figure 8.1 under mutual assessment-evaluation procedures related to client empowerment). Assumptions for such questions are particularly important for women like Stephanie, whose addictions staff may not connect to oppression, as they might with clients of color and from other diverse groups. Practitioners can influence clients' perceptions of their situations simply by the questions they ask and how they ask them, and by their beliefs about the nature of clients' problems and what changes are possible (as metamessages) (Baker and Steiner 1995).

During Stephanie's assessment, she commented that it seemed everything in her situation had conspired to prevent her from entering rehab. Don used the following solution-focused affirmation question to follow up on her comment. "Coming to rehab is a real strength on your part, based on what you've said about all the barriers you were facing. How'd you manage getting here in spite of those barriers?" This question shifted their discussion from the reasons Stephanie had been unable to enter rehab in the past to the reasons she was able to do so currently, emphasizing her strengths and resiliency. As part of this exploration, Don helped Stephanie think through which of her reasons for coming to rehab in spite of the barriers could be used to support her recovery and resolve her problems.

One of Stephanie's main reasons for entering rehab was to relieve the pain of her shame and guilt as an addicted woman who found herself "following in her mother's awful footsteps." Don asked Stephanie a solution-focused miracle question in response (Freedman and Combs 1996): "What if you woke up tomorrow and a miracle had happened: you found this situation was suddenly better and you no longer felt the shame and guilt you mentioned, how would your situation be different?" Other questions included, "Who would notice that the situation was different and what would they notice?" "In what ways would your relationship with that individual be different?" and "What else in your life would have to change before this difference would be noticeable?"

Stephanie replied that the dull ache in her stomach would be gone if a miracle occurred, and that she would be able to look her children and co-workers in the eye without needing to mask her feelings and behavior with cocaine and alcohol. She thought her relationship with her children would be more trusting on their part, and that she would listen to their interests and concerns more genuinely, without fear of failing them the way her mother had failed her. Maybe Duane would tell her when he was under stress, the way she had been able to talk with her grandmother as a troubled teenager. Stephanie also mentioned times when she had abstained from abusing cocaine and was a better mother. Instead of confronting Stephanie about denying the severity of her addiction, Don encouraged her by using the following exception questions (Freedman and Combs 1996): "What positive things were going on in your life during the times when you were able to abstain from cocaine?" and "Which of those things are present in your situation today?"

Exception questions can be used also to help clients monitor and provide feedback on a program's process and outcome evaluations. Such questions are appropriate for some of the mutual and client self-evaluation procedures in figure 8.1, including individual interviews, focus groups, critical dialogue groups, and clients' written and verbal session summaries. Examples of solution-focused evaluation questions are: "How has this program (or this session or type of service) helped in your recovery?" "What changes have occurred in your life as a result of the program in spite of any setbacks you may have experienced?" "What are some things you have done to improve your recovery?" "If there were times when the program was not effective for you, what was happening in your life during those periods that helped you to continue in the program?" "It must have taken determination on your part to not leave at those times; what have you learned from those experiences?" Although Don did not ask Stephanie all of these questions, he asked her what she had learned in spite of her setbacks near the end of her rehab period. Stephanie indicated she finally understood what her grandmother meant about the importance of believing you can live through an experience and committing yourself to it fully. Her journal entries documented that she developed a gradually stronger commitment to recovery while she was in rehab. Stephanie felt that Don's pattern of periodically reviewing and reaffirming the reasons she identified for entering rehab, one aspect of her recovery supports, helped her to become more committed to her recovery.

The Motivational Interviewing Assessment Process

A third procedure for client-centered assessments helps clients and their counselors analyze the former's motivation for recovery. Miller (1983) assumes that clients' attributions, as well as the questions counselors ask during assessment, directly influence motivations for change (see figure 8.1 regarding client-centered, empowerment assessment-evaluation tools). External attributions reinforce clients' helplessness and powerlessness, and therefore their lack of motivation for or beliefs in the possibility of change. Internal attributions encourage clients to acknowledge responsibility for their initial decisions to use substances but also to recognize how becoming addicted and being affected by certain environmental conditions may have influenced their current loss of control. Acknowledging they are not helpless in all aspects of their lives is important, because according to Miller (1983), assuming responsibility for what they can control and credit for what they are able to change leads to more lasting change.

Miller (1983) indicates helpers' assessment questions should utilize clients' attributions to increase the dissonance between their addictive behaviors and knowledge and beliefs that conflict with them. Rather than using direct and forceful confrontation to refute the beliefs and attitudes that may support clients' addictive behaviors, counselors are expected to use exploratory interview questions and feedback to facilitate clients' own conclusions, decision making, and self-efficacy. That approach, in contrast to confrontation, advice giving, stigmatizing, or moralizing, increases rather than decreases their motivation for recovery.

The assessment questions and feedback in motivational interviewing center around the following three strategies (Miller 1983):

1. Providing Affirmations: Using reflective listening in order to:
   a. reinforce clients' self-perceived problems and conflicts related to their addiction(s) and other areas for validation and consolidation ("You've said your use of cocaine has caused family conflicts, what are some examples of those conflicts?"); or
   b. restructure, place certain statements in a different light, or point out the dissonance between various statements made by clients ("You say you haven't been irresponsible in terms of your work, and you've given examples of using meth during your lunch hour and weekends rather than using it while you're on duty. I imagine trying to draw such a fine line between being responsible and being irresponsible at work must be very difficult and unclear at times.")
2. Heightening Awareness: Using consciousness-raising in order to increase dissonance by:
   a. eliciting self-motivational statements that recognize substance-related problems, concerns about the problems, or a need for change ("What things have you noticed about your drinking that concern you?"); or
   b. integrating objective assessment data and normative criteria as feedback to clients, summarizing their self-motivational statements, and allowing them to draw their own conclusions ("I'll try to summarize the different results we now have," "What do you think about the feedback I've shared from the various tests and procedures we've used?" or "Let me see if I can summarize the concerns you've expressed to me, then you can tell me if I've included the most important ones from your perspective").
3. Exploring Alternatives: Directing the dissonance in appropriate directions by:
   a. asking the client what he or she thinks should be done ("What do you think should be done about your situation based on the conclusions you've reached?"); or

       b. suggesting additional alternatives including self-directed change activities (" You may not be aware of this, but some other alternatives include . . ." "What are some steps you've decided to take yourself in this situation?"); and

       c. acknowledging that continuing the abuse is one alternative ("What do you anticipate might happen if you continued your heroin use?").

In Stephanie's situation, because Don was not aware of motivational interviewing strategies, he missed opportunities to help her clarify and assess her motivations for recovery. Had he used those strategies, Don could have built upon the foundation he and Stephanie laid when they assessed her potential solutions and recovery supports (factors that caused her to seek out rehab services). When Stephanie told Don about the shame and guilt she experienced as an addicted woman, he used solution-focused questions to explore what would have to change in order for those feelings to be different. But he did not focus on her concerns about this stigma as a potential positive influence on her motivation for recovery. When she shared her inoculation story and he used the *DSM-IV* and ecomap to help her assess her social supports, Don missed the importance of data from those other three sources about her gender-related social isolation.

Don could have heightened Stephanie's awareness by summarizing the confluence of data about her social isolation from the three combined assessment procedures, as well as her concerns about the stigma of her addiction. He could have also explored some potential alternatives based on Stephanie's increased awareness from the summary and her subsequent conclusions. Specifically, Don could have facilitated a discussion with Stephanie by asking some of the following questions: "Based on the results from these assessment procedures I've just shared with you, what are your conclusions about what the results mean?" "Did I hear you correctly, you're concerned about feeling ashamed of being a woman who has abused cocaine, especially regarding the effects of your abuse on your role as mother?" "You've said your isolation is more clear to you now, and you understand how it has reinforced your substance abuse, and how it has increased your shame about not meeting your expectations as a mother. What do you think should be done to help address and resolve these issues?" "One alternative might be to provide you with a specialized group with other women to address some of these common and unique gender issues. Let's think about what might be helpful from your perspective, and how and where we can get the necessary resources."

In another program in which the staff was being trained in a form of motivational interviewing, an African American counselor, Clarence, had difficulty applying this procedure with some of his clients during assessment. Forty-one-year-old Marvin, an Italian American client who had recently been placed on probation for stealing while under the influence, entered outpatient rehab as a condition of his probation. Marvin's drugs of choice were water (formaldehyde) and crack cocaine. Although Clarence planned to use motivational interviewing to facilitate the assessment process with Marvin, he became stuck by using confrontation to respond to Marvin's adamant denials that he was addicted. Marvin would reinforce his denials by citing how his "overinvolved" Italian family was also trying to convince him of his addiction. Clarence had been recovering for three years at the time, and had been through five other rehab programs before completing a residential therapeutic community program on his sixth attempt. The reason he became stuck with Marvin, Clarence believes in retrospect, is because he assumed Marvin was not sufficiently motivated to commit to and complete rehab at the time.

Being involved in the training while he was actually struggling to complete this assessment with Marvin was fortuitous for Clarence. The trainer helped him to reframe Marvin's "denial" as a lack of motivation for recovery, which ended their dead-end, predictable conflict (Miller 1983) about whether or not Marvin was addicted and how severely. The trainer suggested that Clarence could heighten Marvin's awareness by saying, "This program requires a tremendous amount of motivation in order for each client to be accepted for rehab. From what you've told me I'm not sure you have enough motivation to be accepted in this program." When Marvin protested, saying he was somewhat motivated because his probation required him to accept rehab, Clarence asked him to talk about his motivations aside from being on probation. The trainer advised Clarence to encourage Marvin to continue exploring his situation, to continue providing examples by asking, "What are some other reasons you're here for rehab?" and "What makes you believe you can recover at this time?" The trainer's intervention helped Clarence to resolve the impasse, to which his assumptions about recovery had contributed, and to make his assessment process much more collaborative with Marvin.

Conclusion

This chapter addresses three client-centered assessment procedures based on clients' wisdom and expertise about their recovery supports, desired changes or solutions, and motivations for recovery. These procedures can be combined and then integrated with many of the traditional procedures that most programs use for linking assessment with evaluation. The cases of Stephanie and Marvin illustrate how a program's underlying philosophy, flexibility in providing staff training opportunities to meet emerging client needs, and power-sharing roles can undermine or support the integration of client-centered and traditional methods. In Stephanie's situation, the counselor enhanced the mutual assessment by encouraging Stephanie to be a partner in the process (power sharing), leading to her self-empowerment. However, without specialized diversity training and gender-sensitive assessment tools, he failed to explore related aspects of her motivation for recovery adequately, and therefore did not advocate for specialized resources, such as a women's issues group, to improve her recovery.

In Marvin's program, the staff was being trained in motivational interviewing, so Clarence, his counselor, integrated that procedure into their assessment process. The struggle for Clarence to use this approach effectively was affected by his experiences as a recovering person. Clarence believed that direct confrontation of clients' denial was the only way to support their recovery. He struggled to ask genuine questions about Marvin's motivations for recovery and to allow Marvin to draw his own conclusions about his use of substances without moralizing or labeling his behavior.

What lessons can be learned from these two very different assessment processes? It seems clear that practitioners' use of client-centered procedures is often affected by their own experiences and their understanding of how clients' diversity can affect assessment outcomes. In order to lessen the negative effects of such factors, it is important to use approaches that rely on clients' expertise and meaning, rather than expert models that encourage helpers to engage in power monopolizing roles.

9 Group Approaches to Collective Empowerment in Rehab, Self-Help, and Prevention Programs

> By their very nature group mutual aid systems universalize individual issues, reduce isolation, and mitigate stigma through their powerful yet subtle interpersonal processes. . . . Being active in a group . . . helps develop competence and a sense of personal empowerment.
> —C. B. Germain and A. Gitterman (1995:241)

For the mutual aid and empowerment process, which Germain and Gitterman indicate above is essential for effective group work, to be effective, the members must experience bonding and cohesion. "Bonds among members can dilute power differences that may create tensions and barriers to open communication" (Schopler and Galinsky 1996:1130) and can make the group a safe environment for members to explore their common experiences. Clients in substance abuse rehab have often experienced multiple losses in identity, power, competence, relationships, and possessions. However, stigma associated with those losses, which are common but often assumed to be unique, may cause clients to resist opportunities for group sharing and mutual aid.

Certainly, staff skills and attitudes about substance abuse can either diminish or reinforce the stigma that most clients experience. For example, more highly skilled and compassionate staff can use peer groups to effectively alleviate stigma by modeling social acceptance and coaching peers who are further along in recovery to share their process of getting better (Carley 1997; Smyth 1996). In one rehab program, staff videotape senior clients in the last phase discussing their efforts to recover, and when it is appropriate, their relapses as well. These clients are able to share how they survived, learned from, and can now anticipate signs of relapse. The videotapes are shown to other clients in the middle phases of rehab, to normalize and yet challenge their recovery struggles.

In one example, twenty-five-year-old Edgar called his rehab program from a hotel where he had been staying since his relapse the previous week. He had left rehab abruptly because warrants had been issued for his arrest related to several past charges, and now he wanted to turn himself in, although he admitted he was scared. His counselor met him at the hotel and supported his decision to surrender himself to the police. When he returned to rehab four weeks later after being placed on probation, the counselor worked with Edgar to make a videotape about his relapse and turning himself in to the police.

This tape, an example of a getting better narrative (Carley 1997), was particularly useful later when it was shown during peer group sessions, because legal problems and a pattern of denying and running away instead of addressing them are very common among people in early recovery. When peers hear and integrate the lessons learned, stories such as Edgar's function as inoculation or prevention narratives for the future (Freeman 1998). Similarly, skilled preventionists can use groups, along with peers' taped testimonials, to highlight strengths and resources that help individuals, families, and communities to prevent substance abuse problems (Hawkins and Catalano 1994).

This chapter briefly summarizes the benefits of using groups for empowerment practice, including how group theory is uniquely relevant to the substance abuse field. Then it analyzes the types of groups provided in this field, illustrating through case and organizational examples how each can facilitate collective empowerment. The discussion clarifies too how the mutual aid and social action models can be applied effectively in rehab groups, twelve-step or self-help groups, and prevention programs.

The Benefits of Group Work and Related Theory

Application to Substance Abuse Problems

Critical analyses of research on group work have documented areas of effectiveness and factors to consider for building upon the benefits of groups in the substance abuse field. Research in general suggests, for example, criteria to consider in selecting group members, such as their prior

group experiences (Toseland and Siporin 1986), and how to address drop-
out issues by exploring clients' referral paths to services (Boswick 1987).
Research also shows that using more structured groups with selected populations can lead to better documentation of outcomes (Schopler and Galinsky 1996).

There has been little research on group work from an empowerment
perspective, however, especially regarding substance abuse problems. Such
research may require more attention to clients' voices and to their subjective recovery experiences in addition to objective data. Pending that research, the following aspects of group work have been suggested as important to empowerment practice in substance abuse rehab (Behroozi 1992;
Cartwright 1987; Chau 1990; LePantois 1986; Milgram and Rubin 1992;
Rogers and McMillan 1989; Smyth 1995; Strussner 1993):

1. opportunity to address and resolve the stigma associated with substance abuse, such as shame and guilt related to the abuse and
   the lifestyle, through group mutual aid, provision of factual data
   about addiction, analysis of common underlying feelings and behaviors, and discovering important common and unique
   strengths and sources of power
2. consciousness raising about common influences on the problem
   such as biological or genetic factors, environmental barriers, and
   personal responsibility through group reflection, healing, mutual
   aid, and collective empowerment
3. opportunity to give and receive peer support and critical feedback
   about the quality of reflection and action taken by each member
   and by the group based on knowledge and skills gained during
   the sessions and in the program, involving self-disclosure, offering
   alternative perspectives, and role rehearsal or practicing new
   skills
4. peer modeling of the management of stigma, authority, and
   power and control issues that can affect recovery, including involuntary rehab, relapse episodes, and interpersonal conflicts
5. a supportive context in which diversity issues can be explored,
   which tests staff commitment to empowerment practice and
   peers' abilities to respect, value, accept, and build on the contributions of diverse members.

Related Group Theory and Models

Group work has been called the modality of choice in substance abuse programs because of the benefits identified in the previous section. However, most clients are unaware of those benefits when they enter a program, so they typically resist involvement in the group process. Moreover, clients may believe some aspects of group work, such as open communication and becoming aware of previously unacknowledged feelings, are unsafe and a threat to their recovery. A number of theoretical concepts and approaches help to explain clients' need for and responses to group process, two of which are briefly summarized in this section. These two approaches seem the most applicable to substance abuse problems; however, they can be combined with other group models to provide alternative, often complementary approaches to group practice.

Group Mutual Aid. Schopler and Galinsky (1995) indicate the mutual aid model is based on an assumption that sharing common experiences, interests, and goals can provide relief to members. The purpose in developing a mutual aid system is to manage common interpersonal stressors and to engage in a positive interchange with the environment to minimize external stressors (Schwartz 1971; Gitterman and Shulman 1994). Mutual aid leads to an increase in the quality of the group's creative problem solving by providing clients "a multiplicity of helping relationships" or peer supports (Germain and Gitterman 1995:242).

Germain and Gitterman state that in addition to solving problems related to environmental and personal stressors, a mutual aid system is expected to address behavioral change, educational needs, social connections and skills, and specific tasks related to prescribed group objectives. Trust issues are a key factor in this process. Group members test each other, first with low-risk topics, then with more sensitive and personal concerns (Gitterman and Shulman 1994), especially if they are involuntary clients (Behroozi 1993; Berman and Rossi 1992). As clients become engaged and learn whether they can trust each other, the mutual aid system becomes a reciprocal and self-perpetuating process. The members' common pregroup experiences and the intense work they share during group sessions can lead to bonding and cohesion, which often increases their group participation (Rooney 1992).

In terms of substance abuse, individuals must engage in lifelong efforts to recover from or to resist addiction. One of the primary tools for this ongoing process is mutual aid, which is available in counseling groups, education and prevention groups, informal self-help groups, and social networks, and through indigenous community leaders and individual sponsors and mentors. Developing a mutual aid system in their rehab, prevention, or self-help groups provides clients with microcosms of their natural environments in which to practice work on recovery and related issues. Because clients have often experienced and perpetrated trust violations, the mutual aid model normalizes the testing in which members engage as natural and expected.

Germain and Gitterman's (1994:241–42) five foci for mutual aid groups in general are applicable, therefore, to substance abuse client groups. A mutual aid system can: 1) educate clients about collaboration, trust, addiction-related stigma, resistance to substances, and other issues; 2) help them to change maladaptive behavioral patterns that reinforce substance abuse and enabling; 3) encourage them to reestablish key social connections and processes that can prevent addiction or that have been disrupted by their addiction; 4) share common concerns, experiences, interests, and goals related to their addiction and recovery; and 5) provide resources for problem-solving tasks related to personal, interpersonal, and environmental barriers to recovery and other life issues (Germain and Gitterman 1994).

Group Social Goals and Social Action.   Like the mutual aid model, social action and social goals concepts emphasize empowerment and the development of members' own resources for handling environmental and personal issues (Schopler and Galinsky 1996). Social goals approaches focus "on the worker's role in enhancing individual growth, development, and learning through the use of democratic participation in the pursuit of social action" (Schopler and Galinsky 1995:1132). Social action includes a focus on community building, based on the incorporation of early community organizing principles into this model (Tropp 1971).

Moreover, Freire's (1984) process of consciousness raising, education, planning, and collective social action is consistent with social goals and social action approaches. His four-stage empowerment process emphasizes the value of ordinary people as experts and the importance of their local knowledge in effecting systems change. A number of authors have integrated Freire's empowerment process with the social goals-social action theoretical models and have applied this integrated approach to group practice (Garvin 1991; Lewis 1991; Shapiro 1991). Gutiérrez and Ortega's (1991) application of their integrated empowerment-social action group approach to cultural diversity issues has further enhanced this area of theory building.

In substance abuse rehab and prevention, the goal is to help people acknowledge their existing strengths and to help them build upon their individual, group, family, and community capacities. Consciousness raising about common barriers and limitations is expected to create unity among group members and to reduce their social isolation. It is also supposed to make them aware of the institutional roots of some of their problems (Gutiérrez 1994). This collective knowledge development or education process normalizes the social stigma and power paralysis that typically confront clients and prevents those conditions from continuing as barriers to social action.

Clients need to resume important social roles and increase their self- and group efficacy by becoming competent in changing stressful environmental conditions collectively. They are expected also to provide services to the community, to become socially responsible, in order to compensate for taking from the community while they were addicted (Toubouron and Hamilton 1993). Imbrogno (1987) recommends using peer groups as policy transformation groups. Clients in rehab and prevention programs can use groups to change organizational and social policies related to stressful conditions within the service setting. Furthermore, they can often resolve oppressive conditions in other large systems that may be impeding their recovery and prevention efforts. A variety of other groups are also needed to support clients' social action and mutual aid activities in substance abuse programs.

Types of Groups Used in Substance Abuse Programs

Groups for Clients

Rehab Programs.   Many authors assume that peer influence and support are important aspects of mutual aid, creating positive changes in group members across different types of problems and practice settings (Gitterman and Shulman 1994; Galanter, Castaneda, and Franco 1991). The need to provide clients with maximum opportunities to experience mutual aid accounts, therefore, for the broad variety and the frequency of group sessions in rehab programs. Most offer an array of basic groups daily, for counseling, alcohol and drug education, on-site twelve-step work, relapse prevention, weekend processing, social activities, reentry (into the community) and aftercare, and peer support.

Rehab programs also offer a variety of specialized groups focused on different life domains and special needs. Some have a social action component in addition to a mutual aid system, which helps clients to externalize and resolve common social justice issues and addiction-related stigmas. Groups' focuses include women's issues, men's issues, multicultural issues, art therapy, drama therapy, loss and grief, work orientation-readiness, dual diagnoses, parenting, incest survivors, and adult children of substance abusers (Freeman 1990; Toubouron and Hamilton 1993; Lewis and Ford 1991; Finkelstein 1993; Coleman 1987; Daley 1987).

Self-Help Groups.   In contrast to rehab groups, informal mutual- or self-help groups are based primarily on the twelve-step model. These groups are available to recovering people on and off site while they are in rehab, or they may not be utilized until clients are in aftercare or have completed rehab. People in spontaneous recovery who are not involved in formal rehab programs often participate in these groups as their sole recovery support; they may also use religious supports. Twelve-step groups are organized along at least four dimensions. First, they are organized according to clients' drugs or substances of choice, including Alcoholics Anonymous, Cocaine Anonymous, Narcotics Anonymous, and Overeaters Anonymous (AA, CA, NA, OA). Recovering people and significant others can attend any of these groups, regardless of the drugs involved, although there are groups especially for significant others such as Alanon, Alafam, Alateen, and Alatot (Farris-Kurtz 1992).

Second, these groups are either open to everyone or to recovering people only. Closed groups are more likely to encourage members to share extremely sensitive and toxic issues, but open meetings may also create the same trusting climate. A third, and much more recent, organizational dimension is special needs related to cultural diversity. Self-help groups have been developed to serve primarily or exclusively the needs of women, adolescents, African Americans, Latinos, medical professionals, religious professionals, and gay males and lesbians. An underlying tenet is that the members' common cultural experiences are factors in their addiction and recovery, and that the focus in more generic groups ignores or denies the importance of those experiences and resources. Self-help groups are also organized in terms of the particular themes, issues, or step work addressed during different sessions over time. Examples include the themes of honesty and relationship or couples' issues, or the third step of taking a self-inventory.

Mutual aid in self-help groups tends to be less directive than in formal rehab groups. Support, validation, and critical feedback are often provided through members' sharing their stories and experiences with the individual who is struggling with an issue. An underlying assumption is that members will find their own way to resolve an issue with group support, that of what is shared, they will "take the best and leave the rest" (Alanon 1997). These groups struggle with issues related to social and political action versus the commitment of twelve-step programs to anonymity (Kurtz 1997). Members often recognize that they have collective concerns and that environmental barriers can impede their recovery. However, these groups' commitment to anonymity has prohibited most of them from taking a political stand or advocating as a special interest group for rehab and prevention policy and funding (Meier 1994; Morrell 1996).

Prevention Programs. As in twelve-step programs, in prevention programs all of the work with participants occurs during group sessions, primarily in education groups, although in-session and out-of-session task groups are also used. These education groups target changes in either the members' affective (attitudinal), cognitive (information only), or skill areas, or in a combination of these areas (Tobler 1986). Using a combined framework involves a psycho-education process in which members not only learn particular information but are encouraged to practice collectively applying that information in their natural environments. Group members are expected to identify and utilize protective factors (the presence of abstinent and positive role models) and to resolve risk factors (the availability of alcohol and drugs) in the process of applying their new or enhanced knowledge and skills (Hawkins and Catalano 1994).

Including natural peer networks in groups or exercises that provide a microcosm of a positive peer culture allows the members to develop a mutual aid system (Tobler 1986). For instance, this system can be a vehicle for members to provide critical feedback to each other while practicing refusal skills or exploring how their attitudes about sources of power can affect their resistance to drugs. Often, based on the mutual aid process that develops during in-session task groups, out-of-session task groups may be formed to address particular issues in the members' environment. These time-limited groups can plan and implement social goals and social action in the community, such as getting businesses to donate billboard space for public service announcements related to drug prevention. Occasionally, task groups are continued beyond the life of prevention programs to address ongoing issues in a school or community. Group members may advocate for legislators to fund traditional prevention programs. They also sometimes request funding from private foundations for youth development or recreational programs that provide teens with alternatives to drugs (Hawkins and Catalano 1994; Malekoff 1994).

Groups for Significant Others

Rehab Programs.   Many rehab programs offer groups for family members and other significant individuals in clients' lives to enhance their recovery. Similar to rehab groups for clients, these groups frequently have a mutual aid system to help families and others adjust to positive changes in clients. Another goal is to change significant others' negative interpersonal dynamics and relationships with clients. For this reason, family groups are often inclusive in membership, ranging from spouses or partners, parents, siblings, children, and extended family members to unrelated key individuals.

Clients and their significant others can identify with common concerns expressed by other families, listen to alternative perspectives they may not hear when such views come from their relatives, and gain support and problem-solving resources through mutual aid (Schopler and Galinsky 1995; Pratt and Gill 1990). These multiple-family groups are sometimes supplemented with How to Cope groups (such as Tough Love) and with group play therapy and education groups for the children of clients (LePantois 1986; Flanzer 1992).

Prevention Programs.   Because of the systemic effects of substance abuse on family members, a few prevention programs have experimented with conducting educational groups with families in their homes, often using the parents or parent figures as cofacilitators. Those programs involve training the parent-facilitators in prevention and group process strategies before conducting the family sessions. An alternative model has been to provide the prevention program to groups of adult family members at either school or community sites, such as churches, prior to engaging their children. The goal is to strengthen natural family leadership skills and to resolve potential barriers to prevention with youths and with the community as a whole (Hawkins and Catalano 1994).

Self-Help Groups. Rehab groups for significant others are sometimes supplemented with on- or off-site Alanon, Alatot, and Alafam twelve-step groups (Farris-Kurtz 1992; Flanzer 1992). These operate similarly to twelve-step groups for clients, as noted in the previous section. Often, family members and other key people are encouraged to participate in these self-help groups even if the substance-abusing member refuses to enter rehab or recovery. The main focus is on helping significant others to address their issues related to the substance abuse and relationship problems, rather than on the abusing members' issues (Farris-Kurtz 1992).

Practice Illustrations: Group Mutual Aid in Rehab and Twelve-Step Programs

The Purpose of Interactive Group Strategies

A combination of strategies may be necessary in order to fully exploit the opportunities for empowerment that the range of groups in the previous section can provide. The strategies shown in table 9.1 can be used across modalities, although some are more effective in groups. Interactive strategies, such as the hot seat and clients' presenting their life stories, are designed to facilitate members' recovery and empowerment through group mutual aid and feedback. They can help a client who is stuck in his or her recovery, having reached an unacknowledged impasse, confront it during a session with group support. These issues usually have a major influence on the client's recovery and opportunities for self-empowerment.

A Rehab Program: The Example of Carol

Background Information. In one program's loss and grief group, a twenty-seven-year-old white client, Carol, was struggling to understand why her mother had abandoned her as an infant. However, Carol had said in previous sessions that the abandonment was not related to her recovery and was unimportant. Carol's interactions with peers in the program and with her

TABLE 9.1 Empowerment-Focused Treatment Strategies

	Empowerment Levels or Change Targets		
	Personal	*Interpersonal*	*Political*
Modalities: Individual Counseling	use visualization exercises	develop heritage books	conduct power analyses of personal-institutional conflicts
	analyze cultural stories	write and present concept papers	do role sharing (client-counselor collaboration)
	play disintegration tape to the end		engage in organizational impact or systems change (e.g., gain support for cultural rituals)
	develop triggers and tools checklist		
	complete recovery exercise workbooks (bibliotherapy)		perform community services (e.g., mentoring, voter registration, homeless shelter work)
	write in a journal		
	do relaxation exercises		

Family Counseling	write in a journal	participate in reenactments	develop alternative endings for family disempowerment stories
	develop relapse prevention plan	develop personal growth contracts with other members	conduct power analyses of family and large institution interactional patterns
		conduct power analyses of family triangles/coalitions	
		participate in assertive communication exercises	
Group Counseling	develop solution-focused alternative stories/endings	conduct power analyses on common disempowerment experiences	conduct power analyses regarding social justice issues (e.g., gender bias)
	participate in the hot seat exercise	write and present life narratives or stories	use letter writing, coalition building, and other political action strategies
		analyze relapse-feeling cycle	
		engage in role playing, role rehearsal, and role reversal exercises	
		write and respond to pull-ups	

primary counselor and other staff often involved anger and confrontation. Group members were frustrated because their efforts to provide mutual aid to Carol were not working. As one said, "Carol constantly asks for our support, and then rejects it . . . and us, by the way." Carol had been in the program's three-month day treatment component for two months when her counselor, Chris, decided to use the following exercises.

The Hot Seat and Role Play Exercises. In preparation for the hot seat exercise, Chris had Carol sit in the center of the group and respond, in turn, to questions about the apparent conflicts she was unable to see. Her peers asked what was keeping her from acknowledging the loss of her mother and what purpose it served for her to deny its importance. One member asked why Carol seemed so angry if she had accepted her mother's leaving. When Carol said that maybe this issue was important to her but that she had resolved it, several members shared their examples of similar losses and talked about feeling rejected and unloved as a consequence. Chris followed up by saying it would be unnatural not to be curious about why her mother left; surely Carol had questions to be answered before she could move on. Chris's question and the supportive examples of her peers' losses helped to normalize Carol's unacknowledged shame and self-doubts about "being abandoned."

Chris offered to role play her mother so Carol could ask some of those unanswered questions. During the role play, a moving, self-transformative, healing process began. When Carol asked her mother why she had left, Chris said she loved Carol and believed she was doing the best she could at the time. Carol opened up about what her life had been like as a child, her hurt feelings and longing for her mother, how she blamed herself, and how hard it was now to become a woman without her mother's guidance. She began to cry, and for the first time, she talked about how her explosive anger could be related to the hurt feelings she had just revealed.

The resolution of Carol's impasse through these exercises became more apparent when Carol allowed Chris, as her mother, to hug and comfort her, first as the five-year-old Carol and then as the adult Carol. After a while, Carol in turn began to comfort Chris as her mother, acknowledging how difficult it must have been to leave and lose her daughter. As the role play ended, group members spontaneously hugged Carol, giving her nonverbal and verbal feedback about the positive risk she had taken in exploring and sharing her feelings in response to the exercises.

Evaluation Strategies and Self-Empowerment.   After the session, Chris asked Carol to complete a client session summary for the group (see figure 8.1). Carol wrote that the session gave her a sense of accomplishment because she could hear for the first time the members' common losses and pain. That information and the exercises helped her to understand that her mother's leaving did not automatically mean she hated and rejected her daughter. Carol could see that although she had been hurt, like her peers, she had survived her loss. During and after the role play, Carol felt empowered by the experience of comforting and being comforted by her "mother" and the group. The hot seat was most useful in disrupting her denial. Her peers' questions caused her to critically examine her perspective and overwhelmed her with feelings she had repressed previously. The role play allowed her to risk expressing those feelings openly in the group. Carol wrote that someday, when she is further along in her recovery, she might try to find her mother, to see if they can understand each other and build a relationship.

A Rehab Program: The Example of Shane

Background Information.   Impasses such as Carol's occur throughout the rehab process as clients grow, then sometimes plateau temporarily, in their recovery. In one adolescent rehab program, group members are expected to write and present three to four versions of their life story to help them work through these natural plateaus. This practice developed after staff realized some information in clients' life stories may be intentionally or unintentionally withheld at different stages of recovery (Smyth 1995), or when members are uncertain about the amount of trust and mutual aid they can expect from the group (Gitterman and Shulman 1995). Each version of the life story presentation is videotaped. When group members and a client's primary counselor agree that a particular version is the final one, the most open and trustworthy life story the client can produce, tapes of the earlier versions are played in a group session.

Sixteen-year-old Shane had presented two other versions of his life story before the final version was accepted in his counseling group. In the first two, Shane talked about the deaths of his parents as critical in influencing his drug experimentation and later abuse, but did not share information about the causes and circumstances. He seemed to openly express more and more of his pain, as would be expected from the loss of both parents at a young age, during each taping. The group mutual aid validated Shane's powerlessness and sense of rejection as the members identified many common and unique losses they had experienced. Some of them described negative consequences from their efforts to stuff feelings related to their losses, such as isolating themselves from supports and risking death or injury in dangerous situations.

The Life Story or Narrative Analysis Strategy.   Comparing and analyzing different versions of clients' life stories helps to identify barriers and patterns of growth in their self-awareness, trust in peers, use of critical feedback, and ability to provide mutual aid to others. The goal is to identify and apply knowledge about key underlying issues and omissions that can impede or enhance recovery (see table 9.1). When videotapes of Shane's three versions of his life story were analyzed during a group session, the fact and significance of earlier omissions became apparent. The members could see that as they had provided Shane with validation and support after each presentation and his trust in them had increased, he had gradually revealed more substantive and risky aspects of his narrative and current concerns.

One example was his sharing with the group, in the last version of his life story, the cause of his parents' deaths within a two-year period: HIV/AIDS. A group member asked what it meant to Shane that his parent had died from AIDS. Another asked if he was ashamed. Through these supportive questions and the group's collective analysis, Shane was able to analyze possible reasons for not sharing this information previously. One of his underlying issues was the anger and rejection he felt when his parents died, especially toward his father. Shane and his brother had been sent by his father to visit relatives for the Christmas holidays only a few days before his mother died. He believed his father knew his mother would die before they returned. Consequently, Shane did not have an opportunity to say goodbye to his mother and was afraid to confront his father at the time about what he assumed was his rationale.

Shane was also fearful he might be gay and admitted that drugs helped him to hide from those fears. His father had contracted HIV/AIDS from bisexual relationships and then had infected Shane's mother. Shane acknowledged that, without being aware of it, he had probably worried about being rejected by the group because of this issue and the fact that his parents had had AIDS. When the group and his counselor questioned him about what factors he thought might indicate he was gay, the only one he could point to was his father's bisexuality. The counselor suggested that Shane's questions about sexual orientation seemed normal for his age, that most people question their orientation during adolescence. The questions provided an opportunity for all the members to address sexual orientation, HIV/AIDS, and adolescent development more substantively later in the program's men's and women's issues groups. It became clear from the counseling group session that most of the other members also lacked essential information in those areas.

Another underlying issue was survivor's guilt about his parents' deaths, which from Shane's perspective was more difficult to manage than his other concerns. He and his brother believed their mother must have been HIV-positive when they were born, yet neither of them had contracted the virus. They could not understand why they had been so lucky, while still wondering if they could become infected in the future from their in utero exposure. Shane said his guilt and the possibility of getting HIV/AIDS made him feel like a time bomb that might explode without warning. As a result of the group's collective analysis of Shane's life story and their sharing common losses and concerns about being different, this session became a milestone in Shane's progress during rehab.

Monitoring Changes from Analyzing Life Narratives. In terms of evaluation, videotapes of clients' life stories, such as Shane's, are useful for monitoring significant changes during recovery. Clients' abilities to express previously masked feelings can be noted and the nonexpression of those feelings can be linked with past and current self-defeating behaviors, including addictions, crisis orientations, dishonesty, illegal activities, and negative relationship patterns. Decreases in members' blaming others for their situations can be monitored based on how well they begin to claim ownership of their beliefs and feelings and on the consequences illustrated in their narratives. Group mutual aid can be structured to include an evaluative component by having members provide both verbal and written feedback about peers' progress. The impact of life stories and other narratives also can be monitored by having the members identify which strategies were more or less helpful in their recovery.

For example, Shane's group sessions included relaxation exercises to help him recapture forgotten details of his life story prior to writing the final version. Shane reported that these exercises were the most helpful tools he received in rehab because they provided him with concrete evidence of his improved self-control. He thought the retelling and taping of his life story helped to make it familiar and thus less fearsome. Another narrative strategy, a group member's suggestion that Shane compare his actual life story with his ideal family fantasy, helped him to get in touch with the reality of his losses and to begin to mourn them in earnest.

A Twelve-Step Program: The Example of Moira

Background Information.   Moira was a thirty-five-year-old Latino who had been recovering from crack and heroin for ten months. She lived with her boyfriend, Mike, and their three children. Her boyfriend said he was in recovery too but continued to use his drugs of choice, beer and crack cocaine, periodically. Moira was in the last phase of aftercare following ninety days in an inpatient rehab program. She had been struggling with the dilemma of whether to stay with Mike or leave him because of his relapses and the threat to her recovery. She participated in an NA group in her community, which included some recovering Latino members. In one evening meeting of this group, Moira shared an experience that had occurred that morning.

The Use of Pull-Ups.   Moira explained that she owned a pair of gold earrings that had been given to her a few years before by her grandmother. During the years when she was addicted, she had managed to keep these earrings, sometimes pawning them and then retrieving them when she could, but never selling them outright for drugs. The earrings were especially valuable to her since her grandmother had died while she was in rehab. When Moira awoke that morning, the earrings were gone from the headboard of her bed, where she usually kept them. Her boyfriend was also gone, so she assumed he had stolen them to sell for drugs. Moira said she was so enraged and hurt that she drove around looking for her boyfriend all morning. At some point, Moira realized that she was in the midst of drug houses and companions she once used drugs with, and that she was experiencing an overwhelming anger, which had usually been her excuse to use drugs. After this realization, Moira stopped looking for her boyfriend and just drove around the rest of the day until her scheduled NA meeting. She cried as she shared her anger and frustration over her boyfriend's betrayal with her peers.

The group members provided Moira with pull-ups, a special form of group mutual aid, focused on the positive things she had done during this incident to work on her recovery. Some of this feedback was direct, such as, "It's good you realized anger toward your boyfriend is one of your triggers and stopped looking for him." Some of the feedback was provided indirectly, for example, "I might have kept looking for the b——— and then run over him with my car" or "I can see those earrings are your connection with your grandmother, but by coming here you're showing nothing is more important than your recovery!"

Members shared stories about losing sight of their goals during recovery and then getting themselves back on track. Garrett reminded Moira and the group about a relationship issue he had been struggling with during a recent meeting. His ex-wife, who lived in another part of the country, had suggested that they reconcile. Garrett had moved away two years before when he realized friction and conflicts with her over visitation and child support were impeding his recovery. He had shared his struggle over whether to move back home and reconcile with his wife and children, whom he missed a great deal, with the group. He was concerned about his wife's ongoing alcohol abuse. Through peers' storytelling about their own relationships and their questions about what had changed in Garrett's relationship with his wife, he concluded that a reconciliation was not wise. His last comment to Moira was, "I thought I'd already let go when me and my wife were divorced four years ago, but I learned from the group I'm still holding on to a fantasy relationship."

Monitoring Changes and Personal Growth Indicators. In self-help groups, members who are struggling with a particular issue often react to the group's feedback immediately, or they may provide feedback in a later session as Garrett did. Their responses help other members to understand the impact of their mutual aid on that individual's growth and recovery. Consequently, evaluation and monitoring are very informal and subjective, consistent with the overall goals and format of these groups.

In Moira's case, she provided her NA group with immediate feedback about the session. She said the members' pull-ups helped her keep her sanity. It had not occurred to her before the meeting that she had passed a milestone by not giving in to one of her triggers. She had been thinking what a worthless person she must be for her boyfriend to steal her earrings, especially knowing what they meant to her. The group's support of her resistance to seeking revenge or finding and joining the boyfriend in using drugs clarified the positive steps she had taken in spite of his betrayal. Moreover, Moira commented that a few months before, she might have continued to blame herself for his behavior and ignored their feedback. Garrett's comment about his holding on to a fantasy relationship helped her to see how she had grown. She realized now that she could not trust her boyfriend because of his behavior, not because of some defect in herself. Moira concluded that he probably was not going to change and that "basically, I need to get on with my life."

Practice Illustrations: The Group Social Action Approach in Prevention and Rehab Programs

Overview of Appropriate Mezzo-Macro Strategies

A number of strategies are useful in achieving reforms to enhance the effectiveness of rehab and prevention programs: political and policy reforms, systems changes, political action, community capacity building and development, and therefore clients' collective empowerment. The goal is not only to address and resolve the identified barriers to recovery and prevention but also to help group members develop appropriate political action skills that can be generalized to other needs. The use of power analyses and environmental impact strategies, which are included in table 9.1, are particularly useful in the variety of special issues groups provided for substance abuse problems.

A Rehab Program: An Organizational and Case Example

Background on the Rehab Program.   In one perinatal program for addicted women and their children, many clients' children had been placed in the custody of protective services because of neglect and abuse. Many of these clients had ongoing complaints about seemingly arbitrary child welfare decisions and policies that hindered rather than facilitated their recovery and regaining custody of their children. These complaints often were aired during their women's issues group, where the members attempted to provide each other with feedback and support about their common struggles.

A Client's View of the Service System Barriers and Related Consequences. The plight of Jane, a thirty-one-year-old African American, mobilized the group beyond providing support to taking political action. Jane cried during one group session while relating her latest experience in being caught between child protective services and other systems. Her two children had been placed in a foster home two counties away from the urban community where she lived, requiring a three-hour trip on three different buses each way to visit them. Jane had arrived too late to see her children in her last attempt at visitation, because the last bus was delayed due to a flat tire. The foster mother had been encouraged by the foster care worker to turn Jane away if she came after the agreed-upon time for her visits. She explained that Jane needed to be more responsible about being on time. Missing her visitation meant that Jane would not see her children for another month.

In addition, Jane had been told by the foster care worker that she must secure safe and sober housing away from currently addicted family members before she could have her children visit her at home or regain custody of them. When she tried to explain that she could not get on a waiting list for Section Eight housing until she regained custody of her children, the worker told Jane she was being manipulative and resistive, and did not help Jane identify other sources of drug-free housing or negotiate the possible policy conflicts between protective services and housing systems.

Environmental Impact and Empowerment Strategies

Collective Power Analysis and Conscious Raising. The women's issues group was facilitated by Bob and Alise, two of the program's counselors. With their support, the members did a power analysis of their common experiences with the child welfare protective services system (see table 9.1). This involved identifying who benefited, who lost, and how from the way visitation and other policies were being implemented. For example, it became clear to the members that they and their children lost due to current practices, because they could not possibly meet the unclear, conflicting expectations of the system.

In some situations such as Jane's, power inconsistencies existed due to environmental barriers to the system's policy. The placement of her children in a distant community and the rigidity of protective services staff about the time for visits made it difficult for Jane to accomplish the visits and the system's goal of family reunification. (See chapter 2 for a more detailed discussion about power inconsistencies and inequities.) However, those practices and policies did allow the system to stay in control of placement situations, requiring them to be accountable only to child protective services and the court, not to these clients as parents or to the community.

Group members identified how their unresolved authority issues and realistic fears about the system's retaliation prevented them from individually addressing their situations. In essence, their previous interactions with large systems and people in authority had left them so immobilized and vulnerable that they were afraid to take action, leading to chronic powerlessness or power impairments (Pinderhughes 1988) and problem fatigue (Chestang 1976). Moreover, they agreed with the labels that protective services had used for them at the time of the placements: they were ineffective and unfit mothers. This collective power analysis helped the members to see that power impairment and problem fatigue, along with cognitive distortions caused by drug abuse (Van Wormer 1987), had robbed them of their motivation for and belief in positive change. Now, however, they could identify their strengths and their right to request additional support for improving their parenting skills and regaining custody of their children.

Political Action Planning and Implementation Strategies.   As a result of the consciousness raising achieved through their collective power analysis, the group decided on a plan of collective action. Again with the two facilitators' support and consultation, the members wrote a letter to the director of child protective services requesting a meeting with an administrator to discuss their concerns. They asked that the meeting be held in the rehab program as a convenience to them (and because meeting there could also be a psychological advantage for them). The group prepared a list of questions to ask so that important concerns would not be overlooked and the meeting would be organized and focused. They rehearsed how to ask their questions and anticipated how to address the administrator's reactions to them. Many of these questions focused on structural and procedural problems within the department as well as the conflicts illustrated by situations such as Jane's. The members clarified their goals with each other: first, to be heard and second, to influence policy changes by proposing alternative ways to carry out the department's problematic functions while also meeting the mothers' needs.

The initial meeting, held with an assistant director of the child welfare system, led to a series of later meetings to address some of the identified issues over an extended period of time. The two group facilitators sat in on the beginning of the first meeting to help get it started, and also periodically sat in on the other meetings as needed. They provided information from time to time about how the members could educate themselves about various laws and policies from which the child protective system derived its authority. This continuous negotiation and education process between the members and the administrator led to a number of systems changes and policy reforms that were more supportive of the group members' recovery and custody issues.

Evaluating Systems Change Outcomes

Improving the Child Welfare System's Accessibility and Consistency. One policy change involved assigning a protective services worker to spend one day a week in the rehab program to coordinate services provided there and with other nearby community agencies. This policy and systems change was a further step toward the program's development of the type of integrated services model discussed in chapters 3 and 5. Other on-site community services were being provided in the rehab program, which was moving from a parallel service arrangement toward that more integrated services model.

Another policy reform required that when possible, in cases such as Jane's, future foster care placements would be made in the same county in which the mother resided. The child protective services worker and the rehab program's case managers were expected to help Jane and other clients to coordinate transportation and other resources necessary for successful visitation. A third policy change involved pre-court meetings, which previously had been held only in the main, child protective services office. Those meetings now would be held at the rehab program when they involved clients. These new and reformed policies increased group members' self-confidence and empowerment opportunities. Periodic meetings between the rehab program and child protective services administrators helped in monitoring the effective long-term implementation of these systems change outcomes.

Monitoring Changes in the Rehab Program's System.   This political action process addressed immediate and long-term system changes necessary for removing environmental barriers to current and future group members' recovery. The members developed political action knowledge and skills as a group that they could generalize to other areas. Program outcomes related to their individual skill development were monitored informally through ongoing reviews and analyses of their journals, as well as periodic focus groups. Those groups documented the members' conclusions that this political action activity provided strong organizational supports for their recovery, efforts to regain custody of their children, and self- and group esteem.

These clients' use of their women's issues group as a political action tool was consistent with what Imbrogno (1987) describes as a policy transformation group, which can influence internal and external environmental barriers. The external service delivery system changed in terms of policy reforms in child protective services. The group facilitators' support of the members' political action activities underscores the rehab program's development as an empowered organization. In such organizations, staff and administrators respond positively to clients' efforts to change the internal structure to enhance client empowerment (Florin and Wandersman 1990).

A Prevention Program: An Organizational Example

Background Information and Program Development/Funding.   Youths Establishing Solidarity (YES) developed out of a neighborhood coalition in one midwestern metropolitan area. The community involved was primarily low income and multicultural, including Asian, African, and Latino Americans as well as white residents. The coalition was designed to address a rash of teenage deaths from drug overdoses and gang warfare over an eighteen-month period. As the coalition began to plan and explore strategies for preventing such deaths, it found that the problems were more entrenched and long-term than anticipated. The coalition eventually worked with several community-building consultants, who helped them write a federal community partnership grant proposal focused on substance abuse prevention. During the period of this first grant, coalition members realized that many of the community's problems, including substance abuse, youth violence, teenage pregnancy, school dropouts, unemployment, family disruptions, and crime, were closely interrelated.

YES hired staff members and consultants to implement its program and to begin the process of applying for continuation funding from various sources. For its second cycle, the program was able to obtain funding eventually from two federal agencies, county and state agencies, and a private foundation. This gradually more diversified funding base, as well as the program's scope, allowed it to provide much more comprehensive, community-based, and systems change–oriented services. YES developed a broad continuum of intervention-prevention services for youths and families focused on the following areas:

1. leadership development: training/technical assistance for informal community leaders and prevention and treatment service providers in the following skill areas: grant writing, program development, outcome-based evaluation, dissemination, and advocacy or systems change approaches
2. community building: mobilizing natural leaders in the community, such as business leaders and merchants, the faith community and churches, presidents of neighborhood associations, and law enforcement, to participate in community development and substance abuse prevention efforts (community policing)
3. youth initiative: focus on youth mentorships for developing entrepreneurial skills and microenterprises, peer mediation in community conflicts, motivation and achievement in education, services learning projects, and job training and employment as alternatives to youth violence, substance abuse, and truancy; to include youths thirteen to eighteen years old, young pregnant and single mothers, and nineteen- to twenty-nine-year-old African American and Latino males
4. five-point intervention: placing crisis managers and intervention specialists at five points through which youths and families enter the community care system—hospital emergency rooms, drug court, family court, schools, and law enforcement—involving a centralized referral system, a tracking system, and systematic follow-up
5. alcohol and drug public policy: focus on reducing underage liquor sales and the number of liquor licenses granted through public education and advocacy for policy reform; because alcohol and tobacco remain entry drugs for youth, this offers YES the greatest

opportunity for primary prevention compared to the other components.

Education, Community Mobilization, and Political Action Strategies.
In regard to each of the above five components, YES planned and implemented a number of creative, stakeholder-involved strategies, consistent with its community capacity-building mission. For example, staff members in the alcohol and drug public policy component collaborated with members of two neighborhood associations on reducing/preventing underage access to and consumption of alcohol. The staff identified the two associations as key stakeholders within the target community and for that reason involved them in achieving and institutionalizing various systems changes. They began the collaborative process by inviting the association members to a meeting in which they identified common concerns and then brainstormed tasks to be undertaken as part of a political action plan. The common interests and brainstorming were instrumental in the consciousness-raising process and in identifying critical gaps in their knowledge about city ordinances that influence alcohol accessibility.

Therefore, for several sessions YES members and association members organized themselves into an education group, utilizing guest speakers and consultants as sources of important information. For example, one speaker, the director of the city Office of Liquor Control, discussed requirements for liquor licenses, laws related to underage sells and how selling alcohol to minors is monitored, and how such sells are related to other crimes. Other speakers and consultants included members of the police department, the city council, a youth gang mediator, and several community activists. Another goal was to influence these leaders and policy makers to reduce the proliferation of liquor licenses in the community and the lax enforcement of existing ordinances.

As this educational process unfolded, the members also developed a task group for planning and implementing some of the tasks they had identified. One was mobilizing community residents to attend a meeting with several liquor store owners in the community. This core group of four merchants had been identified as possibly more responsive to community needs than others. The goal was to enlist their help in planning how to influence other retailers to stop selling alcohol to minors. That meeting was a critical turning point because the members of this community residents'/merchants' task group decided to ask all liquor store owners in the community to sign a covenant, a personal pledge to uphold existing liquor ordinances and to proactively cooperate with local law enforcement and residents in helping to monitor and prosecute violators of those ordinances. The task group decided that a merchant and a resident from the task group would be assigned to meet with each retailer. These dyads were to present the group's concerns and some factual data about the negative effects of identified problems on the community and on their businesses, and then request that the retailer sign the covenant. The members of each dyad practiced by role playing their scheduled meetings with the retailers. The primary goal of the covenant was to reduce the demand for the sale of alcohol in the community by 20 percent within three years. A secondary goal was to decrease alcohol- and drug-related crimes, such as assaults and robberies, which occurred around or near the retail liquor stores.

Evaluation of Public Policy Reform Outcomes.   The education group's meetings with the director of the Office of Liquor Control and the city council had a positive outcome: members' increased knowledge and sense of group efficacy about their community mobilization and political action skills. Informally, members reported the results of their meetings with retail merchants, which were also documented formally by the number of merchants who signed the covenant (sixteen out of a possible twenty). The main systems change goal was met: to influence these decision makers. The city council and the director of the Liquor Control Office granted a six-month moratorium on new liquor licenses within the community. This allowed time for the education-task group to provide testimony about how other cities were revising their requirements for liquor licenses to address underage sells. The subsequent tightening of the city's requirements was another positive outcome, although it is too early to assess the long-term results of this policy change.

The task group was only partially successful in reaching its two goals. As noted previously, sixteen concerned liquor store owners in the community signed the covenant. The core group of merchants continued to meet periodically with YES staff and community residents in order to monitor the covenant's implementation. They helped in several prosecutions involving underage sells, a major increase in their civic and service roles. The merchants also helped with problem solving associated with some potential violations. The group had not considered how to monitor a reduction in the overall sales of alcohol in the community, and a reduction of 20 percent in sales to all age groups was probably unrealistic as well. They are now grap-pling with setting a more realistic goal and devising practical methods for monitoring it. Another limitation was not involving youths in the covenant tasks until the media event for acknowledging the signatures was held. Input from this group could have helped in setting more realistic goals and moni-toring systems changes, and in facilitating the youths' skill development.

An unanticipated outcome has been a decrease in the number of street sells of drugs, which often took place around liquor stores in the past, as supported by law enforcement data. In one instance, drug dealers moved an upholstered couch onto the sidewalk in front of a liquor store, from which they sold drugs as cars continuously pulled over to the curb twenty-four hours a day. Teams of residents monitoring the implementation of the covenant and continuous arrests by community policing efforts eventually caused the drug dealers to stop selling there. A few days later, someone burned the couch, a powerful symbol of this group of residents reclaiming their com-munity.

Conclusion

Empowered programs such as the one described in the previous example must coordinate with rehab programs, which serve as the conceptual hub for a continuum of group services sponsored by twelve-step programs, churches, community centers, cultural centers, university continuing edu-cation departments, GED programs, university extension services, health promotion organizations, mental health centers, and substance abuse pre-vention and intervention programs. Rehab programs can help ensure that these sponsored groups, consistent with their own group theoretical models, are designed to maximize clients' power and involvement.

Mutual aid and political action models are two examples of approaches that increase clients' power through skill development in a range of basic and special-needs rehab groups. Long-term skill development occurs in such areas as power analysis, stress management, coalition building, use of critical feedback and support, relapse prevention, assertive communication, con-sciousness raising, education, and advocacy (Hawkins, Catalano, Gillmore, and Wells 1989).

These benefits from rehab groups parallel Shorkey's (1994) assumptions about self-help groups: "A positive sense of personal control and self-determination is important for clients participating in self-help groups. . . . The fellowship component [allows clients to] develop and practice a broad range of important life skills" (152). Furthermore, these groups also reduce the shame and guilt associated with addictions as well as relapse while increasing the members' self-worth and sense of personal power (Shorkey 1994; Ellis, McInerney, DiGiuseppe, and Yeager 1988). Prevention groups offer complementary supports by decreasing members' isolation in communities and by connecting them with sources of power that provide alternatives to drugs, including specialized prevention knowledge, positive role models, refusal skills, advocacy, and mutual aid (Hawkins and Catalano 1994).

10 Family-Centered Rehabilitative Services: Intergenerational and Nuclear Family Empowerment and Evaluation Strategies

The constructivist enjoins therapists to abandon the role of expert and to resist the temptations of power and certainty. The family is seen as an expert . . . it is the meaning that members attribute to events that determines their behavior.

—A. Hartman (1995)

Groups are the treatment form of choice for most substance abuse programs, as noted in chapter 9; however, some clients' personal and interpersonal issues can be addressed more effectively in other modalities. Programs often use family strategies to support and build on clients' progress, using what Shorkey (1994) describes as the fellowship component of groups. Family work may be needed to help the members reorganize and stabilize their functions in order to meet the unit's own needs *and* to sustain the substance-abusing member's recovery.

Although "currently there are fewer people residing in family households, particularly in traditional nuclear family households, than there were in the mid-twentieth century" (Johnson and Wahl 1995:936), the family continues to make up each client's most intimate interactional environment. It is present figuratively in every therapeutic encounter because of its ongoing influence on clients' substance abuse and recovery (Hartman and Laird 1983). Drawing upon the family's expertise about the unit and its members can increase individuals' sources of power (Anderson and Goolishian 1992) and help staff to refrain from using the expert model, as Hartman (1995) points out above.

The work in family sessions can be reinforced by activities and strategies used during group sessions, and vice versa. Focusing on a topic in group sessions, for example, may make addressing it in family work easier, thus providing clients with practice opportunities that can lead to self-efficacy. A thirty-year-old gay male (Kevin M.) in a coed rehab facility had been unable to talk about his sexual orientation and its impact on his addiction in either his group or his family sessions. Kevin believed that most of his peers as well as family members would reject him if they knew he was gay. Yet not sharing this information was increasing his shame and guilt about being gay, and therefore hindering his recovery.

After struggling with this issue alone for a while, Kevin shared his concerns in a group counseling session that his primary counselor was facilitating. The counselor responded supportively and encouraged Kevin's peers to give him feedback about the positive risk he had taken in disclosing his sexual orientation. The members also pointed out some of the effects this "secret" might be having on his family relationships and on his addiction. The feedback enabled Kevin to talk about these issues in a subsequent family session, using advice from his peers about how to initiate the discussion.

His parents were shocked but eventually accepted Kevin's sexual orientation in differing degrees; a younger brother and sister acknowledged they had previously suspected Kevin was gay. Kevin said that if his counselor and peers had rejected him, he probably would have dropped out of the program. Moreover, the group's reaction would have provided him with an excuse to avoid discussing his sexual orientation with his family, as well as his concerns about the latter's painful relationships. On the other hand, Kevin felt that his self-disclosure and the support provided by the group, the counselor, and his family had empowered him. Kevin's risk taking improved the degree of openness and trust in both his group and his family sessions thereafter.

This chapter describes the use of family-centered empowerment strategies for the type of supportive process Kevin experienced, including methods for integrating user-friendly formal and informal evaluation procedures. The chapter concludes with a summary of theoretical approaches related to these family strategies, along with an analysis of the impact of these approaches on empowerment practice.

An Overview of Family Practice Issues and Parameters

Empowerment practice with families with substance abuse problems is based on the assumption that "each family is unique in the challenging array of needs and resources it has available for responding to problems of daily living and for giving meaning to the lives of its members" (Freeman 1993:1). Yet such practice also must address common power inequities and sabotages in families that can reinforce the members' problems and impede their recovery. As can be seen in table 9.1, a number of strategies can be used in rehab services to address both common and unique issues relevant to the interpersonal context of family life. Attention to that context clarifies who should be included in the services and what goals, approaches, and specific strategies will be effective in facilitating family healing and lifelong recovery within the unit.

Who Should Be Included in Family Sessions?

An empowerment approach defines families in terms of the unique forms, structures, and roles that clients are actually immersed in or are attempting to renegotiate, rather than in terms of an ideal unit. Clients should be supported in defining their families for themselves and then in using creative outreach strategies to actively involve the identified members in a variety of family sessions. The members' involvement is important because they can learn how to analyze the effects of their interactions and relationships on the substance abuse and recovery process, and the interaction of those effects with other systemic factors. They have opportunities to develop other skills associated with competence and empowerment, such as decision making and collective action, and to learn how to use practical tools to monitor and evaluate their skill development (see table 9.1).

Welcoming a diversity of families to use a program's services can lead to more collaboration and creativity with clients and their families in defining problems and arriving at solutions. Such diversity may include multiply addicted family systems, ethnic minorities, white ethnic groups, same-sex or gay and lesbian families, single parents, extended and multigenerational families, the poor, recent immigrants, families with members with disabilities, the homeless, and nonblood related families.

General Goals for Family Sessions

The common issues experienced by diverse families imply that the service process should include certain common goals that can be integrated with the specific goals developed to address each family's unique problems. Such goals are applicable whether a family is being seen alone, with other families in groups, in seminars, or in other educational formats involving individuals and families. Services to families are expected to (Flanzer and Delany 1992; Shorkey and Rosen 1993):

1. encourage the family to identify its strengths (e.g., identify solutions that have worked in the past)
2. eliminate ineffective problem-solving behaviors by the unit that are enabling the substance-abusing member
3. develop more autonomous and interdependent functions as a unit and as individual members without the use of substances or enabling behaviors.

A Family-Centered Empowerment Approach

A combination of family services is needed to produce outcomes consistent with the above goals and an empowerment perspective. In traditional programs, services to families have been viewed as adjuncts to the primary client's treatment. The term "client-centered" has sometimes been used to define this emphasis on the primary client. But with an empowerment approach, family services are both an adjunct to the substance-abusing member's services and a primary modality for meeting the unit's needs (Freeman 1993). In this context, client-centered services emphasize both the referred client's needs and the family's needs. A perspective on the client's entire system and the members' active involvement are essential components of client-centered empowerment services. This definition is similar to current definitions of family-centered practice in mental health (Ferris and Marshall 1987), in child welfare (Gibson 1993; Lazar, Sagi, and Fraser 1991; Stehno 1986), and in the profession of social work in general (Hartman and Laird 1983).

Types of Family-Centered Services

When families take the active role implied in the above description of family-centered services, the unit's strengths and special needs can be identified and addressed more effectively. Three main categories of services are included, involving a combination of empowerment-oriented approaches that may be used alone, sequentially, or simultaneously according to a family's resources and needs (Freeman 1993; Heath and Stanton 1991; O'Farrell 1989; Zelvin 1993).

Family Counseling Sessions.   Sessions with individual families and multiple family groups are used to help families address the effects of the recovering members' substance abuse and to understand the interaction of system issues with client and environmental factors that influence the abuse and can affect recovery (Type A: An Adjunct Service to the Referred Client's Services).

Family Interventions.   Prior to addicted members' entry into rehab, family members and other support networks are coached to confront clients (in a solution-focused format) about the severity of their substance abuse problems and the consequences for the entire unit. Or they may confront clients about barriers to recovery and relapses during and after rehab, e.g., in the aftercare or lifelong recovery phases (Type B: Both a Primary Service of Families and an Adjunct to the Referred Client's Services) (see chapter 6 regarding effective family and social network interventions).

Family Education and Support for the Unit's Needs.   The members receive education about normal family development and related issues; help in coping with everyday stresses and problems in a adaptive manner; and mutual support for managing normal transitions, family issues, and environmental barriers to the unit's development aside from issues related to the substance abuse (Type C: A Primary Service to Families).

The Intergenerational Family Service and Evaluation Process

Intergenerational Families' and Large Systems' Power Dynamics

The three categories of services described above can be implemented by empowerment programs, using many of the strategies identified in table 8.1 in chapter 8 to address intergenerational issues. Just as power analyses of political conditions are necessary prior to collective social action by group members, they are important in family sessions. With intergenerational families, however, power analyses and evaluation of the work should focus on barriers and supports to empowerment in both the immediate and extended family network, and on external large systems or social justice issues that affect the family . Analysis of power dynamics includes, therefore, not only family members' personal and interpersonal resources for addressing internal issues but also examples of family resiliency in overcoming external barriers.

Intergenerational Family Practice and Effective Strategies

Case Example: Family Background.   In one outpatient rehab program, a thirty-five-year-old Latino woman (the client), her mother, her husband, and their fifteen- and sixteen-year-old daughters were involved in a multiple family counseling group. The entire intergenerational unit was asked to participate in family sessions because they lived in the same household and a number of family, gender, and cultural factors were affecting the client's recovery. The client, Consuela R., confronted her mother in one family session about knowing but remaining silent about her father's sexual abuse of Consuela as a child. The interaction escalated, with the mother crying and defending herself and Consuela angrily rejecting each effort to explain her behavior in the situation.

The mother tried to explain that her ex-husband had taken a traditionally dominant and "macho" role in the family, and that within the Latino culture, wives often are expected not to question their husbands' behavior. But she denied that she knew about the abuse before Consuela told her about it, at which time she tried to get advice from her priest. The priest suggested that she pray about the situation and that her prayers would provide guidance. While the mother was trying to decide what to do, her older sister heard Consuela telling a cousin about the abuse. The sister then persuaded Consuela's mother to report the abuse to the police.

Family Reenactment and Power Analysis Strategies.   The family counselor asked Consuela and her mother to reenact typical interactions involving the following dyads: mother-daughter, daughter-father, and mother-father. She explained that family reenactments are a practical strategy for uncovering sources of disempowerment and cognitive distortions as well as sources of family resiliency (Hartman 1995; Shorkey 1994) (see table 10.1). Family members were then asked to do a power analysis of each dyad, with

TABLE 10.1 Practice Approaches: Barriers and Supports to Empowerment Practice

	Cognitive-Behavioral Theory	Family Systems Theory	Community Development Theory
Supports	based on constructivist philosophy, which emphasizes tacit knowledge and people's constructed reality as sources of power	emphasis on detriangulation helps family members to identify sources of personal, interpersonal, and political power	focus on the structural roots of personal problems provides a strong rationale for collective consciousness raising and political action related to empowerment
	reduction of personalization and absolutist thinking is consistent with substance abuse recovery goals	family projective process explains how family fears and secrets enable substance abuse and codependency behaviors	roles related to this theory require efforts to shift power from external sources to local constituencies and to increase substance abuse prevention skills and other capacity-building outcomes
Barriers	focus on clients' negative attributions may encourage self-blaming and labeling	family scapegoating and labeling may encourage practitioners to take sides in the unit's power conflicts and sabotages, and perpetuate oppression	the emphasis on decreasing the availability of drugs may cause communities to ignore other systems change or policy reform approaches

	assumes interaction of person and environmental factors but focuses on personal and interpersonal change/empowerment *only*	an overemphasis on stabilizing family relationships may prevent the healthy cutoffs needed by some clients in early recovery from addicted family systems	community-based rather than community-centered approaches may support professionals as *the* experts and decrease consumer and community involvement
Strategies	cognitive restructuring	going with resistance, e.g., "go slow"	education and consciousness raising
	relaxation	reframing	community mobilization
	guided imagery	reenactments and sculpting	policy transformation groups
	social skills training	power analysis of family triangles	coalition building
	thought stopping	homework tasks	leadership development
	modeling and rehearsal	interactive communication exercises	power analysis/investigatory research
	stress inoculation training	role rehearsal, role reversal	needs assesments/assets mapping
			community planning
			political advocacy/action

input from Consuela and her mother about issues that they used to transform the dyads into triangles. Here, the members drew upon information from a family education and support group provided by the program (Type C: A Primary Service to Families), in which they learned about family triangles and power games. Essentially, "a system threatened by intimacy or other stressful feelings can stabilize itself . . . by triangulating an issue such as an addiction, financial worries, or sexuality" (Freeman 1993:4), an inappropriate use of power within the family. The power analysis involved the group members' assessment of who won and lost power in each triangle (including the unit itself) and how.

For example, based on similar family experiences, they noted that in the father-daughter-sexual abuse triangle, Consuela suffered a number of losses—of power over her body, identity, childhood, and feelings through her father's power sabotage (see chapter 2 for a detailed discussion about interpersonal power sabotages). Consuela remembered her father used the cultural value of "respecto" (McRoy, Shorkey, and Garcia 1985) to remind her that she must remain silent about the family secret, otherwise she would be disrespecting his authority. To Consuela's surprise, the counselor and family session members felt that in the mother-daughter-family secret triangle (the sexual abuse), Consuela repeated the same power sabotage process with her mother that had disempowered her in interactions with her father. The counselor pointed out that when Consuela first learned about and used power sabotages through the father's negative modeling, she was not able to decide consciously whether to generalize that behavior to other relationships. Now, however, she could make a choice about whether or not to continue this power sabotage with her mother.

By repeatedly accusing her mother of causing the abuse because she failed to stop it, Consuela's game of "got ya" (Papp 1989) had become a maladaptive but satisfying source of power for her (Selvini-Palazzoli, Cirillo, Selvini, and Sorrentino 1989). During each replay of the game or retelling of the incest story, Consuela both won and lost power because she succeeded in making her mother feel guilty but prevented resolution of their conflicts by maintaining her anger about her mother's failure to protect her. Unfortunately, this unresolved anger and shame about the abuse made her more vulnerable to relapse (Carroll, Rounsaville, and Garwin 1991; Smyth 1995).

Members of the family session then helped Consuela to process ways she could begin to work through her sexual abuse and disempowerment experiences so that she could let go of them. The members had learned that this includes processing what happened rather than pushing it away and address-ing how the experience affects the client's current trust issues with family members and peers. The internalized self-blame that is often masked by the client's anger toward others has to be expressed and resolved as well (Kungman 1989; Pilat and Boomhower-Kresser 1992).

Role Reversal/Role Rehearsal Strategies. The working through process in this case included, for example, the counselor having Consuela and her mother reverse roles and talk about different aspects of the abuse and their relationship while in those roles. This role reversal exercise (see table 10.1) helped each to understand, for the first time, what the experience had been like for the other. As a result, Consuela and her mother were able to develop a sense of empathy for each other as victimized but resilient, and therefore increasingly competent, Latino females. Role rehearsal exercises helped them practice how to keep from replaying their previous power sabotage game, now that they understood its process and consequences for the family unit and for Consuela's recovery.

A variation of this role reversal strategy is to have clients enact roles they may have assumed during a previous stage of development. When Consuela continued to make excuses for her father's role in her abuse, the counselor used this second type of reversal strategy by having Consuela compare a picture of herself as a young child to a current picture of herself. While looking at the childhood photo, Consuela was asked to describe her power and abilities at that time (what she could and could not do), compared to the adult Consuela in the other picture. Next, the counselor asked Consuela to compare a picture of her father to her childhood picture and, while assuming the role of her father and then of herself as a child, to talk about obvious differences in their physical and mental abilities and in their degrees of power. Through this form of role reversal, Consuela was able to see how powerless she had been as a child to physically stop her father from abusing her. She began to understand, finally, that she had experienced a loss of trust in her father and that when she was unable to confront this powerful figure because of his cultural status and role, she blamed herself and her mother instead (Pilat and Boomhower-Kresser 1992).

Personal Growth Contracts and Communication/Solution-Focused Strategies. Consuela's beginning understanding of these cultural and gen-der dynamics in her family made her listen more closely to her husband's concerns about how the mother-daughter power game affected his relationship with her. He withdrew whenever his mother-in-law and wife engaged in it, thus eliminating opportunities for him to be close to and understand Consuela. The husband also withdrew because he became overwhelmed by the hopelessness of the situation and thus felt disempowered himself.

In later single-family counseling sessions, the personal growth contract identified in table 9.1 was used to help the unit address this and other family issues. These contracts require two or more members of a family or social network who are affecting each other's or one member's recovery to plan how they will change their reciprocal, maladaptive behaviors. Such contracts are designed not only to change a system's negative interactional patterns but also to reinforce the positive, interdependent nature of the members' relationships within the system (Freeman 1994; Granvold 1994).

Personal growth contracts help clients to empower themselves by enhancing their self-direction, decision making, and autonomy while discouraging boundary infringements and power sabotages. In this case, the contracts focused on strategies that Consuela, her mother, and her husband could use to reinforce each other's positive changes and to disengage from negative interactions. The contracts addressed the personal growth goals each of them developed as desired outcomes from their sessions. For instance, Consuela's mother wanted to "stand up to Consuela" without being defensive or blaming herself for the sexual abuse. Family counseling sessions helped the mother identify "I" statements or assertive communication skills she could use in different combinations if Consuela continued to confront her about the abuse in a negative manner (see table 9.1), such as:

> "I know you're still hurt and angry about the abuse. Although it's hard to do, I hope you can work through your pain and anger toward me."
> "I wish I'd been stronger with your father and more aware of what was happening at the time. I'm sorry I didn't give you the help and support you needed then."
> "I feel very bad that you were abused by your father. I can't undo the past, but I am here to support you now."

As a goal for her contract, Consuela decided she wanted to make her own decisions about recovery without constantly arguing against her mother's advice and her fears that Consuela might relapse. She decided to use some solution-focused statements suggested by the counselor (Tohn and Oshlag 1995) whenever her mother gave unsolicited advice:

> "I know you're concerned that I might relapse, but I'm the only one who can work on my recovery. You can help by telling me why you believe doing _____ might be helpful. I'll think about what you've suggested and then I have to decide for myself what to do." (Solution-focused message: Do something different.)
>
> "It helps when you give me feedback on some of the things I'm doing to improve my recovery. In spite of the temptation to tell me what to do, you've been strong enough to resist. That's great! (Solution-focused message: If it works, keep doing it.)
>
> "There must be times when I'm doing good things to improve my recovery, when you're not so scared about my relapsing. What's going on at those times?" (Solution-focused message: Search for exceptions when the problem doesn't occur.)

The Evaluation Process, Strategies, and Methods

Monitoring Growth at Different Empowerment Levels. Personal growth contracts also can be used to evaluate the sequence and patterns of changes in clients' and intergenerational family members' interpersonal relationships. For example, the contracts helped the social worker to monitor the reciprocal progress made by Consuela and her mother in decreasing their power games and increasing their related use of assertive and solution-focused strategies. For effective evaluation, such contracts should be reviewed every few sessions to identify and write down examples of family members' progress in reaching goals that might lead to their personal, interpersonal, and political empowerment.

Noting when family members identify new positive sources of power is another important strategy for evaluating outcomes. Sometimes, even though the focus of family services and evaluation is on personal or interpersonal power, the outcomes may have implications for political power. Hagen and Davis (1995) indicate that in circumstances involving gender, racial-ethnic, religious, or other forms of oppression, the personal *is* political. Other authors have emphasized this as well, but especially in terms of family therapy's responsibility to address gender and power inequity issues (Goldner

1985; Hare-Mustin 1987; Elbow 1985; Walters, Carter, Papp, and Silverstein 1988).

An example of this type of personal-political situation was evident when using their personal growth contracts to evaluate changes in Consuela's family. In one individual family session, based on a power analysis, Consuela's mother discussed the outcomes from discovering how the Catholic Church (and her priest in particular) had reinforced her gender and cultural socialization as a helpless, victimized female. The priest had reinforced her inability to decide what to do about her husband's sexual abuse of Consuela. Evaluation of her progress in learning to respond assertively to Consuela's confrontations helped her to see that no matter how good his intentions, the priest blocked her use of personal decision-making power, similar to the power sabotage game played by Consuela. He reinforced her denial of the problem and her responsibility to act by implying that prayer alone might solve it and that therefore, nothing else might be required of her.

In evaluating her progress on the personal growth contract, Consuela's mother noted that she had developed skills in analyzing authority relationships that made her feel more powerful and strong as a woman. She felt her sense of power would prevent her from being intimidated in future interactions with her ex-husband, who still attended some of the same family gatherings, cultural celebrations, and church functions that she did. Moreover, she no longer felt as dependent and powerless in her interactions with priests and other authority figures.

Monitoring In-Session Interactions and Changes.   Informal in-session observations are useful as well for evaluating the effects of family interventions on intergenerational relationships. In the case of Consuela's family, the counselor's informal observations were extremely useful for evaluating family changes and goal achievement over time. An example of unanticipated changes included how Consuela and her mother began to use humor, which lessened the intensity of their interactions but not the seriousness of their concerns. An anticipated outcome observed by the counselor in session was a decrease in Consuela's and her mother's negative interactions and power sabotages. There was an increase in Consuela's positive reactions to her mother's assertive "I" statements (listening rather than interrupting) and in the mother's positive responses to Consuela's solution-focused statements (complimenting her on her efforts toward recovery rather than pointing out what she was doing wrong).

Monitoring Emerging Issues and Parallel Changes in the Nuclear Family. Informal out-of-session observations helped the social worker evaluate the impact of the intergenerational family strategies on the nuclear family's functioning (in addition to providing feedback on the intergenerational family's progress). Often, such out-of-session observations can clarify how to generalize the unit's gains to other nuclear family issues or concerns that surface over time (Hartman 1995). Consuela's husband's contract included his role in helping to monitor changes in the members' interactions outside the family sessions. He was able to write down and share his direct observations of his wife's and mother-in-law's weekly progress in disengaging from their interpersonal power sabotage games, and to give them positive and constructive feedback, with the counselor's support and coaching.

His observer role was suggested by the counselor to validate his assumption that the problem was a boundary issue between mother and daughter and a barrier to Consuela's recovery. Evaluating decreases in the previously unresolved intergenerational conflict made it clear that other issues within the nuclear family were affecting Consuela's recovery and the unit's overall functioning. For example, the couple had a sexual dysfunction problem. Their periodic financial crises and conflicts about the wife's addiction helped them to avoid confronting intimacy issues in their relationship and the younger daughter's behavioral and academic problems at school.

These problems, which started to surface as Consuela began her recovery and her resolution of conflicts with her mother, were addressed in later sessions with the couple alone and in sessions with the daughters focused on the school issues. Several intergenerational family meetings were held also, during which Consuela's mother helped to coach the couple in parenting skills, taking a role sanctioned in many traditional Hispanic families. This family network coaching strategy would not have been effective prior to the counselor's intergenerational boundary and communication work with Consuela and her mother.

Nuclear Family and Large Systems Change Strategies

Nuclear Family Services and Process

Overview. Concerns related to relapse often mask other, underlying or current nuclear family issues that need to be addressed, as was evident in the case of Consuela from the previous section. These underlying issues often surface during sessions where supports and barriers to relapse prevention are being analyzed. The identified barriers may involve current family issues as well as issues related to other large systems such as the school, the legal system, work settings, or the mental health system. As shown in table 9.1, developing a relapse prevention plan refocuses family interaction more productively and can facilitate clients' and family members' empowerment. Using such a plan is often effective because it maps and objectifies the family system and the external environment similar to genograms and ecomaps (Hartman and Laird 1983; Freeman 1994), as can be seen in the following case situation.

Case Example: Family Background.   Clients in one residential program for youths are required to develop a relapse prevention plan in the final phase of their yearlong rehab period. Barry M., seventeen years old, was referred to the program by the court due to his alcohol problems, inhalant use (white out and gasoline), and marijuana abuse, and his alleged rape of an adolescent girl. He began work on his relapse prevention plan approximately two months prior to his release. How to Cope and single family therapy sessions indicated that family members were still having difficulty acknowledging Barry's problems, especially the rape charge. Barry was viewed as the perfect older child in a family of three sons because he was outwardly polite and considerate and because he excelled academically as well as athletically. His white, middle-income family was well respected in their small, rural, and somewhat closed community.

The Relapse Prevention Plan Strategy

Issues Related to Developing the Plan.   In developing his relapse prevention plan (see table 9.1), two of the issues Barry identified as placing him at risk for relapse were his family's (especially his mother's) view of him as the perfect son and his related feelings of guilt at not meeting their expectations, and not knowing how much to tell people about being in drug rehab and recovery after his release. Barry did not think he could get the support he needed from his family to keep from relapsing, since he could not be open with them about his "imperfections." In addition, he believed their demands for him to be perfect could make his situation more stressful, possibly encouraging him to be dishonest and preventing him from using the relapse prevention skills he had learned in rehab.

Another source of stress was an upcoming meeting with the principal of the school to which Barry wanted to transfer, scheduled in two weeks. Barry's parents wanted the school transfer so no one would know he had been in drug rehab and he could get a new start. Barry had been learning in family and group sessions that he should be open about his drug use and recovery in appropriate situations, especially where failure to reveal this information could cause problems later. His primary counselor asked him to present a draft of his relapse prevention plan in a family session and in his peer counseling group for feedback. This was in order to utilize the strengths of the two modalities in combination. The family counseling sessions were an adjunct to services for Barry (Type A), while the peer group was a primary service for the youths' mutual aid and collective empowerment.

Up to that point, the family's role as expert (Hartman 1995) and as a repository of subjugated knowledge about the possibilities of change (White 1989) had been undermined by their myth of Barry as the family hero. That myth limited their considering alternative interpretations of the family identity and process and alternative problem-solving resources (Hartman 1995). Similarly, the peer counseling group had not had many opportunities to challenge the façade Barry used to reflect "the perfect peer" who helped others unselfishly but solved his own problems alone (the hero or lone ranger theme).

The Plan's Format and Problem-Solving Process.   The relapse prevention plan was useful in this instance because its content and format could be used to facilitate the problem-solving process. Such a plan can be formulated as a time line, outline, contract, or flow chart (cognitive map). It typically includes a summary of the following areas, although as noted previously, formats vary across programs:

1. *issues* that the client needs to address in the immediate future during the transition from rehab to aftercare and the *triggers* for those issues (e.g., family conflicts about a codependent relationship between Barry and his girlfriend that could trigger his feelings of shame and guilt, along with anger about his parents trying to control him)

2. *situations* in which those issues might be a problem and how they might manifest themselves (e.g., Barry and his girlfriend had agreed to his parents' request to abstain from sexual involvement while he was in rehab and aftercare. Conflicts might develop with his parents about the amount of time the two of them spent together after he completes rehab and whether they kept their abstinence agreement)

3. *methods, tools, and strategies* for addressing those issues and triggers, including structured activities, journaling, relapse-feelings cycle exercise, reading the Big Book, and communication exercises around risk taking (e.g., Barry would develop a daily plan to help organize his free time involving items from a list of productive activities that he developed, including spending time with his girlfriend. His sponsor would view those plans weekly and help Barry monitor how they were being implemented to enhance recovery)

4. *key people who can support the plan* along with when and how they will be involved in coaching and other supportive roles (e.g., Barry's sponsor could help monitor his daily plans, and an extended family member might help mediate conflicts between Barry and his parents as needed)

5. *key people who might hinder or block the plan* and how to prevent those effects (e.g., Barry needed to identify family members and specific peers who viewed him as perfect—as their hero. Their myths could cause Barry to hide his mistakes and to feel guilty and ashamed about failing to meet expectations, possibly triggering increased stress and a relapse. Preventing those effects would involve Barry deconstructing their myths by clarifying who benefited from them and how and who experienced negative consequences from them and how. The feelings from those consequences, anger or a false sense of power, were to be addressed through tools such as the relapse-feelings cycle exercise)

6. *back-up emergency strategies and resource people* as alternatives when and if first line strategies do not work (e.g., Barry would leave an unanticipated risky situation based on a predetermined cue such as the presence of a risky peer or someone else using substances. Other back-up strategies would include Barry calling a sober peer, the primary counselor, his sponsor, or an adult role model from his church).

Presenting the Relapse Prevention Plan.   The family therapy session included Barry presenting his relapse prevention plan. The members were asked to give him feedback about the areas they agreed with and to make suggestions about other issues that needed to be included. When his mother disagreed that the family viewed him as the family hero, Barry confronted them with examples that he believed proved his conclusion. He pointed out that after more than a year his parents were unable to acknowledge directly that he was a substance abuser ("He only experimented with alcohol and marijuana, and white out is not a drug!") and a rapist ("He had trouble with that girl in the car."). Barry's father said he thought they had progressed in accepting Barry's mistakes but agreed that they still had work to do in that area. He wondered if the present struggles to accept Barry's "wart" could help them be more realistic about their younger sons' limitations.

Combining Cognitive-Behavioral and Family Systems Strategies

Identifying Systemic Cognitive Distortions and Their Effects.   In the family session, Barry explained his relapse-feelings cycle, which he had learned about during his alcohol and drug education group. That process of self-discovery helped him to identify the "undesirable" feelings that led to many of his self-defeating behaviors and his beliefs about the connections between his feelings and his substance abuse. Granvold (1994) indicates that cognitive restructuring (see table 10.1 under Cognitive-Behavioral Strategies) is useful for addressing cognitive distortions or beliefs that lead to undesirable emotions and behavioral consequences by exposing the underlying distortions and modifying the beliefs so they are more consistent with adaptive coping and problem-solving goals.

By learning to follow and observe his relapse-feelings cycle in the drug education group, Barry became exposed to and aware of one of his cycles (or triggers), which involved shame and guilt about not meeting others' expectations. In the past, the stress from these undesirable feelings had led to substance abuse, which he used to self-medicate his feelings and to control other individuals inappropriately (or to disempower them). Barry's cognitive distortions and beliefs included: "The only way to meet my parents' expectations is to be perfect; I must meet their expectations at any cost, if they or others discover I'm not perfect they will reject me; alcohol and marijuana make me feel more perfect and powerful, therefore, they're the only things that'll make me feel okay; if I'm not perfect it means something is wrong with me." Next, Barry had to identify the impact of these distortions on his addiction and recovery.

Family therapy helped Barry's family members to discover and address their parallel cognitive distortions through strategies such as family reenactments, interactive communication exercises, relaxation, and guided imagery, which are included in table 10.1 under Cognitive Behavioral and Family Systems strategies. The sessions helped to uncover the parents' previously unstated distortions, such as: "Barry must be perfect in order to preserve the family's positive image and reputation in the community; if Barry has problems it means we're bad parents and are responsible for his actions (his legal problems and drug abuse); Barry's achievements are necessary for the family's happiness (consistent with such beliefs in all enabling relationships); we should be able to control Barry's behavior if we are good parents; only Barry can carry the family's hopes and dreams for the future." It gradually became clear how the members' denial about Barry's substance abuse and the rape charge allowed them to maintain their view of Barry, and therefore of the unit, as perfect.

Building on Family Themes and Strengths.   In addition to addressing the family's and Barry's cognitive distortions, the counselor reframed Barry's substance abuse, his way of coping with trying to be perfect, as evidence of his loyalty in living up to the family's expectations (even though it was destroying him). This reframe, a family systems strategy, worked because it conveyed a positive connotation by utilizing the family's language and themes (the importance of meeting expectations and being loyal). Moreover, it provided a way for the parents to acknowledge and accept Barry's substance abuse, or a way to get unstuck (Papp 1983; Selvini-Palazzoli, Boscolo, Cecchin, and Prata 1978).

The reframe also released the parents from trying to control Barry's recovery and ironically, helped them to feel more empowered as coaches rather than as drivers of that process. Subsequent family sessions built on the unit's new awareness about their parallel cognitive distortions, their strengths, and their alternative views about family issues, for instance, family barriers to and the members' roles in Barry's recovery. That work included monitoring the parallel problem-solving actions each member undertook to help resolve collective issues.

Evaluation of Nuclear Family Practice

Selecting User-Friendly Standardized Procedures.   Barry's family's progress in addressing those issues was evaluated with three of Hudson's (1982) scales from his Clinical Measurement Package. The Index of Family Relations (IFR) is completed separately by each parent and the youths in a family, while concurrently, the Index of Peer Relations (IPR) and the Generalized Contentment Scale (GCS) are completed by the youths. These standardized, global, and brief rating scales were designed to measure the severity or magnitude of clients' problems at baseline, during the period of service, and after completion of the program. The scales have been normed and validated; the results of those tests have been reported in detail elsewhere (Hudson 1982). These scales were useful with Barry's family because the parents wanted concrete methods for monitoring the family's work and progress (see figure 8.1).

Monitoring and Applying Feedback from Evaluation Tools.   The GCS was especially useful for measuring Barry's periodic depression, which seemed to be a reaction to family conflicts and his shame and guilt feelings. For example, this twenty-five-item scale can be applied to substance abuse and disempowerment experiences as well as related concerns: "I feel powerless to do anything about my life, I have a hard time getting started on things I need to do, I feel that the future looks bright for me, and I feel that I am appreciated by others." After each administration, the scales were scored using Hudson's (1982) mathematical formula and then were discussed with the family (the IFR) or with Barry (the GCS and the IPR). The discussions focused on comparing current and past ratings, analyzing contextual factors that affected the ratings from the clients' perspective, and interpreting what the ratings meant in terms of the unit's and Barry's progress toward goals. The family's involvement in analyzing the scale results helped them to feel more in control of the sessions and heightened their commitment to the process of family growth and development.

Over time, not only did Barry's ratings on the GCS and IPR increase but also some of his cognitive distortions decreased, as indicated by his discussions about specific items such as feeling appreciated by his family and peers. Barry discussed his shift from a belief that he must be perfect as expected to a belief that it was not important for everyone to appreciate him (that it was not possible or important for him to be perfect). He came to believe that his brothers genuinely appreciated him because when he risked revealing his mistakes and self-doubts in family sessions, they did not reject him. The parents' seeing Barry as a real person with "normal" flaws was a more gradual process, with his father becoming more and more outspoken in acknowledging the parents' past "hang-ups about Barry."

Combining Nuclear Family and Peer Group Modalities

As a Vehicle for Changing Large Systems.   In addition to deconstructing the family hero myth in Barry's family sessions, his primary counselor suggested that, simultaneously, he should work on his "be perfect" myth with peers. This was appropriate because Barry's peers continuously made shame-based comparisons between themselves and this standard. Also, the normative stress Barry was experiencing about his upcoming interview with the principal of the school he wanted to attend after completing rehab was a common issue among the program's clients. Although, like his peers, Barry wanted to be honest, he was convinced that if he revealed his drug history and rehabilitation to the principal, he would not be allowed to enroll. In addition, Barry anticipated experiencing feelings of shame once the principal learned about his past.

The role rehearsal strategy was used in a peer-counseling group after the members had discussed the pros and cons of being honest in such interviews. Barry played himself and a peer played the principal. The first role rehearsal involved Barry presenting the reasons he wanted to transfer to the school without discussing his drug history or rehabilitation. The principal refused Barry's request to transfer. The second role rehearsal involved Barry and two other peers playing his parents, along with the same student playing the principal. In that situation, Barry and his parents explained his drug history and rehabilitation as part of their rationale for requesting the transfer. A discussion about Barry's past academic successes and his mistakes followed, with the parents advocating for Barry when the principal initially said he could not enroll. The principal reversed himself and agreed that Barry could enroll under specific conditions about staying out of trouble, after the parents asked him to clarify the transfer policy and whether he had ever needed a second chance to succeed in some area of his life.

After the two role rehearsal scenarios, the counselor asked the peer who took the role of the principal to explain how he experienced the two scenarios and his reactions to Barry in each. The peer said that in the first scenario, Barry had seemed like an okay teenager who could handle himself in an interview. He had seemed straightforward, so as the principal the peer felt he could be direct about denying Barry's request to transfer. He thought the real principal might already know of current problem students in the school and be concerned that Barry might have problems he was not sharing about why he wanted to transfer.

In the second scenario, however, the parents' advocacy and Barry's honesty about his past caused the principal to reverse his decision. Their questions about the policy showed him they were motivated enough to go over his head administratively to push for the transfer. The parents' support of Barry's recovery made him believe they would be helpful in monitoring his behavior and his potential for relapsing in the future.

Later, based on the role rehearsal results, Barry agreed to use a family session to ask his parents to advocate for him and to be honest with the principal about his reasons for wanting to transfer and the specific progress he had made in rehab. Prior to the actual interview, Barry's primary counselor suggested that he research and write a paper on shame and its effects on addiction and recovery, using the program's library of books and videotapes relevant to the topic. This cognitive restructuring strategy, shown in table 10.1, can be effective because it requires the writer to consider an alternative view of his or her problem or an alternative reality. For instance, presenting his paper on shame to his peer counseling group and in a family therapy session required Barry to explain how it affected the way he defined his problems and strengths, and then to explain his problems and strengths from a nonshame based perspective (e.g., from a cognitive-behavioral or transactional analysis framework).

In the peer group, some members raised questions about how they could apply the ideas in Barry's paper to their situations. In a family session, Barry's parents could see more clearly the role of shame and the family hero myth in his addiction and his recovery. With this combination of family and peer group strategies, Barry and his parents were able to convince the principal to allow him to transfer into the new school. Many of these strategies have been used to change policies within other large systems that influence such clients' recovery, such as health care, mental health, housing, juvenile justice, child welfare, and public assistance.

As a Source of Data in Evaluating Outcomes. Evaluation of the combined family and cognitive-behavioral strategies used in Barry's case included two data sources. As part of the mutual aid that group members provide to each other, Barry's peers were able to directly observe and report on significant changes in his behavior or his progress during each session. In addition, his counselor helped Barry construct a self-anchored scale for rating his subjective reactions of shame across various situations to aid in his recovery and transition into aftercare.

Direct peer observations documented changes in Barry's ability to influence large systems. For example, some of his peers reported that Barry seemed more self-confident and able to use his self-advocacy skills after he had successfully role played, planned, and completed the interview in which he influenced the principal's decision about his school transfer request. They also thought the experience showed changes in how Barry thought about his addiction and recovery, and a greater ability to take positive risks on his part by sharing that information with the principal.

Other peers reported that Barry was asking for and using more feedback from them after the group session in which he role played asking the principal for a transfer (this was also after the family session in which he presented his relapse prevention plan). In one instance, a youth who had graduated from the program recently was sharing his post-treatment recovery experiences with Barry and his peers. (Alumni are encouraged to return periodically to participate in group sessions, to support their own recovery and to help peers anticipate barriers to recovery during aftercare that can be addressed currently.) Barry talked about his issues of shame and being perfect. He then asked John, the peer who was in aftercare, and others whether they thought he was making sufficient progress to handle some of the problems youths typically encounter in aftercare. John told Barry, "you're still into your ego thing," which "might trip you up when you're back out there, on the street." He suggested that Barry talk to his primary counselor about writing a concept paper on perfectionism to help him address that area of his recovery.

When his peers introduced the topic as expected in the next group session, Barry indicated he had already began work on the concept paper, which he presented in a later group session. He then included this issue for work in his personal growth contract in order to become more focused during his last few weeks of rehab. Since Barry's shame and perfectionism were interrelated, his earlier concept paper on shame had addressed only one part of the problem. In his discharge meeting a few weeks later, attended by all clients as well as Barry's family and his sponsor, as was customary, participants pointed out examples of his new ability to identify when shame and perfectionism were controlling his behavior. They also noted his more frequent requests for and use of feedback about his actions.

Barry's self-anchored shame scale also was used to evaluate changes. After Barry wrote and presented the paper on shame to his peer group, the counselor suggested developing the scale as a quick source of feedback for Barry whenever he encountered a situation in which he experienced shame, one of his potential relapse triggers (see figure 8.1 regarding this use of scales and other empowerment-oriented evaluation tools). Barry's shame experiences included an instance when he was reprimanded by a staff member for an angry outburst toward a female peer, a related incident when he lied to his parents about the reason for his loss of privileges due to his outburst, and the interview in which he and his parents shared his addiction and recovery history to influence the principal to transfer Barry to the new school.

The process of developing the scale was designed to normalize the management of problem behaviors for Barry and his family. For instance, the counselor helped Barry educate his parents about the role of shame in his addiction and recovery during family sessions. To further increase Barry's sense of self-efficacy, the counselor used Barry's own language to anchor the high, medium, and low points on the scale (Bloom, Fischer, and Orme 1995). Barry's active participation in constructing this rapid assessment and monitoring tool ensured that it would reflect more accurately the subjective nature of his feelings of shame.

Barry's Self-Anchored Scale

Date _____

This situation involved:

I rate my feelings of shame in this situation as follows:

1	2	3	4	5	6	7
I feel I'm only human; I regret my behavior, but I like myself.			I feel like a fool, I'm ashamed of what I did, but maybe I'm not so bad.			I feel like scum, I'm so ashamed, I hate myself and everybody else.

By using the scales in individual, group, and family sessions, the counselor was able to monitor two aspects of the work with Barry. First, the scales clarified aspects of the services provided that helped to decrease his maladaptive feelings of shame and led to other desirable outcomes. Freeman (1993) notes that such feedback is important for identifying which of a program's strategies should be maintained and which should be modified. For instance, analyzing and discussing Barry's ratings on the scales indicated he made more progress when he received immediate feedback from peers who directly observed or were involved in situations in which he experienced shame. Thereafter, those peers were asked to share their reactions to what happened on the spot or during peer counseling and relapse prevention group sessions, and family members were asked to help monitor events and provide similar feedback to Barry during home visits and in family sessions.

A second use of this evaluation tool was in discussing Barry's descriptions and interpretations of situations during family and group sessions, the underlying issues related to his relapse triggers, the sources of his feelings of shame, and how he might have reframed and responded differently to the shame he experienced. It was possible to see, based on changes in his ratings and in how he interpreted the situations over time, that Barry progressed in how he defined and coped with shame. Those changes were particularly noticeable when he made academic mistakes or when he was given feedback about his interactions with or responses to female peers and family members. Significantly, Barry's ratings progressed from mostly 7s to 3s and 4s after he wrote his concept paper on perfectionism and developed his personal growth contract. He was not rating himself in the 1 to 2 range on the scale by the time he completed rehab, but he was able to acknowledge and take pride in his progress up to that point. To continue Barry's work in this area, his counselor suggested that he use the scale as part of his relapse prevention plan in conjunction with his sponsor and family members as he moved into the aftercare phase of his recovery.

Conclusion

The combined family and group work used with Barry and in other examples in this chapter illustrate the range of practice approaches that need to be applied across modalities. A number of approaches can facilitate clients' empowerment; three examples are cognitive-behavioral, family systems, and structural change theories, as shown in table 10.1. Applications of these theories have been integrated throughout the chapter. But it may not be apparent that these and other theories consist of both supports and barriers to empowerment, based on the theories' implicit assumptions and how they are used by providers.

Family systems approaches, for example, can provide supports for recovery by helping the members detriangulate or stop their enabling behaviors. This can lead members to identify new sources of personal and interpersonal power, including a new positive individual identity or existing interpersonal skills. Unfortunately, the emphasis on stabilizing family relationships may discourage clients' adaptive cutoffs from members who present risks, and thus can be a barrier to recovery. In Barry's case, he may need to eventually cut off from some extended family members who continue to maintain their view of him as perfect. However, supports for cutting off developed only after his counselor shifted from a family systems to a cognitive-behavioral approach to identify the family's interrelated cognitive distortions and their threat to Barry's recovery.

This ability to shift from one approach to another in empowerment practice, as needed, is essential for effective outcomes. Service providers who are unable to do so may become barriers to their clients' recovery rather than supports. Flexibility includes using individual and family sessions as adjuncts to group work and also as modalities of choice in situations where clients' family and diversity issues need to be addressed. Chapter 11 presents a full discussion of the choice and combination of modalities in rehab according to cultural diversity, with a focus on individual work in particular.

11 Building on Cultural Diversity in Client-Centered Individual Work: Implications for Self-Empowerment

To assume that because someone is a first-generation migrant from Appalachia, she or he will behave in a predictable fashion may be incorrect. Members of cultural groups generally share certain beliefs, values, and behaviors, but each individual combines these factors in unique ways that reflect his or her particular situation.

—R. L. Berger, J. T. McBreen, and M. J. Rifkin (1996:115)

The goal of group and family work is to build on clients' common experiences and interests in order to accomplish their collective empowerment (Gutiérrez 1995). The practice literature is less clear, however, about the role of individual work in substance abuse rehab. There has been less emphasis on how to use individual sessions to address diversity issues, or as Berger et al. point out above, to acknowledge the uniqueness of the individual. This gap may exist because most knowledge about substance abuse rehabilitation has been developed from practice wisdom and research on group recovery models. Data sources have included both formal rehab programs and informal twelve-step programs (Galanter, Castaneda, and Franco 1991; Schopler and Galinsky 1995).

Furthermore, the literature provides few guidelines about using empowerment and other self-actualizing components of rehab in the less public arena of individual work. As a result, some programs provide one-on-one sessions or individual work for clients primarily to meet state and local funding mandates. Others do so only in response to clients' requests. In one outpatient rehab program, a twenty-five-year-old African American client, Kim, requested individual sessions after relapsing on her fifteenth day of early recovery. Although staff in this program tended to discourage individual work because they assumed it undermined the group process, Kim's counselor agreed to meet with her after hearing the reason for her request.

The one-on-one sessions revealed that Kim had been raped the night of her relapse by an acquaintance, who then left her alone in a rural area. A stranger who picked her up and agreed to take her to the hospital also raped Kim before leaving her stranded for a second time. Kim believed both rapes were her fault. She needed the individual sessions to share her shame and pain about the rapes and her thoughts about suicide. Kim felt she was being punished by God for her relapse, based on beliefs from her Pentacostal religious background.

Later, Kim was able to discuss her relapse experience in group sessions. The members' mutual aid helped her continue to work through what had happened and how she could learn and grow from it. Granting Kim's request for individual sessions was appropriate for initially addressing this client's unique need: to manage the impact of her shame-based religious beliefs on her current crisis and on her potential for suicide.

Such requests for individual work may be denied in some programs for several reasons. Like the staff in this example, providers may be concerned about the extent to which individual work, compared to other modalities, could prolong clients' denial about being addicted or the need for lifelong abstinence. Or they may assume that individual work is more time consuming and therefore less cost effective than group or family sessions (Smyth 1996). Counselors sometimes believe transference reactions and triangulation of staff occur more often in individual sessions, because significant members of the client's therapeutic team (peers, family, and other staff) are not present (Hartman 1995; Shorkey 1994).

Often, based on these and other assumptions, the value of individual work has been underestimated in substance abuse rehab. This chapter contains a rationale for providing individual sessions in such programs and for combining those sessions with other modalities so that clients can experience all levels of empowerment, personal, interpersonal, and political. Case examples illustrate how individual work can address a broad range of cultural diversity among clients, including ethnicity, gender, age, sexual orientation, disabilities, socioeconomic status, and location (rural versus urban communities). The therapeutic strategies and empowerment-focused evaluation tools some programs use to facilitate this process are also described.

The Benefits and Limitations of Individual Work

As noted previously, the goal of individual work is to consider and help resolve unique aspects of each client's substance abuse problems and recovery. This is compatible with the goal of group work and family work, which is to help clients learn from their common and unique experiences through collective consciousness raising. Individual, family, and group work represent, therefore, three parallel, complementary tracks that move clients toward the same destination. Thus, this discussion includes the benefits of individual work as well as how to combine it with group and family work to compensate for its limitations.

Benefits and Goals

An important benefit of individual work is that it affords clients opportunities to address topics that are inappropriate in other modalities, such as conflicts between a client and a staff member, the details of a client's case planning, history taking and analysis, journal analysis, recovery workbook assignments and analysis, and life story preparation and coaching. Individual therapy provides clients with the one-on-one attention needed to address these aspects of rehab and recovery in a private, less threatening venue.

Another benefit is that individual sessions can be used to address issues that clients have difficulty broaching, at least initially, in group or family sessions, as in the example of Kim in this chapter's introduction. Individual sessions can provide the safe environment needed for assessing life-threatening situations such as possible suicide or the need for hospitalization, and offer clients individual support and practice opportunities for opening up intensely personal and/or taboo subjects.

Often, clients like Kim need one-on-one sessions to acknowledge their pain and shame related to sexual abuse or assaults, family suicides, HIV/AIDS, other sexually transmitted diseases, or mental illness in the family. Once they have survived sharing emotionally charged information with a trusted staff member and have been validated for it, clients often experience the self-efficacy they need to bring up such topics in later family and group sessions.

Individual work is also beneficial when different aspects of complex issues, such as cultural diversity issues, loss and grief, and phase work, need to be addressed simultaneously in more than one modality. For instance, gender and ethnic oppression are often addressed in multicultural or women's or men's issues groups, drawing upon the members' common negative experiences and cultural strengths. Simultaneously, the unique aspects of a client's efforts to cope with and address those experiences can be incorporated into his or her personal growth contract during individual sessions.

Overcoming Related Limitations by Combining Modalities

While the above benefits of individual work help to clarify some reasons for providing such services, the use of individual work alone in substance abuse rehab is contraindicated. The limitations of this modality include fewer opportunities for clients to experience empowerment beyond the personal level, to decrease the inherent marginalization and isolation with which most of them struggle, and to address the systemic aspects of their substance abuse and recovery. The following points provide a rationale for combining modalities in order to overcome these limitations (Hester and Miller 1989; McNeece and DiNitto 1994; Rogers and McMillan 1989; Rounsaville and Carroll 1992; Treadway 1989):

1. Although individual work can address the personal level of empowerment well, staff have difficulty directly facilitating clients' empowerment at the interpersonal and political levels when individual work is used alone.
2. Many of the problems experienced by substance-abusing clients are of an interpersonal and systems nature, in addition to the personal problems that confront them.
3. Failure to work on the interpersonal and systems problems and empowerment levels can impede recovery and increase the likelihood of clients either dropping out or relapsing after completing rehab.
4. Therefore, combining modalities may be more cost efficient and cost effective in the long term because it increases the intensity of the services clients receive. Cost efficiency is becoming a larger

issue as this field moves toward more managed care and other cost-saving measures due to national, state, and local policy/funding changes.

Handling Race and Ethnicity

Case Example: Background Information

Issues of race and ethnicity can surface in relation to a program's structure or the client's environment outside the service setting. One example involves a fifty-three-year-old Native American client, Chad, whose wife had died in a home fire eight months before he entered rehab. Barriers related to his rehab program were impeding Chad's recovery. He had just completed thirty days of the program's sixty- to ninety-day inpatient services. It was customary for clients in the middle to late stages of this program to routinely receive home passes to attend church, family functions, off-site NA and AA meetings, and other significant community events. But Chad's primary counselor, Hal, would not give him a home pass to participate in an upcoming sweat lodge ceremony as he requested. Hal's rationale for refusing the request was that Chad was not ready for a home pass. Although approximately 20 percent of this program's clients were Native American, 55 percent were white, and 35 percent were Latino, the staff had received very little training in counseling culturally diverse clients.

Organizational Change and Political Empowerment Strategies

Organizational Power Dynamics.   When the decision to deny Chad's pass was raised in a team meeting by another staff member, Hal became defensive. He said that because the sweat lodge ceremony involved tribal members, giving Chad a pass could lead to his relapsing. Hal, who was white, assumed many of the tribal members had substance abuse problems, based mostly on stereotypes about Native Americans rather than factual information (McCarthy 1993).

The ensuing discussion revealed how little most of the staff knew and understood about Chad's heritage: for example, few knew he was a member of the Lakota Sioux Nation. This discussion led to an administrative decision to hire a Native American consultant initially to provide cultural knowledge and support to Hal, and later to develop an in-service training program for all staff members on counseling Native American clients. In this way, Hal's struggles with cultural competence and self-efficacy were normalized within the organization.

The Cultural Coach Strategy.   The consultant worked with Hal as a cultural coach, helping him identify barriers to and supports for improving his cultural sensitivity. Table 9.1, under the Individual Modality: Political Empowerment category, illustrates the connection between gaining support for clients' cultural rituals and achieving organizational change. Hal's sensitivity was increased in two ways: through written material and discussions about Native American clients and through discussions about the impact of his German American ethnic and farming background on his work with diversity issues.

For instance, the consultant provided Hal with factual information about patterns of alcohol and drug abuse among Native Americans and personal, interpersonal, and structural factors that influence those patterns (Cahape and Howley 1992; May 1982; Murphy and Deblasie 1984; Nofz 1988). Information about Chad's specific tribe, the Lakota Sioux Nation, was essential for addressing some of Hal's stereotypes. The discussions highlighted both the tribal and the individual differences among indigenous people (Berger et al. 1996; Robbins 1994).

The second part of the consultant's coaching strategy was to use values clarification exercises with Hal to increase his awareness of attitudes that hindered his work with Chad and other Native Americans (Herring 1992). She helped Hal to analyze the impact of his ethnic background and values on how he handled power and authority issues, in contrast with beliefs that influenced how Chad responded. Hal identified personal and cultural values that facilitated his work and ethnic pride (being responsible), and other values that impeded the work (a rigid, aggressive way of using power). Within a brief, intensive period of work with Hal and other staff, the consultant's supportive coaching began to change the interpersonal and political climate of the program for Chad and other Native Americans.

The Role-Sharing Strategy.   Simultaneously, to provide more direct opportunities for Chad's political empowerment, the consultant suggested that Hal use a role-sharing strategy with him (see table 9.1 under the Individual work: Political Empowerment category). This required Hal to ask Chad to educate him about sweat lodges and other rituals that indigenous people use periodically to cleanse and purify themselves physically, psychologically, and spiritually (Dufrene 1990; Herring 1992). Hal learned that the intent of sweat lodges is consistent with the program's recovery goals for clients. He began to recognize how this and other rituals were cultural strengths and important sources of power for Native Americans.

With Hal acknowledging Chad's strengths and expertise, Chad became more open to anticipating some of the risky situations he might encounter while out on a pass. They discovered that risky situations included not only being around addicted peers and other nonrecovering people but also being in situations that Chad associated with getting high in the past. An example of the latter was attending a baseball game in a community park where he used to get high. Hal helped Chad think through how to avoid those situations when possible by planning alternative activities in other places. They also worked on identifying and practicing alternative ways Chad could respond whenever he found himself in unanticipated situations.

Organizational and Policy Impact Strategies.   Another part of the consultant's role included recommending to administration that they develop a policy for building on the cultural strengths of clients such as Chad. Consequently, a new policy was instituted requiring staff and clients to identify, during assessment, cultural factors and strengths that could enhance or block clients' recovery and empowerment.

Another requirement was that treatment plans specify how the identified cultural factors and strengths would be used to improve the service process and outcomes. To implement this new policy, the program made two additional changes. First, the consultant provided an organizationwide inservice training program focused on cultural sensitivity in general and on Native Americans and other clients of color specifically. Ongoing staff training updates were to be given at regular intervals.

A second change involved adding cultural issues to the program's quality assurance tracking form in order to monitor the implementation of the new policy over time. This focus and the resulting feedback to staff reinforced the program's emphasis on cultural sensitivity and clients' strengths, and thus the ongoing political empowerment of its culturally diverse clients. Chad specifically gained interpersonal and political empowerment from combining his individual sessions with group work, and from the consultant's cultural coaching and systems change activities (involving the counselor and the administration, respectively). These primarily mezzo systems changes provide a context for understanding Chad's process of self-empowerment at the personal level.

Individual Work and Personal Empowerment

Narrative Strategies. In addition to the above mezzo and micro strategies, Hal's individual work with Chad included a number of narrative strategies, such as:

1. talking or journaling about Chad's key life experiences or personal narratives, past and present
2. deconstructing those narratives to clarify underlying values and beliefs that influenced Chad's behavior and his interpretations of other people's behavior
3. analyzing family and tribal narratives for their healing potential and sources of power
4. responding to cultural narratives suggested to Hal by the consultant
5. applying new solution-focused endings to Chad's personal narratives in order to decrease his problem fatigue (Chestang 1976) and his regression away from his stated goals (Borden 1994).

In one of their sessions, Chad discussed feeling hopeless about and powerless over his life situation as a source of his problem fatigue. Chad was uncertain what was causing this. When Hal asked if there had been another time when he felt that way, Chad shared a personal narrative about his Vietnam War experience (strategy #1 above). One day, Chad and part of his unit were cut off from the main unit by Vietcong fire, and "the enemy" suddenly moved in to attack them. Chad froze when he found himself facing a young Vietcong whose gun would not fire when he tried to shoot Chad.

In the brief moments before one of his buddies killed this young soldier, in Chad's words, he "experienced a staggering revelation." He suddenly realized that the Vietnamese were fighting a war similar to the wars fought by Native Americans, which began with the first European invasion of the North American continent. He saw clearly that he was more like this

Vietnamese soldier in sentiment and experience than he was like other Americans.

From that point, Chad began to doubt the American rationale for the war and this country's promises to liberate the South Vietnamese if they helped to win it. He remembered hundreds of treaties signed by the United States and Native Americans that were never fully honored by the government. After his revelation, Chad started using and abusing alcohol and cocaine. His commitment to the war and to America dissipated. He began to feel rootless and disoriented due to what he later recognized as an identity crisis and divided loyalties. He experienced a rage that was so frightening he began to self-medicate. Predictably, the drugs fueled rather than decreased his rage, which eventually pushed him from problem usage to full-blown addiction.

Sharing this narrative with Hal showed Chad's growing trust in his counselor. Hal's validation and support demonstrated that, indeed, he had heard and respected Chad's narrative. Based on his work with the consultant, Hal decided to have Chad write this powerful narrative in his journal and then deconstruct it during a session (strategies #1 and 5 above). Chad would analyze more specifically how the narrative made him feel about having control over his life and hope for the future.

Hal noted that even though Chad said he did not presently have goals, there was probably a time when he did. Hal encouraged him to remember those goals. Chad recalled that before Vietnam, he wanted to make a difference for Native Americans in this country. He wanted to help restore a sense of hope and dignity to his people and decrease the rate and consequences of alcohol and drug addiction among them.

Hal commented that it was a strength for Chad to remember those goals in spite of his addiction and the other problems he had encountered. Continuing the deconstruction analysis, Hal asked if Chad's narrative about Vietnam moved him closer to or farther away from those goals. When Chad replied that it made his goals seem hopeless, Hal asked if Chad would like to write a new ending to the narrative without changing what had happened so far (strategies #2 and #5 above).

Solution-Focused, Cognitive Restructuring, and Strategic Interventions. Writing a new solution-focused ending or restorying his narrative, as Hal suggested, could make it possible for Chad to achieve or come closer to his goals. Thus, based on Borden's concepts (1992), the re-storied account would be a progressive narrative, in contrast to Chad's old regressive narrative. This homework assignment (Baker and Steiner 1995) required Chad to write in his journal his old narrative, his feelings and reactions, and the long-term consequences he had identified during the session.

A cognitive restructuring process occurred in the session and later when he journaled as Chad realized that his past beliefs and solutions had not worked for him (Shorkey 1994). One of those solutions to the hopelessness and rage, addiction, had become a barrier to his original life goals. The cognitive restructuring, coupled with the in-session analysis of his narrative, allowed Chad to identify and then question his beliefs about not being able to reach his life goals. Chad was then expected to write a new, solution-focused ending to his narrative.

Hal pointed out that this task required time because the new ending had to include only elements that could lead to a reformulation and achievement of Chad's goals. Implicitly, the task shifted Chad's focus away from pathology and hopelessness to resiliency and positive solutions. Hal encouraged Chad not to write the new ending too quickly, however, saying that only Chad would know when he was ready to take that step. This "go slow" strategic intervention helps clients struggling with substance abuse, who often undermine themselves, to refrain from engaging in their typical power sabotage games (see table 10.1).

Like clients with other types of problems, substance abusers are frequently ambivalent about and fearful of change. Consequently, they may engage in the losing game of self-sabotage: "See, I told you it wouldn't work—ain't it awful" (Papp 1989). Clients sabotage their power by resisting change, and as a result, conclude that they have won by defeating the powerful expert counselor. The "go slow" strategy utilizes the client's resistance and enhances his or her possibilities for personal empowerment. The strategy creates a win-win situation because it acknowledges that only the client can accomplish the personal changes necessary to resolve the situation (Papp 1989; Selvini-Palzazzoli, Cirillo, Selvini, and Sorrentino 1989).

Social Network and Cultural Identity Enhancement Strategies. To help reconnect Chad to his social and cultural network, Hal suggested that he talk with tribal and family elders about his narrative work and goals while on a home pass. This would provide Chad with opportunities to get support from positive leaders in his network and to ensure that the new ending to his narrative would be culturally relevant. Those contacts not only helped him to re-story his narrative but also led to his decision to develop a heritage book, based on ideas Hal had learned from the consultant.

Heritage books are one of the cultural identity strategies included in table 9.1 under the Individual modality: Interpersonal Empowerment category. These strategies help clients to reconstruct their identities as recovering people when addiction and other disempowering situations, such as Chad's Vietnam revelation, have shattered them. Heritage books are analogous to the family books that children in out-of-home placements create when they have lost contact with and memories of their families and have become disoriented in terms of their cultural identities (Freeman 1984).

To develop the heritage book, Chad collected pictures and other memorabilia that symbolized his Native Amerian history and traditions. He then organized those materials into book format, based on criteria determined by him, along with a narrative that provided a holistic picture of who he was as a recovering, ethnic person. Chad included collages and other artwork he had completed during rehab to illustrate important feelings and experiences that were part of his emerging identity during early recovery.

Chad later described developing and discussing the heritage book as a healing process that made him feel more connected with himself and more valuable than before. He was able to clarify what parts of the book reflected him as an individual, what parts reflected his cultural group or tribe, and what parts reflected both identities. Chad gradually felt personally empowered, and he felt interpersonally empowered from interviews and discussions with key members of his family and tribe. In addition, his gathering of information from culturally relevant sources, including Native American healers, scholars, and historians (oral and written sources), enhanced his personal identity and his collective or interpersonal consciousness related to Native American traditions.

Other Interpersonal Empowerment Strategies.   Presenting and discussing his heritage book in a peer group was another important step, since identity loss or confusion is a common experience among substance-abusing clients. Group members provided mutual aid and support to Chad and other members in two main areas. First, the members experienced a collective consciousness raising when Chad presented his book. The discussion and analysis helped them to identify common disempowerment experiences and reactions related to their addictions. Codifying or anchoring them often produces a sense of cohesion and interpersonal empowerment (Solomon 1995; Freire 1996).

Second, the process of presenting his heritage book also highlighted unique aspects of Chad's experience as a Native American substance abuser. Group members commented on how clearly Chad's book showed the interaction of special individual, family, tribal, and external influences in his addiction and recovery. Their new insights about Chad allowed them to explore the interaction of different combinations of factors in their own lives. For example, one group member recalled how her Swedish background and Lutheran religious beliefs reinforced stuffing her feelings and avoiding conflicts. As a result of these insights, Chad and some of the other members gained a greater understanding of and sense of control over their situations.

Evaluation Strategies and Tools

Overview of the Evaluation Process.   Hal and Chad used a combination of informal tools to evaluate the effects of the above strategies on Chad's situation. Because some of the intervention and evaluation strategies, such as journaling, involved writing, they decided to add only a few oral evaluation procedures for monitoring. Chad was expected to audiotape a brief summary at the end of each individual session focused on what had occurred during the session and his reactions. The summary was to articulate what was or was not helpful from Chad's perspective. In addition, Hal monitored and recorded his informal observations of Chad in sessions over time.

Monitoring and Documenting Positive Outcomes.   The combination of oral and written evaluation procedures indicated Chad benefited and progressed more from sessions in which Hal used practical strategies that addressed Chad's strengths. Examples included the sessions focused on writing a new ending to Chad's narrative about his Vietnam revelation (when his substance abuse problem began), and those in which he planned and shared the development of his heritage book with Hal. The oral session summaries and written journal entries verified, for instance, Chad's process of deciding how to manage the rage that resulted from his Vietnam revelation in a more adaptive manner. These tools also reflected Chad's growing ability to identify and use his personal and cultural strengths, including his ethnic pride and his strong social network of tribal members.

Hal's informal in-session observations were recorded in regular progress notes for the case. Hal and the consultant agreed that his direct observations should include information about two main areas: Chad's level of involvement in the rehab process (e.g., Chad volunteering comments or suggestions about how certain issues might be addressed in individual sessions and case staffings)and evidence of Chad's growing personal power. The observed changes in this area included Chad's more frequently acknowledging ownership of the changes he was making and discussing why he disagreed with Hal on some issues. Most important was Chad's increased ability to affirm himself by identifying and using personal strengths (his love for himself and for others) or personal and cultural sources of power (cultural rituals related to loss).

Monitoring and Documenting Problems in the Work.   The oral session summaries and other evaluation tools were equally valuable in documenting aspects of the work that were not helpful to Chad. For example, the summaries pointed out that alcohol and drug education sessions were not helpful initially because they did not involve practical activities and they ignored, or did not help him to apply the information to his cultural circumstances. Substance abuse patterns and drugs of choice among Native Americans and the effects of oppression on those patterns were not addressed. This feedback helped Hal and other staff to integrate more effectively the cultural education provided by the consultant, increasing the cultural relevance of the drug and alcohol education sessions for Chad and for other clients of color. These changes gradually showed Chad that his culture was valued and that he was genuinely being encouraged to take a more active role in his case planning and recovery. The program's positive responses to Chad's feedback in the session summaries helped to document Hal's and Chad's influence in making the work more client-centered and culturally relevant.

These changes were critical for helping Chad to manage and learn from a relapse that occurred while he was on a pass during his last week of rehab. Although staff were initially convinced that Chad should be dismissed from the program, Hal was instrumental in getting them to decode the real message underlying his relapse. The team was able to see that the relapse indicated Chad was stuffing his feelings related to termination, not trying to manipulate the staff as they had assumed initially. The case staffing included input from Chad and led to a plan for helping him to address his feelings about termination.

The plan included strategies for helping Chad deal with the unresolved loss of his wife eight months before he entered rehab, which surfaced during the staffing. Since he had been addicted when his wife died, Chad had never fully mourned or grieved for her. Here again, tribal traditions helped him to cope with and ritualize his loss in culturally meaningful ways (e.g., a briefer but much more intense and expressive mourning period than some cultural groups' traditions). For Chad, journaling about cultural narratives that reflected some of his fears about and experiences with loss and endings was very effective as well. (Chapter 12 describes an empowered helping process for facilitating clients' management of termination and other losses.)

Managing the Often Unacknowledged Areas of Diversity

Case Example: Background Information

Sometimes, generally unacknowledged areas of diversity such as age, class, disability, or location may indicate a need for individual sessions during rehab. Carl's case illustrates the impact of this combination of unacknowledged cultural factors and certain organizational variables on his empowerment and recovery.

Carl, a fifty-six-year-old white client from a small, rural, and extremely impoverished area, entered a thirty-day rehab program because of his methamphetamine addiction. Carl was diagnosed as manic depressive (bipolar) when he was in his early thirties, although in retrospect, he recalled experiencing very dramatic mood swings beginning in his twenties. He refused to take his psychotropic medication regularly because he did not want to become dependent on it. He had been hospitalized frequently when he decompensated. Carl had been divorced for fifteen years and was cut off from his ex-wife and adult children. His only supports consisted of two friends from his hometown who also had substance abuse problems and belonged to the same motorcycle club.

The rehab program is located in a nearby metropolitan area and serves a predominantly younger, white, and economically diverse population, most of whom are polyaddicted. This program accepts a few dual diagnosis clients like Carl, but it does not have specialized services or staff for them. Services are coordinated with those of a nearby mental health center that provides mental health assessments and medication education and maintenance. In addition to its fifty-bed, thirty-day inpatient program, this rehab facility has a larger sixty-day outpatient program.

Intervention Strategies for Personal Empowerment

Reframing the Client's Diversity and Resistance.   Carl was resistant to rehab and remained uninvolved during his first few days in the program. The contrast between him and his peers in terms of age, social class, residence location, and type of disability was a major factor. Carl felt isolated and vulnerable, so he refused to risk opening up in peer group sessions. He coped with his shame about his dual diagnosis by saying he did not believe in the program's psychological "claptrap." His only reason for being in rehab, he told his counselor, was a court mandate due to a DUI charge.

During his first few individual sessions, his African American counselor, Esther, tried to provide opportunities for Carl to empower himself and get involved in rehab as quickly as possible, given the time limitations. Esther noted that Carl was very concerned about protecting his privacy in the small rural area where he lived and avoiding becoming the brunt of "redneck" jokes by peers in the program. She pointed out that the more knowledge Carl had about what triggered his methamphetamine abuse, the more power and control he would have over his life. This knowledge would include ways to manage other people's curiosity and negative comments about his colorful language and rural lifestyle.

Esther's reframe of Carl's responses to his first few days in rehab contained two important aspects that helped him to empower himself. It normalized Carl's responses by renaming his behavior as a natural concern about his loss of power and control over his life rather than resistance, and a desire for privacy rather than paranoia about being different. This worked because it had a positive connotation and was consistent with Carl's emotional reaction to what seemed to be an unsafe environment. Esther's reframe also helped Carl to identify a meaningful rationale for working on his recovery, one he chose rather than one that was imposed on him.

Using Recovery Workbook Exercises and Checklists.   Although this decision to commit himself to recovery increased Carl's participation somewhat, Esther told Carl she knew he continued to have reservations about the program. He was honest with her, therefore, and admitted that recovery was still not a priority for him. However, Carl did agree to complete a recovery workbook with Esther focused on triggers related to his substance abuse and tools for recovery. This knowledge development workbook enabled Carl to identify and process with Esther certain information that only he knew about his drug abuse. For example it helped him to analyze the following areas related to his abuse cycle:

1. past situations where he felt he was not in control of his life, was threatened in some way, or experienced strong negative feelings
2. what was occurring in those situations at the time (triggers for his substance abuse and other dysfunctional responses to the situations such as physical violence)
3. physical and psychological warning signs that preceded his substance abuse (a burning sensation in his stomach and feelings of outrage and shame when he felt he was being disrespected, especially by younger and more educated and affluent acquaintances)
4. the amount of time between the triggers, the warning signs, and the beginning of his binge cycle
5. what he typically did in between the triggers and warning signs before he actually used meth (his meth abuse and relapse patterns): refusing to take his psychotropic medication or altering the dosage and frequency; staying up for extended periods without adequate sleep and food; hanging out more with his addicted friends in the motorcycle club
6. how he felt and what he thought and did after or during his abuse cycle (feeling revengeful, exaggerating his beliefs about his power and competence, engaging in verbal and physical fights with strangers and "innocent bystanders," and committing property crimes and driving violations with his two addicted friends).

This workbook strategy allowed Carl to be more in control of what information he revealed during his rehab, while also helping him and Esther to cover a lot of important material in a brief period. Carl's insight and knowledge about his substance abuse cycle increased his self-confidence and competence. His sense of power from this new knowledge made Carl eager, instead of resistant, to learn about various practical tools for improving his chances of recovery.

Applying Recovery Tools in Relapse Trigger Situations.   These tools included methods Carl could use to avoid and/or manage the trigger situations, individuals, or issues he had identified in his workbook and discussed with Esther. Examples such as developing a new sober support group and replaying his disintegration tape helped Carl to see how he could manage his triggers if he decided to recover. Table 9.1 includes the disintegration tape strategy as an example of a personal empowerment tool for individual sessions; it can be used in other modalities as well.

This strategy is an antidote to telling toxic addiction war stories, which typically impedes recovery. Esther pointed out that when Carl felt vulnerable and fearful and wanted to feel more powerful, he would talk about and glamorize his meth binges and the dangerous escapades he engaged in while under the influence. By suggesting he replay his disintegration tape during sessions when he told war stories, Esther helped Carl go beyond his usual stopping point in the stories, aspects of his binges that made him feel strong, accepted, and daring (the euphoric part of the cycle in #6 above). This meant he had to fully discuss and analyze or deconstruct the down side of the cycle, which, he learned from replaying his whole tape, was often forgotten but easily predictable. That part of the cycle involved remembering his feelings of shame, worthlessness, and fears about frequently being in jail with more experienced and physically violent inmates. He also remembered feeling overwhelmed when he had to pawn his motorcycle and other personal possessions to make bail, and feeling totally out of control when he lost yet another job due to his addiction.

Combining Individual Sessions with Other Modalities

On-site Peer Group Sessions.   The combined use of the disintegration tape and other strategies in individual sessions reduced Carl's vulnerability and addressed his strong need for privacy, control, and safety from peer rejection. His skill development from completing parts of the workbook and Esther's validation in spite of his reading problems gave Carl a sense of accomplishment and increased his self-esteem. These changes in his individual sessions served as a bridge to Carl's increased involvement in peer group sessions, where there were more opportunities for interpersonal and political empowerment. For example, Esther and other counselors helped Carl to risk sharing in group sessions his anger and pain from peers' negative remarks about his lifestyle or social class and rural home community. This positive risk taking validated Carl's improved communication skills and increased his interpersonal empowerment related to peers and staff members.

Specialized Psychoeducation Sessions Outside the Setting. Another factor in his increased group interaction was Carl's diminished embarrassment about his mental health disorder. The workbook helped Carl to identify shame about his disorder and the effects of not taking his medication as two of his triggers for bingeing. Subsequently, Esther arranged for Carl to attend several psychoeducation sessions at the mental health center focused on his dual disorder and the effects of medication on his bipolar symptoms.

Carl's new knowledge in these areas became an important source of personal and interpersonal power, because it normalized his disorder as one of the many limitations that people live with. He was able to share his new beliefs and values about his dual disorders in the rehab program's peer group sessions. This helped to educate and influence both peer and staff perspectives.

Evaluation Strategies and Tools

A *Triggers and Tools Checklist.* Esther wanted Carl to be actively involved in evaluating their brief period of work together. Information gathered from completing the workbook allowed them to develop a checklist of triggers and tools for Carl as both an intervention strategy and an evaluation tool (see table 9.1 in the Individual modality: Personal Empowerment category). In terms of evaluation, the checklist served as a client self-monitoring tool. It included Carl's list of identified triggers, which he was to check whenever he found himself in a threatening situation; a description of his warning signs; a list of identified tools he could select and apply; and what outcomes occurred. Thus, the checklist helped Carl to monitor and analyze threatening situations during rehab that were similar to those in which his past drug abuse had been reinforced.

Data from the checklist revealed some of Carl's current trigger situations, including interactions with particular staff members and peers as well as specific situations Carl could anticipate having to handle when he returned to his home community. For example, monitoring with the checklist indicated that Carl experienced a greater threat to his recovery in situations involving younger male clients about the same age as his twenty-year-old son, from whom he was cut off.

Working through several of these conflictual situations simultaneously with Esther and in group sessions (one of his identified tools) gave Carl new insights into his intergenerational value differences with younger peers as well as ideas about how he might approach reconciliation with his son after completing rehab. Feedback from both the group sessions and his self-monitoring forms made Carl more open to using other tools on his checklist, such as timing himself out and replaying his disintegration tape. The feedback process also revealed that Carl reported more effective outcomes when he used these strategies because he could control how and when to apply them.

Direct Observation and Verbal Feedback. Esther's direct observations were another source of information for evaluating Carl's progress. Prior to beginning the workbook and other exercises, Esther observed that Carl's focus was primarily on resisting her efforts to get him involved in rehab. After their first few individual sessions, in which he developed initial insights about his conflictual peer interactions as his triggers, his focus shifted to concern about the fact that his peers in the program and members of his home community viewed him negatively. He admitted this bothered him, but he did not know how to respond. This admission seemed to be a turning point in Carl's willingness to work more consistently on his recovery by addressing those conflicts more actively in group and individual sessions.

Esther noted that his focus shifted again during his last two weeks in the program, when he began to understand more clearly how certain tools could enhance his recovery. For example, Carl learned how knowledge works as a recovery tool when Esther arranged for him to attend education sessions at the mental health center focused on his bipolar depression and his substance abuse problems. Esther's feedback about the positive changes she observed helped Carl become more committed to his recovery. He noted that his resistance gradually decreased over the four weeks because the tools he learned to apply increased his control over his life, his primary motivation for remaining in rehab, aside from the court's mandate.

Managing Diversity in Terms of Gender Issues

Overview

Gender issues can also affect clients' empowerment opportunities and recovery. Often in cases such as Kim's, described in this chapter's introduction, gender interacts with other areas of diversity, including ethnicity and religion. Although women's and men's issues groups are useful for addressing common problems in this area, as noted previously, individual sessions can provide the initial or simultaneous support and validation needed for clients to explore their unique concerns.

Case Example: Background Information

Kim, a twenty-five-year-old African American client, entered an outpatient rehab program for treatment of her addiction to crack and alcohol. Her live-in boyfriend, forty-year-old Bill, was an intravenous heroin addict who had introduced Kim to crack. Bill had been in several rehab programs previously and had promised to enter rehab with Kim but then had changed his mind. Kim's three children were in foster care due to neglect, and she was fearful that her drug abuse would cause her to lose them permanently.

Intervention Strategies

Journaling, Externalization, and Affirmation Strategies.   Kim's counselor, Adrianna, suggested that she journal in an unstructured way at least once a day, preferably at about the same time, about her thoughts, feelings, or events that occurred. Kim was expected to journal more often if the need arose. Some of her entries were made immediately following the two rapes, while Kim was still thinking about suicide as the only way to handle her pain. But prior to and after those events, her entries focused on her motivation for coming to rehab: enticing Bill to enter rehab with her.

Kim's preoccupation with her need for Bill prevented her from seeing herself as a separate person who was worthwhile in her own right. Her values about relationships became clear from these journal entries. She wrote, "I'm nothing unless I'm in a relationship" and "eventually Bill will make me happy, I know he will!" Kim's rehab included a women's issues peer group. Feedback from members of this consciousness-raising group, education on gender socialization, learning how to use affirmations, and journaling did not seem to affect Kim's fixation on Bill.

Adrianna believed this preoccupation served two negative purposes in Kim's current situation: it distracted her from working on recovery and it prevented her from handling the long-term effects of the rapes, beyond her initial crisis reaction and suicide ideation. So Adrianna pointed out Kim's emphasis on Bill and others in the journal rather than on herself as a person. She suggested that Kim use a more structured approach to journaling for a few days, following each unstructured entry with a structured analysis of the content. This is a useful approach for helping addicted clients get unstuck in their journaling (Plasse 1995). Kim was to count the number of times she referred to herself in relation to other people versus the number of times she referred to herself as a separate person. The assignment was designed to help Kim externalize or objectify the problem she was having in seeing herself as an individual.

In a one-on-one session a few days later, Kim was able to acknowledge that the counting assignment gave her insight about her "big" preoccupation with Bill in her journal. She also referred to similar feedback from the women's group that she could now hear for the first time. Labeling the problem redundantly as a "big" preoccupation also helped Kim to keep it externalized and therefore separate from Kim the person (Freedman and Combs 1996). Adrianna suggested that for the next two weeks, Kim should write at least two affirmations about herself in the journal following each entry in which she was able to focus on personal needs other than her need for Bill. Thus, Adrianna combined externalization and affirmation strategies to strengthen Kim's use of journaling for reflective work (see table 9.1 in the Individual Modality: Personal Empowerment category).

Visualization Exercises.   Building on Kim's insights from journaling about her self-marginalization, Adrianna used the ecomap to help her identify more adaptive sources of social support than Bill in her environment. The ecomap is a cognitive restructuring mapping tool (see figure 8.1) or a visualization exercise (see table 9.1 in the Individual Modality: Personal Empowerment category) that can strengthen clients' perceptions about and use of their environmental resources. By using the ecomap, Kim identified a former teacher and members of a neighborhood church as available supports with whom she had lost contact after she began her four-year relationship with Bill.

This church was less fundamentalist, and had an urban mission and more tolerance for helping recovering people, than the Pentacostal church from Kim's earlier years. Kim was able to attend NA meetings held in this urban mission church as well as receive meals in its soup kitchen. The former teacher provided a place for her to live after her relapse and the two rape incidents fifteen days into her forty-five-day outpatient rehab program. At that point it became clear to Kim that continuing to live with Bill was a trigger for relapse because of their pattern of conflict and her view of herself as incomplete without him. His ongoing substance abuse in her presence was an added trigger.

The ecomap was useful too during individual sessions in which Kim began to identify other sources of disempowerment in her environment, such as recovery risks within her extended family. For instance, she had not been able to say in the women's issues group that her mother was a prostitute. In individual sessions, she revealed that her mother was angry because Kim was no longer a source of drugs after the relationship with Bill ended, during her last two weeks of rehab. Her mother's anger and blaming Kim for her problems had encouraged Kim to self-medicate in the past, and these current demands could increase Kim's potential for another relapse. Her mother's problems and the interpersonal dynamics between them led Kim to decide to cut off from her mother for a while and use her former teacher as a more appropriate model of women's interdependence.

Evaluation Methods

Documenting Personal and Interpersonal Empowerment.   The ecomap was an evaluation tool as well as an intervention strategy. Adrianna and Kim compared the initial ecomap with periodic revisions and with final revisions made when rehab ended. The revisions indicated Kim's shift from primarily addicted and exploitative relationships in early rehab to nonaddicted and supportive relationships near the end of rehab. These new relationships, with her former teacher and a sponsor from her church, were both empowering.

Kim's journal was a second source of data for evaluating her response to rehab. As noted previously, her initial entries focused almost entirely on her need for Bill and their relationship issues. Later entries, particularly those after the externalization and affirmation assignments, indicated a new focus on Kim's identity as a person and as a woman. Those entries reflected a consciousness-raising and personal empowerment process as she began to view herself as a separate and worthwhile person. For example, some focused on Kim's career goals and steps she was undertaking by herself to meet those goals.

Documenting Changes at the Political Empowerment Level.   In addition, Kim's journal entries at the end of rehab described her new experiences in providing community service, a key component of her rehab program. Aftercare plans in the program require some form of community service to help clients learn appropriate ways of using their leisure time. Another goal is to help clients learn how to contribute positively to their communities, to give back something for their chance to recover and for what they have cost the community during their addiction (see table 9.1 in the Individual Modality: Political Empowerment category). Kim's journal entries indicated a sense of efficacy from becoming a group leader in her church's mentoring circle for young girls. She wrote, "I know something about being a woman now that can help these girls be stronger than I was at their age."

Conclusion

Empowerment practice in individual sessions during rehab should result in the type of self-efficacy expressed by Kim in the above journal entry. An important part of such practice is the combination of reflective, interactive, and systems impact strategies that each helper and client collaborate on during rehab. Chapters 9 and 10 clarify that essential aspects of recovery work occur in family and group sessions; this chapter illustrates the important parallel process in individual therapy. The time limitations imposed by managed care policies require integrating these modalities to maximize clients' empowerment opportunities and remove barriers to their recovery.

Rehab programs need a combination of cultural resources to meet the needs of diverse clients. Comprehensive training programs are necessary for staff members' development and growth over time in the area of cultural competence. Knowledge about professional helpers' own culture should be included as well as information about the cultural groups of which their clients are members. Unacknowledged cultural gaps involve disabilities, location, gender, and certain ethnic groups such as Native Americans.

There a need for both long-term and periodic training to help staff and clients identify supports and barriers to empowerment and cultural efficacy and ongoing supports, such as cultural coaches. The goal should be to enhance staff and clients' competencies while achieving the organizational and social policy reforms necessary for effective empowerment practice with diverse clients.

12 Phased Services During Aftercare and Termination: Evaluation of Empowerment Outcomes

Once resolved (at least temporarily), a now-preventable problem
becomes the target for other distinctive practices to prevent relapse.
—M. Bloom (1995:1898)

The third stage of treatment is maintenance or aftercare, which helps clients to solidify gains made during the first and second stages, to prepare for termination of services, and, as noted by Bloom above, to prevent relapse. It is assumed that providing specific relapse prevention training in this stage helps clients learn to manage high-risk situations while they still have treatment supports. However, they may not be convinced that they have the power to manage risky situations in everyday life. Therefore, the transition from rehabilitation, the second stage of treatment, to aftercare and eventual termination should help to enhance clients' self-efficacy for managing recovery after treatment ends (Smyth 1995).

Further, phased or staggered services can increase opportunities for client empowerment throughout termination or the transition out of services (Fortune 1995). Phased services help clients realize that although they are receiving less frequent and intensive services, they can effectively apply the skills they have learned to manage their recovery. In one situation, Dwayne, a thirty-one-year-old African American client, was in his first week of aftercare services. During a group session, Dwayne mentioned his concern about living near a grocery store where drug sales occurred frequently. In the past, each time he went to this store, he bought drugs. His peers encouraged him to find a different place to shop, pointing out that the old store was a risky, slippery situation.

The counselor suggested that Dwayne use his relapse prevention tools to manage this. Playing his disintegration tape could help him to understand how the store had become one of his relapse triggers (see chapter 11 for a detailed discussion of this relapse prevention strategy).The tape reminded him of two important aspects of his cycle: how good it felt to be greeted and accepted by his "home boys" in front of the store and the crack high he had anticipated. Realizing that this was only one part of his disintegration tape made it difficult to keep denying the cycle of violence, stealing, homelessness, and relationship losses that followed each of his relapses.

This example points out the value of "in the moment," practical treatment supports provided to clients during aftercare and highlights some individual factors that add to the complexity of this treatment phase. The impact of Dwayne's loss of family members and nonaddicted peers on his ability to manage high-risk situations during recovery is evident. Often in this stage, loss experiences during and at the end of treatment "stir up emotions about clients' previous losses" (Fortune 1995:2400).

A service program's handling of aftercare and termination may present additional barriers to effective recovery. For example, assigning clients to new counselors when they shift from rehabilitation to aftercare is a common practice. Often this is done without allowing clients an opportunity to discuss their reactions to the change, including possible feelings of rejection and unclear expectations about the new service (Siebold 1992).

In addition to these individual and program factors, certain policy reforms affect this transition by restricting access to and maximum periods for services (Creager 1991). Managed care restrictions have changed many inpatient programs from thirty. sixty, or ninety days to fourteen days, with clients being transitioned into thirty- or sixty-day outpatient programs for the remainder of their treatment. Moreover, these policy reforms include more restrictive admission criteria for the recently modified fourteen-day inpatient programs (Halim 1996).

Clearly, a number of interrelated factors can affect the aftercare stage of treatment, relapse prevention, and lifelong recovery. This chapter analyzes elements of clients' individual and family loss histories, rehab and prevention programs, and policy that influence the aftercare stage and termination. In each section, the impact of these factors on empowerment outcomes is discussed as well. The chapter concludes with a discussion of what aspects of the aftercare or maintenance stage support reintegration, based on current evaluation research, and what aspects are barriers to effective client reintegration.

Managing Individual and Family Factors

Loss and struggles to cope with it are universal experiences. Clients who are addicted or who have substance abuse problems may have experienced additional losses. Some may be related to ordinary life events and developmental transitions, while others are more directly related to clients' use and abuse of substances. Both types of losses may resurface before and during aftercare, necessitating the provision of special services for addressing them.

Ordinary Life Events and Losses

Types of Losses.   A number of authors have identified different categories of loss experienced by most people over the life span that can undermine or enhance their personal growth, depending on the individual's and family's coping abilities and other strengths (Bowlby 1980; Kamerman 1988; Kübler-Ross 1969; McNeil 1995; Silver and Wortman 1980). One system categorizes losses in the following four areas: physical and mental functioning, status and roles, significant relationships, and familiar possessions and surroundings (Freeman 1984). Examples in these categories include loss of sexual functioning or cognitive ability, an occupation or role in a peer group, relationships with family members or friends ended by death or divorce, and mementos or living arrangements.

Challenges to Coping with Loss.   Addicted clients may experience more difficulties than other people in normalizing such losses and their reactions to them. Both addicted and nonaddicted family members can heighten a client's self-blame by attributing the stress they experience from a loss to the client's substance abuse. This allows them to deny the loss or its impact while reinforcing the addicted member's shame and guilt.

A lack of opportunity to work through mourning and grief related to previous losses can result in cumulative, chronic sorrow (Freeman 1996), which can diminish the ability to cope with future losses. A person's potential for achieving mastery over losses by moving toward acceptance and integration may be affected. Integration allows people to obtain meaning from the loss experience and then to internalize that understanding as a component of their personhood and identity. Failure to integrate the experience can produce a sense of incompetence and incompleteness, with alternating feelings of guilt, shame, disempowerment, and rejection that can inhibit further personal growth and empowerment in this area.

These overwhelming feelings can be used as a rationale for self-medication, which numbs or masks them with the rush of power or invincibility that some people experience from the abuse of substances. Often, the underlying and unfinished grief is expressed in some of the themes included in table 12.1, which are consistent with Kübler-Ross's stages of loss and grief. The table demonstrates how current events and transitions in clients' lives can cause them to move back and forth between loss stages and related themes. The first quote following each loss theme illustrates a reaction to an ordinary loss or transition, while the second quote illustrates a response to an addiction-related loss. The example of Dwayne in this chapter's introduction shows movement between the stages of denial and depression or between themes such as "The Lone Ranger" and "Poor Me."

Program Supports. Once individuals achieve stabilization in early treatment, rehabilitation and aftercare can provide opportunities to address these themes and the unfinished loss experiences that tend to resurface throughout treatment. This occurs because most people experience heightened vulnerability during rehab when their value systems and lifestyles are challenged (McNeil 1995). Also, they may be getting in touch with feelings they have not experienced previously or in a long time, reliving important events that they buried successfully in the past by staying high. Moreover, clients are confronted with twelve-step work that involves taking an inventory of past wrongs and atoning for those mistakes, among other recovery activities.

Clients need supports to confront these new and frightening feelings and significant past events that they have suppressed. They need education about loss and grief and opportunities to unlearn old ineffective coping styles and develop more healthy patterns, to say good-bye after working through irrevocable losses, and to atone for and reconnect with retrievable relationships that are important for their recovery. Freeman (1996) points out that making other services available to these clients "without providing education and counseling for helping them to manage their losses is likely to be ineffective" (71).

Addiction-Related Losses

Types of Losses and Loss Themes.   Clients with substance abuse problems experience additional losses related to their drug use and abuse, often without being aware of the losses or the impact on their lives. Examples include the loss of physical control experienced during sexual and other assaults while under the influence, repeated job or career failures (losses of status and familiar surroundings), falls and other accidents (losses of functioning), and escalating debts that accrue from substance abuse (loss of resources). Failed attempts to end the addiction may reinforce the losses of control and nurturing relationships that result from or are exacerbated by the abuse.

All family members and significant others experience these losses too, as "substance abuse becomes the central organizing theme of the unit" (Freeman 1993:5). The addicted family or peer group member frequently is not fully aware of the emotional impact of these losses or of the additional stresses that this lack of awareness creates for the unit. Families react in different ways in order to manage the stress and disorientation resulting from these experiences. They may become emotionally and physically detached from the addicted member as well as from each other, or they may overfunction to mask or compensate for the emotional gap that is created when the addicted person's involvement with substances intensifies (Shorkey and Rosen 1993).

Freeman (1996) and Smyth (1995) indicate that one of the most profound losses experienced by addicted clients, however, is the loss of their relationship with their drug(s) of choice and drug lifestyle once they enter treatment. Using Kübler-Ross's stages of loss and grief to frame addiction-related losses in table 12.1 clarifies how clients' initial denial themes are often an effort to preserve their connection with their substance(s): "I don't have an addiction problem" or " My addiction is no big deal."

Bargaining themes such as "Running in Place" are an effort to postpone the loss of identity and lifestyle from giving up the addiction. Addicted clients bargain to relinquish their substance(s) for good if they can have one final hit, reasoning that "One hit can't hurt me!" Ignoring their knowledge that the addiction must be given up altogether and that one hit leads to another is clearly "Running in Place," since the client goes neither forward nor backward in terms of recovery.

TABLE 12.1 Kübler-Ross's (1979) Loss and Grief Stages and Freeman's (1994) Related Loss Themes

Stages	Examples of Clients' Themes from Ordinary Life Events and Addiction Experiences
Denial	*Not Me!*: "It (the loss) didn't happen." "I don't have an addiction problem."
	Tea and Sympathy: "It (the loss) isn't important to me, but I see it bothers you." "My addiction is no big deal to me, I'm sorry you have a problem with it."
	The Lone Ranger: "It's over (the loss), I'm out of here." "My addiction is a problem sometimes, but I don't stay anyplace long enough for people to get to know me."
Anger and shock	*Et tu, Brute*: "She said she left because of my affair, but I don't think she ever really loved me." "Even my mother thinks I'm an addict; that's the ultimate rejection!"
	Let's Just Do It and . . .: "Yes, it (the loss) happened, it wasn't fair, but I did what I needed to do and then got on with my life." "I'm here (in treatment) because I have to be, but as soon as I can, I'll . . ."
Bargaining	*I'll Cry Tomorrow*: "I won't give in to my feelings now, maybe later. . . ." "I don't need to deal with how I got addicted or why, I just won't use anymore."
	Running in Place: "I've stopped missing him, but maybe he'll come back sometime in the future." "I know I can't get into the drug scene again, but one hit can't hurt me."
Depression	*Poor Me*: "No one has ever felt this bad before." "I didn't set out to be an addict; why did this happen to me?"
	There Is No Future: "My life is over without my child." "What am I going to do without drugs? What kind of life is that?"
Acceptance	*Got It!*: "Nothing happens without a reason; God has a plan." "I used to demand life on my terms when I was using; now I'm struggling to accept life on its terms."
	I'll Do as Much as I Can: "I'm struggling to accept it (the loss), but I know I'll be working on what it means to me for a long time." "I have the tools I need, all I have to do is use them, one day at a time."

Staff Roles During Early and Middle Phases of Rehab.   The expression and impact of these themes vary during different stages of treatment (Freeman 1996). And as clients move back and forth through loss stages and themes, their collective and individual needs change. All clients in early treatment or the stabilization stage can benefit from education about and normalization of loss and grief, including the loss of their drug(s) of choice. Normalization helps them to understand that denial is a common reaction that maintains the addiction and loss themes, such as "Not Me" and "Tea and Sympathy."

Staff may see and need to acknowledge variations of other denial themes in this table during early treatment. "The Lone Ranger" theme can manifest itself as "I can be in treatment and out again before they discover how bad my problem is; then I won't have to really give up _____" (their drugs of choice). Staff can point out how other clients have expressed such themes and how they change with progress in treatment and movement through other loss and grief stages. Being able to label and understand common themes helps clients to gain some initial control in this early period of recovery.

In contrast, many clients in the middle or rehabilitation stage need help to begin the common process of working through losses that affect their management of current feelings and development of effective coping skills. Apparently Dwayne, discussed in this chapter's introduction, had not learned those skills or worked through his losses adequately in the middle stage of rehabilitation. Or perhaps, as expected during aftercare, he needed help in applying the skills more effectively.

Staff Roles During Aftercare.   Aftercare is the stage where those skills can be practiced and refined during group sessions, while further in-depth working through of addiction-related losses and other losses can be addressed as needed. Clients in this stage may continue to express depression themes such as "Poor Me" and require peer feedback to acknowledge universal losses, to mourn them, and then to move on toward acceptance or "Doing the best I can" (see table 12.1).

Whereas many of clients' common and individual needs can be met by peer group services, some of their unique loss issues may be more appropriately addressed in individual and family counseling during aftercare. In the case of sixteen-year-old Kellie, a biracial white and Native American girl who had been adopted by a white family at the age of two, anger over the loss of her natural family became the focus of treatment during the middle phase. Her adopted family would not provide Kellie with information about her natural family because they were afraid she would begin to identify herself as Indian instead of white, and from their perspective, that would mean she had rejected them. Group counseling helped Kellie identify how her anger toward her adopted family had become the rationale for her crack, alcohol, and marijuana addictions. Peers helped her to identify some of the triggers in her family relationships and in her behavior and thinking that could lead to relapse.

During aftercare, however, Kellie was able to explore in more depth the loss of culture she had experienced by being cut off from her natural family and her tribe. She knew very little about this part of her heritage. Confronting the pain of that loss during individual and family sessions in this stage, after she had developed and practiced essential relapse prevention skills, allowed Kellie to more safely confront her adopted family. She was able to openly talk about their attitudes and share how much those attitudes pained her.

Previously, she had been able to express only the anger connected with her loss. As a result of the family and individual sessions, Kellie revised her relapse prevention plan to focus on learning more about her heritage. This exploration was important for her healing and recovery process, movement toward the "Got It" theme in table 12.1, and for addressing identity, an appropriate developmental task.

In other instances, clients' unique needs may require that the loss work usually recommended for the aftercare stage occur earlier during rehabilitation. Individual and family strengths essential for developing an effective recovery program may be blocked and inaccessible to clients who have been severely traumatized (Smyth 1995). The most severe cases of child sexual abuse, spousal battering, community violence, emotional abuse, or multiple losses may require focus in the middle stage of treatment, and the usual education and skill development services for managing loss and grief may not meet these clients' needs sufficiently (Gorski 1989).

Also, when family members adopt dysfunctional roles to cope with a member's addiction, those roles can become very chronic and rigid. This can make them unresponsive to initial education and skill development services (Freeman 1996) and thus impede early recovery. If treatment plans are not modified to address these relatively unique situations prior to aftercare, clients are likely to blame themselves for their lack of progress, to feel disempowered, and to relapse and drop out of treatment early.

Managing Program Factors Related to Losses

Aspects of a program's structure and process of treatment can create new losses for clients and influence how well previous and existing losses are addressed. The transition out of services may be affected too, as when clients drop out of treatment early or leave as planned but without appropriate closure on losses and other concerns. Therefore, the following aftercare goals are important for clients involved in formal and informal rehab services, prevention, and natural recovery:

1. effective application of loss and grief education and skills in order to work through and accept losses, including the termination of services;
2. development of effective coping patterns for handling future losses and other stresses, and the application of relapse prevention tools learned during rehabilitation to problems in everyday life;
3. implementation of changes in lifestyle, daily living skills, and interpersonal relationships or social supports that are necessary for effective recovery and empowerment without substances (Gottlieb 1987; Gutheil 1993; Marlatt and George 1984; Shure and Spivack 1988).

Formal and Informal Treatment Factors

As noted in chapter 10, providing relapse prevention training and tools early in recovery and integrating them into a relapse prevention plan sets the stage for ongoing client empowerment and self-efficacy. In aftercare, program supports for implementing the plan effectively can potentially enhance these positive outcomes to an even greater extent.

Empowerment occurs through a process of anticipatory coping (Caplan 1989), identifying and planning how to address stresses in high-risk relapse situations. Self-efficacy training (Bandura 1989) is important for generalizing what is learned from anticipatory coping to problem resolution in the actual life situation. Client involvement, phased services, and specialized training for staff are critical for facilitating these aspects of the aftercare stage and an empowered termination process.

Client Involvement and Phased Services.   During aftercare, formal services can be staggered so that the frequency and intensity are decreased based on each client's incremental progress in applying anticipatory coping and self-efficacy training to his or her recovery. At the same time, the frequency and intensity of informal services, such as transitional housing, twelve-step programs, other support groups, recreation, and community service may need to be increased (McCrady and Irvine 1989; Malloy 1990; Smyth 1995). This parallel transition process is necessary so that new and existing informal community supports can supplement, and eventually replace, formal treatment. However, the client's active involvement in planning and implementing the transition is central to this phased service process (Daley 1989; Smyth 1995).

In one sixty-day outpatient program, Effie, a twenty-eight-year-old Italian American woman, met with her counselor three times per week for the first thirty days of recovery. Even though she had experienced two isolated "slips" (single instances of combined alcohol and Valium abuse), her counselor recommended that Effie be shifted to once-weekly sessions during the next thirty days. Effie wondered if she was ready for this change; she thought she needed the support of more frequent sessions to manage the stress of family gatherings once or twice monthly where alcohol was always served. She was concerned too about managing the relationship with her boyfriend, who continued to abuse cocaine and had become a drug dealer to support his addiction.

However, the counselor believed that Effie had made sufficient progress to be moved to once-per-week treatment, and so the change was made. A more appropriate response from the counselor would have been to use Effie's relapse prevention plan as a framework for exploring her concerns: exploring the basis for her concerns and processing with her the relapse triggers that were part of each situation.

Solution-Focused Collaborative Strategies.   Then, anticipatory coping could have helped Effie identify exceptions (Nickerson 1995), or situations in which she already felt empowered and was able to use her relapse prevention tools effectively. For instance, Effie was managing successfully conflicts with one co-worker without self-medicating as she had in the past, and was resisting the temptation to go out to "drinking" lunches or happy hours with other well-meaning co-workers.

She was managing the peer conflict by reviewing her triggers checklist in her head and by suggesting that potentially conflictual discussions be continued at a later time (when she could think more clearly) whenever she recognized a trigger from the checklist. In the case of social invitations, she consulted her appointment book, where she had written "You don't have to touch fire to know that it burns" as a reminder of her self-efficacy training, and then assertively declined the risky invitations.

Using this solution-focused strategy of finding the exception (Nickerson 1995), the counselor could have helped Effie think through a similar application of her relapse prevention tools in the two risky situations she was still concerned about. Her sense of empowerment from managing risky work interactions could have been used to create hope and new possibilities for handling the other two areas more effectively.

Analyses of Power and Loss Themes.   A power analysis of family coalitions and roles could have revealed previously unidentified triggers that threatened Effie's recovery. One trigger recognized in later recovery was her loss of dignity and status as the older sibling. The loss occurred gradually as she became addicted, family members labeled her as irresponsible, and her value and role in the family diminished. Memories of this earlier loss might have been precipitated by the impending loss of the social worker, implicit in the plan for less frequent counseling sessions. The theme of "Et tu Brute," or "I didn't expect this from you too," in table 12.1 illustrates the painful connection Effie acknowledged later between her past and impending losses.

Need to Negotiate Changes in the Aftercare Plan.   Therefore, in addition to the identified strategies, perhaps the most important approach should have been to modify the plan to change Effie's counseling schedule. Services could have been staggered more gradually so that her concerns about her boyfriend and family relationships (barriers to her recovery) could be acknowledged and addressed.

Instead, Effie appeared somewhat detached and reflective during her one weekly session the following week. In the second week of the new schedule, she did not show up. The counselor learned through other clients that Effie had relapsed. She reentered the program four months later, feeling guilty and ashamed because she had ignored signs of her impending relapse but unaware of the program's role in the process (Surls 1994).

To avoid exacerbating the type of disempowerment and loss of control experienced by Effie during her relapse, rehab programs should solicit, acknowledge, and integrate clients' input on all treatment decisions. There is no doubt that Effie learned important information about recovery from her relapse. Moreover, the relapse might have occurred even if the counselor had used some of the treatment strategies discussed in this section. But the entire situation could have been handled more productively with Effie's input and the additional support available from phased services.

The Nature of Effective Phased Services.   Phased services require a commitment to facilitating positive forms of learning, from clients' preventing or being confronted with the realities of relapse. Positive learning experiences are possible when a range of phased services are available for meeting the goals identified in the overview to this section. These services can improve not only relapse prevention and coping skills of clients such as Effie and Dwayne but also their management of termination and development of self-efficacy. The following services should be provided at various intervals and levels of intensity, based on the population being served and each client's needs and issues to be addressed (Annis 1986; Elbow 1987; Fortune 1995; Gutheil 1993; Siebold 1992; Smyth 1995):

1. Team referrals should be made to aftercare (the referring and receiving counselors and other staff work together with the clients through a transition period between rehabilitation and aftercare, involving clients in treatment plan decisions and encouraging them to discuss their reactions and concerns).
2. Ritual markers should be used to validate the clients' transition (and loss) from rehabilitation to aftercare (and from aftercare to termination of services), including memory books, rites of passage involving elderhood or alumni status, naming ceremonies to mark the loss of the old identity and taking on of a new identity, exchanges of photographs, and celebrations involving food and other ethnic specialties.
3. Loss and grief education should be continued along with analysis of clients' loss themes (see table 12.1), which can be identified through ritual markers, journals, life narratives, and power analyses. Help should be provided for working through losses and other barriers to an effective recovery and transition out of services.
4. Anticipatory guidance and training in coping skills should be provided for clients to manage high-risk situations, old unresolved losses, and new losses and concerns.
5. Self-efficacy training should be used to help clients apply anticipatory coping skills to actual problems in living, increase compe-

tency, and enhance personal growth through self-feedback and affirmations from peers and staff.

6. Peer group and family counseling should address interpersonal and communication issues clients encounter when implementing changes in lifestyles and daily living skills related to the family, peer network, employment, social, and political action domains.

7. Continuation of relapse prevention training is required; clients' skills can be reinforced with the help of aftercare clients who train peers still in the rehabilitation stage.

8. On-site peer mentoring and volunteer community services should be important aspects of twelve-step recovery work and self-efficacy training.

9. A combination of on-site and off-site twelve-step meetings, transitional housing, and vocational training/work opportunities should be used to aid in the transition out of services.

10. Other services identified by individuals and peers as essential to recovery and relapse prevention should be included.

Specialized Training for Staff. In order for the above complement of aftercare services to be effective, rehab program staff need programmatic supports. They need specialized training in critical areas in order to become self-empowered helping professionals who can facilitate client empowerment. Such training needs to be consistent with important program factors: philosophy, mission, and goals for empowerment, as discussed in chapter 8. Essential areas of training for aftercare services include anticipatory coping, self-efficacy, loss and grief issues, termination, and relapse prevention.

Usually, staff training for helping professionals in these and other topics is presented as a tool for helping clients to grow and develop. In the substance abuse field, however, both recovering and nonrecovering staff members may have unfinished losses regarding their own addictions or those of family members or peers that can impede their ability to use such training to benefit clients (Anderson and Wiemer 1992). For instance, Effie's counselor from the previous example, Ilene, had been in a coaddicted relationship with her husband when she began recovery, similar to the relationship between Effie and her boyfriend. When Ilene's husband entered a recovery program first, she experienced a sense of abandonment and rejection.

In talking about her work with Effie later during supervision, Ilene questioned whether her personal abandonment issues had been addressed sufficiently in her own recovery. She concluded that her unresolved loss might have caused her to ignore Effie's request for more time to work on ending the relationship with her boyfriend, whom Ilene thought of as the "abandoned" party in that relationship.

In addition to personal addiction-related losses, staff members have often experienced the types of universal losses and transitions discussed earlier. These can surface when staff attempt to help clients address their addiction losses and work through termination (Fortune 1995). Thus, a different, four-pronged focus is needed for training staff in these aftercare topic areas, including (Anderson and Wiemer 1992; Brill and Nahmani 1993; Fortune 1987; Van Wormer 1987):

1. education and skill training in the identified aftercare topic areas
2. education and skill training for addressing and managing personal and professional issues that may be barriers to effective work with clients in the topic areas
3. training in effective instructional methods, skills, and materials to improve the education and skill training provided to clients during aftercare
4. training in identifying and resolving program factors that are barriers to effective aftercare services through mobilization of administrative supports.

To ensure that staff members achieve these process-oriented goals, all program administrators should be involved in the training provided for aftercare services. Administrators should then work with counselors to provide the program supports necessary for successful implementation of the training and for empowerment of staff (Anderson and Weimer 1992; Freeman 1988).

Prevention Program Factors

Challenges to Maintaining Prevention Outcomes.   Although prevention programs have not included aftercare services traditionally, many preventionists have explored the problem of maintenance and generalization of outcomes with various populations (Coates 1990; DeJong and Winsten 1990; Lawson 1989; Schinke, Botvin, and Orlandi 1991). This research has identified factors that enhance the maintenance of protective components for alcohol and other drug abuse prevention. Program factors include training in skills such as resistance and problem solving, while community factors include the presence of positive and sober peer and adult mentors, along with opportunities for bonding and empowerment (Hawkins and Catalano 1992).

One promising approach to maintaining protective factors after a program ends involves a multicultural perspective on community substance abuse prevention. Bloom (1995) says of multicultural programs such as Orlandi's (1986) that maintenance is enhanced because participants are "involved in developing and monitoring (these) prevention programs, both to optimize their strengths and special knowledge and to motivate them in a program they 'own' " (1899). These programs recognize unique strengths as well as differences in language, cultural values, patterns of addiction, and oppression and disempowerment experiences.

They often illustrate, however, how culturally incompatible values can be hidden in the structure of a program, leading to group disempowerment and lack of maintenance. For example, a program's emphasis on cultural tolerance can be undermined by its curriculum if the case examples contain biased descriptions of cultural patterns in the group being served or in other groups. It is less likely that such a program's curriculum will be viewed as culturally sensitive or that resistance skills will be learned or maintained.

Prevention Aftercare Strategies.   To maintain prevention skills and empowerment experiences through a transition stage similar to treatment aftercare, effective multicultural and culturally sensitive programs need to develop relevant services. These can include alumni support groups in schools, churches, cultural clubs, community centers, and in youth associations such as Boys and Girls Clubs, 4-H groups, Boy Scouts and Girl Scouts, and the YMCA and YWCA. Programs might collaborate with Alanon and Alateen twelve-step groups in cosponsoring aftercare services and support groups, illustrating creative networking between formal and informal prevention resources. These aftercare and peer support services could become a standard part of prevention programs.

A complement of phased services paralleling those in treatment aftercare could be included, such as anticipatory coping and self-efficacy training. Addressing loss and grief issues would be relevant also. Many individuals completing prevention programs have had the typical losses experienced by most people, and no doubt, they incur additional losses from dropping out of substance abuse peer networks or from relinquishing family enabling roles. Prevention aftercare services could range from three to six months, depending on the needs of the youths or other population groups being served.

In one prevention program serving black, white, and Hispanic youths, an aftercare component developed spontaneously when the clients identified additional tasks necessary for maintaining their gains from the program. They planned and organized a research project to explore the prevalence of substance abuse among young people in their community, a dissemination conference to impact policy, and a peer prevention support group in their school during a yearlong "aftercare" phase (Malekoff 1994). This example demonstrates prevention aftercare activities that other self-directed and empowered youths could engage in to maintain their substance abuse resistance skills. Moreover, adding an aftercare component to prevention programs can make the traditional continuum of care a true continuum as shown in figure 12.1, instead of the linear range of separate services that exists currently.

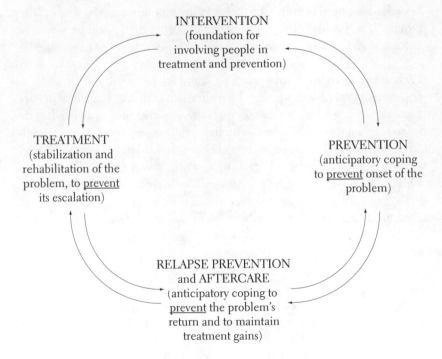

FIGURE 12.1 Modified Substance Abuse Continuum of Care

Natural Recovery

The Role of Resilience Factors.   Natural and indigenous factors also can affect people's recovery and prevention experiences. Individuals who recover from or resist substance abuse without formal or informal services such as twelve-step programs may exhibit a natural resiliency and problem-solving ability. Thus, knowledge about what Kurtz (1992) calls natural healing or recovery may be enlightening in two ways. First, research has documented factors that contribute to this process, such as religious or spiritual involvement, concerns about personal health, work environments' nontolerance of drug use, and using natural supports as a means of social control (having a positive and expressive family or not wanting to hurt the family) (Kurtz 1992; Ludwig 1985; Tuchfield 1981; Vaillant 1988).

A fifty-four-year-old African American man decided to recover naturally after his two young grandchildren repeatedly refused to be near him whenever he had been drinking. Burt had been a binge drinker since his late twenties with cycles of alcohol abuse that occurred every three or four months, when he would drink continuously for weeks. He was a construction worker; the workplace culture involved heavy drinking on payday and in many instances, on a daily basis during or after work. He had close relationships with family members except when he binged; then there were periods when he was avoided and rejected, especially by his grandchildren.

The day he decided to recover after a particularly long binge, Burt placed a bottle of vodka on his bedroom dresser. He said he was finished with drinking because it had cost him his grandchildren's love. Keeping the bottle in sight reminded him of the consequences of drinking and how hard he needed to struggle each day to recover. Burt withdrew from his peer network of co-workers who drank heavily and from risky social and recreational events. He maintained contact only with a few sober friends and engaged in nonalcohol-related family and social activities periodically. He became a more spiritual person, often reading the Bible and listening to religious programs on the radio. After six months of abstinence, he poured out the vodka. He remained abstinent for twenty-three years, until his death.

Some researchers have identified unique contributing factors to natural recovery in specific populations. For instance, Granfield and Cloud (1996) studied a sample of middle-income addicted individuals. Contributing factors in their natural recovery included maintaining a job, career, or business throughout the period of addiction; having nondrug-using friends to turn to when they decided to recover or moving to a new community if their peer networks consisted of mostly substance abusers; and becoming involved in sober, organized social groups as additional resources.

Value of Resiliency Data for Rehab Programs.   Most likely, a combination of individual, family, and environmental factors help to determine if and how natural recovery occurs. These supports probably affect recovery in a similar manner for clients involved in the aftercare stage of formal and informal treatment. Kurtz (1992) notes that they provide the individual with new sources of self-esteem, hope, forgiveness, and self-efficacy. Therefore, staff should help clients to assess, develop, and utilize natural recovery supports to enhance their progress during aftercare.

Information from research about why people in natural recovery avoid formal and informal recovery services can be enlightening. Granfield and Cloud's (1996) study of forty-six people in natural recovery identified the following programmatic barriers: ideological conflicts about the disease concept and assumptions about clients' powerlessness over their addiction; concerns about association with substance abusers who focus constantly on their addictions; and the disempowerment experienced by some people of color, gay men and lesbians, women, and strong individualists in reaction to the white, male-oriented culture of formal and informal services.

While these results from one study of middle-income people in natural recovery are not generalizable, they can help sensitize staff to potential barriers to recovery and empowerment. The respondents in this study emphasized the importance of having natural, sober support networks that felt inclusive and accepting of them in their recovery, in contrast to the exclusiveness they perceived in formal rehab and twelve-step programs they had attempted to recover in or knew about second hand.

Burt, the man in the previous example, decided to recover naturally because he believed programs and support groups dictated what recovering people should do without listening to the person who knew best. By implication, staff in formal rehab programs and peers in twelve-step and other informal groups should encourage clients to help identify and change similar barriers to effective aftercare in their programs.

Policy Influences on Loss and Aftercare

Although various policy issues have been addressed in other chapters of this book, policy that impacts the aftercare phase in particular warrants spe-

cial attention here. The aftercare phase represents a bridge for clients between their rehab programs and reintegration into the community, whether
they are involved in a residential, day hospital, or outpatient program. Generally, addicted individuals have gradually ceased to function well as members of a family or community prior to their recovery. They need rehab
supports to develop new, more adaptive connections in their communities
(Smyth 1995). Policy reforms affect programs' attempts to maintain aftercare
as a support and vital bridge to client reintegration, and their effects have
implications for client empowerment and management of losses during recovery.

Client Empowerment Issues

Health Care Policies.   A national health care plan, including provisions
for mental health recovery services for substance abusers, has been debated
widely (Poole 1995). A number of different versions of the plan have been
proposed, but one common aspect is restricted access to rehab programs.
The proposed restrictions seem to be part of the war on drugs philosophy
and concerns about not allowing mental health provisions to dominate allocations for general health care services (Freeman 1997).

It is safe to assume that aftercare will have even greater significance for
clients' recovery as health care and substance abuse block grant policy reforms are made. Such legislation is likely to restrict maximum service periods
for the stabilization and rehabilitation stages of recovery, but both research
and practice wisdom indicate the importance of maintaining long-term aftercare programs. Daley (1987) concludes that "clinicians need to help substance abusers devise long-term aftercare programs" because "relapse rates
are lower and relapses tend to be less severe for those persons who have
aftercare plans and are linked up with self-help and counseling resources"
(140).

Public Assistance-Employment Policy.   Policies that provide social supports to addicted clients also can restrict their access to long-term aftercare
services, and therefore to empowerment opportunities. For example, welfare
reform, or the Personal Responsibility and Work Opportunity Act (H.R. 4
1995), does not consider the needs of addicted clients. Many who are receiving outpatient substance abuse rehab services may require financial assistance but may not be able to work prior to the aftercare phase (NASW

1996). Moreover, many addicted clients lack marketable job skills, training, and career-oriented work opportunities (O'Donnell 1993). Hence, the already limited number of jobs that pay a living wage may not meet the special needs of this segment of the population (Poole 1995).

Housing Policy. Often, many of these clients are homeless when they enter rehab and require transitional housing prior to their completion of the early and middle phases. Current housing policy is beginning to focus more on transitional housing, but in the reintegration phase rather than during the early and middle periods of recovery. An adequate income and housing are essential for effective early recovery and community reintegration, because these resources provide the necessary buffers for maintaining recovery. In essence, these supports allow recovering people to develop self-management skills in regard to their recovery and their economic and social self-sufficiency. They provide a foundation for continued client empowerment and relapse prevention.

Client Loss Issues

Policy and Low-Priority Rehab Services. Although new managed care policies are designed to reduce costs while improving service quality, the caps on these policies may limit service comprehensiveness and availability (Chamberlain 1995; NASW 1996; Saucier 1995). Services identified by policy makers as without empirical documentation of direct effects on recovery, such as loss and grief groups, family groups, relapse prevention training, community involvement, and long-term aftercare may be reduced in scope or eliminated completely.

The Powerful but Limited Role of Early Recovery. Some research and practice wisdom indicate such services *are* essential for successful reintegration. They provide opportunities for clients to address unresolved losses, family issues, other relapse triggers, and stresses that reinforce addiction and impede recovery. Those services also provide important opportunities for clients to develop and practice anticipatory coping and other relapse prevention skills that help extend rehabilitation beyond the period of initial sobriety attained during early and middle recovery. The person may have stopped abusing their drugs of choice, but this dramatic change is estimated to represent approximately 10 percent of the work of recovery. The other 80 percent, which occurs during aftercare and the ongoing process of recovery, is when losses can be addressed and resolved and empowerment is possible.

Conclusion

From this discussion, it is clear that a number of interrelated factors, including universal and addiction-related losses, can affect the aftercare phase and clients' transition out of services. In addition, many myths exist among service providers and policy makers that can affect aftercare outcomes, and therefore clients' community reintegration.

Staff members often believe that clients relapse because they have not followed the program's recommendations or that chronic relapsers cannot be helped. These and other myths can affect the nature of services staff provide and how they evaluate rehab and reintegration outcomes. Daley (1987) concludes, for example, "staff may not adequately educate substance abusers and family members about relapse" because of such beliefs, and "they may limit the number of admissions for those who relapse" (140).

Research documents the folly of such myths and their impact on conclusions about service effectiveness. Focusing only on relapse rates in evaluating rehab and reintegration outcomes is too narrow because it ignores a key part of the self-management cycle and because relapse is a natural part of recovery. Aftercare trains clients to pay attention to both the recovery and the relapse aspects of this cycle and to use their tools to increase recovery and decrease the potential for relapse.

Clients' self-empowerment and self-esteem are likely to be increased when the focus is on gaining competence to manage the whole cycle. Therefore, learning from potential or actual relapses is assumed to be as important as using relapse prevention tools successfully and becoming involved in non-drug-using social networks. A range of other criteria have been documented by research as essential for successful rehabilitation and reintegration outcomes (Annis 1986; Bandura 1989; Carroll, Rounsaville, and Gawin 1991; Dayley 1987; 1989; McCready and Irvine 1989; Molloy 1990; Smyth 1995):

1. completion of a long-term aftercare phase of rehab in addition to early and middle phases

2. successful application of relapse prevention tools to daily stresses and triggers as part of the self-management cycle to increase recovery, decrease the potential for relapse, and increase understanding of recovery from experiencing both aspects of this cycle
3. development and use of nondrug- or alcohol-related networks, including a supportive and accessible sponsor
4. obtaining stable transitional or permanent drug-free housing and adequate employment or job training
5. development and use of a variety of nonalcohol- or drug-related leisure activities for appropriate management of time
6. involvement in community service projects to strengthen the bond and connection with the community and its resources, which may include political action and systems change as needed
7. implementation of a plan of personal growth for improving areas of functioning related to recovery: coping skills; interpersonal relationships; loss management; and work, job training, or education goals
8. involvement in twelve-step recovery work or in some other peer support group with a positive, nonalcohol- or drug-related focus (e.g., Women in Recovery)
9. a gradual shift to include other social connections in the support network, such as community religious institutions and groups, spiritual traditions, cultural clubs, or community centers
10. maintaining ongoing contacts for mentoring newly recovering people through alumni status with a rehab program, twelve-step groups, or other informal connections.

It is clear from these informal criteria that community reintegration begins during the aftercare phase and continues beyond clients' termination or transition out of services. Also, reintegration is a process that takes place over many months and years, not a single event. An important next step for the practice field in evaluating this process is to identify behavioral indicators for these and other criteria, then explore them more thoroughly under research conditions to identify a similar cluster of criteria and indicators of successful prevention outcomes.

Part 4

Empowering, Microcosm,
and Empowered Substance
Abuse Programs:
The Voices of Special Populations

Part 2 of this book analyzes how the three subsystems of the multilevel substance abuse service system can work together and the typical barriers and supports that programs encounter. In contrast, part 3 describes an empowered substance abuse service process across the continuum of care, involving both self-help and service provider strategies. Essentially, part 2 focuses on the service system's structure while part 3 addresses an empowered change process for clients and the impact of the system's structure on that process. The discussion in those two parts of the book is, naturally, focused on the dynamics across various types of rehab programs.

Part 4, on the other hand, examines how all of these elements interact within each of four exemplary programs that serve special populations. The four chapters clarify how the needs of each population influence the empowerment process and the structure of the respective programs and vice versa. Clients' characteristics and experiences are considered along with the effects of interpersonal variables and factors in the larger surrounding environment. In each chapter, clients' voices, their own words and nuances of behavior, their often stunning narratives, their very subjective realities and experiences are presented to reflect the dynamic empowerment process in action.

Chapter 13 examines a community-based residential rehab program for a multicultural population of adolescents that, through state public policy reforms, is moving toward becoming more community centered. This chapter describes how staff struggle to operationalize empowerment practice with clients who often suffer from developmental power cutoffs and impairments (or status barriers). The clients' creative responses to empowerment opportunities highlight their resiliency and commitment to recovery, along with the impact of practice in a secondary setting on this process. Their narratives illustrate the importance of their beliefs and developmental stage to their recovery and empowerment.

Chapter 14 focuses on recovery and empowerment in a community-centered day treatment program for perinatal women and children. As part of a broad-based umbrella organization, this program comes closest (among those described in part 4) to the comprehensive, integrated, community-centered system described in chapters 3, 4, and 5. The special gender-related political empowerment needs of this multicultural group and the unique program factors that facilitate that empowerment are clarified in the discussion. These clients' narratives reflect the effects of societal and programmatic oppression, as well as their own gender biases and socialization, on their recovery.

The focus of chapter 15, empowerment practice within a dual diagnosis program, involves a predominantly white but also multicultural population of adults. The program consists of combined outpatient and day treatment services within a mental health or secondary setting that is community based rather than community centered. The clients' control and power needs are analyzed in terms of medication compliance issues, acceptance of their dual substance abuse and psychiatric conditions, their strengths, and their involvement in innovative systemwide empowerment policies and implementation strategies.

Finally, chapter 16 describes a culture-specific rehab program for African American adults. This program provides multiple residential and outpatient substance abuse services in a primary setting, including services for the homeless and for women who are part of a parallel service arrangement of on-site programs and projects sponsored by a number of other organizations. The services and conceptual framework are based on Africentric values, traditions, and philosophical approaches that address cultural identity, community responsibility, and political empowerment as integral aspects of recovery.

13 New Alternatives: A Drug and Alcohol Rehab Program for a Multicultural Adolescent Population

> When I was first in treatment, I was living a double life—
> pretending to change, but I didn't think anyone could tell. It got to a point I
> almost believed it myself. Then my counselor asked me if I was sincere about
> recovery or just trying to get by. I was shocked by her question. It hurt to think
> she didn't trust me.
>
> —Shane S. (1995)

Most researchers and authors agree that the ideal strategy with children and adolescents is primary prevention involving education, skill development, and opportunities to practice using the new knowledge and skills (Schinke, Botvin, and Orlandi 1991). However, the severity of the current problem among this country's youths indicates that rehab should be a high priority as well (Kleber 1991). Smyth (1995) assumes that because youths' histories of substance abuse tend to be shorter than adults', age-specific services are required for adolescents to recover successfully. Such services are designed to address patterns of use, developmental tasks, and environmental stressors that influence addiction in unique ways. This chapter summarizes background information on the clients of an age-specific rehab program, identifies multilevel components of effective rehab in the program, and provides an analysis of empowerment issues for this population, their empowerment and disempowerment experiences, and practice implications for the program.

Background Information on the Client Group

Impact of Development on Use Patterns and Related Issues

New Alternatives serves adolescents between thirteen and seventeen years of age (the mean age is fifteen). Clients come from all socioeconomic backgrounds and family compositions. School performance is one age-related area of functioning that is often affected by their substance abuse. Some of the youths are school dropouts or have a history of academic failure; others have managed to do well in school for a period of time in spite of their substance abuse. Although the program acknowledges that these clients may confront other developmental issues such as identity problems, peer conflicts, or stress from emotional, physical, or sexual abuse by caretakers, its main admission criterion is that clients have a primary diagnosis of alcohol and drug abuse or dependency. Most of those admitted to the program are multiple or poly drug abusers. This pattern has made effective rehab, and particularly relapse prevention services, more difficult because these clients' triggers for and rewards from substance abuse have tended to be more complex.

Another commonality in this age group is that a majority of the clients have also sold drugs on a regular basis (Kaminer 1991; Schinke, Botvin, and Orlandi 1991). This has required the program to include services for helping youths involved in drug sales to make broader lifestyle changes. Those clients' immersion into drug and other illegal networks is often greater than that of the typical adolescent drug abuser (Williams 1995). Some of their drugs of choice are also age-related, such as gasoline and white out, because these and other inhalants are inexpensive and easily accessible for youths (Botvin and Tortu 1988; Young 1987). The program serves clients from most of a southern state's thirty-five counties, because there are very few residential programs for this age range within the state.

Impact of Diversity on Referral Patterns

This residential program has the capacity to serve a combination of sixteen males and females. Fifty percent of the boys admitted to the program are Caucasian and 50 percent are African American, while 70 percent of the girls are Caucasian and 30 percent are African American. The program would like to recruit more adolescents from other ethnic groups, particularly girls. But few females of color receive services from the psychiatric hospitals and hospital substance abuse units that refer many of the white girls, so referrals have remained low or nonexistent for females from some ethnic groups. Overall, most of the program's referrals are from juvenile court, based on status offenses, property crimes, drug sales and possession, and acts of violence. New Alternatives is a long-term program; rehab ranges from nine to eighteen months, with the average length of stay being one year. Program administrators believe their referrals from juvenile court and other social control organizations have increased because the program provides the long-term services necessary for addressing these clients' moderate to severe age- and gender-related problems.

Client Empowerment Issues

Entry Into Rehab

A number of empowerment issues have surfaced in New Alternatives that are relevant to other adolescent programs. One issue is related to this client group's typical routes into rehab. As noted previously, referrals usually come from social control agencies such as juvenile court and child protective services, as well as from health and mental health organizations. Therefore, in initial and ongoing early rehab, some of these nonvoluntary clients seem passive and accepting of services at a superficial level but, like Shane at the beginning of this chapter, may only appear to be in active recovery (Gibson 1993; Hawkins and Catalano 1992; McDonald, Bradish, Billingham, Dibble, and Rice 1991; Williams 1995). Questions about their sincerity may cause them to feel disempowered, yet those questions must be raised in order to help youths move from customer to client status (Rasheed 1996). Shane later identified the counselor's strategically timed question as a positive turning point in his slow recovery.

Other youths have been angry and hostile toward adults about their loss of power and freedom, and toward the social control systems that have required them to accept services. These attitudes have made it more difficult for staff to help empower adolescents initially, because, as one graduate of the program said, "they scare the staff. . . . But instead of getting rid of kids that yell and cause problems, the counselors should ask them why they're angry!" This young former client shared her opinion with staff in order to help them assess the sources of youths' anger and disempowerment in more depth, along with their recovery potential (their strengths and resilience). As a result of this and other feedback, staff and clients have struggled to get beyond these negative attitudes and resistance tactics, which are early barriers to empowerment for both.

Continuance in Rehab

Another empowerment issue with this population involves legal limitations on their decision making and therefore on their power to drop out of rehab or control their lives in other ways. For example, adults can leave rehab at any point without legal consequences if they are not court ordered to accept services. Ironically, although it is sometimes detrimental, an adult's dropping out can represent an irregular pattern toward eventual acceptance and completion of rehab. This may lead to self-efficacy and empowerment once the adult experiences successful recovery in spite of what appears to be, at least initially, a rehab drop-out or failure pattern.

Youths, on the other hand, whether or not they are mandated to accept services, cannot drop out or run away without legal sanctions because running away is a status offense (HHS 1990; Jarvis 1990; Freeman 1994). New Alternatives manages this issue by teaching its clients the consequences of leaving or running away, along with methods for identifying the triggers and warning signs and alternative ways to cope with the stress that precipitates running away. These strategies place adolescents in charge of whether they run while providing them with knowledge, skills, and other tools for managing the underlying issues, thus helping them to empower themselves (Williams 1995). Although runaway rates are extremely low for this program (only one incident occurred in the past two years), staff continue to be concerned about how mandatory rehab and other disempowerment experiences can disrupt recovery for youths.

Client-Specific Services

Developmental differences between adult and adolescent substance abusers have tended to affect the latter's empowerment opportunities in client-

or age-specific services. For instance, differences in use histories and patterns mean that adolescents seldom have a chance to "bottom out" like some adults who decide to recover, or to experience some of the severe consequences that make acceptance of rehab more likely. The definition of "bottoming out" is unique to each individual and adult clients often enter rehab without reaching that stage, but age and a combination of other factors can contribute to the briefer substance abuse histories that many adolescents experience. They require age-specific services focusing on initial and ongoing consequences of drug and alcohol abuse for youths to increase their opportunities for self-efficacy.

The developmental tasks of some youths in this program have been postponed or addressed ineffectively because substances have masked their related feelings and cognitions. All teenagers face challenges of friendship or peer relations, courtship, career planning, identity, and separation from the family of origin. Completion of such tasks is necessary for successful movement through adolescence into young adulthood (Freeman and McRoy 1987). New Alternatives staff assume that if they fail to help their clients address these areas effectively as part of their ongoing recovery, stress from struggling with or avoiding the tasks can be triggers for relapse and barriers to the youths' ongoing development.

These aspects of the program's clientele require more empowerment-oriented, innovative, and age-specific intervention strategies to move them into rehab and to prevent dropouts. Examples include drama therapy with a substance-abusing peer network and a recovering professional athlete influencing a high-risk teenager who is also a fan to enter rehab (see chapter 6 for a more detailed discussion of the intervention process). New Alternatives uses age-specific alcohol and drug education and counseling strategies as well; for instance, peers are cofacilitators in education groups and positive rap talent shows, and a physical development ropes course is a counseling intervention. As a result, clients' strengths are utilized more effectively in the recovery process (Kaminer 1991). Many of the program's other client-specific strategies and program factors are summarized in the following section.

The Program's Internal Structure and Context

The organizational analysis framework discussed in part 2 of this book, and especially in chapter 5, is useful for clarifying New Alternatives' internal and external context. The former consists of the program's structure and operation, while the latter includes the program as a subsystem within the larger, multilevel substance abuse service system. The other two subsystems are the community and policy/funding subsystems, which are discussed later in this chapter. The program subsystem, or the program's internal context, is discussed in terms of its early development and its philosophy, services, and empowerment-related program factors.

Early Program Development

New Alternatives was started in March 1991 as a specialized component of a twenty-eight-day rehab and detox program for adults. Many of the services were generalized from the adult program and had to be adapted later as age-specific issues surfaced. For example, it became necessary to make family involvement a requirement in the youth program in order to identify immediate barriers to clients' continuance in rehab and supports for recovery. Assessment data revealed high rates of sexual abuse, negative school attendance and performance patterns, and intrafamilial substance abuse problems from which the youths, unlike adults, could not isolate themselves after they returned home from rehab.

In addition, many clients in the adult program were negative models for the youths due to the proximity of the two programs and the short-term nature of adult services, which provided a very brief stabilization period. For these reasons, the adolescent program was moved into a separate but nearby facility after one year. The program moved again in 1993 to a more rural, outlying area when state and county funds provided resources for building a new facility.

Program Philosophy and Conceptual Framework

New Alternatives assumes all youths are at varying levels of risk from the present drug culture, so staff "are prepared to work with children with a variety of backgrounds and problems," understanding that "youth beginning to experiment with tobacco, alcohol, and other drugs will repeat the same behaviors of more serious drug offenders (e.g., disrespect of adults and authority, general rebellion, anger management problems, dishonesty, and the inability to experience and show feelings)" (*Staff Handbook* 1995). The program's philosophy is that addiction to alcohol and other drugs is a chronic, progressive, and eventually fatal disease, and that rehab leads adolescents through a healing process toward wholeness.

This philosophy implies also that in order to do this, services should address youths' emotional, physical, spiritual, and social needs and the total, difficult developmental transition they are confronted with (*Staff Handbook* 1995). Families are viewed as intrinsic to this recovery process. Although the term "empowerment" does not appear in program procedural manuals or other written materials, one staff member summed up the program philosophy and framework by emphasizing, "We understand that kids feel better when they accomplish a task or goal, or learn something, or do things they didn't believe they could do" (Interview 1995).

Nature of the Program's Services

Program Components and Staff. New Alternatives has both residential and day treatment services, divided into five phases. As can be seen from figure 13.1, phase 1 involves an orientation in which participants gradually become invested in the program, while phases 2 and 3 require full and intensive involvement, phase 4 includes program participation and bi-monthly weekend home passes, and phase 5 allows clients an extended thirty-day home visitation.

Phase 5 is viewed as a transition period that allows clients time to prepare for the move back into the community while they are still participating in the program. This phase requires attendance at weekly counseling and twelve-step groups, completion of weekly written progress reports, and weekly urinalysis. Staff believe phase 5 helps youths identify unacknowledged relapse triggers and increases their sense of competence about recovery.

Each phase involves different responsibilities and outcomes in the recovery process. For instance, among other goals, phase 1 requires clients to identify self-defeating behaviors such as guilt or blaming others, phase 2 requires them to demonstrate leadership skills in relation to peers in their unit, and phase 3 requires them to initiate problem-solving efforts to resolve interpersonal or organizational conflicts with peers, family members, or staff. To enhance decision making and self-efficacy, when youths believe they are

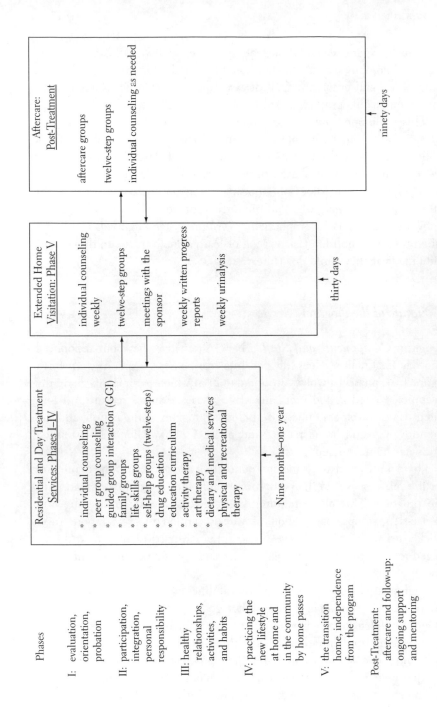

Aftercare: Post-Treatment

aftercare groups

twelve-step groups

individual counseling as needed

← ninety days

Extended Home Visitation: Phase V

individual counseling weekly

twelve-step groups

meetings with the sponsor

weekly written progress reports

weekly urinalysis

← thirty days

Residential and Day Treatment Services: Phases I–IV

* individual counseling
* peer group counseling
* guided group interaction (GGI)
* family groups
* life skills groups
* self-help groups (twelve-steps)
* drug education
* education curriculum
* activity therapy
* art therapy
* dietary and medical services
* physical and recreational therapy

Nine months–one year

Phases

I: evaluation, orientation, probation

II: participation, integration, personal responsibility

III: healthy relationships, activities, and habits

IV: practicing the new lifestyle at home and in the community by home passes

V: the transition home, independence from the program

Post-Treatment: aftercare and follow-up: ongoing support and mentoring

FIGURE 13.1 Program Services and Phases: New Alternatives

ready to move to the next phase, they can petition for a phase meeting in which they present an analysis of their progress to all the staff and clients in the program (their caring community). A joint decision is then made about whether the petitioner is allowed to move to the next phase, and feedback is provided about how the caring community views his or her progress. During my study of the program, three clients were in phase 1, six were in phase 2, four were in phase 3, two were in phase 4, and three were in phase 5.

Figure 13.1 contains the service components included in the program. New Alternatives is described as milieu therapy; therefore, all components are viewed as primary because each addresses some aspect of addiction and recovery. For example, art therapy sessions may involve creating colorful masks that reflect the feelings discussed in peer groups that clients previously stuffed or self-medicated. Clients make collages to illustrate the life histories they have presented and analyzed in individual and group counseling sessions. The ropes course not only teaches interpersonal and social skills but also helps clients to address directly personal and interpersonal barriers to recovery that surface during the group activities on the course and in school classes and family counseling sessions.

A diverse combination of staff members provide these integrated services. An M.S.W., the senior human services provider, supervises the program's five substance abuse counselors, four house parents, three aides, and consultants in adolescent substance abuse rehab and clinical areas. The senior provider reports to the director of the program, who also oversees the education department, food services, and various therapies: art, activity, and outdoor. The milieu or integrated nature of these services requires staff to coordinate their work closely within each component and across components. In art therapy, counseling and art therapy staff cofacilitate sessions; in the wilderness and drug education components, they are encouraged to develop joint projects for clients.

Major Theories, Approaches, and Rehab Strategies.   The program uses a combination of Reality Therapy, family therapy, psychoeducation, group mutual aid and positive peer culture, experiential learning, problem solving, and case management strategies. There is a heavy emphasis on values clarification, self-responsibility, and learning from natural consequences (Turner 1996). Clients are expected to volunteer to coach and mentor peers in education classes and to provide a great deal of constructive feedback and mutual aid in peer counseling groups (Galanter, Castaneda, and Franco 1991; Schopler and Galinsky 1995). They are encouraged to observe an honor system about not cheating or breaking rules while also being responsible for reporting peers' infractions in order to maintain a caring community and nonenabling relationships. Family involvement is required to prevent triangulation of staff and parents and because the approaches used by the program emphasize the importance of structural family changes to support the youths' recovery (Freeman 1994; Hartman 1995).

Empowerment-Related Program Factors

Type of Empowerment Organization and Program Factors. New Alternatives fits within the microcosm program category that I have added to Florin and Wandersman's (1990) original two categories of empowerment programs (see table 1.4). Adolescents can influence the service system in specific empowerment-related ways. Table 13.1 includes examples of organizational program factors that provide opportunities for the clients to achieve political empowerment, including mechanisms for them to provide feedback to staff about program services, participate in treatment team meetings, and request and present petitions at phase meetings to determine their movement through the program. These examples are related only to the internal program context.

Occasionally, the program focuses on helping a youth rehearse requesting and advocating for a policy change in other large institutions such as a community's public school system or child protective services. However, because this type of political action and systems change is not an integral part of its services, New Alternatives does not fit within the more developed category of empowered programs (Florin and Wandersman 1990). Thus, although empowerment is addressed effectively by some internal factors, the program does not go far enough in providing such opportunities related to the external environment, which could more effectively help to increase clients' autonomy, decision-making, self-efficacy, and political action skills in terms of the developmental needs discussed in a previous section.

In spite of these limitations in externally focused political empowerment, program factors, including the examples in table 13.1, help clients to empower themselves at the personal and interpersonal levels. Journaling and client-staff collaboration in developing relapse prevention plans are examples of personal empowerment program factors. In contrast, the phase 5 peer-calling network and the program's mutual aid groups help clients to achieve empowerment at the interpersonal level.

Type of Organization and Empowerment Needs of the Population. As noted in a previous section, adolescents' resistance to mandated services and their special developmental needs make empowerment particularly important for this population. These clients need to address power issues with authority because of their program entry patterns and to develop some autonomy and decision-making skills through age-specific program factors involving power sharing.

One way to assess the fit between these empowerment needs and the level of empowerment services is to evaluate the program's goals in this area. New Alternative's overall goal is to involve each adolescent in the participation and design of their own recovery process. The program has a set of related objectives, including remaining alcohol- and drug-free. Other objectives are for clients to take responsibility for their own actions and consequences; develop a personal, positive, inner strength; and develop a respect for self and community by refusing to sell drugs or create disturbances.

Although these three objectives imply empowerment, they are more related to personal and interpersonal levels of empowerment, consistent with the program factors discussed in the previous section. The objectives indicate that New Alternatives was designed to address the political level of empowerment only to a limited extent internally, and not at all externally. The program's external context is discussed next in terms of empowerment supports and barriers.

The Program's External Structure and Context

New Alternatives' external context affects youths' recovery and empowerment experiences in a parallel manner to factors in its internal context. The program's organizational auspices, which are a buffer between the internal and external context, influence the nature and quality of services. As explained previously, the external context consists of the community and policy/funding subsystems in which the program exists.

TABLE 13.1 Examples of Empowerment-Oriented Program Factors: New Alternatives

Empowerment Levels	Major Themes		
	Professional Services	Peer-Led Services	Professional-Client Collaboration
Personal	clients learn to journal, write life history, narratives, develop heritage book on cultural background	peers are assigned to orient and help transition new youths into the program	clients and staff collaborate on developing a relapse prevention plan and on individual service plans (ISP)
	clients learn self-management techniques to prevent running away	peers are encouraged to volunteer to tutor youths with academic deficits	clients can request time out as needed as part of their self-management skill development
Interpersonal	in preassessment meetings, youths present to staff their reasons for needing services and type of life they desire	peers facilitate peer counseling groups and mutual aid to members	family members, staff, and peers collaborate in giving youths feedback in phase meetings and in decision making
	youths can request a termination meeting if program is not working for them	youths call and write Phase V and aftercare peers to provide support/ positive peer-calling network	family participation is required for family meetings and in the development of goals to support youths' progress
Political	feedback on the quality of the program is regularly solicited from youths by staff	peers pledge to follow an honor system and to report violations, creating a positive peer culture in the program	youths participate in staffings and treatment team conferences
	youths are sometimes coached on how to influence other systems, e.g., their school district		youths present their request for a phase meeting to move to the next phase of treatment

Organizational Auspices

New Alternatives is part of a county mental health center whose structural organization is primarily geographical. Each of the four regions includes mental health, mental retardation, and substance abuse services. One division also has specialized services for the elderly. Three other functional divisions are included in the mental health center: Special Operations (medical records and supported living), Stabilization Services (in-home crisis services and partial hospitalization), and the Comptroller (budget and contract management). All seven divisions are administered by a CEO and by a Medical Director who reports to the CEO. The central office administrator for New Alternatives is a director of one of the geographical divisions, although the program is physically separate from the mental health center.

According to the organizational auspices continuum in figure 5.1, New Alternatives fits between "Substance Abuse Services in a Secondary Setting" and "Parallel Services Arrangements with Substance Abuse and Other Services." The secondary setting is the mental health center, while certain parallel services, including public education, psychiatric consultation, cultural enrichment, and twelve-step groups, are provided on site by other organizations.

One important aspect of the program's organizational auspices is currently impacting empowerment opportunities for consumers and staff. Previously, the mental health center's services were organized in terms of populations and special needs. Substance abusing youths might have been served by an adolescent unit, a mental health unit, and a substance abuse unit that often had conflicting priorities and whose staff competed for resources across the different divisions. A 1995 organizational change resulted in the current geographically based divisions. Staff within each are expected to share clients, resources, and ideas more effectively and efficiently across mental health, mental retardation, and substance abuse components (Interview 1996).

Mental health center administrators believe the current structure has removed unnecessary organizational layers and barriers to client and staff empowerment. Clients' needs are multidimensional rather than unidimensional, as implied by the old structure; thus the new focus on multiple needs has increased service accessibility (Interview 1996a). Staff have benefited as well because of increased intragency collaboration and decreased conflicts about values and methods (see figure 5.1 under Advantages and

Disadvantages of services in a secondary setting and parallel services). Similar changes have impacted the community subsystem and its empowerment, and the empowerment of the program's participants.

The Community Subsystem

A consumer reform movement within the state has shifted the focus of mental health services to include community and consumer input into decision making and policy development (Interview 1995c). The movement began with parents who became angry when they were prevented from gaining lifetime care and education for their mentally retarded children. The initial confrontation between the parents and mental health administrators resulted in political action by a coalition of special interest groups and community leaders, which led to a statewide initiative by legislators to reorganize the entire mental health system. The process was consistent with the consciousness-raising, investigatory research, and political action phases of Freire's (1989) empowerment approach, illustrated in figure 6.1. The system-wide reforms became effective in 1996. Currently, community service boards make funding and other policy decisions that govern New Alternatives and all other mental health center programs throughout the state. A majority of each board must consist of the consumers of disability services and their family members; human services professionals are included as well.

In some ways, changes caused by this reform movement can make New Alternatives a more community-centered rather than community-based program in the future. Chapter 4 contains an extensive discussion about the differences in these two types of programs and their impact on empowerment. Community-centered programs provide more empowerment opportunities at personal, interpersonal, and political levels than community-based programs. Although it may be too early to determine the outcomes of the reform, the community and consumer service boards may increase each program's accountability to the community (Interview 1995d) and the community's capacity building and level of self-sufficiency (see table 7.2, item 10 on community influences on external systems).

The quality and timeliness of substance abuse rehab for youths also may be improved. As a result of recommendations from community service boards, new student assistance or early intervention programs must be provided by mental health centers throughout the state, in addition to existing day and residential treatment services for adolescents. New Alternatives is in the process of developing a student assistance program. In the interim, it provides drug intervention and rehab services to adolescents in a nearby juvenile detention center. It is the only program in the region to provide such services to this segment of the population (Interview 1995). The focus is on helping to empower these youths by increasing their understanding of how their involvement in illegal activities and detention is linked with their drug use or abuse. This program could further enhance client and community empowerment by increasing opportunities for clients to influence and contribute to community well-being and for the community to take on additional roles in the program's operation (see table 4.1).

The Policy/Funding Subsystem

The recently developed community service boards discussed in the previous section are part of a larger policy-making structure that was authorized by a 1993 state health and mental health bill. Nominations to these boards are made to the county boards of health, and then members are appointed by the county authorities. A check-and-balance system requires that the boards of health consider nominations from advocacy groups and clinical professional associations and that county authorities appoint a consumer of disability services, a family member of a consumer, an advocate for disability services, or a local leader or businessperson with an interest in mental health, mental retardation, and substance abuse. Each county can appoint one board member per 50,000 residents. The nominations must reflect each disability group as well as the race, gender, ethnic, and age characteristics of the region's population. Each member serves for a two-year period.

These community service boards have widespread policy and service planning and implementation powers that can affect the quality of empowerment services. For example, they can contract for services, set fees, receive and administer grants and other donations, buy and dispose of real estate, and accept appropriations or supplies from governmental entities. In addition, their knowledge and philosophical orientations may establish service priorities that are barriers to empowerment, especially for young consumers. New Alternatives' administrators are concerned about how differences among the three disability groups may be interpreted by these boards and therefore may influence their understanding of the different resource allocations needed. For instance, developmental disabilities are chronic and require continuous, lifelong care, while substance abuse problems require acute care and repeated rehab episodes over time. This means that substance abusers, particularly developing youths, need intensive services for periods that extend beyond the episodic patterns of initial and ongoing recovery.

In addition, the emphasis of managed care policies on short-term services and restricted access to services could be a barrier to the type of long-term, developmentally-focused services provided by this program. It is possible, therefore, that such policies can inhibit opportunities for the long-term skill development and self-efficacy needed by youths for successful recovery.

Under the current reorganization plan, the community service boards also make recommendations to regional boards that were authorized under the same state legislation. The regional boards have a direct link to the state health department and therefore to the state divisions of mental health, mental retardation, and substance abuse. The state health department disperses funds to regional and community service boards and only has a general planning function. Policy decisions, including decisions about actual funding allocations, are now made by the regional and community service boards. Again, it may be too soon to determine how these empowerment-oriented consumer reforms can benefit this program's clients. However, in 1995, the mental health system had a funding shortfall. In the past, the system was able to appeal to the department of health or to the legislature for an advance on its funding for the next year. The reorganized, more community-accountable structure does not allow for such contingencies. As a result, New Alternatives and other programs had to eliminate some of their services and stop admitting new clients for several weeks until the new fiscal year began.

The Empowerment Process in Action

From the previous discussion, it is clear that New Alternatives' external and internal context influence how recovery in general, and clients' empowerment experiences in particular, develop within the setting. This consciousness-raising process is described below in terms of two clients' empowerment and disempowerment experiences, with emphasis on some of the unique dynamics in each situation. In addition, variations in such experiences across many of the program's clients are analyzed.

One Client's Empowerment Narrative

Background Information.   Shane is a sixteen-year-old Caucasian boy who was in phase 1 at the time the following empowerment experience occurred. Shane's mother died from AIDS when he was ten years old, and his father died from the same condition two years later. His father had become HIV-positive while both parents were in the military. Shane and his older brother went to live with their mother's sister and her husband after their father died. Shane began using drugs when he was ten, primarily because his brother used drugs and it was something they could do together. Shane also became involved in shoplifting and residential burglaries to support his drug use and for the high those activities gave him. His brother, still a drug abuser, had been through several rehab programs unsuccessfully. One day in his life skills group, Shane admitted he was worried about his brother's continuing drug problems and the potential effect on his own recovery after completing rehab. Several peers pointed out that Shane was worrying about everyone else instead of focusing on learning about himself.

Shane's Narrative.   I sat there awhile, staring at the floor. No way could I stop worrying. I knew I couldn't live without drugs because my brother, Lyle, couldn't stop using, and he's stronger than me. I kept staring at the floor; I thought if I did that maybe the group would leave me the hell alone. I had a hard time talking in front of people at that time—I wouldn't have talked to you like this a few months ago. Then Pat, she was leading the group that day, asked me to stand up and do a role play. She said we'd role play how it felt when voices in my head told me to worry about different things. It felt funny, but I went and stood in the middle of the group, to do what she said. Every time I told the group what my worry voices said, Pat would have one or two of my peers come over and stand until there were eight or nine of them around me. Like when my worry voice said, "What about all those people you robbed—think about how angry and afraid you made them," Pat sent Tonya and Amir over to stand by me.

Then I said out loud my worries about Lyle, my aunt and uncle, my mother's death, my father's death, and wanting to get back on drugs. Pat had the group members standing by me tie things around my arms, legs, and chest—scarves, shirts, anything—and then told them all to pull hard. She asked me what it felt like being pulled in different directions. I said it felt like I might crash and hit the floor any minute. I was too unbalanced, I couldn't do anything. Pat asked if I could change the things that were pulling on me. I said no, if I tried pulling one way, one of them pulled me off balance even more. When she asked if it felt like I was stuck, I just shook my head yes. I closed my eyes for a second; I was trying to keep the picture in my head—me being pulled, feeling real tangled up about things.

Conclusions About the Meaning and Impact of the Experience. In describing his conclusions about this experience, Shane said, " A light bulb came on—finally I understood the only thing I could change was trying not to use, I felt a little relief. . . . I fooled people when I was in treatment before, but I know I can't hide in this program." Shane felt the role play helped him to understand that other people—his peers, Pat, his aunt and uncle— were working with him on his recovery even though it was primarily his responsibility. It was the first time he allowed anyone to see how scared he was about his previous life and his ability to recover. The role play showed him he could survive exposing his feelings and other "weaknesses," including his sense of responsibility for his brother's continued drug abuse.

Shane felt most vulnerable about the loss of the relationship with his brother. Successful recovery meant he would have to stay away from the only other surviving member of his immediate family. That could be a greater trigger for relapse than other issues. The two of them were friends and brothers; their closeness developed within the context of their drug abuse and coenabling behaviors; and developmentally, Shane was still struggling with the issue of friendship and loyalty.

The role play helped Shane to empower himself for two reasons. It externalized his problems so that he could separate himself from them (Nickerson 1995): the worry voices that reinforced feeling ashamed and his assumption of responsibility for every negative event that happened in his family. The role play also pulled him physically in different directions, helping him to feel experientially his subjective and emotional reactions to being stuck in the middle. Shane's empowerment experience reflects the client-professional collaboration and peer-led themes of interpersonal empowerment identified in table 13.1. Those themes highlight the importance of having an audience to witness and support the type of transformation Shane experienced in the role play and when telling about that experience (White and Epston 1990). The public venue provided greater opportunity for the validation and self-efficacy he described so clearly.

Further evidence of his self-efficacy emerged when Shane was asked to define "empowerment" after giving his narrative. He defined the term as "knowing and understanding things." He was also asked if and how this definition applied to his story. Shane felt it applied because he learned important information about parts of his life that he could not change and that had caused him to feel bad about himself in the past. He made a connection between having this "self-knowledge" and being able to stop the drug use and cope with his other worries. After several weeks, continued support from peers in group sessions helped Shane view the role play in a different light that strengthened his empowerment. He reframed being pulled in different directions during the exercise as evidence of his peers helping him to stand up (until he could begin to stand on his own).

Clients' Empowerment Narratives: General Issues

The example of Shane's empowerment is useful for clarifying how such experiences evolve, even though each may be significantly different. Analysis of clients' collective experiences in New Alternatives is equally useful for understanding factors that can influence this process. As part of my research, I asked twelve clients in phases 1–4 in this program (including Shane) to describe rehab situations that they felt extremely good about or that caused them to feel good about themselves. There were a number of commonalities and differences across their situations. The responses focused on the content and on the meaning and consequences.

The Content.   The majority of empowerment experiences described by the youths took place during formal aspects of the program such as a phase meeting, a treatment team meeting, the loss and grief group, a counseling group, or the life skills group. Few of these situations involved informal interactions, such as family visitations, teacher-student discussions about assignments after class, card games, or meal time. That the clients' narratives describe formal services indicates that most of these experiences involved the interpersonal level of empowerment and professional-led, peer-led, and professional-client collaboration themes (see table 13.1). Only three client narratives reflected empowerment at the political level, such as petitioning for a phase meeting or participating in a treatment team meeting.

Both peers and staff were identified as influential in most of the positive outcomes. A number of adaptive staff and programmatic responses to power issues were identified, for example, trading off and acknowledging/supporting personal power (see items 3 and 4 in table 2.2). Clients' empowerment narratives identified many instances when peers and/or staff pooled resources by brainstorming how to resolve an issue or used an exercise that made them aware of their power to act. Often, the staff and peer responses heightened the youths' awareness of their issues and sense of competence in managing them. One youth, fifteen-year-old Ralph, successfully petitioned for a phase meeting in which he described his progress: moving from having "a big head and being too cocky" to admitting he has problems, talking about his feelings, and asking for help. More important, peers and staff were able to identify other positive changes they had observed in his responses to authority of which he was not aware. This was an example of successful political empowerment because it changed what Ralph perceived as the program's "bad boy" label for him.

Other identified issues included gaining insight about a loss; handling first-time affirmations from parents; becoming aware of how to change family relationships that could inhibit recovery and trigger a relapse; and being macho versus being able to cry in group sessions. As this list indicates, the clients' empowerment narratives focused almost exclusively on their personal issues and described peers, family members, or staff as supports. An exception was one client's narrative about becoming empowered from learning about how a negative peer relationship was impeding her recovery.

In that example, staff and peers had confronted seventeen-year-old Tonya at various times about her impatience, intolerance, and self-righteousness about other people's negativity. One day, when Tonya had a conflict with a peer about his negative attitude, a teacher asked her, "What is it about you that can't let go of this issue about Aaron's negative reactions to females? . . . He's an okay person, it's his behavior that's bad; you're a good person, but your behavior is a problem. If you can't forgive and tolerate his imperfections, how are you going to forgive your own mistakes and recover successfully?" Tonya felt good about this experience because she learned how her attitude toward Aaron had become a barrier to her own recovery. She heard for the first time that this particular teacher cared about her and saw her as worthwhile in spite of her problem behavior. Tonya knows now it is possible to accept others (herself, staff, family members, neighborhood friends) while not accepting or condoning their negative behaviors. She also understands that it is impossible to force others to change, but she has the power and control to change herself.

The Meaning and Impact of Clients' Empowerment Experiences. Clients' responses to questions about the meanings and outcomes of their empowerment narratives document the influence those experiences had on their recovery. Tonya's empowerment experience helped her to reinterpret feedback from staff, peers, and family members that was critical of her behavior. She now believes that their concerns about her negative behaviors, such as flashing the boys in the program, do not imply that she is being rejected, and that she is a worthwhile person in spite of those behaviors. Her self-esteem increased and her identity was enhanced as a result of this experience. Others felt a sense of accomplishment (being allowed to move to the next phase of rehab) or competence (convincing a principal to allow enrollment in school, despite the principal's bias about drug abusers). Another youth gained insight by becoming aware of how difficult it is to walk away from drug-using peers while on a home pass, in spite of having rehearsed how to manage this scenario in group sessions.

One Client's Disempowerment Experience

Background Information.   Melody is a sixteen-year-old African American client who was in phase 3 (having been in the program for six months) at the point when she was interviewed for my research. Many staff and peers had confronted her about isolating herself and having a negative attitude about being in the program and following the rules. Melody was adopted as an infant; her parents were in their forties at the time, so they were older than most of her peers' parents. Melody believed her parents were too strict and that her father, in particular, did not love her. She began huffing gasoline when she was eleven years old, started smoking marijuana when she was fourteen (in the beginning she stole from her father's supply of marijuana, prescribed for medicinal purposes), and then began to smoke crack when she was fifteen. Melody also inhaled white out periodically. The disempowerment experience that she described took place during an individual counseling session with her primary counselor, Evelyn.

Melody's Narrative.   My counselor said she wanted to see me. I went to her office, but she just sat and looked at her desk for a few minutes. Then she said everyone was fed up with me. I was always in trouble. She'd just heard I'd flashed the boys during study period yesterday. She said she was tired of going to bat for me. She was sick of my negative attitude. She'd tried to stand by me, now she was through with me like everybody else. I wasn't interested in getting better. I was standing still in treatment, like I was standing in a septic tank. All the while she was talking she wouldn't look at me, until she said that about the septic tank. Then she looked up at me awful mean. I could see she meant what she said—that she was real frustrated with me.

Some staff told me she was gonna give up on me sooner or later; I knew she might, but I was still surprised. The last thing she said was to think about if I could really change, if I really wanted to change. I felt like I'd been kicked in the chest when I left her office. I could hardly breathe and was sweatin hard. I hid out in the bathroom so nobody could see me cryin. Every time I saw her the rest of the day, I felt low, and ashamed of myself.

Conclusions About the Meaning and Impact of the Experience. Melody said that this experience was the low point in her recovery. She knew she was not doing well because her behavior was the same as before she entered rehab, even though she was no longer using drugs. She was caught in a cycle in which her negative behaviors escalated as she received more and more negative feedback. The session with Evelyn made her aware that she was repeating this addiction cycle, although she believed being in rehab had made a difference. Melody felt scared and powerless; now she really wanted to change but was not sure she could do so by herself.

While Melody could see why Evelyn and the other staff were upset with her (her behavior was awful), she believed the staff were harder on the girls than the boys. They seemed to expect the girls to have more problems but put the boys on a pedestal. Melody felt none of the staff would listen to her and Tonya's explanation about why they flashed the boys. Because there had been an increase in rule infractions at that time, the staff called an amnesty meeting in which all the clients were encouraged to share their unacknowl-edged rule infractions and secrets that could affect their recovery. Melody had to show remorse for flashing the boys and other negative behaviors. She felt the amnesty meeting confirmed her shame and isolation. To Melody, the staff seemed to be saying they "knew she was bad, but didn't know she was that bad."

Melody's conclusions about the effects of this disempowerment experi-ence are interesting. She described the short-term impact as negative: Evelyn's reference to Melody standing in a septic tank clarified how low she was in the mire (in addiction thinking and behaviors) and the danger of remaining stuck. But in the long term, Melody believes the experience gave her hope about overcoming her "faults" and benefiting from the program.

She said staying focused on her recovery was a constant battle that she was winning slowly with help from Evelyn and the other staff, who refused to desert her in the end.

Melody's narrative reflects the professional-led theme of personal disempowerment, which resulted from the counselor's effort to confront Melody about allowing herself to become stuck in her recovery after some initial progress. The counselor's use of the septic tank metaphor conveyed knowledge about rural culture but reinforced Melody's childhood fear of falling into a septic tank. The metaphor heightened Melody's powerlessness while also providing a clear impetus for change. Thus, the counselor's goal of movement was achieved but, at least initially, the client felt disempowered.

Clients' Disempowerment Narratives: General Issues

The process of exploring disempowerment experiences of clients in New Alternatives was similar to the process of examining their empowerment experiences. The twelve clients interviewed were asked to share situations during rehab in which they did not feel good about what happened or about themselves. They were also asked to define "disempowerment" after sharing an example of this type of experience and to discuss to what extent their definition applied. The content and consequences of their collective experiences were then analyzed and compared.

The Content.   Most of the disempowerment experiences shared by these clients involved individual and group counseling sessions, with one exception. Several of the clients cited the amnesty meeting described by Melody as their most disempowering experience. The counseling sessions they described involved two types of situations. One was the unplanned expression of clients' most vulnerable feelings, such as crying in group, revealing the pain of sexual abuse, discussing anger toward parents, and feeling rejected after establishing a close relationship with a primary counselor. Ironically, feelings described as disempowering by some clients were noted as examples of empowerment by others. For example, a female whose family did not express feelings openly felt disempowered and exposed in the group when she cried while describing being assaulted and raped. A male who cried when describing the death of his grandmother expected to feel bad but instead felt empowered from group members' support and sharing of similar losses.

A second type of counseling situation described by participants as disempowering involved negative feedback from peers and/or staff, for example, being told not to "wallow in her depression," being asked if he was "faking recovery," and being told that the females were not working as a team like the males. Fifteen-year-old Mattie had been pairing off with a peer to gossip about other peers while also holding grudges against peers and staff. When she was confronted about her behavior in a group session, she first denied the feedback was true, then later acknowledged it was true after further discussion. With her counselor's support, Mattie decided to return to the first step of "admitting she is powerless" (spiritualizing power). As part of this first step work, she wrote a letter to her peers in which she examined and apologized for her behavior. When Mattie told the counselor that she was depressed by having to acknowledge her regression in the program, the counselor told her not to wallow in her depression.

The Meaning and Impact of Clients' Disempowerment Experiences.

In the above example, the counselor's comment stopped Mattie and her friend's interaction and caused Mattie to withdraw for a period of time. She and other clients described such disempowerment experiences as sources of shame and evidence of their rejection by others (power sabotage or interpersonal disempowerment). These clients implied or stated clearly that the approval of peers, family, or staff was critical for self-acceptance, and that consequently, disapproval signaled that they were worthless (personal disempowerment). For a number of reasons, some of these clients were unable to critically examine or deconstruct the messages they heard from others. They accepted the negative messages without question and internalized the implied self-blame.

For example, sixteen-year-old Richard interpreted his experiences during the amnesty meeting as evidence that he was weak and untrustworthy. He felt coerced to share new information about stealing from his grandparents before entering rehab and having sex during a weekend pass. He said the amnesty meeting made him feel like "I'd been dissed" (disrespected). The staff's goal was for him and his peers to acknowledge and forgive their own mistakes in the meeting. Instead, this coercive experience reinforced Richard's negative self-identity and powerlessness in decision making. He talked with a peer about how negative messages from the amnesty meeting affected him, but could not talk about his feelings and perceptions in individual or group counseling.

In the example of Melody (the septic tank metaphor) and others, hearing negative messages allowed them to become unstuck and to move on toward recovery. The strong relationship between Melody and her counselor may have been a factor as well as Melody's awareness of being stuck. The turning point was her interpretation of the counselor's metaphor: that the more she tried to extricate herself without help, the more mired she became in a cycle of negative behavior. Melody decided that she could not change without the help of peers and staff, and thus began a new stage of her recovery at that point.

When Shane's counselor asked if he was faking his recovery, he eventually accepted that negative feedback even though he felt disempowered. The same counselor initiated the role play with Shane that was described in a previous section. Perhaps her negative feedback, which led to his disempowerment, made Shane more reflective about his behavior and more receptive to the self-knowledge and empowerment that he experienced later from the role play. The examples of Shane and Melody indicate that some youths can integrate certain disempowerment experiences in a way that strengthens them with time and self-reflection. For other youths like Richard, such experiences during this period of identity development and consolidation may be so devastating that they become barriers to self-healing and growth.

In addition to these examples of personal and interpersonal disempowerment, many of the female clients in this program described common experiences of political disempowerment. Over time, but especially related to the amnesty meeting, female clients felt staff blamed them more for problems in the setting than the males. Whether or not staff agreed with their conclusion, the females' reality was a common perception that they were seen as less valuable and capable than the males. This perception seemed in turn to affect how the female clients heard and interpreted feedback from peers and staff.

Practice Implications

These descriptions of empowerment and disempowerment in action have a number of implications for effective practice in this adolescent program. Table 13.1 illustrates program factors that staff and clients identified as contributing to the latter's empowerment, including participation in treatment team conferences, presenting life histories in group, being involved in the honor system, journaling about feelings, collaborating with staff on relapse prevention plans, and going through the engagement or trial stage of early recovery. Similarly, clients were able to identify program factors that decreased the effectiveness of services and negatively affected their collective and self-efficacy.

This analysis of empowerment barriers confirms the need to address gender issues more sensitively and explore how the program impacts those issues for male and female clients. Counseling sessions could include information and exercises on gender roles, identity, socialization, oppression, power analyses, and empowerment alternatives. Ideally, those topics should be the focus of both gender-separate and coed groups. This addition could enhance not only the program's existing client-specific services related to gender issues but also services for developmental issues (identity development).

Another implication is the importance of empowering staff by providing training to increase their competence in client-specific services for adolescents and empowerment practice. Training goals could be to clarify staff roles in client empowerment and disempowerment and identify methods for increasing staff empowerment. Research revealed commonalities and differences in how clients perceived and were affected by their experiences in the program, and some clients' immediate reactions differed from their long-term reactions. Staff can be trained to help clients empower themselves (for example, to conduct power analyses) and learn how to grow from both empowerment and disempowerment experiences over the long term. Most important, staff can be taught how to refrain from inadvertently causing or contributing to client disempowerment.

Although staff currently solicit feedback from clients informally, a third practice implication is the importance of instituting a more formal system of program evaluation. The director has planned and will soon implement structured data collection instruments that will provide more systematic pre-/post- data on behavioral, attitudinal, and academic changes in clients over time. In addition, it would be helpful to include systematic data from clients and staff in focus groups, critical dialogue groups, and individual interviews to document preservice or baseline rates of problems, client outcomes, and the process of service delivery. More systematic collection of informal data (direct observations by staff and clients' written summaries of sessions) can help identify supports and barriers to empowerment practice with adolescents. For example, my research, involving direct observations and qualitative interviews, identified supports such as mutual aid in peer counseling groups and phase meetings as well as barriers like the current negative format of amnesty meetings. This combination of qualitative and quantitative measures can increase opportunities for client involvement in evaluating the program and in modifying it accordingly. Greater client involvement in program evaluation (internal political empowerment) is consistent with this client population's developmental needs.

A related and final practice implication is that the program should simultaneously increase client involvement in external political empowerment activities. This author's research documented New Alternatives' creativity in enhancing clients' personal and interpersonal empowerment and their political empowerment within the program. For instance, the program encourages clients' sponsors to attend phase meetings as their advocates, especially in the later phases of rehab. One method for enhancing these youths' opportunities for external political empowerment would be to increase the involvement of sponsors and other community members in the program's structure and operation. For example, meetings with the new community service boards could provide clients with opportunities to influence board decisions. Board members could be encouraged to take a more active role by serving on program committees. Clients could become involved in community service and systems change projects related to their recovery, including volunteering in homeless shelters and conducting peer prevention sessions in public schools.

Conclusion

This description and analysis of services provided by New Alternatives for its adolescent clients has revealed interesting data on the special needs and strengths of this population. Their resilience while working through the recovery process is noteworthy, since their recovery is complicated by a number of developmental and gender issues. The analysis has also clarified components of empowerment practice that are essential for helping this population address those issues. Some of the components exist in the program currently, such as client-determined phase meetings and a collaborative assessment of progress. Other examples represent gaps in the program's current services, including information on gender socialization, oppression, and efficacy as well as client involvement in community or systems change projects.

These clients' rich narratives clearly reflect their experiences in the program, their struggles, feelings, hopes, disappointments, subjective realities, and interpretations of significant events. Peer and staff influences are apparent, and whether they are intentional or inadvertent, it is possible to trace how they lead to client empowerment or disempowerment in each unique situation. Most important, these narratives and earlier descriptions of the program and community structure clearly reflect the interaction of power dynamics with unique client variables over time in youths' paths toward recovery.

14 Restore and Repair: Perinatal Rehab Services for Women and Children

> My eleven-year-old was out of control when I first went to treatment. I had trouble sayin' no to him, 'cause I was havin' flashbacks about when I neglected him. Doin' crack—before treatment—I wasn't worried about that. My peers tole me over and over, things'd get worse at home unless I got more structured. They wasn't dictatin' or judgin' me, so I started listenin' to what they said. They challenged me to do better by my kids.
>
> —Cassandra N. (1996)

Problems experienced by addicted women of child-bearing years often require complex, gender-related medical and psychosocial services. These problems include sexually transmitted diseases such as HIV/AIDS; high-risk pregnancies or infertility; physical or sexual assaults during prostitution, drug dealing, or other illegal activities; homelessness; and inadequate parent education and parenting skills. These women's children, like Cassandra's son in the above example, may suffer from parental neglect and abuse, and also from severe peri- and postnatal drug withdrawal symptoms, low birth weight, developmental delays, and cognitive and intellectual deficits (Chisum 1986; Freeman 1992).

Solutions involve a range of comprehensive services, including parent education, specialized foster care for drug-involved children, drug education and counseling, on-site drug-related OB/GYN and pediatric medical care, special transitional housing for women and their children, transportation, child development and child care, special education for children, adult education, work training and employment, and family counseling (Brown 1991; Finkelstein 1993; Wilke 1994). A barrier to effective programming is that most service models have been developed for men. Only a few gender-specific models have been developed for women recently (Finkelstein 1993; Reed 1987; Sandmaier 1992); most other programs, even those modified for women, do not address gender-related policy, community, family, and personal barriers to women's recovery.

This chapter clarifies one program's gender-specific services for overcoming such barriers, the underlying client empowerment issues, and the program's structure and context. An analysis of the empowerment process is included, using client narratives from my research; then practice implications are presented. To set the stage for this discussion, the following section summarizes background information on the program's clients.

Background Information on the Client Group

Impact of Diversity on Use Patterns and Related Issues

The Restore and Repair Program serves approximately 60 to 75 low-income women with children per year and has a capacity for 20 clients at one time. The drop-out rate is approximately 40 to 50 percemt. These women are generally polyaddicted, with alcohol and crack cocaine being the two most common drugs of choice. They have an average of three children, with a range from one to ten children.

The women are an ethnically diverse group. The majority of them, however, are African American (75 percent) or Hispanic (17 percent), while the remainder are white (5 percent) or Asian American or Native American (3 percent). Their age range is from 19 to 45 years. Most of them are unemployed, although many clients in the last phase of rehab are employed or have been placed in a job training program. Approximately 90 percent of the program's clients are high school graduates; nevertheless, some are either illiterate or have significant deficits in reading and math. Fifty percent of those who are high school graduates have also completed one to two years of college.

These clients do not fit some of the stereotypes about addicted women, which include an early onset of drug use during adolescence and a fairly brief period of addiction (Freeman 1992). Their average age of first drug use is 21.6 years and their average period of addiction is 7.4 years. It is not clear how most of these women avoided using drugs at an early age or whether particular individual or environmental factors protected them from early use. Another possibility is that they used other drugs initially, such as marijuana and alcohol, with only minor consequences until they began to use highly addictive crack cocaine later.

The result has been a common pattern of late onset or late impact of drug use.

The women's drug use patterns are consistent with a trend noted in the literature among female cocaine abusers of child-bearing years. Studies show that the average age of female cocaine abusers has risen from 21 to 29 (Brody 1989; Hale 1994), and the current mean age of women entering this program is also 29 years. This trend suggests that for any number of reasons, women may be experiencing longer periods of addiction before they are able to develop a relatively stable recovery. As a result, providing services for these women has become more difficult (Interview 1995).

Impact of Diversity on Referral Patterns

This trend toward longer periods of addiction and the women's prior rehab histories have influenced referral patterns to this program. A majority of the women have received rehab services prior to entering the program, so many are referred by other providers. Often these clients received services in short-term residential programs. They were referred to Restore and Repair because it is a long-term day treatment program; clients' average participation is one year, with a range from eight to fourteen months. The program is designed to help these "rehab hardened" clients remain in their communities while providing them with skills and practice opportunities to change personal and community barriers to recovery (Interview 1995).

Other clients are referred to the program by hospitals and physicians, the criminal justice system, protective services, or homeless shelters. Not surprisingly, those women have numerous medical, legal, child custody, and housing problems. Another pattern is that most clients are in crisis upon referral because they often have multiple mandates for accepting services. The most common mandate is from child protective services, which requires them to quickly develop an acceptable reunification plan for their children, who are often in a variety of out-of-home placements.

Client Empowerment Issues

Entry Into Rehab

An emphasis on mandated services for regaining custody of children can affect women's readiness for treatment (Freeman 1992). Shame and guilt from the stigma of female addiction are other factors (Finkelstein 1994). As a result, some women do not follow through on referrals to this program or participate fully in intake as a way of coping with their lack of control over the situation. They often express their powerlessness through angry outbursts toward other clients, withholding of vital information, irregular attendance during the first weeks, and failure to follow through on initial referrals for other services such as housing and health care that are essential for effective recovery (Interview 1995). Approximately 35 to 40 percent of clients entering this program do not have legal and/or physical custody of their children.

Restore and Repair attempts to address these entry issues through a process of consciousness raising. Staff explain that entering rehab for the sole purpose of regaining custody of their children can sabotage the women's recovery. The emphasis is on self-motivation, or obtaining services for themselves, in contrast to the gender pattern of putting the needs of others first. By giving the women permission at intake to focus on their need to heal and empower themselves (as a prerequisite for learning how to become a better parent), the women begin to feel affirmed and valued (Interview 1995).

Another empowerment issue is the women's lack of awareness about their specific patterns of addiction. They often have unique, easy access to drugs through boyfriends or spouses who introduce or reinforce their drug use, other males who give them free drugs, and their involvement in prostitution (Freeman 1992). This can make them more reluctant to accept services, and because they are unaware of the political aspects of such gender exploitation (Finkelstein 1994), they may blame themselves for this entry barrier. Further, some of them believe they are incomplete without relationships with males, which increases their reluctance to accept services and their self-blame for this reaction.

The staff believe self-blame and overreliance on males for drugs and validation are barriers to self-empowerment. Thus, initial services include imparting information on gender socialization, getting in touch with the women's inner wisdom, building trust and supports among the women, putting their current intimate relationships on hold, and not establishing new relationships. Self-validation, although difficult for the women to understand and practice at first, is nevertheless emphasized as a basic tool for initial recovery (Interview 1995).

Continuance in Rehab

Helping the women to build trust among themselves is difficult for staff. Many clients do not trust their own feelings and instincts, and having been abandoned and rejected by female family members and role models, they may also mistrust peers and staff. Some have generalized those feelings to all women. One client in the program said, "The majority of us have trouble trusting other women—we're closed-minded that way, but we need to open up." This mistrust, the underlying anger and pain, and competition have led to power sabotages and power cutoffs among some of the clients and female staff in the program.

Sometimes, if anger has been a trigger for drug use in the past, it can become a trigger for clients' dropping out of rehab and relapsing. Staff have observed this pattern in some clients during initial rehab sessions before they become oriented to the program, or when they reach certain plateaus in later phases of rehab. To address such barriers to maintaining clients in rehab, staff help them to develop a sense of unity among themselves, which decreases the women's distrust of themselves, peers, and staff. It creates the emotional climate necessary for self- and group efficacy and for helping these clients continue their recovery (Interview 1995).

At least initially, the women place great emphasis on "cleaning up" physically, because they have neglected their health, hygiene, and personal appearance while abusing drugs. They tend to overemphasize improvement in these areas, often competing among themselves to dress and look better to gain self-affirmation and empowerment. As the program begins to emphasize internal and external changes—learning about who they are as individuals—clients' fears and anxieties resurface, and they may feel as disempowered and worthless as they did when they abused drugs. At times, those feelings can trigger their dropping out and relapsing. For prevention purposes, staff use loss and grief education to help the women acknowledge and address their losses of self-concept and -esteem, relationships, health, pride, and femininity (Interview 1995).

Gender-Specific Services

Identifying barriers to rehab entry and continuance, and therefore to empowerment, highlights client-specific services that are essential for perinatal programs. Restore and Repair, for example, provides gender-sensitive services to address these clients' trust problems and cultural bias against making their needs a priority. The women are encouraged to delay obtaining custody of their children or starting new intimate relationships until they have done some of the required internal work. Child development and parenting classes improve their competence and self-efficacy for regaining custody at a later time (Burns and Burns 1988). Other services help clients to connect what they have learned about who they are with their expectations for male-female relationships and other roles. Group sessions can increase their self-esteem and therefore the range of choices they can identify and apply in those relationships as they recover.

Restore and Repair has developed gender-sensitive drug and alcohol education groups that emphasize the unique biochemistry of women as it affects their addiction and recovery process (Finkelstein 1994; Wilke 1994; Lex 1991). Lundy (1987) indicates that the focus of this program's groups, the impact of sex-role conflict and gender bias on women's addiction patterns and drugs of choice, is a core aspect of gender-sensitive services. Other services focus on adolescent and adult development, because many of these clients function at a younger age than their chronological age. Education on developmental stages helps them to cope with and resolve gender identity and gender socialization conflicts. Often, such issues were not addressed sufficiently earlier in life, if at all, due to trauma from childhood incest and rape, parentification, early parenthood, family disruptions including divorce, and emotional or physical abuse (Marcenko, Spence, and Rohweder 1994; O'Hare 1995).

The Program's Internal Structure and Context

Restore and Repair's internal structure and context reflect the type of gender-sensitive services discussed above, because the program was designed in reaction to male-oriented women's programs. This section describes the program's early development, its philosophy, its services, and the empowerment-related program factors it includes.

Early Program Development

This intensive family day treatment program for pregnant and parenting women with children from birth to three years of age was developed in 1990 in a large West Coast city. The program is located in the same low-income community where many clients live and in which drug use and sales, as well as other illegal activities, occur continuously. From the program's inception, it has operated six hours daily, six days per week, on a year-round basis to provide the supports necessary for women to recover in their natural environments.

A family focus has been essential from the beginning because many of these clients continue to live in households where family members and significant others abuse substances or have other addictions. Some of them are not yet aware of how these relationships affect their recovery, while others are waiting for space in subsidized housing, transitional housing, or sober living group homes. Even clients who do not live with their families often encounter relatives, friends, acquaintances, or neighbors who are involved in daily drug activities. These family and community stressors can impede the women's recovery; therefore, Restore and Repair addresses such factors directly to enhance clients' recovery and self-efficacy (Interview 1995). Lifetime rather than time-limited aftercare services are included in the program to help clients normalize and manage ongoing stressors.

Program Philosophy and Conceptual Framework

This program's philosophy is grounded in empowerment concepts. The program encourages women to develop and apply life skills in their daily situations. An underlying assumption is that skill development leads to self-efficacy and empowerment. It also leads to a critical consciousness of the impact of gender and parenting issues on women's addiction and of community supports and barriers that affect their addiction and recovery.

Consequently, the women are expected "to participate in social action and to mentor newcomers. These activities empower them to be self-reliant and to be part of a community during treatment" (*Staff Procedures Manual* 1995). This expectation is supported by the program's conceptual framework, because it emphasizes a community-centered, holistic, comprehensive, and collaborative approach to service provision. Thus, the one-stop shopping model, which provides a broad array of early interventions on site, is a core aspect of the program's organization.

Nature of the Program's Services

Program Services and Staff. Figure 14.1 reflects the broad array of services that Restore and Repair and other community organizations and agencies provide on site. The program is responsible for coordinating all these services on behalf of clients. For example, client and staff advocacy have led to on-site meetings and precourt hearings between the Department of Children's Services (DCS) and clients when the latter have had concerns about how custody and visitation policies were impeding their recovery. DCS staff spend time on site each week to receive and process clients' applications for public assistance, food stamps, day care subsidies, and Medicaid.

The array of services also includes Cocaine Anonymous (CA) and Alcoholics Anonymous (AA), which host meetings several times weekly. These meetings are open to the community; staff and clients believe this "mixed participation" makes the meetings more rich and diverse in gender, ethnicity, age, and time in recovery (50 to 60 percent of the participants are from the community). The combination of participants also keeps meetings reality focused and practical. In addition to these services, the program's staff conduct screenings in nearby clinics and hospitals that have identified drug-abusing pregnant and postpartum women. These screenings are an assessment and intervention tool, since they are often the only opportunity for staff to engage the women and encourage their acceptance of rehab services. Because their children are at high risk for many of the problems identified in the introduction to this chapter, as shown in figure 14.1, day care, transportation to and from the program, child development, parent education, and parent-child enrichment services (Mommy and Me) are included in Restore and Repair.

This figure clarifies how these and other services are provided during four distinct phases. Phases II and III represent the core, while Phase I is a probationary period for assessing the clients' motivation and objectives for recovery through the development of a treatment plan. Phase IV is the alumni or lifetime aftercare phase. The probationary phase can last from thirty to sixty days, depending on how long it takes to stabilize the client physically (detox) and psychologically, and to orient them socially. In both Phases II and III, clients become involved in all program activities and services. Phase II involves full-time participation for six days, with an emphasis on changing behaviors and attitudes that can impede recovery; Phase III continues that regimen but requires participation for four rather than six days so clients can work on educational, vocational, and employment goals (*Client Handbook* 1995). During the period of my research, three of the program's clients were in Phase I, four were in Phase II, five were in Phase III, and eight were in Phase IV.

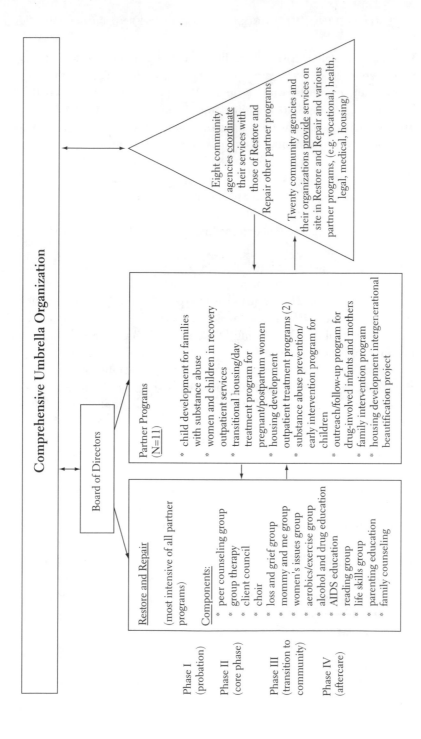

FIGURE 14.1 Organizational Auspices of Restore and Repair

The program's staff consists of a medical director, program director, senior counselor, counselors (four), case managers (two), a lead teacher for the day care center, and child care workers (four). A majority of the staff are female and African American; there are also some Latino (Spanish-speaking) and white staff members. The medical director is an OB/GYN physician on the staff of one of the community's major hospitals and affiliated with other hospitals and clinics that serve the same clients. These alliances have facilitated service coordination among the various providers. An undergraduate degree is the minimum requirement for the program director and senior counselor positions. All other positions require a combination of education (e.g., completion of high school or a specified number of college hours) and experience.

Counselors provide individual therapy for their primary clients and group therapy. The case managers are key actors throughout the four phases of the program. However, they are especially helpful in obtaining such basic resources as legal and health services when clients enter the program. Equally important, during Phase III, they make referrals for career counseling, education classes, job training, job placements, supported work, and transportation to work and job training programs. M.S.W. interns in yearlong practicums provide specialized group and individual sessions for incest survivors, grief and loss issues, and family counseling. These interns are supervised by an M.S.W. social work consultant who provides ten to fifteen hours weekly in direct services, staff consultation, and supervision.

Major Theories, Approaches, and Rehab Strategies. Restore and Repair uses the group counseling process as its major strategy, involving consciousness raising from experiential exercises, confrontation, peer support and feedback, and active listening, which helps clients discover their common experiences. Although the program's written materials focus on empowerment concepts, the program struggles to balance self-discovery and knowledge about group process (Berman-Rossi 1992) with a more traditional encounter group model (Rooney 1992; Shaffer and Galinsky 1989). Consequently, at times staff's efforts to help clients empower themselves backfire. Some clients indicate that disagreements about the focus of services are often dismissed by staff as evidence of clients' denial or manipulation. Staff's negative confrontation of clients in those situations has been overemphasized as well.

Reality therapy develops self-knowledge by helping clients to recognize the relationship between their values, attitudes, and behavior and the consequences that follow. For example, one client became aware that she used anger about her partner's putdowns as an excuse for her addiction and a recent slipup. The disease theory of addiction is another component of the program's theories and strategies. Clients are taught that addictions are a disease, but certain cultural biases and personal factors, such as sexism and addictive thinking about quick fixes, can reinforce and maintain their addictions (Interview 1996).

Case management is a necessary component because of the program's philosophy about the effects of environmental barriers on the women's recovery. This approach makes it possible for the women to resolve and/or cope with daily barriers to recovery while they are supported by the program's broad array of other services. Therefore, it is not simply a practice approach for staff but also an educational tool for teaching clients how to solve problems as part of their resocialization and self-empowerment process. Essentially, case management is the catalyst for that process (*Staff Procedures Manual* 1995).

Empowerment-Related Program Factors

Type of Empowerment Organization and Program Factors.   Restore and Repair fits within the category of empowered programs identified by Florin and Wandersman (1990) and included in table 1.4. Table 14.1 provides clear examples of program factors that lead to consumers' personal, interpersonal, and political empowerment. For instance, personal empowerment frequently occurs in women's issues groups, which develop clients' critical consciousness about their common experiences. Opportunities for interpersonal empowerment are increased for Phase II and III clients who become Big Sisters or mentors to new clients. The use of the hot seat and other peer feedback exercises can be another source of interpersonal empowerment.

Clients are required to participate in a range of social or community action activities outside the program that empower them politically. Examples include marching to support a new transitional housing project for recovering people that some members of the community are protesting, or participating in community outreach and relationship building through the program's open house or community advisory board (Interview 1996).

TABLE 14.1 Examples of Empowerment-Oriented Program Factors: Restore and Repair

Empowerment Levels	Major Themes		
	Professional Services	Peer-Led Services	Professional-Client Collaboration
Personal	gender-specific alcohol and drug education, including issues of oppression and gender bias, and effective parenting classes are provided	clients are assigned tasks in the program's day care center to develop parenting competence and to support-extend day care services for themselves and peers	peers and staff collaborate to provide critical feedback in hot seat exercises and other experiential activities for specific clients
	the women are taught how to affirm themselves daily through exercises, journaling, strengths assessments, and other activities	peer expediters remind and support clients in job assignments in the program and help escort them to outside appointments	
Interpersonal	staff coordinate the program's services with community sober living houses and supported work arrangements to increase clients' autonomy and social supports	clients mentor their peers as Big Sisters to enhance the recovery of mentors *and* mentored	clients and staff plan fund raisers and implement them collaboratively

	family therapy groups provide clients with opportunities to change system barriers to recovery and increase their supports	peer groups are led by clients to address client-client issues and other interpersonal growth issues	staff collaborate in coaching clients to advocate for and change other institutions and systems such as public welfare, protective services, and the legal system
Political	staff complete a reunification plan, including client tasks and advocacy strategies for impacting the court and protective service systems re out-of-home placements of clients' children	clients collaborate on developing and implementing social action activities in the community	the client council meets regularly as part of the program governance and policy development with staff members
	staff solicit and act on feedback from clients about the program's quality in community meetings with clients	peer alumni association does community fund raising for the program and volunteer community projects	

Political empowerment is encouraged within the program as well. A client council provides formal input into ongoing policy development and decision making that affects the program's operation. Periodic community meetings are scheduled for clients to share their thoughts and concerns informally with staff. In spite of these opportunities, some clients indicate that often their input is ignored or discounted in problem or crisis situations. Program factors that influence those experiences are discussed in more detail in "The Empowerment Process in Action" and in the following section.

Type of Organization and Empowerment Needs of the Population. This pattern of feeling discounted in staff-client relationships is often a painful reminder of similar situations these women have experienced in their natural environments prior to and during rehab. The pattern also evokes questions about whether they can trust other women, especially those in authority positions. During my research, several clients said they sometimes test staff in these two areas, either consciously or unconsciously, by acting out. Such behavior is also a cry for help because, as one client pointed out, "I was trying to learn to take control over my life, the frustration made me act crazy, and then later on, I'd feel shitty when my peers and the counselors avoided me."

The staff's struggles to balance empowerment practice with traditional encounter group strategies may contribute to this pattern of clients feeling discounted. Many of the factors shown in table 14.1 help staff to apply an empowerment orientation, consistent with the goal of empowered organizations as noted in a previous section (Florin and Wandersman 1990). Other factors, however, when used inappropriately, may encourage staff to embrace the encounter orientation, creating an oppressive climate. For example, the hot seat is used in groups to provide support for client self-discovery and efficacy from an empowerment perspective. But direct observation and client interviews indicate that sometimes the exercise is used to confront clients in an angry, hostile manner, which leads to disempowerment rather than empowerment.

Another example involves the program factor of actively soliciting client feedback. Some clients are reluctant to risk sharing their concerns with staff in the open community meetings. They have observed that some of their feedback has been discounted or reacted to defensively. However, when clients have used the more anonymous program suggestion box, as they are encouraged to do, their feedback has not been acknowledged or addressed.

This discrepancy between the program's goals as an empowered organization (Florin and Wandersman 1990) and its implementation of empowerment practice has made fully meeting the needs of some of the women more difficult.

The Program's External Structure and Context

In addition to these internal factors influencing the quality of Restore and Repair's empowerment practice, some external factors—the program's organizational auspices and the community and policy/funding subsystems— are also relevant. These three areas interact in their influence on the program's services and outcomes.

Organizational Auspices

Based on the organizational auspices continuum in figure 5.1, Restore and Repair fits under "Comprehensive Umbrella Organizations." From its inception in 1990, this program developed as part of a larger project that included eleven other family service programs. Figure 14.1 illustrates the range of individuals and families the programs serve and their various services to the larger low-income community.

Restore and Repair provides the most intensive level of care, although each program utilizes the services of the others. For instance, to improve its outcomes, Restore and Repair refers clients' children aged five years and older to the umbrella organization's prevention/early intervention program for children. Elderly and adolescent family members of clients, as well as other appropriate community residents, are referred to the intergenerational grounds beautification program in a nearby housing project.

In addition, twenty other agencies provide services, such as vocational counseling and medical care, on site. A rationale for the development of this umbrella organization with its array of community agencies is to provide more comprehensive and coordinated services at one easily accessible center. The goal is to eliminate fragmentation in the service delivery system that can impede clients' recovery. Another aim is to increase organizational accountability among the programs involved and their accountability to the community (see figure 5.1). The arrangement enhances clients' autonomy and self-sufficiency because it provides numerous services for them to select from and opportunities to influence policies that affect those services (Moore 1994).

The Community Subsystem

This program and its comprehensive umbrella organization were designed to be community-centered, which implies community involvement in the program and vice versa. The program's community advisory board, composed of local professionals and leaders, is involved in its policy development. Although former clients are expected to become members of the board (*Program Procedures Manual* 1995), none have joined presently. There are informal opportunities for board members to meet current clients in the program, but ongoing formal mechanisms have not been developed to increase their interaction and input.

Informally, the community participates in and supports the program in a number of ways. Often, community members refer and accompany substance-abusing residents to the program for screening and intake. An informal network of community members informs Restore and Repair about the activities of clients who stop attending or relapse, where they have moved or what shelter they are staying in, what drug houses they frequent, and their community supports and barriers. Program staff use this vital information during home visits—required whenever a client is absent for two or more days—designed for intervening with and reengaging clients. This informal process illustrates that the community views the program as community-centered, that it is accountable to the community and the community is accountable to it.

The program requires that clients become involved in the community as volunteers and in social action projects. Other programs sponsored by the umbrella organization are community-centered because they have a similar community development orientation. For example, the housing project beautification program involves youths and the elderly working together. It is designed to reclaim gang members among the community's young people and to use the skills and strengths of isolated elderly people in educating and mentoring. In this process, the youths develop leadership and vocational skills that benefit the long-term needs of the community for self-sufficiency and cultural relevance (*Program Procedures Manual* 1996).

The Policy/Funding Subsystem

Restore and Repair has a diversified funding base, which contributes to its current health and sustainability (Chapin 1994; Kunnes, Niven, Gustafson, Brooks, Levin, Edmunds, Trumble, and Coyle 1993). Funding comes from various private grants and county, state, and federal alcohol and drug agencies. Across the other eleven programs sponsored by the umbrella organization, funding sources include state and federal child and family service agencies; city and federal alcohol and drug agencies; the United Way; state and federal housing authorities; state mental health, probation, and health services; and federal agriculture and transportation departments.

While this diverse base has contributed to the programs' longevity, various agencies' conflicting policies about documentation, service priorities, client eligibility, the level of client and community involvement, and service accessibility have created some difficulties. For example, the state is considering how new managed care policies for residential programs can be applied to day treatment and other outpatient programs. Officials have requested data from Restore and Repair and other such programs to assist in their decision making, and the program has found itself in a policy catch-22. It is being asked to supply information that can decrease its autonomy and the accessibility of its long-term services to high-risk clients. However, if it fails to comply, it could lose state funding. Although no decision has been made about when and how managed care policies will be applied to various outpatient services, Restore and Repair has intensified efforts to document why its clients require more long-term services (Interview 1996).

Another policy/funding barrier to service accessibility involves the city's perinatal rehab expansion project, which includes this program and six others. The project's policies and funding structure are designed to increase the availability of culturally focused perinatal services to pregnant and parenting women in the city and in several surrounding counties. A centralized screening and assessment process reaches and engages Asian American, Latina, African American, Native American, white, and poor women in need of services. Each of the programs serves a designated population among these groups. For example, one serves Asian and Pacific Islander and African American women; another serves Latinas, African American, and lesbian women; a third serves the general population of women. The goal has been to standardize a range of services including alcohol and drug recovery, drop-in centers, transportation, child care, bilingual staff, housing, medical care, and culturally focused counseling.

However, women in Restore and Repair's community are often referred to perinatal programs far away from their neighborhood, and women in other, distant communities are referred to this program. Because of transportation logistics, those referral decisions have made it difficult for women to visit their children in out-of-home placements or to find employment or job training in geographically accessible areas. Some women's requests for referrals to programs that serve clients from their ethnic group or from a different group have been ignored. Clients in those situations tend to drop out or become resistant to efforts to involve them in rehab. Restore and Repair often helps them to work through their reactions, and when it is feasible, advocates on their behalf with the perinatal project. This advocacy role has earned the program a reputation for not being a team player in the project's policy implementation.

The Empowerment Process in Action

In spite of the negative labeling this program has experienced in the policy area, it has continued the advocacy role associated with empowered programs. To clarify how Restore and Repair operationalizes this and other roles, this section presents clients' narratives about their empowerment and disempowerment experiences. These accounts provide a unique picture of life and recovery for individual women in the program, and in contrast, for the group as a whole in terms of common experiences.

One Client's Empowerment Narrative

Background Information.   Joanie, a twenty-four-year-old African American, had been in the program approximately three months. Her two children, aged three months and two years, had been placed with her aunt after being removed from her custody by child protective services when the youngest was born drug involved. Joanie was addicted to crack cocaine and alcohol. She had been living on her own since the age of sixteen, and had moved to the West Coast from her hometown in the South three years previously. Her narrative describes her experience during a community CA meeting held on site in the program. Joanie had the floor because she wanted to talk about a personal crisis during the past week.

Joanie's Narrative.   I took my time walking to the front of the room. I hadn't talked much in meetin's before, so I was kinda jittery. I held my head down, wonderin' where do I start? Pretty soon, someone said, "Take your time." I waited a little more, then I started talkin' about my family. My father died when I was real young—I was only three at the time. My mother had lots of boyfriends after that. She'd go off and stay with them sometimes. My Aunt Flo, she lives here now, would take care of me and my sisters.

When I was about twelve, my mother married one of her boyfriends, Mr. Jessie. He moved in with us. Before, every time she'd leave, I'd be scared she wouldn't come back, so I thought, now things'll get better. But right away he started messin' with me—sexually I mean. I finally told my oldest sister Bobbie, and she told my mother, who said I was lyin.' So he kept doin' it. I used to stay at Bobbie's whenever I could, but he'd always make my mother bring me home after a few days. Sometimes he beat her. I started drinkin' to take my mind off things. I quit school and got a job when I was almost sixteen—moved in with Bobbie for good. She was married by then, and her husband said he'd kill Mr. Jessie if he ever bothered me again.

A couple years later, my mother died. I was still angry with her for not believing me. I had started doin' crack by then, so I just put my hurt feelings on the back burner. Last week, everything came to a head, and I wanted to pick up, bad, but I didn't. I got a letter from my cousin about my stepfather. He got drunk one night and burned the house down. He died in that fire. I tole the CA group, "I know I shouldn't feel this way, but I'm glad the bastard's dead." Everybody was real quiet. I couldn't tell what my peers was thinkin' after I said I was glad he's gone. Then, after a while, a women in the back said, "Oh well."

Conclusions About the Meaning and Impact of the Experience.   Joanie said her peer's comment in the CA meeting indicated she and the other participants were not judging her. Not being judged was obviously an important part of this experience for Joanie. Up to that point, she believed she had done something wrong; otherwise her stepfather would not have molested her. The comment also suggested to Joanie that others in the meeting had a similar reaction to her stepfather's death. If other people could understand her feelings about him, then perhaps she, Joanie, was not so bad after all.

When she decided to talk about her reaction in the CA meeting, Joanie said, she felt guilty, and that feeling brought her unresolved grief and anger about the sexual abuse and her mother's death to the surface. Anger and rejection had been triggers for her past substance abuse, so Joanie found herself at risk for relapsing during the current crisis (Nelson-Zlupko, Kauffman, and Dore 1995). She had fantasized about forcing her stepfather to admit the sexual abuse and hoped that then, somehow, her deceased mother would know about it and believe her finally. With his death, the fantasy ended and Joanie's sense of a lost opportunity exacerbated her crisis.

Interestingly, Joanie felt she had ended her story in the CA meeting as she struggled with guilt feelings and wondered what her peers were thinking. She expected them to give her advice about how to keep from relapsing, similar to her counselor's advice in an individual session. But the woman's "oh well" comment caused Joanie to continue her story. She expressed her anger and guilt in more detail, and then said how those feelings affected her. She told the group, "I know I'm weak, but I'm also strong, how else could I make it this far? I can't let him [the stepfather] rob me of my sobriety now. I can't let him keep me feelin' bad about myself. I don't want to give up!" Then she talked about what she might do to keep from relapsing, drawing upon both the individual session with her counselor and her peers' support in the CA meeting.

Joanie felt empowered from this experience, because as she defined the term, it meant she was "able to make good choices in the middle of her crisis." Her conclusion suggests she was empowered at the personal level by making choices about sharing her story in the meeting and maintaining her recovery. Joanie also experienced self-efficacy at the interpersonal level by influencing or "moving" her peers with the genuineness of her story and her feelings. She felt that a spiritual bond developed with them, involving both the men and the women, as she talked about her crisis. This experience illustrates peer-led empowerment as shown in table 1.3, which for Joanie consisted of the self-help group's compassion, empathy, advice, hope, and willingness not to judge her. It also reflects the theme of professional-client collaboration, because the counselor's previous advice and active listening seemed to set the stage for the self-efficacy Joanie later experienced in her twelve-step group.

Clients' Empowerment Narratives: General Issues

An analysis of fifteen other clients' empowerment experiences clarified some of the common issues, themes, and outcomes for these women. Among other questions, the clients were asked to describe situations during rehab about which they felt extremely good or that caused them to feel good about themselves. Their responses are organized in terms of the content of their narratives and the impact and consequences they attributed to their experiences.

The Content. The majority of the experiences described by these clients occurred during formal services such as individual counseling, group therapy, women's issues group, peer counseling, and the big group (where all group therapy clients are combined). Only a few experiences occurred in informal or unusual situations such as hallways, the lobby area, the program director's office, and community agencies. The issues addressed seemed to cluster in three areas: larger systems, significant relationships, and clients themselves. Examples of systems-related or political empowerment issues involved conflicts about child custody, coping with a housing relocation that could trigger relapse, obtaining transportation resources, and managing bias from interagency collusion. The data analysis indicated that often, the systems issues facilitated empowerment at the other two levels as well as at the political level.

In the case of a white client, Nicole, the manager of her sober living group home threatened to move her to another home because of conflicts with her roommate. The other home was next door to where her ex-boyfriend lived; he had been her drug partner prior to her recovery. She was afraid she would start up their relationship again and relapse. When the manager would not change her mind, Nicole discussed her dilemma with her counselor. The counselor and program director advocated with the housing manager to allow Nicole to remain in her current living arrangement. Their effective advocacy is an example of political empowerment involving the theme of professional services (see table 1.3).

Simultaneously, the counselor and case manager had several joint counseling sessions with Nicole and her roommate, Karen, a black client in the program, in order to resolve their conflicts. These clients' reciprocal feedback helped them to identify more realistic expectations for themselves and each other, as well as their underlying racial biases. The process led to their interpersonal empowerment in terms of the peer-led and staff-client collaboration themes. Individual counseling helped Nicole to acknowledge and address the loss of a child who died while she was abusing substances. She experienced self-efficacy from recognizing patterns in how she coped with stress. She became aware that inappropriate anger toward Karen and others in the past had allowed her to avoid very painful feelings about the loss of her child.

Examples of interpersonal empowerment included using peer feedback, deciding whether to trust other women, confronting fears about family violence, taking risks through sharing with peers and staff, and handling sexual abuse. One black client, Carrie, said her empowerment occurred when she realized that her sharing in the group contributed to another client, Helen's, insight and growth (interpersonal empowerment). Carrie had stated that she enjoyed being sexually abused by the minister of her church. The counselor validated her perceptions about this experience but pointed out that Carrie's understanding her exploitation was equally important.

The ensuing discussion and guided imagery exercise helped Carrie to recognize how she had been taken advantage of and that it was not her fault. At the end of the session, Helen said that listening to Carrie's situation was helpful. It validated that she too had been exploited by a trusted family friend's sexual abuse, and that the experience was real whether or not she could ever convince her father that it had occurred.

Other examples dealt with clients' personal empowerment from having their thoughts and actions validated. A twenty-year-old white client, Sharon, who had difficulty talking to her primary counselor directly, journaled about a relationship that was troubling her. When she shared that narrative in individual therapy, the counselor commented that bringing the journal with that entry to the session represented a big step. A thirty-one-year-old Latina, Adrianna, encouraged by her peers, decided to move out of her family of origin's household, where addicted relatives also lived. In individual counseling she pointed out additional reasons for the move and cultural supports (a self-help group) that her peers had not identified. The counselor reinforced Adrianna's independent thinking and decision making, pointing out that the peer group needed to hear the rest of her story: how she had used their feedback to arrive at her own decision.

The Meaning and Impact of Clients' Empowerment Experiences. These clients were able to clearly describe what their empowerment experiences meant in terms of staff-client relationships, intimate relationships, personal coping, and long-term recovery. Sharon, the client who journaled about a difficult relationship, began to trust her counselor as a result of the positive feedback. That trust allowed Sharon to accept or reject the counselor's future suggestions rather than to follow them without question. Carrie, who had been sexually abused by her minister, felt the session stopped her from seeking out men sexually to gain love.

Nicole felt the program's advocacy for her with the housing manager helped her to become more competent in problem solving. Encountering barriers now means an opportunity to cope better, to learn something new that increases her ability to control her life. Nicole also felt that her experience was a turning point in her recovery, "life changing," because she learned how her ideas and feelings affect her behavior.

One Client's Disempowerment Narrative

Background Information.   Maribella is a thirty-five-year-old Puerto Rican mother of three children. She is a single parent and lives occasionally with her boyfriend, who is also recovering. Maribella has one and a half years of college and has worked as a computer technician. Her drugs of choice are cocaine and heroin. She had been in four rehab programs previously but only completed one of them. Maribella had recently transferred from a residential program to Restore and Repair; she had been there for twenty days when the following experience occurred during and after a peer counseling session.

Maribella's Narrative.   It was in peer group and one of the clients was going on and on about being afraid she would lose her son if she came down too hard on him. He was jerkin' her chain about not being there for him when he was little—while she was druggin' and in the life. I knew what she was feeling like, because I been there with my oldest son, Mike. He was gang-bangin' and skippin' school until I got him in line. I had Poppi spend time with him and started being more responsible—having a curfew and making him respect me. He hangs out sometimes, but he's not in a gang now, you know, he's calmed down. I said to Cassandra she would lose her son for sure if she didn't try and be more structured.

Sharon and some of the other clients gave Cassandra advice about being a good parent too. Cassandra doesn't have confidence in herself—none of us do—her self-esteem is low so I tried to make her feel better. I told her Latinas have to be hard on their sons or else they lose them to the streets. I could see she was frustrated at first, but then she started to ask what to do about her son, because he was just on the brink, you know? She wanted to try some of our suggestions—just because she was so frustrated. And I could tell she was very scared of relapsin.' I felt good about helping her since she's sincere about her recovery. When the group was over, Victoria stopped me in the hall. She was the staff support person for the group that day. She asked me why I came on so strong in the group, like a junior counselor. Then she said I should take the cotton out of my ears and put it in my mouth so I could listen instead of talking so much. After that, I clammed up; I didn't feel comfortable speaking up in group. When some of my peers asked why I was so quiet and said I gave good advice, I just shrugged my shoulders and kept quiet. The group didn't feel safe anymore.

Conclusions About the Meaning and Impact of the Experience. Maribella describes herself as normally feisty and confrontive, but Victoria's comment about her trying to be a junior counselor in the group left her speechless. Maribella said, "I felt like I was nothing." She thought she would never trust another woman again, especially one in authority over her. Her former husband had just gone to court and gotten legal custody of Mike, their oldest child. Her mother-in-law had testified that Maribella was not a good parent. Maribella felt her ex-husband had waited until she worked hard to become a better parent, helping Mike to resolve his problems, before he tried to get custody. She knew she still had many problems, but she believed she had been betrayed by both her ex-husband and his mother. She explained that she had not been trying to make the situation with Mike look better in the group than it really was, but she needed to feel good about some part of her life.

Maribella concluded that her sudden quietness in the group had two outcomes. First, it forced her to control an angry reaction to her counselor's putdown at a point when she was feeling very vulnerable. Her usual reaction would have been to deny the validity of the feedback and to attack the counselor in return, thus sabotaging her own power and recovery. Instead, she kept quiet although she felt very disrespected. Her reaction to the counselor made her think more clearly about the real reason for her anger—her own behavior—whereas she normally expressed anger inappropriately and then quickly forgot about it. Second, keeping quiet made her a more active listener in the group. Maribella decided it was possible to learn by sitting back and listening. She could learn about herself and apply information she was learning about others to her life. Her definition of disempowerment—

a displaced negative attitude or behavior that can be a learning experience —
is consistent with her conclusions about this episode.

Maribella experienced disempowerment at the personal level related to
the theme of professional services, as shown in table 1.3. Obviously, the
counselor made a judgment that Maribella's role in the group was harmful
to her recovery and that of her peers. Her concerns may have been heightened by this client's rehab history and her recent transfer into the program.
But the counselor's negatively confrontive approach was a power cutoff for
Maribella because it left her feeling personally powerless. It reinforced her
low self-esteem and the vulnerability that resulted from the recent child
custody decision.

A more positive confrontive approach might have made this client start
listening without causing her to feel worthless and powerless. The counselor
could have begun with a question about how Maribella was coping with the
custody decision and the effects on her interactions with family, with peers
in her group, and others. Her behavior in the group could have been pointed
out as a possible confirmation that she was feeling bad and perhaps over-
compensating as a result. The self-discovery from this process could have
led to personal empowerment and learning in a more positive context.

Interpersonally, the experience illustrates the peer-led theme in table 1.3.
Maribella's disempowerment affected her understanding and use of peer
support in the future. It caused her to doubt her ability to influence and be
useful to her peers. The more positive confrontive approach discussed above
might have clarified which behaviors could be useful to peers and which
could not. That approach might also have enhanced her leadership in the
group, while making her open to peer feedback that challenges that role
when necessary.

This experience shows how two people can be involved in the same
situation and come to different conclusions about it. In a separate interview,
Cassandra described the same group incident as Maribella, in response to
the question regarding situations about which she felt extremely good.
Cassandra's reaction is described in the example at the beginning of this
chapter. Although they both experienced the group incident positively at
first, Maribella's conclusions about it changed as a result of the counselor's
confrontation. She believed she had lost face with the group even though
the members did not hear Victoria's feedback to her. In her interview with
this author, Maribella identified the situation as one about which she felt
extremely bad, even though she had learned from it. She felt it was a clear
example of disempowerment.

Clients' Disempowerment Narratives: General Issues

Overwhelmingly, the fifteen clients' disempowerment narratives dealt with issues of self-esteem, trust, and risk taking. Trust and risk taking seemed relevant in many of the same experiences, involving both personal and interpersonal disempowerment. A thirty-year-old black client, Phyllis, was unable to talk with her counselor about guilt related to her mother's death. The mother's diabetes had been exacerbated by her drug addiction and by Phyllis's pattern of sharing drugs with her. The counselor said Phyllis would talk about the situation when she was ready, and only Phyllis could decide when that was. In spite of the counselor's understanding and support, Phyllis could not talk about the situation. Not being able to risk sharing her feelings of guilt implied to Phyllis that she could not be trusted, causing her to feel personally disempowered.

Risk taking was the focus also in the women's issues group. In one session, the facilitators asked clients to share information about their addictions they had not shared before. Many clients discussed their experiences with prostitution for drugs and the effects. Carol had previously told peers she had never engaged in prostitution. Yet while listening to their experiences, Carol realized she had engaged in the same activities in her home for money with acquaintances and their friends as her peers had done with strangers on the street. Carol's insight pointed out the seriousness of her addiction for the first time. She felt disempowered interpersonally because she had felt superior to her peers in the past, and now she believed they would distrust her if she risked telling them the truth.

Some clients experienced interpersonal disempowerment and decreased self-esteem in group therapy sessions. One woman, fifty-three-year-old Ginger, received peer feedback that she acted like she was in "Club Med" and that she was "uppity." Ginger felt powerless in the face of this feedback, because she felt her primary counselor and case manager should have warned her about the impression she might be giving. A twenty-eight-year-old Latina–Native American client, Venida, was asked by her counselor to refrain from wearing dresses, pumps, make-up, and jewelry for thirty days, so she could focus on who she was inside. Venida reacted passive aggressively to this suggestion, seeming to accept it but later saying she did not remember the discussion. In her view, the inside and outside work were the same. While she tried to focus on and address her internal issues, Venita's already low self-esteem decreased even more and she relapsed. The result was a overwhelming sense of failure and disempowerment.

Only two types of political disempowerment were included in these clients' narratives. One was clients being discounted in terms of their input into treatment plans. A thirty-year-old Vietnamese client, Kmung Lee, who continued to have positive urinalysis results for drugs in her system, was reported to DCS by her primary counselor. As a result, Kmung Lee did not regain custody of her children in a subsequent court hearing. She said she understood her counselor's responsibility in making the court report a requirement of the treatment plan, but she felt disrespected and powerless when she was excluded from the professionals' decision making in developing that plan. Moreover, she lost face within her family network, because although they distrusted the child welfare system and courts, their input was not solicited; nor were they considered as potential placements for the children.

The handling of feedback about programmatic issues was also a source of political disempowerment. Barbara, a twenty-seven-year-old black client, was frustrated about not getting sufficient time in individual counseling to make her Phase III plans for job training. After asking her primary counselor for more time proved ineffective, Barbara yelled in the program's lobby one morning, "I need some more counseling time; somebody help me!" Although all of the counselors, including Barbara's, were near the lobby area, no one responded. Later that day Barbara was called into the director's office and was given feedback about her unwomanly behavior. Barbara felt politically cut off and prevented from moving forward in her recovery as a result.

The Meaning and Impact of Clients' Disempowerment Experiences.
Barbara's and other clients' reactions indicated their disempowerment experiences were significant, but in different ways. Some clients used these experiences to move their recovery in new directions that increased, rather than decreased, their self-efficacy. For example, after reflecting on her experience, Barbara decided that she should have made a personal appeal to the director or to another staff member instead of acting out. Also, Barbara realized that her behavior could have been harmful to her counselor without achieving the goal she desired.

Barbara then talked the situation over with the social work student who facilitated her family therapy group. The student coached her on how to approach the director about her need for more individual counseling time.

As a result, the director assigned another counselor to Barbara, one who had been assigned to her when she first entered the program and with whom she had developed rapport.

Other clients felt they learned more about trust and boundaries from their experiences. Maribella felt that being called a junior counselor helped her to see that her other rehab attempts had failed because her trust issues were not addressed. She was still struggling with those issues during her current rehab program, while continuing her learning through an active listener role. Venida, the client who relapsed after she stopped dressing up and using make-up, felt her experience had a dramatic effect on her recovery, because now she was less passive aggressive in her reactions to peer and staff feedback. She trusted them to give useful responses now without blaming them for her relapse. Venida said she "was a relapse waiting to happen. Stopping the drugs is only ten percent of recovery; the rest is the inside work on your cultural identity, liking yourself as a woman, facing the fears, your self-esteem, trust, and control issues. I love myself now, so as an indigenous–Mexican American in recovery, I give the inside more attention than the outside."

Practice Implications

This arduous process of self-discovery and -knowledge that Venida and others in the program described documents the impact of power issues on these women's recovery. While their narratives have highlighted many program factors that facilitate this process, they have also pointed out how the program's empowerment practice can be improved. These practice implications may not be generalizable to other perinatal programs; however, they certainly raise questions about the nature and quality of empowerment practice with women and children.

A key implication for Restore and Repair is the need to improve the clarity and operationalization of its conceptual framework. Although empowerment concepts and language permeate the program's written materials and its intentions in this area are a strength, the program is clearly struggling to integrate two conflicting orientations. An empowerment orientation is inherently incompatible with the medical and encounter models, whose underlying philosophies support the disease concept of addiction. A strong effort is needed to retrain and resocialize staff to replace these two models, which will be difficult because of a traditional bias in many rehab programs in favor of the disease concept (Freeman 1992). Considering the empowerment needs of women discussed previously, a revision of this conceptual framework is essential.

Moreover, Gutiérrez, GlenMaye, and DeLois (1995) indicate that even when an organization's empowerment orientation is well conceptualized, staff often have difficulties operationalizing it effectively with clients. Administration can provide organizational incentives such as training opportunities and direct feedback to staff to support their empowerment practice. Many of the problems encountered by Restore and Repair's staff should be acknowledged as inherent in this model and in the process of change; only then will staff remain motivated to improve the model's application at all organizational levels (Gutiérrez et al. 1995).

Therefore, a related implication is for the program to involve clients and staff in helping to redevelop its conceptual framework and improve methods for its operationalization. Chapter 5 provides a detailed discussion of the use of staff-client retreats and long-term planning processes to improve empowerment practice in rehab programs. Freeman's (1995) procedure for Multicultural and Empowerment Organizational Assessment could facilitate staff-client collaboration (see table 5.1).

The need for ongoing formal and informal mechanisms for soliciting and using client feedback should be addressed during this inclusive organizational change process, since that seems to be at the heart of these women's trust and risk-taking issues. My research revealed that most clients' political disempowerment involved these two issues, along with low self-esteem. The use of team work concepts and team training between staff and clients could enhance the outcomes of this organizational change process (Harrington-Mackin 1994). More comprehensive program evaluation procedures will be needed to closely monitor those outcomes, including the team-building process.

The need for improved team work is related to another practice implication for Restore and Repair. Although my research documented many ways in which this program has maintained its community-centeredness, this is an area in which improvement is needed also. Women's history of oppression and gender socialization biases indicate that stronger institutional incentives and supports are necessary to provide opportunities for their political empowerment. Former clients and other recovering people in the community are an untapped resource for this program. Using the team concept to make their representation on the program's executive board a requirement or having a consumer liaison work with the board could be effective. Linking board service to clients' community service requirements and leadership development could also strengthen the program in this area. Practical, user-friendly board training is an important organizational support for the involvement of consumers and other recovering people in the community, and for their self-efficacy.

Effective consumer involvement requires recognition that these women are not a homogenous group, and that they need different opportunities and incentives. The women's diversity is also important regarding a third practice implication. The program seems effective in addressing gender issues: distinguishing the women's unique recovery needs from those of men and maintaining a predominantly female staff. Moreover, the program has ensured that staff of color are in the majority to reflect the ethnic diversity among these women. Restore and Repair can improve its recognition of diversity by providing more culturally sensitive services. It is important to identify how differences between African American women, white women, and Latinas, and differences among African American women and among Latinas affect their addiction and recovery. The needs of lesbian and bisexual women should be addressed as well. Many staff pointed out that they have not had referrals from this population, but it is likely that such women have not identified themselves or that they have gone elsewhere for rehab services. Also, since co-occurring eating disorders are not unusual in incest survivors and drug-abusing women, treatment in this area needs to be addressed to enhance the recovery and empowerment of these women.

A final implication relates to how current social program reforms have singled out women and children as the primary targets of cost containment policies (Freeman 1996). The Personal Responsibility and Work Opportunity Act, or welfare reform, is one example. Restore and Repair is structured so that women in Phases I and II are fully immersed in the program. Most of them are not employable during those phases because of the debilitating effects of their addiction and the intensity of recovery in day treatment services. In addition, many of them lack adequate work skills and have poor employment histories. They may also have strengths and talents that have not been tapped into adequately during previous work or job training experiences.

Welfare reform work requirements could disrupt the long-term intensive rehab services these women need in order to become employable during

Phase III and on into the future. Managed care reforms are another example of punitive policies that are already decreasing access to long-term rehab programs for special populations such as women with children. This and other perinatal programs can develop collaborative strategies aimed at influencing reform requirements to meet the needs of high-risk women and at preventing their further disempowerment, either personally or politically.

Conclusion

While the needs of all substance-abusing and addicted individuals are important, concerns about high-risk women are a priority because of the impact of their addictions on the future of the family. Therefore, families' and communities' stakes in the rehabilitation of this population are extremely high. Pregnant and postpartum women such as those in this program are the victims of a tripartite oppressive environment, related to their gender, ethnicity, and socioeconomic status.

The effects of this environment must be considered in order to understand their addiction development and recovery process. Thus, gender-sensitive services in Restore and Repair and other effective programs should address how oppression influences women's addiction as well as their power to mobilize personal and environmental supports for their recovery. This change process involves counteracting the existing power-reducing forces and replacing them with power-engendering supports. It encompasses changes in the women's inside/outside personas, as noted by Venida, and in factors within and outside the program. Women must be actively involved in this process of consciousness raising, power analysis, and action at personal, interpersonal, and political levels. Only then can the question, "Who will save these women and their children?" be answered without reservation, "The women themselves!" Restore and Repair and other perinatal programs can provide the empowerment opportunities; these women will do the rest.

15   Recovery Works: Rehab Services for Adults with Dual Diagnoses

> I was on my way to rehab this morning. Down on 9th and Bartle by the river. My sister came stumbling outta the alley with a coupla her drug buddies. She was so wired—she didn't hardly know me at first. We hadn't seen each other for months. When she asked for money for a hit, I told her I wasn't enabling her no more! She even tried to get me to hang out with them for a while. I told her, "If I take jus' one hit, I'll be right back down here with the resta you dopeheads, acting paranoid agin." I felt real bad—talking to her like that. But what else could I do? My bus pulled up right then, so I got outta there.
>
> —Eddie B. (1995)

At least 50 percent of all people with psychiatric disorders are substance abusers, and a large number of them are addicted (Sciacca 1991). Many of these individuals with dual diagnoses have multiple stressors, such as Eddie's chance encounter with his addicted sister in the above example and his paranoid symptoms. These clients' psychiatric symptoms and patterns of coping with stress encourage them to distance themselves from family members and others with whom they have close relationships, often for survival reasons. Ironically, however, such cutoffs can lead to greater social isolation, which increases the risk of relapse in both substance abuse and psychiatric disorders.

While a tendency toward social isolation and other adjustment problems is common, these clients are diverse in their individual strengths, diagnoses, drugs of choice, levels of functioning, social supports, and motivation for and commitment to recovery (Read, Penick, and Nickel 1993; Weiss, Mirin, and Frances 1992). Their empowerment opportunities and other experiences with service providers may vary as well. Until recently, two separate service systems addressed these clients' diverse needs, but often inadequately, because the mental health and substance abuse fields have conflicting philosophies, service priorities, methods, and outcome criteria (Minkoff 1992). New programs, called MICA (for "mentally ill and chemically addicted"), have been developed in most states to provide integrated services within one system. These services are holistic and comprehensive, based on a psychosocial rehabilitation rather than a psychiatric disability model (Cnaan, Blankertz, Messinger, and Bardner 1989; Surls 1994).

But clients with dual diagnoses pose serious challenges to these new MICA programs. Medication compliance is low among some of these clients, because they equate taking psychotrophic medications with abusing illegal substances and with a loss of control. Others have polydiagnoses involving chronic physical diseases such as HIV/AIDS, which require additional specialized services. Clients with multiple diagnoses may experience competence and self-efficacy less often than other substance abusers because their needs can overwhelm their natural resiliency and other strengths. Thus, providing integrated, specialized, and client-specific services by trained and motivated staff, even in the new MICA programs, remains difficult (Blankertz and Cnaan 1992; Goldman and Willenbring 1990).

Client-specific services for dual and polydiagnosis clients are the focus of this chapter. Background information on this diverse client group is presented as the foundation for a discussion of their unique empowerment needs. An analysis of the internal and external structure of one program, Recovery Works, is included. Clients' narratives are used to illustrate the empowerment process in that program, based on my research, and the practice implications from that research are summarized.

Background Information on the Client Group

Impact of Diversity on Use Patterns and Related Issues

Although Recovery Works has 50 clients enrolled at any given time, only about 30 clients participate in its outpatient/day treatment services each day. Sixty-eight percent of these clients are males and 32 percent are females. Among the female clients, approximately 60 percent have children under 18 years of age, and almost all of those children are in the care of extended family members or in other out-of-home placements. Sixty-nine percent of clients in this program are white; 14 percent are

African American; 11 percent are Latino; and 5 percent are Asian American, Native American, or biracial. They range in age from 21 to 66 years, with the majority in the young and middle adult ranges (21–29 and 30–45 years) (Interview 1995).

Most clients admitted to the program have either mood disorders (44 percent), personality disorders (29 percent), or thought disorders (18 percent). Seven percent have psychotic disorders not included in other *DSM-IV* classifications (i.e., schizo-affective disorders) (American Psychiatric Association 1994). To be admitted, clients must also have a substance abuse problem and a history of unsuccessful completion of other programs (*Program Procedures Manual* 1993). Therefore, all of the program's clients have received services in various inpatient and outpatient mental health units and clinics in the past, where the primary focus was on their psychiatric disorders. Only 17 percent have received services in substance abuse programs for the general population, and only 3 percent have been in other MICA programs (Interview 1995).

A recent pattern in Recovery Works is that an increasing number of clients with borderline personality disorders also have a history of polydrug abuse. Many young adult males in this subgroup have moved in and out of multiple service systems, including the mental health, psychiatric, legal, employment, and health systems, without receiving adequate care. Often, the staff perceive them as more demanding, hostile, and physically aggressive than clients with other diagnoses, perhaps because of these clients' youth and highly reactive interpersonal styles (Pulice, Lyman, and Mc-Cormick 1994; Safer 1987). In order to manage their interpersonal conflicts and psychiatric symptoms, many clients learned to use substances at an early age and to experiment with various combinations of substances (Interview 1995).

Aside from this subgroup, however, 62 percent of the program's clients have a pattern of polydrug abuse. The distribution of various substance abuse disorders among them has remained relatively consistent since the program began: cocaine dependence 37 percent, with 21 percent crack cocaine; alcohol dependence 31 percent; cannabis abuse 25 percent; prescription drug abuse 24 percent; and cannabis dependence 5 percent. The combination of substance abuse and psychiatric disorders has made this program's clients a highly transient, often homeless and unemployed group. In this regard, they are similar to clients in other MICA programs across the country (Blankertz and Cnaan 1992).

Impact of Diversity on Referral Patterns

Homelessness and unemployment are common problems for substance abusers, but more so for dual diagnosis clients because of their symptoms (Blankertz and Cnaan 1994). Most of them live in unstable housing situations or on the streets; thus, their referral patterns are different from those of other substance abuse clients. A majority of the program's clients are referred by inpatient psychiatric hospitals (23 percent) or self-referred (21 percent), while another 15 percent are referred by homeless shelters. The associated hospital's mental health crisis unit refers about 16 percent.

Such referral patterns are common in this group of clients because they "are difficult to engage and often enter the system only while in crisis" (Blankertz and Cnaan 1994:537). Crisis referrals to Recovery Works stem from multiple factors that must be addressed immediately, such as the natural course of clients' chronic disorders (recurring episodes of acute depression, anxiety, or hallucinations); lack of medication compliance; family stress; loss of housing; unemployment; and social network disruptions (Blankertz and Cnaan 1994; Galanter, Franco, Kim, Metzger, and DeLeon 1993; Lovell and Sakolovsky 1990).

Clients' Empowerment Issues

Entry Into Rehab

Because this program's clients generally have been involved in other mental health services prior to admission, they are accustomed to the culture of treatment settings. Many psychiatric inpatient programs rely on professionally determined services and measure outcomes by individuals' compliance with the programs' medical and psychosocial regimens and by symptom reduction (Galanter, Egelko, DeLeon, and Rohrs 1992). Therefore, when clients enter Recovery Works, they expect to fulfill a similar powerless role. Instead, they are required during the entry period to observe how the program operates and to determine if it matches their needs and they will fit in (Interview 1995). Potential clients are not required to participate fully in the program, but they are expected to sit in on all groups and are involved in screening and intake procedures. They are encouraged to ask staff and peers questions about what they observe during this pre-engagement phase.

This initial valuing of clients' input acknowledges their power over the situation. It allows them to apply extremely important, although at other times inconsistent (due to frequent changes in their psychiatric symptoms), self-knowledge.

Upon entry, clients' power issues may cause them to continue resisting medication or to act out by exaggerating their symptoms or isolating themselves. Denial is another form of resistance. Some clients believe substance abuse is the lesser of two societal stigmas, so they admit it may be a problem but deny the chronic and pervasive consequences of their psychiatric disorders. All of these resistance or coping strategies are a reaction to what they perceive to be a no-win, powerless situation.

Program staff have been trained to go with clients' initial resistances. They may point out that a client is isolating him- or herself as a form of protection until it is clear whether peers and staff can be trusted. This response recognizes that only clients have the power to decide who they will or will not trust and when. Staff may acknowledge when someone has decided not to take his or her medication even though they believe the decision is not a good one. While the client is not on medication, staff suggest that he or she keep a record of the symptoms that develop, what precipitates them, and which coping strategies are effective or ineffective.

These clients can experience self-efficacy from generating their own data about the consequences of their decision to stop taking medication (Interview 1995). A new client who stopped taking her medication for two weeks said, "I forgot how bad my voices [auditory hallucinations] were, they went away after I started the medication, so I thought they were gone for good. Now I know I was just fooling myself." Although it was painful and scary, this experience made her face a reality she could no longer ignore: that her symptoms were part of a lifelong condition controllable in part by medication when it is taken on a regular basis.

Continuance in Rehab

The lifelong self-management process is difficult for most dual diagnosis clients, so they sometimes regress as a natural part of rehab. When these crises occur in later phases, staff frequently become more controlling and condemning (Kay, Kalathara, and Meinzer 1989). Consequently, some clients experience disempowerment and rejection, which causes them to drop out of rehab and relapse. The program does not automatically discharge clients for relapsing, but it will do so if they sell drugs to other clients. Even if clients insist on leaving AMA (against medical advice), they and their primary counselors are required to collaborate in developing a reentry plan describing what positive steps the client will take before returning. It is tacitly acknowledged that only clients have the power to determine if they succeed or fail in rehab (Interview 1995).

Another symptom management issue involves clients who enter and drop out of different programs continuously in a revolving-door pattern. These clients are considered recovery professionals who basically come to rehab for detoxing and for respite from their psychiatric symptoms (Cohen and Burt 1990). Staff try to resist becoming hopeless about these clients, yet not to overinvest in their recovery. They attempt to help these clients empower themselves long enough to stay in rehab but believe their efforts are not effective with most (Interview 1995).

Social isolation among dually diagnosed clients is another issue that increases the risk of dropouts. Isolation reinforces these clients' beliefs about their vulnerability and lack of self-sufficiency in comparison to others, and decreases their self-esteem. Recovery Works addresses this power issue by helping clients to develop a community or family of peers who are responsible for each other's well-being. The emphasis on mutual responsibility and collective power helps to maintain these typically isolated clients in rehab. All of them benefit when a peer progresses and all "are responsible for maintaining a system of bi-directional helping to support and encourage peers who are experiencing problems" (*Client Handbook* 1994).

Client-Specific Services

A central aspect of client-specific services in this program is helping clients to recognize the consequences of their substance abuse and psychiatric impairments. In addition, they are taught in problem-solving and Rational Recovery groups how each condition reinforces the other and learn self-management skills for preventing and recovering from relapses in both conditions. In education sessions, relapse is reframed as a natural part of recovery and as a source of eventual empowerment because it provides knowledge about effective coping. Clients' concerns about the stigma of mental illness and addiction are addressed as well.

Further, client-specific services offer clients many alternatives to decrease their powerlessness and resistance to rehab. The goal of this inclusionary, decision-making approach is to generate only client-acceptable services (*Client Handbook* 1994). Prior to program enrollment, staff present capsule versions of potential new groups and other services to clients. The clients vote to determine which will be offered during the next four months. The focus and content of about 20 percent of the program's 25 groups and other services are changed during each enrollment period.

During enrollment, clients develop their individual schedules for the next four months by signing up for various new and continued services they have approved by voting. They can consult with their primary counselors in the process, much like college students meeting with advisers before enrolling in their classes each semester. Having to choose between two or more desirable services that are offered simultaneously often reinforces the clients' decision-making skills and increases their autonomy. It also increases their promptness and attendance rates for the groups and other activities they include on their schedules (Interview 1995).

Another part of the program's client-specific services is providing the same knowledge and skills in different types of services, using different approaches that appeal to clients' various learning styles. For instance, information about the symptoms and consequences of dual disorders and their management is presented differently in various groups such as the mental health and drug education, MICA, health and wellness, and weekend process groups.

Development of skills related to those topics, such as planning and implementing a new diet and exercise regimen in the health and wellness groups and learning to present information on psychiatric and substance abuse disorders to peers in MICA groups, is accomplished in different ways. Clients learn to provide critical peer feedback (pull-ups) and mutual help in different formats within twelve-step groups, encounter groups, and Rational Recovery groups. The latter is an alternative to twelve-step groups for clients who do not believe in God or in a higher power (*Client Handbook* 1995). Skill development in Rational Recovery groups is guided by RET (rational-emotive therapy) concepts and a psychoeducation model. In twelve-step groups, a narrative and peer support format guides this process of knowledge and skill development, whereas in encounter groups, the peer feedback model commonly used is much more confrontational and intensive.

The Program's Internal Structure and Context

The structure and context of Recovery Works support the use of mutual help and other peer-led services as sources of empowerment and effective recovery. The nature of such supports is clarified in the following discussion about the program's early development, philosophy, services, and empowerment-related organizational factors.

Early Program Development

This program began in 1988 in a medium-sized urban city on the East Coast after it became clear to state administrators that dual diagnosis clients were not being served adequately by either the mental health or the substance abuse system. Programs in both systems would discharge clients whenever their "secondary" disorders became unmanageable, or staff would try, often unsuccessfully, to coordinate totally different services between different programs that operated out of two conflicting systems (Interview 1994). When Recovery Works was developed as one of the state's first MICA programs, its goal was to coordinate services by minimizing conflicts between approaches used to address the two types of disorders.

Since that time, the program's goal has shifted to integrating the two service approaches, so it is therefore more complex. Seventeen different but interrelated dimensions are used to assess clients' needs in terms of their psychiatric and substance abuse disorders and to organize the recovery process. Figure 15.1 lists those dimensions as they are addressed during different phases of rehab, while table 15.1 summarizes the specific program factors that help clients to achieve global change in those areas.

Program Philosophy and Conceptual Framework

Global change, rather than minimal change or symptom reduction, is an important part of this program's philosophy. It is assumed that global or complete lifestyle changes occur when the two types of impairments are viewed as two primary interacting conditions and are addressed conjointly. This mind-body-social development change process occurs also through a

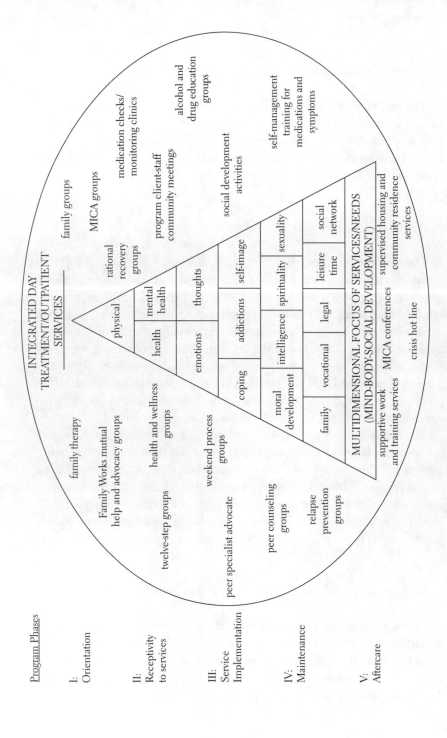

Program Phases

I:
Orientation

II:
Receptivity
to services

III:
Service
Implementation

IV:
Maintenance

V:
Aftercare

INTEGRATED DAY TREATMENT/OUTPATIENT SERVICES

family groups

MICA groups

medication checks/
monitoring clinics

alcohol and
drug education
groups

rational
recovery
groups

program client-staff
community meetings

self-management
training for
medications and
symptoms

social development
activities

family therapy

Family Works mutual
help and advocacy groups

health and wellness
groups

twelve-step groups

weekend process
groups

peer specialist advocate

peer counseling
groups

relapse
prevention
groups

supportive work
and training services

MICA conferences

crisis hot line

supervised housing and
community residence
services

MULTIDIMENSIONAL FOCUS OF SERVICES/NEEDS
(MIND-BODY-SOCIAL DEVELOPMENT)

physical

mental
health

health

thoughts

emotions

coping

addictions

self-image

intelligence

spirituality

sexuality

moral
development

vocational

legal

leisure
time

social
network

family

FIGURE 15.1 Program Phases and Services: Recovery Works

series of trials during rehab, based on a client's growing desire to stop using drugs and to accept and manage his or her psychiatric impairments (Interview 1995). Global change is only possible, therefore, through a program environment that supports the client's agreement on the need to change and to use his or her inner resources to do so (*Client Handbook* 1994). This philosophy acknowledges that some clients will not be successful during their first trials in rehab because their desire for global change may only develop gradually over time.

Empowerment is both stated and implied in different parts of the program's materials. For example, the importance of client empowerment and ownership of change is highlighted in the client handbook, while the program brochure states that "services are tailored to meet each cllient's unique and individual needs." Further, everyone, including clients and staff, is considered a specialist based on his or her unique experiences and inner wisdom about life and recovery. The program's conceptual framework involves a holistic approach that integrates aspects of this philosophy along with the seventeen dimensions shown in figure 15.1.

Nature of the Program's Services

Program Components and Staff. This program has an integrated outpatient and day treatment program: outpatient services are half day, while day treatment services are all day. The program serves clients for periods from eighteen to thirty-six months through five related phases. As can be seen from figure 15.1, these phases involve orientation, receptivity to services, service implementation or use, maintenance, and aftercare. The general goals for all clients in each phase are based on issues that have been identified through client feedback during community meetings and other activities and by staff. Examples of client issues identified during the orientation phase include lack of trust of service providers and social isolation. Goals for this phase include having staff members demonstrate their value and affirmation of clients and enhance clients' bonding with peers and the program.

In contrast, issues identified during the service implementation phase include clients' anxieties about change and their struggles to recover from relapses. Understandably, goals for this phase include accepting and achieving global change. One client relapsed immediately after participating in a staffing in which he received overwhelmingly positive feedback about his progress. When he returned to rehab several weeks later, he said the experience showed him that he was not ready for the changes that had occurred. The feedback revealed to him for the first time the enormity of the task he had undertaken. His fears about accepting and completing it caused him to return to his old patterns of self-medication and decompensation. As expected in this phase, the program helped him to resist these old patterns and establish new patterns that could lead to global change rather than simply symptom reduction.

Recovery Works' staff consists of the program director; a senior counselor; addiction counselors (3); case managers (3), one of whom is a specialized vocational counselor; a nurse (1); a peer specialist; and an office manager (Interview 1995). The director, who has a Ph.D. in psychology, is the program's first and only director. He believes that staff who were with the program from its inception are more committed to working with either the substance abuse or psychiatric problems of clients. However, gradually, through more selective hiring and more specialized training, the current staff is committed to the program's integrative approach. The senior counselor is an M.S.W., but the position requires a graduate degree in any helping profession. Requirements for the counselor positions include an undergraduate degree plus experience for certification in addictions counseling, while the case manager positions require an associate degree and one year's experience in a similar position.

The peer specialist position was created by state administrators to allow previous clients to become staff members who are an important part of the service team. These specialists co-lead peer groups in the program and an advocacy/support group for people with dual diagnoses in the community. They help clients plan collaborative social development activities to prevent isolation and to enhance daily living skills, mentor individual clients in the recovery process, and help to staff a crisis hot line for this population group (*Staff Procedures Manual* 1993).

Major Theories, Approaches, and Rehab Strategies. Recovery Works uses an integrated psychoeducational, cognitive-behavioral, case management, peer empowerment, family systems approach. There is a heavy emphasis on helping clients become informed about their psychiatric impairments, medication uses and consequences, brain chemistry related to illegal and psychotropic drugs, psychosocial and substance abuse rehabilitation, addiction, and relapse prevention (Cnaan 1988; Galanter et al. 1993; Minkoff 1989). Peer specialists and client volunteers facilitate client empowerment. Along with other program staff, they are responsible for some psychoeducation services. The goal is to increase clients' knowledge, social development, and self-management, and therefore, their self-efficacy and empowerment.

Three types of family services are provided, guided by family systems and psychoeducational theories and approaches. Family therapy provides an understanding of family dynamics for improving relationships and communication in individual families or groups of families. Family group is a two-sequence mental health and drug education/problem-solving group for significant others. Family Works is a mutual support, advocacy, and problem-solving group run by families for which staff serve as consultants. Battaglino (1987) assumes that family support groups are essential for improving "the quality of life for their loved ones" by targeting "the professional community, the political arena, and the social environment" for change (48). In addition, such groups enhance opportunities for empowerment because they involve self-help and professional service collaboration (Traunstein 1984; Medvene 1984) (see figure 15.1).

As a result of this combination of services, clients who were formerly helpless redefine who they are and learn how to help themselves and their peers. They learn to externalize their psychiatric symptoms and relapse risk factors in order to gain control over them. In cognitive-behavioral and systems terms, they learn the rules of a new game or new system (Hartman 1996; Power, Jerrom, Simpson, Mitchell, and Swanson 1989; Nurius and Berlin 1994; Shorkey 1994), called the development of group- and self-efficacy. This combination of approaches is implemented in the variety of formats or venues shown in table 15.1.

Empowerment-Related Program Factors

Program factors summarized in table 15.1 indicate that this program fits between the categories of microcosm programs (added by the author) and empowered programs (Florin and Wandersman 1990). Those authors assume that empowering programs only provide opportunities for clients to experience personal and interpersonal empowerment. In contrast, microcosm programs provide for clients' political empowerment within the service setting, and empowered programs encourage political empowerment in the

TABLE 15.1 Recovery Works: Examples of Empowerment-Oriented Program Factors

Empowerment Levels	Major Themes		
	Professional Services	Peer-Led Services	Professional-Client Collaboration
Personal	client relapses and refusals to take medication are approached as client self-education, discovery, and self-management experiences entry period is designed for helping clients to observe and assess whether the program can meet their needs and to "try out" services	client work crews help them to develop collaboration skills through joint tasks/activities graduates return to mentor and support current clients and to increase their self-efficacy	clients who are discharged from the program collaborate with their primary counselors to develop a reentry plan clients set their own goals in collaboration with their primary counselors
Interpersonal	weekend process groups are used to help clients plan and debrief about weekend stresses and supports that influence recovery clients are involved in supportive work arrangements in Phases III and IV to improve their self-sufficiency and level of competence	system of peer bidirectional helping is encouraged in peer-led counseling and mutual aid groups (pull-ups, hot seat, etc.) peers present information on substance abuse and psychiatric disorders in MICA groups	Family Works, a self-help and family-staff collaborative service, advocates for program and community resources client social development activities are planned and implemented by clients and staff to enhance self-management and reduce social isolation
Political	Recovery Works's hospital board reserves one seat on its advisory board for consumers the program's consumer advocacy group meets with the director monthly to provide feedback and influence program policies		clients vote on/develop individual schedules with primary counselors for new program curriculum every four months and provide consumer input into community services peer specialists advocate for systems change in the community and large institutions, and cofacilitate or monitor the quality of the program

larger external environment as well (Florin and Wandersman 1990). The table makes it clear that clients often gain personal and interpersonal empowerment opportunities through setting their own recovery goals and giving critical peer feedback and support to other group members.

Recovery Works also provides opportunities for clients to influence the political structure of the setting. The client voting and enrollment process related to the offering of new services and clients' input at community meetings are strong opportunities for them to impact the program's political structure. However, this program provides only a few opportunities for clients to experience political empowerment in the external environment—in the community and in regard to large systems practices, organizational policies, and related public policies.

Type of Organization and Empowerment Needs of the Clients. Many of these clients experience numerous problems in negotiating other systems such as the legal, health care, and public welfare systems. This is especially true for women with young children who lack basic resources and for young adult males who act out periodically, for example, those with borderline personality disorders (Galanter et al. 1992). These and other dual diagnosis clients need help in developing trust in MICA service providers who emphasize the client-centered nature of their integrated programs. Some program factors provide opportunities for trust building and allow clients to influence the nature of the program. Coaching and skill development strategies designed to improve clients' social development often create opportunities for them to influence external systems as they try out their new skills in the natural environment. For example, one seat on the program's hospital advisory board is reserved for past clients, and staff and current clients are sometimes involved in meetings with external agencies in order to influence the quality of services those agencies provide.

Theoretically, systems change experiences should be generalizable; however, clients indicate they have been unable to generalize those infrequent experiences to the external environment. This causes them to feel ineffective, incompetent, and powerless in some situations involving other systems. Therefore, they need to develop more political influence skills that directly address barriers they encounter outside the MICA and recovering communities. Recovery Works should address such barriers more comprehensively because failure to do so can influence clients' rates and patterns of relapse. Strategies for affecting these barriers are included in the section on practice implications.

The Program's External Structure and Context

The issue of political influence and how it is addressed in the program is also shaped by the external structure of Recovery Works, which consists of the program's organizational auspices and the community and policy/funding subsystems within which it operates.

Organizational Auspices

Recovery Works is part of a large hospital's mental health department. The department's other services include inpatient psychiatric care, an outpatient clinic, and psychiatric emergency services, including a crisis unit. The large, comprehensive general hospital provides an array of physical health services and occupational, respiratory, radiation, and physical therapies. Although the program is located several blocks away from the main hospital, its staff members are considered hospital staff and the clients are viewed as consumers of the hospital's services. In addition, the director meets regularly with the mental health department's administrators, along with other program directors, and confers with them about certain policy decisions. The staff attend and participate in departmental staff meetings on a regular basis. They also collaborate with other hospital staff in individual cases and regarding special services such as the psychiatric emergency room and coordinate staff resources by providing joint mental health training opportunities.

Based on these structural ties, this program fits within the area of substance abuse services in a secondary setting, according to the organizational auspices continuum shown in figure 5.1. As noted above, an advantage to services in a secondary setting is the opportunities for collaboration and coordination, which enhances the delivery of client-specific services that contribute to clients' empowerment in the program. Another advantage is that the hospital, and particularly the mental health department, is a major referral source for the program's clients, often when they are in crisis. Increased timeliness and appropriateness of referrals to the program have allowed staff to more effectively address some important barriers to empowerment, discussed in "Client Empowerment Issues."

A disadvantage of the secondary setting is that the staff's psychosocial rehab philosophy and acceptance of an integrated service delivery system often create conflicts and barriers to collaboration with regular hospital staff. Recovery Works staff indicate their more specialized services are often a low priority when resource decisions are made at the departmental and hospital levels (see figure 5.1). Both factors have often contributed to staff disempowerment and inability, at times, to use empowerment strategies effectively.

The Community Subsystem

Recovery Works is a community-based rather than community-centered program. While it relates closely to the MICA and recovering communities, their various service providers, and clients' families, it does not seem to be accountable to the larger surrounding community. For instance, mechanisms to facilitate this, such as having community members on its advisory board (which now includes former consumers and professionals) are not in place. In addition, the program's clients are not responsible for performing community service activities and are not often engaged in political action to change adverse conditions and large systems' practices or policies that limit their empowerment and effective resolution of barriers to their recovery.

A number of organizational mechanisms help this program to coordinate services for and increase accountability to the MICA and recovering communities. The director meets with a consumer advocacy group once monthly and solicits input about how to improve clients' access to the program and the quality of its services. The group consists of current and past consumers from the program and other consumers in the MICA community (Interview 1995). As noted previously, past clients are represented by one seat on the hospital's advisory board, which provides opportunities for them to influence policies and decision making. The program's peer specialist consults with individual consumers and MICA consumer groups in the community; other staff help cofacilitate COPES (Consumers Organized for Public Education Support) groups in the community and are board members and informal advisers for a network of specialized community residences for consumers.

The Policy/Funding Subsystem

State administrators in the mental health system that monitors substance abuse programs became more and more concerned during the late 1980s about the status and quality of services for clients with dual diagnoses. Services were fragmented and ineffective because they were designed to address only one component of those clients' needs, either their psychiatric or substance abuse disorders. Therefore, in 1990, the mental health system developed a statewide psychosocial rehab model of service delivery. However, because the medical or psychiatric service model was well entrenched, administrators decided to pilot the integrated substance abuse and psychosocial rehab services in new programs.

Twenty new MICA programs were developed throughout the state. They had organizational ties to local mental health services, but they were expected to model their services on the new state integrated model rather than on the traditional model used within their host organizations. The new model emphasizes a normalization philosophy that assumes that certain symptoms are a natural part of psychiatric disorders. This philosophy also assumes that the symptoms and the stressors that precipitate them will frequently require admission to some type of client-specific holding environment, which should be as close to the client's natural community and social network supports as possible.

Holding environments established consisted of community club houses, respite services, emergency room crisis units (outpatient), and short-term inpatient psychiatric trauma units (Interview 1996). Proactive planned admissions to these holding environments (rather than mostly unpredictable admissions) are assumed to be necessary throughout the natural and chronic course of such disorders. Other client-specific services are expected to develop from programs' actively soliciting and applying clients' input about services and programming issues. Thus, this policy-level philosophy does encourage and support Recovery Works' emphasis on empowerment practice.

Current funding patterns and decisions for MICA programs are designed to fit this empowerment philosophy. For instance, 51 percent of all governance and policy-making roles in these programs are expected to be reserved for consumers. Between 1987 and 1991, state funding for individual services shifted from 80 percent of the mental health budget to 25 percent, with the difference being allocated for family and community-centered services. Peer specialist positions were created and funded for each program, each regional office, and the state central office. The state now solicits proposals for grants focused on institutional change. These consumer-oriented, political action grants are designed to train and support clients in advocating for the removal of empowerment barriers in MICA and mental health programs and in other state institutions (Interview 1995).

How have these philosophical, policy, and funding issues affected empowerment practice in Recovery Works? While there is more funding for services within MICA programs, state resources for community support services such as transitional housing and supported employment remain inadequate. These services are critical for building and maintaining clients' self-sufficiency and for preventing avoidable relapses. In the hospital's mental health department, conflicts exist between the staff's MICA philosophy of psychosocial rehab and the psychiatric disability model (which has not been completely eliminated in traditional mental health programs). For instance, other departmental administrators do not agree with Recovery Works' emphasis on funding for social development activities beyond basic activities of daily living. Staff assignments related to changing the curriculum every four months to enhance client-specific services and empowerment have been challenged administratively from time to time. The program's policy of not automatically discharging clients who slip or relapse has been questioned by other mental health staff, particularly when they are helping to coordinate services for family members or significant others.

The Empowerment Process in Action

In spite of the above barriers, the state's innovative requirement that funding patterns be consistent with an empowerment philosophy has created unique opportunities for clients' social development and self-efficacy. The clients' narratives attest to this while documenting specific factors that support or hinder them both individually and collectively.

One Client's Empowerment Narrative

Background Information.   Anna is a thirty-seven-year-old Chinese American who had been in outpatient rehab for three months for her alcohol and marijuana addictions. Her diagnosis was bipolar depression, for which she was taking lithium. She lived with her family until she was thirty years old, when she moved in with a woman with whom she had a five-year relationship. That ended when her partner committed suicide. Anna began her current relationship soon after this loss. In a Rational Recovery group session focused on "letting go of dysfunctional relationships," Anna talked about the recent ending of her relationship with her current partner, Chris. Prior to this session, Anna had "come out" in discussions with individual peers but had not discussed her sexual orientation in the group.

Anna's Narrative.   I surprised myself by volunteering to talk about my relationship with Chris. I knew some of my peers thought I was a freak, but this past weekend was so stressful, I had to get things off my chest. I told them Chris was coming around every night since she moved out, trying to get me to drink with her. She threatened to beat me up—knife me—anything to get me back. She's still trying to control me by holding on to our relationship. I waited to see my peers' reactions. Kevin had nodded off, or so I thought, until he asked me was I holding on to the relationship too. I said no way, but then thought about it for a little while. Another peer, Karla, started to say something but my counselor, Ben, shook his head. I told them, "I guess you could say we're both holding on to the relationship, in different ways. Maybe I'm scared to be alone. My parents won't have anything to do with me, I'm not close to anybody else—except my brother."

Ben asked the members to talk about difficult relationships they had been in. I couldn't believe what happened then, the things they said; I could actually see myself in some of their situations. Craig said he wouldn't give up his drug partners at first because they filled up an empty space inside him and made him forget about trying to recover. Bill mentioned one of his past relationships had a lot of drama like mine—he got high off the drama and it made him forget about his voices and paranoia. Marie held on to a negative relationship because the stress made her more manic, and being manic gave her an excuse to "pick up." Listening to them, my doubts just went away. I could see I was right in breaking up with Chris, even though I didn't know what to do next.

Conclusions About the Meaning and Impact of the Experience.   Anna concluded that this group experience made her feel good about herself because it removed her doubts about an important decision she had made. Breaking up with Chris represented an effort to bring closure to a negative, self-destructive relationship and to exert control over her life by making her own decisions. In essence, she was trying to regain the power she had ceded to Chris. Ben's encouraging group members to talk about similar relationship struggles and the stories they told were affirming to Anna. Those strategies reflect the professional service and peer-led themes in table 1.1.

Her peers' stories normalized Anna's concerns about her relationship with Chris and made her less fearful that her peers would reject her because of her sexual orientation. The stories helped Anna to understand why she had been ambivalent about ending the relationship and that her reaction was common during early recovery. Anna said being mixed up (her ambivalence) was like having a "brain cloud" over her head, whereas seeing her doubts disappear was like having the sun's rays burn the cloud away.

Accordingly, Anna later defined "empowerment" as the clearing away of brain clouds. From this definition and the above conclusions, it is likely that Anna experienced personal empowerment. She clearly felt she gained power by developing confidence about her decision making. The experience made Anna more open to working on self-esteem issues that had prevented her from addressing the battering and stalking by Chris in the past. She could see that the drama over her relationship with Chris distracted her from working on those and other issues, such as the stigma of her psychiatric disorder, becoming comfortable with her sexual orientation, handling her grief over her former partner's suicide, and examining her present commitment to recovery.

Based on how she processed this experience later, Anna seemed to experience interpersonal empowerment as well. She concluded that she had the power to improve her relationship with her older brother, in order to build a stronger support network. He was already supportive of her entry into rehab and of her desire to end the relationship with Chris. She acknowledged that she could not change her parents' rejection, which was based on her sexual orientation, substance abuse, and chronic depression. Accepting that fact encouraged her to think about how she could use the group and her brother as current and future sources of support.

After the group session, Ben asked Anna if the family control issues she had described could be cultural. Anna recalled she had moved in with her first partner in an effort to diminish her parents' control over her life. Her family, like Chris, had encouraged her to stop taking her medication because they distrusted Western medicine and saw mental illness as a stigma. Anna talked about the importance of family loyalty and respect for elders in the Chinese culture; it is still expected in more traditional families that adult children, especially females, will live with their parents until they marry. Anna's moving out and her sexual orientation were a direct affront to the family and its cultural values. The counselor's relabeling of these issues helped Anna to see them in a different, less negative, context. This relabeling or cognitive restructuring reinforced Anna's changing beliefs about what she could and could not control, helping her use her sources of self-efficacy and let go of her sources of powerlessness (Ellis, McInerney, DiGiuseppe, and Yeager 1988; Nurius and Berlin 1994).

Clients' Empowerment Narratives: General Issues

My analysis of Anna's narrative and the empowerment narratives of twenty-four other clients in Recovery Works revealed a number of patterns. These are discussed below in terms of the content of the clients' narratives and the impact the experiences had on their lives.

The Content.   In contrast to other programs in this study, approximately half of the clients' experiences occurred during informal rather than formal aspects of rehab, such as a social event in the community, a spontaneous discussion with the director in his office, an encounter with a counselor in the hallway, a conversation between two peers during a cigarette break, and interaction during one of the program's informal community meetings.

One of these informal encounters was shared by three different clients during separate interviews. It involved a social development group activity of going out to dinner at a restaurant. On one outing, the service was extraordinarily good. When the waitress brought the check to the table at the end of the meal, it became clear to the restaurant's staff that they had mistaken this group of clients for a party of doctors from the same hospital. The accompanying counselors from Recovery Works pointed out to the empowered clients that their exemplary social behavior had influenced the restaurant's assumption about their social and professional status.

This example illustrates another pattern that emerged from the study. Clients' empowerment experiences often involved a combination of coaching by staff and peers and their own practicing of newly acquired skills (see other examples of this professional staff-client collaboration theme in table 15.1). Before their restaurant outing, these clients had been coached in and had practiced how to order a meal, dress appropriately, and engage in socially appropriate interaction and manners comfortably in such situations. Coaching and practicing new skills have been found to be critical for the development of self-efficacy and social competence (Blankertz et al. 1992; Cnaan et al. 1989; Galanter et al. 1992).

This skill training process was also illustrated in other examples. Lee, a thirty-two-year-old Latino client, experienced political empowerment when he was selected to attend a state MICA conference during a community meeting. That empowerment was intensified, however, when he was coached about his role and about how to influence the conference process by senior peers who had attended previous conferences and who had longer periods of sobriety. Kay, a twenty-six-year-old African American client, experienced personal empowerment during a weekend process group when she talked about the death of her mother and her first custodial visit with her children, which had both occurred during the preceding weekend. After listening to her story about these two events and expressing support, her peers engaged Kay in a role play that helped her practice the ritual of making funeral arrangements, about which she was extremely anxious. The role play normalized her anxiety and conveyed the group's belief in Kay's ability to get through the ritual without relapsing.

Another pattern was that, as a group, these clients' narratives tended to include all three empowerment levels. Some of the previous examples focus on clients' personal and interpersonal empowerment. Other examples at those two levels include a client who felt affirmed when his counselor shared a user-friendly book about his psychiatric disorder with him, and a client who used humor to relieve a peer's stress about his hallucinations by reframing them as UFOs.

An example of political empowerment involved Bernard, a forty-four-year-old white client with a personality disorder. Bernard had experienced a family crisis over the weekend involving threats and physical violence by his brother. When he called the COPES crisis line, he was told that his problem was not a crisis because he was not the individual who was out of control. When Bernard stopped by the director's office on Monday to say hello, he shared what had happened. The director listened to Bernard's story and asked how the response had affected him and how he managed the crisis situation at home. He reinforced Bernard's conclusion that his request had been handled inappropriately by the crisis line. Later, when the director scheduled a meeting with the crisis line staff, he asked Bernard and another consumer to accompany him to discuss how the services could be improved. Bernard's self-esteem and -efficacy increased because the director followed up on his promise to check out his complaint and included him in the process.

The Meaning and Impact of Clients' Empowerment Experiences.   Many of these clients were clear about what they learned and how they grew from their empowerment experiences. As a group, they contrasted those experiences with past social and personal "failures." The clients who related the restaurant example thought their experience demonstrated that they could influence how the restaurant staff and others viewed them: as socially acceptable people who happen to have psychiatric impairments (interpersonal and personal power). Other clients felt their experiences taught them that social and political action can develop from feeling good about themselves and their peers.

Bernard, who experienced the crisis line incident, felt good about the situation because the director "treated me like I knew what I was talkin' about. He didn't take sides or nothin' with the COPES people. I mean he took a chance, having me go with 'em to talk about the crisis line. I hadda stand by what I said happened. I guess I mighta backed out or screwed up, but he believed I could do it, so I went with 'em and stood my ground."

One Client's Disempowerment Experience

Background Information.   Brian is a twenty-four-year-old white client who had been in rehab for four weeks when the following disempowerment experience occurred. He had been referred to Recovery Works by a homeless shelter and was on probation for writing bad checks and for assault and battery of another recipient at the local welfare office. Brian was taking Prozac after having been recently diagnosed as schizophrenic. He was difficult for staff to engage and used compulsive journaling to distance himself from peers and staff. He always carried a stack of notebooks in which he journaled constantly. Brian also isolated himself from peers and family members. The disempowerment experience he shared occurred during his first family session in the program, which he did not want to attend.

Brian's Narrative.   Two things made me mad about the family group. I didn't wanna go in the first place. I knew it'd be the same as always, my parents blaming me for all the family problems. I told the group, I had enougha feeling bad about that. Then one of the counselors, Owen, told me I should be going to NA every week to keep from relapsing—I admitted to the group I been on meth for about six or seven months. I looked at my father; he was sitting there with his head down when the dude mentioned NA—probably remembering the time he tricked me into going to AA when I was thirteen. He said, "Brian, stop making excuses, you gotta go sometime." Some'a the clients and their family members started telling me what they get from NA and Alanon; they ganged up on me—didn't understand at all. The other family counselor, Shirelle, said maybe going to NA should be part of my probation. That really got to me; I was tired of their crap. I stood up and walked out of the room. I could feel 'em staring at my back. I heard Shirelle say, "He's getting too excited" as I slammed the door.

Conclusions About the Meaning and Impact of the Experience. Brian felt disrespected because he was not listened to by the group members or by Shirelle and Owen, the counselors. He had hoped his father, especially, would defend him because he knew how Brian felt about twelve-step groups. Brian's father had been a recovering alcoholic since Brian was thirteen years old. Having been told by a counselor that his children had been badly affected by his addiction and needed counseling and support to adjust to his recovery, he decided to take Brian to an AA meeting, but without explaining where they were going and why. Brian remembers feeling great shame from observing his father and other participants talk about their addictions and personal problems.

He was at an age when being accepted by his peers and being like everyone else was essential, so he felt this experience set him apart. The intense vulnerability and powerlessness he felt first scared and then angered him, feelings he relived during the family meeting. Even his physical reactions were the same, including sweating, feeling numb and unable to talk, and feeling goose bumps from people staring at him. Brian's description of his inability to control himself or influence members of the family group is an example of personal and interpersonal disempowerment. The experience reflects the professional service and peer-led themes shown in table 15.1.

Brian's legal problems were a byproduct of his anger control issues. He often became aggressive, such as when he assaulted a man in the welfare office or stormed out of the family meeting. In fact, Brian stated that he felt so scared in the meeting, he might have hurt someone had he not left the room. Yet he was also ashamed of leaving and of not coping effectively with the feedback he received. He felt embarrassed during the next few days whenever he was around his peers, feeling also that he could not do anything to improve their opinions of him.

Often, when Brian felt down like this in the past, he had used meth and isolation to self-medicate and hide his feelings. So he was tempted to use again, and although he did not, he felt isolated from his peers, his family, and the staff. A few days later, he was assigned to a peer mentor or big brother. Through that connection, he was gradually able to get more involved in his recovery and in rehab.

Clients' Disempowerment Experiences: General Issues

Brian's narrative and those of other clients in the program highlight some common issues as well as some differences across their disempowerment experiences. Often these differences were a matter of degree rather than substantial variations. The content and clients' feedback about the meaning of the experiences are summarized in this section.

The Content.   Almost all of the disempowerment narratives shared by these clients were at the personal and interpersonal levels; only one was at the political level. In that example, thirty-two-year-old Keith, an African American client, was required to apologize for being physically and verbally aggressive toward another client. This type of behavior had not ever occurred in the program, so the director developed a new policy to address similar situations in the future. He announced the new policy in one of the community meetings attended by COPES representatives, along with clients and staff in the program. Then he told Keith to make his apology. Keith said this experience caused him to "lose face" as a leader among his peers and reduced his stature in the program. Though Keith admitted the situation could have been worse, because he could have been discharged, he felt his recovery was undermined by this public humiliation.

Examples of personal disempowerment include a client who learned about the probable effects of her cocaine addiction and HIV-positive status on her unborn child in the mental health and drug education group. Anger from her powerlessness to change the situation was directed at a doctor in a regular rehab program who had not provided her with this information, and at herself for her prior lifestyle. Another client talked about being pressured by his primary counselor to move to a less restricted transitional housing situation. This client felt his counselor did not understand his fears about the effects of the move on his symptoms, such as increasing his isolation and hallucinations. In his current, more communal housing, he was forced to interact with peers and staff, whereas he would have less natural peer interaction and supervision in the new housing. He felt guilty because he was resisting becoming more independent and was disagreeing with the staff.

The example at the beginning of this chapter illustrates a client's interpersonal disempowerment. Eddie, a thirty-eight-year-old white client, was frustrated that he could not influence his sister or rescue her from her drug buddies and her addiction. He knew she was risking violence and even death in her lifestyle of drugs, homelessness, prostitution, and shoplifting. Yet he was also angry with her for trying to get him back on drugs when she knew he was on his way to rehab the morning of their chance encounter. His anger and powerlessness persisted, in spite of supportive feedback from the peer specialist with whom Eddie talked about the incident as soon as he arrived at rehab that morning.

The Meaning and Impact of Clients' Disempowerment Narratives.   The main impact of these experiences was on clients' attitudes about their power in relation to other people's. Some clients were fatalistic about their disempowerment experiences, while others said they might have felt less powerless and reacted differently if their situations had been handled more appropriately. For instance, Eddie felt his chance encounter with his sister was a no-win situation, and that his recovery and family loyalty were bound to be tested sooner or later. He even realized from talking with the peer specialist that his reaction was necessary to protect his own recovery and healthy functioning. However, accepting that fact and acknowledging his powerlessness to force his sister into rehab did not stop him from believing he had "abandoned" her. Eddie believed he would simply have to live with the guilt from this experience for the rest of his life.

In contrast, Keith, who was required to apologize for his aggression toward a peer in a community meeting, believed his disempowerment could have been avoided. Thus, he learned about the inappropriate use of authority from this experience. Keith thought the director used his authority to punish him, although he always talked about being compassionate toward clients. Keith said the two of them should have talked first about the new policy in a private meeting. Then they could have worked out how the apology would be handled, even if a public way was still necessary. This way, Keith believed, he could have prepared himself to cope more effectively with the public apology. A private discussion might have helped Keith to understand that his loss of respect occurred during the aggression incident rather than when he apologized for his behavior, a distinction he seemed unaware of even while recounting this incident.

Practice Implications

Power cutoffs such as the one experienced by Keith, as well as clients' empowerment experiences, indicate that social development activities, self-management skills, and coping with the stigma and normal stresses associated with their impairments are central to these clients' recovery. Their stories are supported by the literature's emphasis on the need to improve these clients' self-sufficiency and quality of life (Battaglino 1987; Cnaan et al. 1992). The discussion of background information on this population and its empowerment issues identified many areas in which Recovery Works is addressing its needs very well.

However, two identified areas are not being addressed adequately. Staff and clients agree that there is insufficient funding for a continuum of transitional housing for clients with dual diagnoses, from the most to the least restricted or supervised. Supported training and employment opportunities have increased in the last few years as MICA programs have been developed, but a greater range of comprehensive services is needed to meet the clients' diverse interests, abilities, and limitations.

Improved services in these two areas could reduce these clients' social isolation and other forms of maladaptive coping that increase the risk of relapse in substance abuse and psychiatric disorders. Also, gender-specific transitional housing and supported work opportunities are needed even though women comprise less than 35 percent of the population served by Recovery Works. Thus, one practice implication is for staff and administrators, client advocacy groups, significant others, related agencies and organizations, and the larger community to develop collaborative political action and systems change strategies to impact mental health policy and resources.

Another implication is the importance of training these clients to become politically active as a group by challenging barriers to empowerment in other systems, such as the health care, legal, and public welfare systems. A number of clients expressed frustration from trying to access resources and engage in other problem-solving activities. Group sessions on how to challenge external systems effectively could provide more resources for supporting these clients' recovery and efforts to gain or regain self-sufficiency (Imbrogno 1987). Policy impact groups could be called Political Education, Advocacy, and Systems Change Groups and could be both peer-led and staff-facilitated.

A third implication is also related to policy impact. The discussion on empowerment and the internal and external structure of Recovery Works clarified how well clients are actively involved in the program's operation. After using primarily informal procedures to monitor its operation for the first few years, the program is just beginning to implement an evaluation process. Relatively effective outcomes in client involvement and empowerment should not be difficult to measure and describe through formal program evaluation (Fetterman 1992). Clients should be involved, which will provide more opportunities for them to ensure that evaluation data are used to enhance the program's existing client-specific services. Clients' and peer specialists' skill development can be improved through conducting needs assessments, facilitating focus groups, interpreting research findings, and engaging in dissemination and other forms of policy reforms and political action.

A final implication is the need to clarify conflicting staff policies and provide additional supports for staff to engage in empowerment practice. A number of programmatic mechanisms exist for maintaining staff skills and motivation, including periodic retreats, bimonthly team-building meetings, specialized training, regularly solicited input into the program's design, and the director's support in working through conflicts with hospital staff.

Additional supports could relieve some of the staff's role strain in its relationships with departmental employees and administrators. Examples include providing specialized training to departmental staff with whom Recovery Works staff typically collaborate. Moreover, the process for managing conflicts between clients and program staff in team meetings is not sufficiently clear to the participants. If this and other issues related to empowerment practice are not clarified in a way that is consistent with the program's underlying philosophy, both clients and staff may suffer negative consequences.

Conclusion

Programmers and practitioners may exaggerate the limitations of dual diagnosis clients while ignoring their strengths. An analysis of clients' backgrounds and experiences and the process of empowerment practice in Recovery Works has revealed the range of diversity among these clients as well as their common needs. What is amazing about their stories is how well these clients are able to give voice to their recovery experiences, highlighting in detail the intermingling of strengths and problems related to their substance abuse and psychiatric disorders.

What critical lessons can practitioners, service providers, and policy makers learn from such stories? One is the need to distinguish between the differential roles of seemingly supportive program factors or resources in the empowerment and disempowerment processes. The program's policy of making dual diagnosis clients responsible for their actions as part of their self-management and collective empowerment is one example. Disempowerment resulted when one peer leader was required to make a public apology to the community for his violent behavior toward another client but was not involved in deciding how to resolve the situation. In contrast, empowerment occurred when another client's very serious failure to take her medication caused the staff to involve her in generating her own data on the consequences. That process increased her knowledge about her substance abuse and psychiatric disorders and about her strengths in a way that significantly improved her recovery potential.

16 Dareisa Rehab Services: A Culture-Specific Program for African American Adults

This is my second time in the program. I came in the first time just to keep from goin' to jail. Not that I couldn't do the time, I been in jail before. I got busted for dealin' heroin and crack. I didn't so much participate in the program the first time—I just occupied a seat. This time, I'm connected like I wasn't before, the program taught me who I am. I know it sounds like a put-on, but this program changed my historical roots from slavery and shame, to Africa, and self-respect.

—Perlena B. (1996)

Some researchers assume that traditional, nonculture-specific approaches to rehab are equally as effective with clients of color as they are with white clients. Color-blind approaches imply that the self-destructive patterns of problem use and addiction are common across different racial/ethnic groups and that therefore, those patterns should be the primary focus for helping all clients to recover (Tucker 1985). Other authors assume that even if such approaches have short-term benefits for some clients of color, culture-specific approaches are necessary for most of these clients' long-term recovery (Amuleru-Marshall 1991).

Others assume that culture-specific approaches are essential for African Americans' recovery because, for example, "the impact of drugs and the resultant 'chemical slavery' has been devastating to the African American community" (Rowe and Grills 1993:21). This devastation is apparent in the rates of related health problems such as cirrhosis of the liver and heart disease, and in the rates of crime, family violence, unemployment, school drop-outs, and violent deaths, which have led to a loss of human potential and other resources (Clifford and Jones 1988; Rowe and Grills 1993). Drug abuse has had a similarly devastating impact on other oppressed and disadvantaged groups, implying a need for culture-specific approaches with Latinos, Native Americans, women, gay males and lesbians, and the elderly (Blume 1992; Delgado 1995; Evans and Sullivan 1990; Lawson 1989; Lewis and Jordan 1989; Rogan 1986).

Traditional rehab services focus primarily on clients' substance abuse problems. Generally, other problems are viewed as natural outcomes of their addiction and individual dysfunctioning, or at least as areas they may have the power to change individually. Hence, those problems are addressed in order to enhance clients' recovery. However, clients of color and from other oppressed groups' individual problems are often accompanied by problems stemming from institutional barriers that are beyond their individual control in development and resolution. Thus, such problems are contributors to as well as consequences of these clients' substance abuse and powerlessness (Harper 1991; Tucker 1985). Culture-specific rehab is designed to deflect the impact of these environmental barriers, or oppression, on their substance abuse problems and so is assumed to be essential to these clients' recovery (Gordon 1993; Rogan 1986).

In addition to helping clients of color identify and address sources of powerlessness, culture-specific rehab should help them to identify sources of power within this context. Their cultural strengths, beliefs, values, meanings, positive experiences, and ways of being in the world can be a source of collective power for combating their substance abuse (Freeman 1992). Clients from white ethnic groups also may benefit from addressing the cultural context of their addiction and recovery during rehab. Hayton (1994) asserts that "effective treatment of European Americans requires the same culturally sophisticated approach that accounts for effectiveness in other cultural groups" (113).

However, for African Americans and others who suffer from oppression, addressing their cultural context can be, perhaps, more crucial than for whites. African Americans should be helped to clarify their cultural identity and its effects on their addiction and recovery, or as Perlena eloquently states in the above example, what they identify as their cultural roots. In fact, Rowe and Grills propose that effective Africentric services should be guided by an alternative framework "for understanding the culturally normative behavior of African-Americans in drug treatment and recovery, based on an appreciation of core African-centered beliefs"(1993:21).

This chapter describes one such Africentric program in terms of its early development, its clients' background characteristics, and their empowerment issues. Their experiences with empowerment and disempowerment in Dareisa Rehab Services are described in their own words, based on my research, illustrating the influences of the program's structure. Some key practice implications from this research, for both empowered Africentric programs and culture-specific programs that serve other special populations, are then discussed in conclusion.

Background Information on the Program and Client Group

Early Program Development

Dareisa is a residential and outpatient rehab program that developed on the East Coast during the 1980s. Although it addressed cultural factors that influence clients' recovery from its inception, the shift to an Africentric approach occurred after the program had been in operation for several years. It became apparent that many clients in rehab lacked a center or a source of coherence and meaning in their lives prior to their drug use and abuse, a condition exacerbated by their addictions and other problems. Also, clients struggled with many environmental problems and barriers that tended to overwhelm their individual and cultural strengths, increasing the risk of dropouts.

Africentricity offered a culturally meaningful way to marshall and build on these clients' stengths and to address internal and external or institutional barriers to self- and cultural esteem (Interview 1996). The program began as a long-term facility, in contrast to past and current trends, in order to address clients' chronic, pervasive, and systemic problems, which often led to powerlessness and hence to power paralysis. It is located in a semirural area to protect clients' confidentiality, to address their shame-based self-esteem issues, and to protect them initially from the multitude of risk factors present in their immediate communities until they are able to enhance their existing strengths and develop new ones (Interview 1996).

Program Philosophy and Conceptual Framework

Dareisa's philosophy assumes that "an individual cannot be viewed in isolation of his or her family, community, or cultural group, therefore, re-covery and positive lifestyle changes can only occur in the individual's social

and cultural context," which includes the development of "self-pride in an-
cestral origins and history" (*Staff Manual* 1995:1). This approach requires
an intense, demanding daily routine and ongoing, collective positive reinforcement. It is consistent with the program's empowerment priorities: to
provide opportunities for clients to mature holistically—emotionally, spiritually, educationally, culturally, politically, and socially.

This holistic, collectivist philosophy is also consistent with the program's
framework of Africentricity and cultural bonding, involving the concepts of
mutual responsibility and "knowledge is power"; peer and staff cultural role
modeling; and the importance of having an orderly, structured environment.
It is based on Asante's (1989) teachings and on Oliver's (1989) definition of
Africentricity: "the internalization of values that emphasize love of self,
awareness of traditional African heritage, and personal commitment to the
economic and political power of African Americans and other people of
African descent" (16).

Impact of Diversity on Clients' Use Patterns and Related Issues

This Africentric program has the capacity to serve 80 adults at a time;
approximately one third are female and two thirds are male. Consistent with
its philosophy, the program serves mostly African American clients (95 percent) but often has a small number of whites, other clients of color, and
biracial clients (e.g., African American and Native American or African
American and white). These clients range from 21 to 73 years of age, although there are far fewer at the upper end of the range. Their educational
backgrounds are equally broad, ranging from completion of the second grade
to master's and doctoral degrees. About 30 to 35 graduate from the program
each year. Prior to the advent of managed care policies, most clients stayed
in this residential program from eight months to one year (Interview 1996).

Many of these clients' histories indicate they began their drug use at an
early age and eventually abused a wide range of drugs. For example, a thirty-
three-year-old client, Bob, began his cigarette and alcohol use at age six. He
added marijuana as a teenager and then progressed to crack, heroin, and
intranasal abuse of cocaine by the time he entered his first rehabilitation
program. Some of Dareisa's clients, like Bob, relate their early drug use to
the easy accessibility of substances, particularly alcohol. Other clients associate their early substance abuse with an economically impoverished child-

hood and/or extensive polydrug use and negative role modeling within their families and social networks (Interview 1996).

Impact of Clients' Diversity on Referral Patterns

Because many of these clients have experienced heavy and prolonged drug use, referrals from the legal system are very common (33 percent of the total). Their offenses include drug possession and dealing, and other drug-related charges such as DUIs, prostitution, family or community violence, shoplifting, armed robbery, and burglary. Dareisa's success rates with long-term substance abusers have led to another source of referrals: program graduates, family members, and their acquaintances (30 percent). These word-of-mouth referrals about the unusual African-centered services the program provides help to attract clients who have been unsuccessful in their prior attempts to recover (Interview 1996). Then too, some of these referrals are self-referrals, like Perlena in this chapter's introduction, who return to Dareisa for second and third trials based on their own knowledge of the program and their motivation to try rehab again.

Many clients are referred by black churches and community organizations (25 percent), which is typical in black communities (Wright, Kail, and Creecy 1990). Other rehab programs refer about 10 percent because they believe these clients require more long-term services and/or the culture-specific services Dareisa provides. A smaller number of referrals are from hospitals and mental health centers (2 percent), perhaps because of the mistrust some African Americans have had for those institutions historically (Gordon 1994; Harper 1990).

Clients' Empowerment Issues

Rehab Entry and Culture-Specific Services

These referral patterns and the surrounding circumstances often influence clients' initial experiences in the program, including whether their needs for positive sources of power are met. Dropping out is one of their responses to initial concerns about autonomy and how to cope with the stress of recovery. Dareisa's dropout rate is highest from the point of entry into rehab through the first ninety days. Often dropping out is due to a combination of factors that contribute to or increase clients' powerlessness over their life situations. Some dropouts are special needs clients such as those with dual diagnoses, women with young children who have difficulty making adequate arrangements for their care, and those with chronic family problems that distract them from rehab. Clients who are legally mandated to participate in rehab also have a high drop-out rate, because such mandates can increase their resistance to accepting services (Interview 1996).

To decrease dropouts and powerlessness, Dareisa transitions new clients into the program by placing them in tribes with existing clients who have the same primary counselor (*Client Handbook* 1994). These counselor tribes serve as alternative families or small social networks. They provide clients with support and help in developing their collective power through planning and implementing tasks that help to improve the program. Also, the organization of clients into tribes is part of the program's Africentric, positive peer culture, which helps in solving their entry problems and in getting them to bond with peers and with the program.

Many clients from all ethnic groups have low self-esteem, which affects and is affected by their substance abuse. In addition, Dareisa's clients frequently have low cultural esteem from prior oppressive experiences, which they have coped with through self-medication and other ineffective methods. Entering rehab tends to reinforce their low self- and cultural esteem because they view the need for treatment as further evidence of their worthlessness and lack of control over their lives. Consequently, this program has developed a culturally rich physical and psychological environment that sends affirming messages to clients about themselves as African Americans and about their ethnic group as a whole. Abundant pictures and accompanying text on the walls illustrate important contributions, leaders, and events related to African American history and to the group's current status, along with historical and current facts about African life, customs, values, achievements, and traditions (Interview 1996). Perlena, from this chapter's introduction, found that this culturally rich environment helped her to develop a new sense of connection with her peers and with other African Americans.

An extensive library provides similar cultural knowledge and information about addiction and recovery focused at different reading levels. Clients use the library to complete written and oral rehab assignments during the first thirty days of the program and later (*Client Handbook* 1994). A technology resource and media center provides related information through high-tech video equipment, tapes, computer games, and other materials that appeal to different learning styles. Both the library and the resource center are designed to increase clients' knowledge and self-efficacy. They also provide opportunities for clients' skill development (*Client Handbook* 1994) while in early rehab because technologically, such experiences can increase their ability to meet future work requirements. The purpose of these resources and the culture-rich physical-psychological environment is to bombard new clients especially, but also continuing clients, with constant reflections of their individual and group worth, an important source of ethnic power and pride (Interview 1996).

Rehab Continuance and Culture-Specific Services

Many aspects of traditional rehab can increase African Americans' powerlessness (Rogan 1986); therefore, multiple client-centered and culture-specific strategies are used throughout the course of this program to build on clients' unique strengths. Examples range from the program's philosophy about and use of traditional self-help groups to client leadership roles in the program to the nature of services provided. Clients are not involved in twelve-step groups until the last phase of rehab (*Client Handbook* 1994) because as African Americans, they have experienced ongoing powerlessness from many instances of oppression. Staff assume that the NA, CA, and AA philosophy can heighten these clients' ethnic powerlessness because it requires them to acknowledge their helplessness to control their addictions and other aspects of their lives (Interview 1996).

Instead of involving them in twelve-step groups, this culture-specific program teaches clients the seven African principles of collective living and harmony, or the Nguzo Saba (*Client Handbook* 1994). These principles include: 1) Umoja (unity), 2) Kujichagulia (self-determination), 3) Ujima (collective work and responsibility), 4) Ujamaa (cooperative economics), 5) Nia (purpose), 6) Kuumba (creativity), and 7) Imani (faith) (Asante 1985, 1990; Gordon 1992). The principles are applied to clients' recovery and to their lives in general in order to increase their personal, interpersonal, and political power (Interview 1996).

The principle of Ujima, collective work and responsibility, for example, is applied to the work of the counselor tribes within the program and to clients' community service projects. Clients learn through counseling groups and other services that, as African Americans, they have a responsibility to themselves and to the village to contribute daily to the community's well-being (Interview 1996). One client, Darlene, defined Ujima as African Americans' collective commitment and responsibility to save and reclaim all high-risk black children. Her group experiences included exploring how her addiction and criminal offenses and those of other members have undermined their cultural community's self-sufficiency and well-being. They analyzed how their prior lifestyles were inconsistent with Ujima and the other principles, and identified triggers that continue to distract them from living by the principles and could lead to relapse. This type of Africentric bonding and commitment to each other and to the community has improved Darlene's and other clients' maintenance rates beyond their initial ninety days in the program (Interview 1996).

In addition, based on African traditions, tribal elders, or clients with seniority in the program, serve as program leaders (*Client Handbook* 1994). They help to coordinate services, mediate conflicts among clients, and facilitate resolution of clients' crisis situations to prevent rehab disruptions. They are also an important part of the program's governance, providing input into policy development and implementation. Another aspect of these culture- and gender-related services is that clients are expected to participate in a circle that offers mentoring and social supports to young people. Female clients participate in circles for girls, and male clients in circles for boys, in detention facilities, community organizations, churches, schools, and social clubs.

In traditional Africa, these circles have been used to pass down the wisdom of elders and cultural traditions to young people. The circles teach them how to live appropriately according to African values and principles (Gordon 1993). In Dareisa, clients' wisdom and experiences are used to help youths build upon protective factors in their lives, such as good family communication, and decrease risk factors, such as school failure and a lack of positive, nonaddicted role models. The benefits for clients include opportunities to fulfill their cultural responsibilities to the village and to increase supports for their maintenance in recovery. Thus, the circles provide important ties to clients' cultural and recovery communities.

Other culture-specific services include naming ceremonies and the development of heritage books. In naming ceremonies, clients select a new, significant African name that is a public acknowledgment of their transition to a new African-centered, recovering identity (Gordon 1993). The heritage books chronicle each client's African and African American background and experiences in pictures and narrative, in order to increase their understanding and integration of self-knowledge, which is necessary for recovery (Interview 1996). Bob, the client from a previous example who began using substances at age six, believes that developing his heritage book and participating in one of the program's circles provided a spiritual-cultural connection that was missing in his life. Such connections are a result of cultural bonding, which begins with clients' initial rehab experiences and is present throughout their tenure in this program; they aid in ongoing recovery.

The Program's Internal Structure and Context

Nature of the Program's Services

Program Components and Staff.   The culture-specific services discussed in the preceding section are provided throughout four progressive and related phases that include both outpatient and residential components, as shown in figure 16.1. Phase I is orientation to the Africentric and recovery aspects of the program and development of positive attitudes, self-discipline, and a basic understanding of substance abuse and its effects on the mind and body. Phase II focuses on building clients' self-knowledge, understanding of their cultural history, and increased responsibility to the peer recovering community and to the larger African American community. During this phase, clients are expected to work toward educational and vocational goals while increasing their skills in identifying and resolving problems (*Client Handbook* 1994).

In Phase III, clients establish more meaningful relationships with family, friends, and the external community; become role models for new clients; practice and expand their coping and problem-solving skills; and transition to a new Africentric and recovering identity. Phase IV is the reentry phase, which involves greater participation in work, training, or educational activities and in community living, as well as a gradual decrease in the intensity and frequency of participation in the program (*Client Handbook* 1994). All four phases involve individual, group, and family sessions, along with special seminars, meetings of the counselors' tribes, morning orientation meetings, and impromptu and planned general community meetings with all staff and clients.

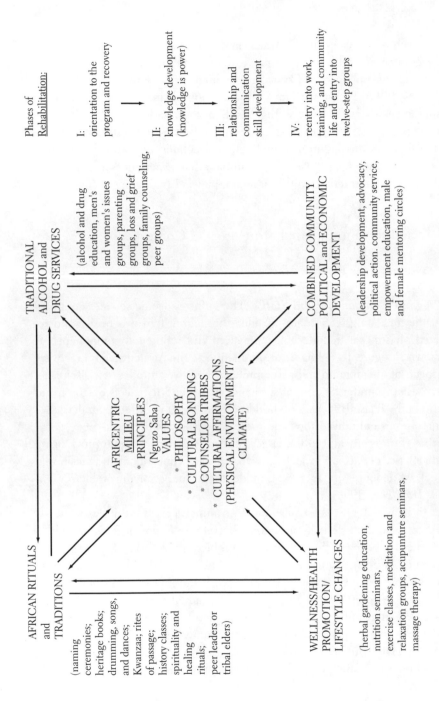

Phases of
Rehabilitation:

I:
orientation to the
program and recovery

II:
knowledge development
(knowledge is power)

III:
relationship and
communication
skill development

IV:
reentry into work,
training, and community
life and entry into
twelve-step groups

TRADITIONAL
ALCOHOL and
DRUG SERVICES

(alcohol and drug
education, men's
and women's issues
groups, parenting
groups, loss and grief
groups, family counseling,
peer groups)

COMBINED COMMUNITY
POLITICAL and ECONOMIC
DEVELOPMENT

(leadership development, advocacy,
political action. community service,
empowerment education, male
and female mentoring circles)

AFRICENTRIC
MILIEU
* PRINCIPLES
(Nguzo Saba)
VALUES
* PHILOSOPHY
* CULTURAL BONDING
COUNSELOR TRIBES
* CULTURAL AFFIRMATIONS
(PHYSICAL ENVIRONMENT/
CLIMATE)

AFRICAN RITUALS
and
TRADITIONS

(naming
ceremonies;
heritage books;
drumming, songs,
and dances;
Kwanzaa; rites
of passage;
history classes;
spirituality and
healing
rituals;
peer leaders or
tribal elders)

WELLNESS/HEALTH
PROMOTION/
LIFESTYLE CHANGES

(herbal gardening education,
nutrition seminars,
exercise classes, meditation and
relaxation groups, acupunture seminars,
massage therapy)

FIGURE 16.1 DAREISA: An Anricentric Rehab Program

Figure 16.1 includes the range of services in which clients participate throughout the four phases of this program. As can be seen, the program's integrated combination of services comprises four main components: traditional alcohol and drug education, Africentric rituals and traditions, wellness and health promotion, and community political and economic development. Services in these areas are interrelated through the program's Africentric milieu or its cultural bonding environment (i.e., the Nguza Saba and African philosophy and values).

For example, specialized men's and women's issues groups in the traditional alcohol and drug education component integrate the seven African principles (the Nguza Saba) as standards against which clients analyze the consequences of addiction for African Americans in particular. The wellness and health promotion component includes education about growing herbs that have been used in traditional Africa and by elders in African American communities for preventive health and self-healing. The male and female mentoring circles described in a previous section are part of the community political and economic development component. They are consistent with the program's Africentric milieu because they reinforce the use of elders to socialize youths in culturally meaningful ways. Communities' political development is enhanced indirectly through modeling and leadership development, which benefit both the clients and the youths.

Examples of more direct political and economic development activities in figure 16.1 include the program's advocacy for resources to help clients develop culturally related microenterprises (e.g., a soul food catering business) and the male clients' participation in the 1996 Million Man March in Washington, D.C. The African rituals and traditions component includes the naming ceremonies described previously and teaching clients about African drumming and dance. These activities are culturally meaningful ways to educate African American clients about their traditions. They can lead to increased self- and cultural esteem, and they model how to use leisure time positively (Interview 1996), an essential part of effective recovery.

The staff are also expected to immerse themselves in the program's Africentric milieu. Many of them identify with African traditions and values through the adoption of African names and clothing, and the Nguza Saba as a code for daily living. The staff consists of an executive director, deputy director, site manager, operations manager, health coordinator, clinical supervisor, counselors (5), and clinical staff aides (3). Most of the administrative positions require at least a master's degree; however, the executive director has a doctorate in psychology. The exception to the requirement is the position of operations manager (food service manager). A nutrition consultant with expertise in African American and Caribbean diet and cuisine is a resource to the food service manager in meal planning and preparation. The consultant is also used as a health educator in client groups and in seminars related to the program's wellness component.

The site manager and the clinical supervisor are currently working toward their M.S.W. degrees. The counselors are required to have a degree in addictions counseling; two of them are presently completing their degrees as a condition of their employment. All of the staff have had extensive training in multicultural and culture-specific rehab services as well as Africentric programming. Dareisa provides an ongoing professional development component as part of its emphasis on education for staff and clients, based on the belief that knowledge is power (Interview 1996).

Major Theories, Approaches, and Strategies. Dareisa uses a therapeutic community approach to rehab, with an emphasis on social learning theory. Consequently, practicing new roles and the program's positive reinforcement, coaching, cultural modeling and mentoring, cultural rituals, positive labeling, and skill development strategies are important influences on clients' recovery. However, both the program's literature and its services and procedures indicate that aspects of other theories are involved, including family systems, ethnic identity development, psychoeducation, case management, economic development, and community development approaches; these are integrated in innovative ways. For example, family systems and ethnic identity development theories help to explain how organizing clients into counselor tribes for which they choose names and having them develop reciprocal roles for engaging in activities to maintain the program is such a strong source of cultural bonding and collective power. Because many of these clients have experienced cutoffs from their families of origin, the tribes are often useful as alternative, sober social supports.

Empowerment-Related Program Factors

Type of Empowerment Organization and Program Factors. This program is an empowered organization based on Florin and Wandersman's (1990) assumptions that such programs help to shift power from the service setting and from large external institutions to clients (see table 1.4). Examples of program factors that provide opportunities for developing clients' personal, interpersonal, and political power are shown in table 16.1. Personal empowerment, for instance, is achieved through empowerment education and peer feedback (push-ups and pull-ups), while interpersonal empowerment is related to the use of inspirational black speakers in seminars and to education and support of clients in collaborative herb growing in the African tradition.

Examples of political empowerment include community service projects as well as the peer-led political action and advocacy activities in which clients are expected to engage. Community service projects include cleaning up neighborhoods, painting houses for residents who are poor and elderly, registering community residents to vote, and attending public forums in order to influence community-level policy changes. Political action has included clients' petitioning the state to turn over unused office buildings to house the homeless and participating in an African American political rally against the realignment of voter precinct boundaries, which would decrease residents' electoral power. Such activities help these clients to understand at a practical level the impact of their collective power.

For instance, Jeff, a thirty-eight-year-old client with six months' recovery, was arrested one day in the program on a prior warrant for drug dealing just as male clients began planning their participation in the 1996 Million Man March in Washington, D.C. He was released on bail unexpectedly, shortly before the march was scheduled. He said, "No one from rehab knew I'd been released or would come looking for me for a while. But I couldn't let my peers down, we'd been planning to participate in the march together. And I knew if I didn't go back to rehab, I wouldn't make the march . . . and I'd relapse. So I went back to the program on my own. When we were there, at the march, I'd never seen so many black men together before, doing something positive, making a political statement to the world!"

Type of Organization and Empowerment Needs of the Population.   Clients like Jeff are often unaware of their individual and collective power, even after receiving Africentric and empowerment education. It is only when they operationalize their power that they believe it is real and generalizable, consistent with the program's emphasis on social learning theory. For African American clients in particular, this acknowledgment and exercise of power needs to be culturally meaningful in terms of the stressors, oppression, and institutional barriers they encounter in the real world. Examples of clients'

TABLE 16.1 Examples of Empowerment-Oriented Program Factors: Dareisa

Empowerment Levels	Major Empowerment Themes — Professional Services	Peer-Led Services	Professional-Client Collaboration
Personal	a culturally enriched physical and psychological environment is used to educate and affirm clients in the history, values, leaders, and traditions of Africans and African Americans lifestyle changes are required for cultural bonding, such as language modification (no ethnic denigration); elimination of meat, tobacco, and sugar from the diet; exercise; and meditation/relaxation techniques	African dance, drumming, and songs are a form of hands-on cultural education, a bonding process, and a leisure time organizer to improve self-management and self-efficacy tribal elders (clients with recovery seniority) expedite, coordinate, and mediate services and crises/glitches in the program's operation with peers	Africentric rituals such as naming ceremonies, gifts of kente cloth for program graduates, development of heritage books, etc. are coplanned and -implemented to improve self- and cultural identity/esteem staff and clients develop and present multimedia dissemination and education materials about the program, recovery, and cultural traditions

Interpersonal	clients are organized into counselor tribes, develop a positive collective identity, and operate as a social support network	peer-led morning orientation meetings focus on black facts, historical events, and African traditions that facilitate recovery	staff and peers collaborate on providing push-ups and pull-ups to clients to aid in their recovery
	the Nguzo Saba are used as principles of collective living and harmony and as spiritual/moral guidelines for cultural maintenance and effective recovery	peer groups plan, plant, and harvest herbal gardens for wellness and self-healing in the African tradition	program graduates return and cofacilitate community meetings with staff for current clients in which they share their triumphs and struggles with recovery
Political	staff facilitate, broker, and advocate for client economic development opportunities that are culturally relevant (e.g., microenterprises)	peers cofacilitate African circles for male and female youths for mentorship and support, leadership development, and cultural education	clients with seniority in rehab, tribal elders, provide regular input into program policy development and reform
	staff organize inspirational seminars for clients involving black political and social activists and economic developers	peer-led political and advocacy activities are encouraged, such as participation in local and national political rallies, public forums, public cultural events, and petitioning of policy makers (e.g., to influence homeless policy)	staff and clients collaborate on community service (or service learning) projects: neighborhood cleanup, voter registration, training and job development

feedback about supportive program factors demonstrate that this criterion of cultural relevance is often met for them:

"I learned how we are as a people, very spiritual, and able to help each other to survive."

"The principles tell us where our power is, in following and living the Nguzo Saba."

"The focus on knowing the sources of your pain and knowing about your ancestors gets you in touch with your feelings. You realize your pain isn't unique and how other black people before you survived and stayed strong."

The Program's External Structure and Context

Many of these internal variables, which have caused clients to describe their experiences in Dareisa so positively, often interact with various factors in the program's external context, including its organizational auspices and its community and policy/funding subsystems.

Organizational Auspices

Dareisa provides multiple substance abuse services in a primary setting. It is also part of a newly developing parallel service arrangement, so it fits within two areas on the continuum of organizational auspices in figure 5.1. Related substance abuse programs include coed residential services, coed outpatient services, services for dual diagnosis males (substance abuse and AIDS), services for dual diagnosis females, services for addicted homeless people, services for inmates in a state correctional facility, and transitional housing and aftercare services for recovering men and women following their completion of rehab.

Having this range of primary substance abuse services within one program means that Dareisa is able to provide client-specific treatment to a number of subgroups of addicted, special needs clients (see advantages and disadvantages of primary settings in figure 5.1), for example, women and homeless people. Moreover, the program has been able to monitor how particular aspects of client-specific services work best with each subgroup that it serves. A disadvantage is that, increasingly, staff are required to participate in more specialized training programs, because knowledge, technology, and service delivery methods are rapidly changing in these population-specific services. This has been especially true for staff who work with clients with HIV/AIDS (Interview 1996).

Recently, the program has added other on-site services in a move toward establishing a number of parallel service arrangements. This has required Dareisa to develop both informal and formal agreements with other organizations and agencies whose services are essential for clients' recovery. For instance, housing, health, and legal agencies are now located on site to reduce miscommunication, fragmentation, and other service barriers for clients. Jeff, the client who was arrested in the program on an outstanding warrant prior to participating in the Million Man March, is one example of interagency miscommunication prior to the new service arrangement. The probation office was supposed to mediate all warrants or court appearances for Dareisa clients to prevent such unexpected arrests and jail releases. Since the probation office and other agencies now have part-time staff on site, interorganizational collaboration has been enhanced through a more time-consuming but increasingly effective coordination and planning process.

The Community Subsystem

Colocation of multiple services and a number of other factors have made Dareisa a community-centered program. Even though it is in a semirural multicultural area away from clients' homes, the program manages to infuse participants with a sense of community responsibility, because it emphasizes their responsibility to the multicultual community surrounding the program and to the general African American community. Clients' recovery is enhanced through their involvement in service projects, such as the mentoring circles and political advocacy for developing housing for the homeless. Clients have also engaged in community service within the larger African American community (which often has included their home communities), focused on voter registration and neighborhood cleanup activities.

Moreover, since approximately 55 percent of the program's referrals are from former clients, family members, community residents, black churches, and black community organizations, it is clear that the larger African American community views the program as responsive to its members' needs. That community is actively involved in some of the program's operations as well. The board of directors and advisory board are comprised of former consumers and other laypeople from the African American community, as well as ethnically diverse individuals from business, finance, health, mental health, religious, and law professions.

The Policy/Funding Subsystem

The program's focus on economic and political development has increased over the years as major changes have occurred in the sociopolitical environment and in public policies related to substance abuse rehabilitation. Changes in funding patterns at the federal level, involving greatly reduced categorical funding and slight increases in integrated funding (Freeman 1996; Kunnes, Niven, Gustafson, Brooks, Levin, Edmunds, Trumble, and Coyle 1993), have caused Dareisa to seek more diversified financial resources. Currently, the program receives funding from a range of federal sources, including departments and agencies related to substance abuse, maternal and child health, housing, HIV/AIDS, and labor. In addition, it receives private donations and grants from individual donors, companies, and foundations, along with local and state grants for community development and establishment of enterprise zones.

The program's efforts to diversify its funding base have provided more resources for combating the negative impact of managed care policies on its services. Such policies have, by and large, impacted substance abuse rehab most often by limiting clients' initial access to and long-term involvement in services (see chapter 3 for a more detailed discussion). The program has dealt with these barriers in two main ways. First, it has appealed the new fourteen- to thirty-day service limitations, often successfully, on behalf of clients with the most severe and chronic addictions and family circumstances. Second, Dareisa has developed more individualized treatment plans for other clients who need but have been denied access to more long-term rehabilitation. Some of those clients have been admitted to the larger coed residential program for short-term services and then been transferred to one of the smaller programs for more specialized, long-term services (e.g., to the women's program or to the homeless rehab program). Other clients have received various combinations of services over time involving the residential, day treatment, and aftercare/transitional housing components of the program. For example, some clients have received services for thirty–thirty–ninety days in those three components, while others have received services for thirty–sixty–ninety days, based on new managed care limitations.

In spite of the program's innovative strategies to address managed care barriers to rehab, staff members feel the quality of services often has been compromised. They believe the shorter periods of supported recovery, housing, and employment are causing the program to be less effective with some clients, because the culture-related aspects of their addictions and recovery require more long-term attention (Interview 1996).

Another, more indirect strategy used to handle the impact of managed care on rehab services has been an increased emphasis on prevention. Dareisa has organized a Speakers' Bureau that involves staff members and past and current consumers in speaking to various groups and organizations in the community at educational seminars; public forums; discussion groups; churches, mosques, and synagogues; schools; business groups; government agencies; and community organizations, as well as on radio and television programs (*Program Manual* 1990). The speakers educate laypeople not only about the signs and consequences of addictions but also about the culture-specific nature of the program's services and the policy/funding barriers it encounters. These efforts have often resulted in other funding, donations, and in-kind support for the program in addition to helping it achieve its prevention goals. The Speakers' Bureau uses the program's library and resource center as the main source of the written and videotaped materials it presents or disseminates at each event.

The Empowerment Process in Action

In spite of the above policy/funding barriers to service effectiveness, many aspects of Dareisa's program structure influence clients' unique, Africentric empowerment and disempowerment experiences. Common themes across those experiences are described and analyzed in the sections that follow.

One Client's Empowerment Narrative

Background Information.   Perlena is a forty-year-old woman with two children, aged eighteen and nineteen. Her husband divorced her two years prior to this experience, when she relapsed for the third time. A Baptist bishop, he felt Perlena's continued addiction to heroin and alcohol and her last relapse proved she was not really trying to recover. He also believed his position was in jeopardy because people were becoming aware of her "ungodly lifestyle and sinful associates." After her divorce, Perlena became a dealer and sold heroin and crack, which led to a jail sentence and to her current parole status.

Perlena has a high school education. She once co-owned a successful catering business with family members which, along with the responsibilities of being a bishop's wife, created overwhelming personal stresses for her. Initially, Perlena's parents had custody of her son and daughter, who currently live with their father and his second wife. This was Perlena's second attempt at rehab in Dareisa (she had been in two other rehab programs previously). During the third month of her current stay, because of an incident in the women's issues group, Perlena says she learned to stop playing the blame game and being ashamed of her past mistakes. The main topic of the session was chosen by the clients: how they feel about themselves as black women and about other black women, and how this issue has affected their addiction and recovery.

Perlena's Narrative.   Several of my peers gave their opinions about how black women feel about each other. Essie said, "There's no sisterhood, we're always putting down ourselves and other women. Basically, we're ashamed of ourselves as black women; being addicts just makes the shame worse." I said, "I'm ashamed of me, the addict, but nobody has the right to put me down. When word got around the church about me usin' drugs, people just shut me out, especially the women, they'd look right through me like I wasn't there. Or worse, they'd glare at me—like they hated me. I felt like nothin.' Lookin' back, I can see they gave me an excuse to keep gettin' high." Shirley said, "I guess you never put down another black woman yourself?" Her question surprised me, but it made me think. I told the group about a girl we used to make fun of in high school—Ruby—we made fun of her clothes, how she talked, and how she looked. She dropped out of school in the tenth grade. The other girls thought the whole thing was funny. But I felt bad about it—I knew my mother would be upset if she knew, she always said don't disrespect anybody. Terry said she was "the Ruby" in her high school, the one all the other girls picked on and hated. She said it made her feel worthless. I could see tears in her eyes, I felt bad for her. Barbara, the counselor, asked if me and Terry could help each other, as two black women carryin' around a lotta pain. I said I felt bad about hurting another black woman; I know what the hurt feels like now, and I can't forgive myself. Terry leaned over and hugged me; she said, "I forgive you, Perlena."

Conclusions About the Meaning and Impact of the Experience.   When recounting her interaction with Terry, Perlena said she felt a powerful sense of relief and a self-acceptance she had never experienced before. The incident made her realize how hard she had been on herself. She had not forgiven herself for being an addict and hurting others; nor had she forgiven the church women for shutting her out without trying to help her. Their reactions reinforced her view that she must be a black superwoman who did not make mistakes or tarnish the image of the bishop's wife. Connecting two painful experiences—the putdowns she participated in during high school and the putdowns she experienced from church women—helped her to see how some of her experiences as a black woman contributed to her shame and addiction. Not surprisingly, Perlena defined "empowerment" as "seeing the light, knowing yourself, and not letting shame or other people dictate the choices you make."

Terry's parallel high school rejection provided an opportunity for her and Perlena to begin a mutual healing process in the women's issues group. Terry's hug and forgiveness brought some closure to Perlena's unfinished business with Ruby (the classmate Perlena had not seen for years). Acknowledging the pain she had caused and accepting Terry's forgiveness helped Perlena to forgive herself, reinforced by Terry's conclusion: although the ridicule Terry experienced from her classmates contributed to her self-hate, only she was ultimately responsible for the bad choices she had made. Perlena realized that, like Terry, she needed to stop her blame game. She could eventually seek the forgiveness of her children and other family members, but if they did not forgive her, she had already begun to forgive herself.

Based on this experience, Perlena decided she needed to redefine why she was in rehab and in recovery. She needed to be there for herself rather than for her children. Perlena's interpretation of her narrative indicates she experienced empowerment at both personal and interpersonal levels. Personally, she developed some important self-knowledge about her own barriers to recovery, such as believing she did not deserve compassion because she could not change her past negative experiences. Interpersonally, she recognized that the image she had presented in her relationships—that of a successful black businesswomen who had status as the wife of a bishop and who did not make mistakes—of which she had not been fully aware in the past, was no longer necessary. Self-medication had allowed her to maintain that façade and a belief that it was working for her. But peer feedback from this group session indicated that it had not worked as well as Perlena thought.

One group member said Perlena had been grandiose when she first entered rehab, that she put on airs about being middle-class and different when she was an addict just like her peers. The session was the first time this peer felt Perlena had been genuine. The positive feedback about risk taking, revealing her experiences and pain in the group, encouraged Perlena to be more open in her ongoing peer interactions.

Perlena's relationship with Terry in particular became closer, in spite of a twelve-year age difference between them, because of Terry's reassuring and supportive hug during the group session. The hug indicated that Terry understood Perlena's shame and remorse about hurting another black woman, while recognizing that Perlena had been hurt and shamed in a similar manner herself. Their mutual empowerment helped the two of them to develop and draw upon a sense of unity and strength as black women that neither had ever experienced before. Another interpersonal consequence was Perlena's increased understanding of the counselor's role in the group process. She recognized that the counselor's willingness to allow the group members to set their own agenda had been helpful, as had her efforts to open the discussion and show the members how to handle some of their issues directly, such as when she encouraged Terry and Perlena to help each other work through their common pain.

Clients' Empowerment Narratives: General Issues

An analysis of the empowerment narratives of twenty-two other clients in the program, in addition to Perlena's, helped to identify common and unique aspects of those experiences. The patterns are reflected in the content of the narratives and in the consequences the clients attributed to their experiences.

The Content.   Most of these clients' empowerment experiences occurred in various components of the program, which indicated initially that there were few commonalities in where the events occurred and what they involved. It is possible, however, that Africentricity may be the common element, due to its integration throughout the program's various components. Clients' narratives highlighted the importance of this cultural integration and infusion for their empowerment. Their experiences included seeing their herbs bloom for the first time in the program's herb garden; receiving a piece of Kente cloth as a graduation gift from the program; observing a male peer being assigned additional chores for using derogatory language toward black females; having feelings of personal and racial shame validated in group sessions, but then challenged as barriers to recovery; being acknowledged for tasks completed by the counselor tribes; and being made an expediter as a symbol of elder status and continued recovery.

A second pattern was the program's continuous reinforcement of clients' empowerment experiences over time. Many clients reported an initial empowerment event, and then a heightened sense of power from a second experience that built on the first and made it even more meaningful. For example, one client, Bernard, was asked to help develop a new videotape for the program's Speakers' Bureau, based on his technical expertise and skills from his previous work in television production. This empowerment experience validated his self-worth and personal power, providing him with a glimpse of the person he might become as he continued his recovery, someone who contributes to rather than takes from his community. Bernard's power from that experience expanded when he participated in his naming ceremony weeks later. This second event symbolized his official passage to a new identity and reminded him of the strong sense of hope he had experienced when he was first asked to develop the video.

Another example involved Perlena from the previous section. Her empowerment experience in the women's issues group led to the development of a feeling of sisterhood among the members. Perlena described the cumulative bonding that occurred from that session onward: "We said as black women, we have to stop everybody else from definin' who we are, we can't allow it anymore. We know about our African roots now, and we're different from what we were." Perlena's personal and interpersonal power was expanded later when she participated in the program's community voter registration drive. When she registered a black teenage mother and the girl's mother to vote at the same time, Perlena said, "I felt a sisterhood with them—the mother and daughter coming in together—we all know voting is important for our community in spite of the problems. It was like the natural high I got from the women's group when Terry hugged me—I could see we had a common struggle and a common goal."

The Meaning and Impact of Clients' Empowerment Experiences. Each time clients such as Perlena and Bernard connected their initial empowerment experiences to later positive events, they reexperienced and expanded their initial sense of power. The meanings they attributed to those first experiences deepened and became clearer with the retelling of their stories. In Bernard's case, a way of operationalizing his desire to contribute to his community became more clear and specific when he participated in the naming ceremony. The mentoring role conferred by this rite of passage led him to commit himself to teaching black youths media skills through a community center as part of his aftercare plan. His decision strengthened Bernard's transition into aftercare services while focusing his use of leisure time in a more culturally relevant way for recovery purposes.

Often these clients' initial and later experiences involved empowerment at different levels, thus increasing the impact of those experiences on their recovery. Perlena's initial experiences in the women's group involved consciousness raising about the need for black sisterhood and the gaining of personal and interpersonal power. Her participation in the voter registration drive involved political empowerment, which caused her to reexperience and expand on her power gains from the women's group. It reminded her also that collectively, as black women, she and her peers and the women in the community could make a difference. Bob, from a previous example, experienced personal power and insight from writing about his early exposure to substances in his heritage book. His written plan for using the African principles to resist those influences during recovery was an additional source of personal power. Bob described a related and stronger sense of interpersonal power when he began to apply those principles in his work with youths in one of the program's mentoring circles.

One Client's Disempowerment Experience

Background Information.   Paul is a thirty-five-year-old factory supervisor who entered Dareisa because of its distance from the city in which he lives. He was concerned about meeting some of the people he had supervised if he entered a rehab program near his home. Paul had been a freelance house painter for the preceding year because he said it gave him more freedom than factory work, although he admits he was fired by the factory after working there for thirteen years because of his addiction. He had been in the program for thirty days and was scheduled to be transferred to Dareisa's homeless program the following week when the disempowerment described in the next section occurred.

Paul believes his ego led him to abuse methamphetamine and then crack, because he thought he could never become addicted. He was raised by his paternal grandmother after his mother died when he was eight years old. He and his father have always had a distant relationship. Paul's father recovered from alcohol abuse years ago through a religious conversion. He has encouraged Paul in his recovery but is skeptical about this particular Africentric program and about rehab in general. Paul's disempowerment occurred during a meeting with his counselor tribe following an incident in which Paul bribed James, the van driver who was transporting clients to appointments, to stop for cigarettes. The use of tobacco and unscheduled stops by the drivers are prohibited by the program.

Paul's Narrative.   Malik explained why the tribe was meeting, he said some clients hadn't heard about what happened (he's the clinical supervisor, he was subbing for my counselor). He said I needed some feedback—a push-up—that I was in deep trouble. Then he asked me to talk about the situation—what was I trying to do? I told him, "I've already been disciplined, I got two weeks of hump chores and a special community cleanup project. I'll be discharged from rehab if I break any other rules in the next month. I'm on probation—so what else is there to talk about?"

Malik said, "We need to hear from you about what happened." Everybody was looking, waiting for me to say something. I felt like I was being grilled, singled out for their anger. I told him I thought I was being judged by all of them. I don't need that. I admit I shouldn'ta bought the cigarettes, shouldn'ta asked James to stop or gotten him in trouble. But, you know, he coulda said no, he's got his own mind. Cigarettes are no big deal—it's not like I asked him to stop for crack or something like that.

Malik asked what triggered my need for cigarettes. I said, "There wasn't no trigger, things are going well. I'm transferring into the homeless program next week, I'm getting ready for that, my father said he might come to visit soon, things couldn't be better."

The oldest guy in the group, John W., said, "Well, maybe the tension was buildin' up? That's probably your trigger, man. We all been there, you was just scared." I told him, "You're my trigger, old man. If you know so much, at seventy years old, how come you're in here with the rest of us?"

Nobody said anything. John W. just looked at me. I felt worse than when the meeting started. I could feel their disappointment and frustration with me. Nobody talked to John W. like that, and I was being oppositional instead of working the problem through the group. But usually, when I'm under attack, I fight back. John W. just got in the way, I wasn't responsible for what happened!

Conclusions About the Meaning and Impact of the Experience.   In discussing his conclusions about this experience, Paul said, "Although I was attacking everybody and denying how serious it was, inside I felt like a fraud." Accordingly, he defined "disempowerment" as low self-esteem, saying also that it involves doing something without thinking or realizing the consequences that will occur later. Paul noted that this definition applied to his behavior in the tribe's meeting, especially to his attack on John W., and to his coercing the van driver to stop for cigarettes. The experience reinforced his already low self-esteem and a lifelong pattern of "shooting myself in the foot" when things were going well. For Paul, succeeding was more frightening than failing. If he succeeded, people would soon discover he was a fraud, that he was not as intelligent or personable or competent as he appeared to be.

When asked if he still felt that way, Paul said no, that what happened in the tribe's meeting after his outburst against John W. made a difference in his life. Paul continued his narrative from the point where the members sat quietly, surprised and stunned by his outburst.

Malik said, "John W. is too shocked by what you just said to react. He's used to being respected as an elder of this tribe, so he's probably surprised." Malik pointed out, "He's seventy years old, he's made mistakes and learned from them, he has seniority in the program, he gives feedback and he takes it. So while he's thinking about what to say — about what feedback to give — if you don't mind, John W., I'll try to give Paul some feedback."

Malik pulled three chairs into the middle of the circle, for me, John W., and himself. He sat next to John W., facing me. He said, "Paul, I'm going to give you feedback, not like we usually do, but by telling you a story. This is a different kind of story, because you're in the story. I want you to imagine you're on a long journey, there's a blizzard, the snow's blowing very hard, it's so thick you can't see anything a few feet in front of you, and it's very cold and dark. Imagine you've been on this journey a long time, so long you've lost your way. Gradually, you've given up hope that you'll find any shelter. You're cold, wet, and tired — your legs and feet are numb from the cold. You can barely move them. Then you see a light shining through the snow. You follow it; you're not sure if it's real, but you follow it. Finally, when you think you're about to collapse, you reach this house with a light in the window. Someone opens the door, welcomes you with a warm blanket and something hot to drink, then sits you in a chair by the fire. You warm up slowly, your body relaxes. You lay your head back and soon, you drop off to sleep."

The members began to ask Malik questions about this story of a journey and to give their interpretations of what it meant. When Malik asked Paul what he thought, Paul said the journey represented hope. Malik said, "What if, instead of putting a light in the window for you to find your way and welcoming you with a warm blanket, the person gave you just enough help so you were able to find your own way through the snow? Wouldn't you be better off from learning how to find the way yourself, so the next time you're lost, you could find your way again?"

Paul said Malik's interpretation of this story changed the way he thinks about himself: "I'm on a journey to find my self-esteem. I try to use the feedback or push-ups to help me find my way, but I have to complete the journey myself. So now when I get feedback and I get upset, I ask myself if I'm upset because I'm looking for the light in the window—the easy way out—instead of using the feedback to find my own way. Finding my own way's harder, but what I'm learning will stay with me for the rest of my life." Paul's interpretation of his personal and interpersonal disempowerment shows how his painful outburst was turned around by the clinical supervisor's narrative strategy, leading to unanticipated growth for Paul and for the other members.

Clients' Disempowerment Narratives: General Issues

Although Paul's experience was unique in some ways, it was also similar to those described by the other twenty-two clients who participated in my research. The similarities are apparent in both the content of the experiences and the individuals' interpretations of them.

The Content.   A common aspect of these clients' disempowerment experiences was the identification of individual and institutional barriers to recovery. Some barriers were directly related to the program. For example, twenty-two-year-old Ted experienced disempowerment while trying to get readmitted to Dareisa. He relapsed within three weeks after his graduation. When he called to see if he could be readmitted, he was told he would have to wait until he had at least thirty consecutive days of recovery. He was placed on a thirty-day waiting list. Each time the program contacted him after that and he admitted he had relapsed again, he was placed on another thirty-day waiting list. Finally, his former primary counselor interceded to get him readmitted when he learned that Ted had attempted suicide. Ted said the program's readmission policy was so harsh it conveyed the message that he "wasn't worth saving." His narrative strongly underscored the personal and political or systems disempowerment he experienced in this situation.

Other institutional barriers identified in clients' experiences involved systems outside the program. Twenty-five-year-old Margaret was charged with abandonment by protective services after an aunt who had agreed to keep her children while she was in rehab left them alone and disappeared. The program succeeded in helping Margaret to get the charges dismissed and find an alternative caretaker for her children, although the loss of control she experienced initially disrupted her recovery.

Marvin, a thirty-year-old high school dropout who was in the program's reentry phase, was referred to a combined GED–undergraduate degree program by one of the clinical aides. But when the college admissions counselor discouraged him from entering that program "because his background was inadequate," Marvin felt he had been discriminated against because of his substance abuse history and race. He said, "I'm used to being told I'm not ready, or not good enough, but I thought this program was supposed to give people a second chance." These clients' experiences are examples of political disempowerment involving the professional services theme (see table 16.1).

Examples of personal and interpersonal disempowerment also were evident. Twenty-seven-year-old Donesha felt guilt and disempowerment when her friend overdosed on heroin after Donesha entered rehab. The friend's parents would not take Donesha's call when she phoned to offer her condolences. They told a family friend that Donesha had gotten their daughter hooked on drugs and then had abandoned her.

Another client felt disempowered when he was dismissed from his position as expediter in the program. Forty-one-year-old Charles was in Phase III when he developed an intimate relationship with one of the female clients, which was against the program's rules. His primary counselor and the director met with Charles to discuss possible consequences. Although they decided to remove him from his position as an elder in the program rather than discharge him, Charles felt a great loss of personal power as a result.

Conclusions About the Meaning and Impact of the Experiences.   Many of these clients believe their disempowerment experiences validated and reinforced their low self-esteem. Ted, the client who had difficulty getting readmitted to rehab after relapsing, said the harsh readmission policy conveyed a message that he would not be forgiven. He had been told over and over again that he was a model client during rehab, so he wondered if the staff took his relapse as a personal failure, because they believed he could not fail. Margaret thought the abandonment charge filed by protective services meant she was an unfit mother for leaving her children with her aunt, who later abandoned them. Margaret felt she was in a no-win situation because she could not identify any other options at the time. She assumed that she had to either leave her children in a questionable caretaker situation so she could get into rehab or stay on drugs and continue to neglect and abuse her children herself.

Other clients concluded that the Africentric aspects of this program cushioned some of their painful disempowerment experiences. Paul's disempowerment narrative in the previous section illustrates how the use of Africentric tribal groups for developing strong cultural and family bonds may have prevented him from being devastated by his experience. Moreover, Malik's Africentric intervention helped Paul to understand more clearly how the Ujima principle works in recovery. Paul learned that tribe members are responsible for providing feedback to each other, but each member must direct his or her own unique journey. Paul believes the story was a reminder to all the members that going from the blinding, cold snow outside into a house to fall asleep by a warm fire could be a prelude to complacency. From Paul's perspective, accepting feedback might prevent this.

Malik's intervention also emphasized the Africentric concept of eldership. When John W. added his feedback to Paul "about his journey," Paul felt both of them benefited from restructuring their relationship in a more positive direction, as a young black man and his respected elder. In contrast to his previous attitude, Paul believed their new relationship enhanced rather than diminished his struggle to love himself and improve his competence.

Implications for Practice in Culture-Specific Programs

This discussion about clients' narratives highlights some underlying practice implications for Africentric programs and for culture-specific programs in general, including the importance of helping clients to develop a culturally relevant, life-organizing framework and restraining or adapting the use of traditional rehab services.

A Life-Organizing Framework

Sustaining Beliefs. Developing a new, culturally relevant belief system is one aspect of the life-organizing framework, which also includes cultural education and environmental change experiences to help clients organize and center their lives. First, culture-specific programs should introduce clients to a belief system that provides them with a code to live by and principles to govern current and future growth-oriented relationships (Gordon 1993). Such a belief system allows clients to interpret their life stories in ways relevant to their recovery and to their cultural backgrounds and strengths.

In Dareisa this aspect of the life-organizing framework consists of an Africentric philosophy, value system, and principles of collective living or the Nguzo Saba. Although this program is continuing to improve its Africentric approach, the use of counselor tribes, a cultural bonding milieu, rituals such as naming ceremonies and mentoring circles, and community service and political action activities already help clients change their beliefs about the possibilities for transforming themselves and their life situations.

As clients integrate these culturally centered beliefs, they are expected and encouraged to apply them to all aspects of their lives and recovery. Undoubtably, this concept of a transforming and sustaining belief system can be generalized to other populations and culture-specific programs. For example, programs for women could use feminist philosophy and theory to organize a set of beliefs that help them to sustain and center their lives. Programs for Native Americans could use the culture wheel and Native tribal value systems for the same purpose.

Cultural Education. This aspect of the framework is equally important for a culturally relevant recovery. Education includes helping clients to learn experientially about their cultural group's history, traditions, strengths, sources of group efficacy, and ways of being, with the goal of increased self-knowledge and cultural esteem (Rowe and Grills 1993). This process can create a sense of belonging and unity, which facilitates brainstorming about common cultural issues related to addiction and other areas and then working through the necessary long-term self-healing and recovery.

An analysis of empowerment practice in the Dareisa program demonstrated how clients use their cultural education to resolve both day-to-day and long-term problems. Paul's example included a current rule-breaking incident (using tobacco) and a long-term pattern of reacting negatively to feedback about consequences. The tribe meeting involving Malik's narrative intervention reinforced cultural education sessions in which Paul and his peers learned about the concept of "eldership" in the African tradition, the role of griots and other elders in transmitting cultural knowledge to young people. Malik's using John W.'s status as an elder to remind the group about that concept reinforced what they had learned.

Cultural education is applicable to culture-specific programs in general. Programs for Hispanics, for example, could provide cultural education about that group's history and traditions and the impact of colonization and oppression. Within-group differences could be clarified by involving consumers (Delgado 1995) and culturally sensitive historians representing the broad range of subgroups within the Hispanic culture, including Mexican Americans, Puerto Ricans, Cubans, and Nicaraguans.

Integrating Environmental Impact Experiences. Removing systemic barriers to recovery and empowerment and assuming responsible cultural roles in the community seem essential for clients to adopt a view of themselves as culturally valuable and powerful (Freeman and O'Dell 1993). The integration process provides clients with alternative solution-focused stories, making the typical war stories they use to reinforce addiction and other maladaptive coping mechanisms irrelevant (Interview 1996). Furthermore, when they engage in and integrate effective environmental impact experiences as part of their identities, clients are able to cope more effectively with future cultural stress and oppression. Thus, integration of these meaningful experiences is also important in relapse prevention.

As noted previously, many empowerment stories shared by Dareisa' s clients involved effective environmental change experiences within the setting and in the community. However, those clients needed multiple opportunities to practice their environmental impact skills before they could develop the type of self- and group efficacy described by the clients who participated in the 1996 Million Man March. Identifying, teaching, and encouraging clients to practice using culturally relevant environmental impact skills as part of their recovery is likely to be essential in any culture-specific rehab program.

Adapting Traditional Rehab Services

Direct Services. It seems essential too in these programs to modify traditional direct services that prevent clients from developing cultural self-knowledge and experiencing empowerment. Many traditional rehab programs emphasize clients' simultaneous involvement in twelve-step groups, short-term residential or outpatient care, family therapy, and job placement services. While the combination is appropriate for most clients, these services do not realistically address systemic barriers that confront African Americans and other clients of color or members of oppressed groups, and thus could potentially impede recovery.

Dareisa recognizes that power inequities, a chronic lack of cultural esteem, negative role models in the family and community, and racism in the labor market and in other institutions affect its clients' addiction and recovery process (Rogan 1986; Rowe and Grills 1993). Therefore, the program excludes twelve-step groups until clients begin aftercare, provides long-term rather than short-term residential treatment, helps clients to develop alternative family and peer networks in rehab and in the community, and focuses more broadly on economic development opportunities rather than just job placements. Programs for other clients of color have little chance for success unless they too adapt traditional services to address the cultural realities their clients must confront in recovery.

Indirect Services. To surmount these environmental and individual barriers to recovery, culture-specific programs should also engage in comprehensive indirect services, such as dissemination, advocacy, coordination with prevention programs, rehab program design innovations, and resource development. Traditionally, rehab programs advocate for resources, such as additional beds, or "supplemental" services, such as recreation programs. This narrow view of advocacy is no longer sufficient in programs that serve special needs groups because the relevance of empowerment and culture-specific services to recovery is clearer.

Dareisa's focus on a broader range of indirect strategies has led to more diversified sources of funding and programming, and to the colocation and coordination of services especially relevant to its clients. In some African American communities inundated with drug abuse and drug dealing, Dareisa's dissemination and prevention coordination strategies have been both welcome and effective. Other culture-specific programs may need to focus on a broader range of indirect services in order to be effective with, for example, Native American or Asian American clients.

Conclusion

This discussion about one Africentric program's empowerment and culture-specific services demonstrates that flexibility and adaptability are two important characteristics for culture-specific programs. It also clarifies how difficult it is to plan and implement this type of highly integrated program, which, by its nature, invites more involvement and scrutiny by consumers than other, less client-centered types of rehab programs. Although Dareisa strives to improve its services regularly, it is clear from my research that the program's internal structure facilitates some clients' empowerment while blocking that of others.

A consumer-driven evaluation is needed to clarify how specific policies and practices influence clients' disempowerment, particularly in the political area, which was noted as a concern by a number of clients. Evaluation also could document how other policies and practices, such as cultural education and various Africentric rituals, are a major resource for clients' self-empowerment and recovery.

Epilogue

Lessons Learned from Empowerment Research:
Implications for the Future
of Empowerment Practice

He who is being carried does not realize how far the village is.
—African proverb

A common concern in the research literature and among substance abuse staff and administrators is the need to improve the quality of program evaluations and other practice and policy research in this field. An emphasis on empowerment can make this goal easier in some ways, yet more difficult in other ways. Empowerment practice requires that services be consumer-centered and that clients and staff be actively involved in designing, implementing, and evaluating them along with the impact of relevant policies (Gutiérrez, GlenMaye, and DeLois 1996).

Consumer involvement in the development, analysis, and reform of relevant organizational and public policies ensures that they will address clients' strengths, concerns, and needs (Chapin 1995). In addition to participating in policy research, consumers can help make efforts to improve the quality and relevance of program evaluations and other practice research less arduous by sharing their knowledge about their families and communities, the available supports and potential barriers to recovery, and often, how those barriers can be overcome. Programs can develop more innovative strategies for conducting research at nontraditional community sites and for identifying and evaluating the effects of natural resources and environmental barriers on consumers' recovery and prevention activities.

However, client involvement can complicate empowerment practice and research because it frequently is more time-consuming and requires programs to be more accountable to different stakeholder groups in different

ways. Including consumers and community members on research committees and advisory boards helps to establish important collaborative relationships for conducting, analyzing, improving, and disseminating research. But
these partnerships require service providers to help educate consumers about
research and service delivery methods while supporting the unique knowledge and skills clients contribute to making those processes more culturally
sensitive and consumer-centered (Freeman 1996).

Hence, the benefits of consumer involvement in empowerment research
and service delivery far outweigh the difficulties. If clients are excluded, as
the epigraph of this chapter warns, they will be unable to increase their
individual and collective competencies and will not know "how far the village is." Consequently, this epilogue assesses how well empowerment research in the substance abuse field addresses the effects of consumer involvement in practice and policy research and in service delivery. It
summarizes the components of empowerment practice with special populations and analyzes the extent to which research has documented consumer
empowerment at political as well as personal and interpersonal levels. Strategies for improving this research are discussed, based on the lessons learned
from my own and others' work, and implications for future empowerment
practice and policy development are discussed.

State of the Art in Substance Abuse Empowerment Research

Research on Children and Youths

Research on empowerment practice in prevention has identified program
factors that contribute to youth leadership development and self-confidence
at personal, interpersonal, and political levels. For instance, Malekoff's
(1994) action research developed partnerships between youths and social
workers to examine substance abuse problems in a multicultural community consisting of white, black, and Hispanic residents. Some of these middle school students had participated in a prior immigration and accultur-
ation project for Hispanic youths. They were concerned about substance
abuse problems in their community. Therefore, they helped to develop a
survey instrument, identified the sample, and administered the survey in
five different language versions to 450 middle school students, then
planned and implemented a community conference to disseminate the

results. The researchers developed a preventive empowerment model based on Freire's (1982) approach, which provides opportunity for community members to listen, engage in dialogue, and take political action. Their empowerment model emphasized role flexibility and leadership skill development during the conference where "youth informed, enlightened, empathized, and confronted" while "adults listened, learned, and followed" (Malekoff 1994:50).

Conference outcomes included a plan to involve youths as well as adults in a community development/empowerment process that resulted in a drug-abuse prevention program for youths in collaboration with a local high school, a support group for day care workers concerned about the effects of family drug and alcohol abuse on the children they served, a local task force to address interethnic group violence, and an ongoing drug-free club created and run by adolescents for peers. Opportunity to develop and practice leadership skills was a key component of youth empowerment in this study, because it involved role flexibility or role switching between youths and significant adults in their environments (Malekoff 1994) (see table 1.1 under Professional/Client Collaboration at the Interpersonal and Political Levels).

Similarly, in terms of youth empowerment, Wallerstein and Bernstein (1988) documented that having adolescents interview family members, community residents, and adults in rehab or jail about substance abuse problems and how to resolve them led to empowerment outcomes at all three levels. The youths gained a greater sense of control and ability to influence others from analyzing media messages and changing policies that increase adolescents' access to and consumption of substances, conducting preventive peer education sessions with younger, latency-age students, and utilizing information that they collected from their interviews with substance abusers to change systems. (See table 1.1 under Peer-Led Services at the Political Empowerment Level.) These researchers used a control group–repeated measures design, written pre- and post-tests, and an eight-month postprogram follow-up survey. They were able to document maintenance of gains in the experimental group's risk perceptions about substance abuse, control over life and ability to influence others, and self-reported abstinence rates compared to the control group.

Other researchers report parallel findings regarding consumer-centered program factors and youth empowerment outcomes (Chang 1993; Botvin and Wills 1985; Freeman and McRoy 1986; Massey and Neidigh 1990;

Palmer, Davis, Sher, and Hicks 1989). Some peer empowerment prevention programs for youths are noteworthy too because they document the participants' nonuse or nonabuse of substances from periods of a few months to two years after the programs ended (Hansen 1988; Lynn 1986; Massey and Neidigh 1990; Molloy 1989).

Certain program factors have resulted in a reciprocal empowerment process when youths of different ages are included. Porter, Lerch, and Lewis (1986) report that using volunteer senior high school students in prevention activities with junior high students empowered the older students by making them feel special, encouraging them to maintain appropriate social behavior, and enhancing their self-confidence. Conversely, these authors' qualitative study revealed that older students' personal narratives of their struggles and decision making to not use or abuse substances inspired and empowered the younger students in their efforts to abstain (see table 1.1 under Peer-Led Services at the Personal and Interpersonal Levels).

A number of other researchers have studied empowerment practice with this population while receiving rehab services. Freeman's (1990) qualitative study of eighty-three white, black, and Latino youths, fourteen to eighteen years of age, focused on how well their rehab program facilitated their empowerment process and recovery. Three outpatient and inpatient counseling groups were studied over a four-month period, using direct observation and interviews. Audiotapes of the group sessions helped to identify empowerment and disempowerment themes in the group process and program factors that affected this process and other outcomes. Black and Latino youths' disempowerment themes involved the struggle to develop a positive individual and ethnic identity and to resist the rewards of substance abuse, which include minimizing racial stress and other environmental factors. Not having culturally appropriate supports in the program for discussing those issues further disempowered these clients. White youths' disempowerment themes included the struggle to meet other peoples' age-related role expectations for them without help in rehab to normalize those struggles. The findings document what the youths expect from rehab in order to meet these ethnicity- and age-related empowerment needs: help in learning social competencies, such as alternatives for coping with stress without using substances; guidance in discussing and working through ethnic conflicts and developing a positive identity; and life skills training for meeting new developmental role expectations (Freeman 1990).

Studies on Ethnicity and Poverty

In other studies, researchers have examined empowerment practice related to substance abuse in low-income communities, communities of color, and multicultural communities. Research in the prevention area emphasizes that drug use is a community problem, requiring comprehensive approaches that address multiple factors in order to be effective (Kolbe 1986). Skirrow and Sawka (1987) indicate that programs also must derive their goals and norms from communities in order to create environments conducive to empowerment.

Fitzpatrick and Gerald (1993) studied 215 residents from four neighborhoods who were at high risk for alcohol and drug use as well as drug-related arrests, school dropouts, and crime. From an empowerment perspective, the researchers assumed that the planners of a future community prevention program needed to understand the residents' concerns and beliefs about their problems in order to involve them in the development and use of program services. The findings document conflicts between the subjects' ongoing observations of community substance abuse problems and their perceptions that the problems were not severe (reflecting community norms that encourage use). The study demonstrates that community barriers such as pro–drug use norms may prevent residents from collectively addressing substance abuse problems and empowering themselves in the process.

Wheller's (1992) study findings support using solution-focused needs assessments for planning prevention programs that do not pathologize communities and are sensitive to the members' perceptions about what methods can work. His study identified aspects of an education program that could be effective with a low-income community in Australia and did a follow-up evaluation of that program once it was implemented. The findings demonstrate a short-term, unspecified reduction in alcohol consumption by the community's youth population (Weller 1992). The author concludes that consumer involvement in planning the program may have influenced the positive outcomes and the residents' ownership of the process.

Some studies of community action programs have attempted to mitigate the effects of disempowerment in low-income communities with high alcohol and other drug abuse rates. Lurigio and Davis (1992) indicate that when residents observe active drug sales and proliferation of drug houses, they begin to believe neither they nor the police can gain control over the community. As a consequence, they view their communities and themselves as inadequate and powerless. In spite of such ongoing disempowerment experiences, some community action programs have involved residents in effectively reducing drug-related activities and taking back their communities through drug hot lines, crime stoppers, and neighborhood watch projects (Rosenbaum, Lurigio, and Lavrakas 1989; Eck and Spellman 1987).

Lurigio and Davis (1992) surveyed 400 residents from four large urban inner-city communities, using a representative sample from each that was either mostly white, mostly African American, majority white (one third African American), or more diverse (African American, white, and Asian). The purpose was to compare residents' perceptions about crime, drugs, and disorder in their communities in areas that had substance abuse rehab programs with residents' perceptions in areas that did not have programs. The rehab programs were part of a national citizens' antidrug initiative that had been in effect for two years prior to the study. The authors documented their effectiveness in decreasing the fears of residents living in the designated program areas (compared to residents in nonprogram areas). The programs had altered conditions that were subtly related to the residents' fears: conditions of social disorder, physical decay, and a lack of social control—and had increased the residents' collective efficacy through their successful outcomes in fighting back against drugs (Lurigio and Davis 1992) (see table 1.1 under Peer-Led Services at the Political Level).

In another study focused on a Hispanic community, Gordon (1991) used qualitative interviews and direct observation to clarify factors that influenced rehab service providers' effective identification, intervention, and provision of culturally sensitive recovery supports for residents who were alcohol abusers. The findings verified the existence of both staff and organizational barriers in the service programs. Staff barriers included divergent rehab philosophies (client-centered versus organization-centered) and negative perceptions of clients' motivations for entering rehab. Organizational barriers, such as a lack of program incentives for staff to address the cultural strengths and needs of Hispanic alcoholics and ethnocentrism in some organizations, prevented the interorganizational collaboration necessary for sharing culturally relevant resources. These barriers were assumed to influence residents' empowerment and disempowerment experiences not only while they were in rehab but also in their post-rehab contacts with the same organizations and service providers over time.

Other studies have examined consumer involvement in organizations from a community perspective, which views drug abuse and drug sells as one of many indicators of community breakdown, besides homelessness, unemployment, crime, violence, and lack of economic growth. The focus of this type of research is on multiple rather than single community problems. Chavis and Wandersman (1990) found that a sense of community is the key variable that influences consumers' and residents' perceptions of control and therefore, their meaningful involvement in community development and drug-abuse prevention. Perkins, Florin, Rich, Wandersman, and Chavis (1990) concluded that consumer involvement is related to level of social cohesion and community satisfaction. These findings clarify how empowerment can result from fulfilling a citizen duty or from collective consumer involvement, which in turn leads to decreased feelings of helplessness among community members.

Women and Empowerment Research

Women have been included as the focus of substance abuse prevention research, but only as part of studies on child and adolescent populations (see Malekoff 1994; Wallerstein and Bernstein 1988; Porter, Lerch, and Lewis 1986 in a previous section on prevention research on youths). Therefore, most of the available data on empowerment practice with women is related to rehab programs and services; much of it demonstrates that drug-using and addicted women experience higher levels of guilt, shame, depression, and anxiety about their drug involvement than men who use or abuse drugs (Nelson-Zlupko, Kauffman, and Dore 1995; Underhill 1986). Social stigma may cause them to suffer more disempowerment experiences than men, thus precipitating these reactions, because they are rejected and oppressed by family members' and society's gender-related biases (Finkelstein 1993).

A number of qualitative studies have been conducted on women in substance abuse rehab in order to identify gender-related empowerment and disempowerment issues from their perspective. Most of this research has been focused on their disempowerment experiences. Woodhouse (1990) used ethnographic and life history techniques to interview twenty-five women in a gender-specific rehab program, individually and in focus groups, about their life experiences and significant people in their addiction and recovery. Most of the women in the sample, who ranged from eighteen to thirty-two years of age and were polyaddicted to crack, heroin, and alcohol, had experienced a series of violent events including rape, incest, and battering by partners and others prior to and during their addictions. These disempowerment experiences caused them to isolate and medicate themselves and to not trust other women (as well as the men who committed the violence), leading to gender-related recovery barriers.

Klee, Schmidt, and Ames (1991) conducted in-depth interviews with sixty-five women (African American, white, Latino, and Native American) who were in outpatient and residential rehab programs, involving a social model with support groups and aftercare, for alcohol problems. Disempowerment themes reflected in family or partner relationships consisted of numerous instances of criticism, conflict, avoidance, abandonment, and sabotage (e.g., a partner giving the woman alcohol so he could have more time for outside social activities or take advantage of her sexually). Robinson (1984) interviewed sixteen white and two African American women who had been in recovery for periods ranging from less than six months to sixteen years. Sources of empowerment included family members or friends who supported them in seeking out rehab services and in continuing their recovery; sources of disempowerment included family members who drank with them, were addicted themselves, threatened divorce if they got involved in rehab, or financially supported their continued addiction.

Dually Diagnosed Homeless Popluations

Empowerment practice with multiply impaired, chemically addicted individuals has been studied to identify their special needs, strengths, and limitations. The mostly residential programs under study are based on the premise that these individuals are detached from functional roles in society, often experiencing episodes of disempowerment as part of a mutual withdrawal/ rejection process. These psychosocial rehabilitation programs are designed to reintegrate clients into society through a bonding process that supports individual freedom, choice, and autonomy to decrease their sense of powerlessness (Blankertz and Cnaan 1994). These programs differ from therapeutic communities, which foster solidarity through a collective conscience rather than individual autonomy and use collective decision making to punish deviations from their mutually established rules (Berg 1992).

Blankertz and Cnaan (1994) compared the level of client-centered services within a therapeutic community program with services in a psychosocial rehabilitation program. The latter provided holistic, individualized services to dually diagnosed clients for whom relapse was considered an expected part of the recovery process. The program was described as integrating "a low demand environment with clear expectations for progress" (540). Although program factors related to client empowerment were emphasized as critical to recovery, empowerment outcomes were not addressed specifically in the study. Only outcomes related to abstinence from drugs and alcohol were monitored and reported, along with reductions in clients' mental health hospitalizations and increases in their successful functioning in environments that required adequate skills of daily living (permanent residency).

Using a time series design, these researchers collected data with a combination of existing and self-developed instruments on 200 clients' personal and homeless histories, activities of daily living and skill levels, addiction severity, and severity of mental illness. Twenty-nine percent of clients in the psychosocial rehabilitation experimental group (15) in residence for more than 60 days exited the program successfully, compared to 7.9 percent (3) in the therapeutic community comparison group. Although these success rates are low, the difference between the experimental and comparison group outcomes is statistically significant. Blankertz and Cnaan conclude that individualized psychosocial rehabilitation is a major influence on outcomes because most of these clients cannot thrive or recover successfully in therapeutic communities and other environments that are too restrictive and rigid.

Other researchers have found that a combination of individualized, client-centered services and other program factors has a similar positive effect on recovery outcomes with dually diagnosed homeless clients experiencing powerlessness. Those program factors include peer-led groups, orientation and modeling procedures, and token economies used with dually diagnosed clients (Galanter, Franco, Kim, Metzger, and DeLeon 1993) or with that population in combination with homeless drug-involved mothers addicted to crack and heroin (Galanter, Egelko, DeLeon, and Rohrs 1992) (see table 1.1 under Professional Services at the Personal Level). Pratt and Gill (1990) used a number of consumer involvement strategies with a population of clients who were mentally ill and addicted. These authors developed a client research study group in which members analyzed relevant research literature, were encouraged to participate on a research evaluation committee in this dual diagnosis program, and disseminated relevant information to other clients as self-empowerment strategies (see table 1.1 under Professional/

Client and Peer-Led Services at the Interpersonal Level). However, the researchers were unable to document whether these clients' increased positive attitudes about their active involvement in the program were a direct outcome of the experimental group's empowerment experiences.

Studies on Severely Addicted Clients

Research on services for resistive, uncooperative, and severely addicted clients has focused on factors that affect their successful recovery compared to clients with less severe substance problems: specialized approaches, interventions with their spouses alone, and community support approaches. Many of these factors lend strong support to and reflect empowerment concepts, although some researchers may not classify them as examples of empowerment practice.

Cognitive-Behavioral Relapse Prevention Approaches.   Carroll, Rounsaville, and Gawin (1991) studied a group of severely addicted cocaine abusers in comparison with a group of less severely addicted clients. The two treatment groups received services that used a cognitive-behavioral relapse prevention approach, while a comparison group of mildly addicted clients received "interpersonal therapy." These researchers found that the cognitive-behavioral approach was more effective with the severely addicted clients than interpersonal therapy, while the two groups of mildly addicted clients did equally well in both types of therapy. The concrete relapse prevention skills acquired by severely addicted adults through the cognitive-behavioral approach provided them with a sense of power over their situations and practical tools for handling daily barriers to their recovery. Similar studies have documented the value of social skills training for recovering adults (Carroll 1998; Cooney, Kadden, Litt, and Getter 1991).

Methadone Maintenance Procedures.   Another specialized approach with resistive and severely addicted clients is methadone maintenance. Early research on this method produced mostly negative, or at best questionable, outcomes. Friedman (1993) indicates that early researchers concluded that maintaining clients on a safe dose of methadone, a long-acting synthetic narcotic substituted for the opiates the clients had used, essentially substituted one addiction for another and failed to help addicted clients change their drug-use behavior.

More recent research in this area, however, has shown some promising results. Nowinski, Baker, and Carroll (1992, 1995) have documented the effectiveness of Project MATCH, a methadone maintenance program involving chronically and severely addicted clients. Stabilizing such clients in methadone maintenance therapy has allowed them to utilize work and vocational training and group counseling services, outcomes that have often been associated with personal and interpersonal empowerment and self-efficacy. It is not clear yet to what extent this approach and these results have been replicated with similar clients in other programs. Researchers and service providers may still be concerned about whether and when to discontinue methadone maintenance and the potential impact on clients' recovery.

Approaches with Significant Individuals and Social Networks.   Other approaches to working with uncooperative clients have focused on engaging members of their social networks (Zelvin 1993; Thomas 1994) or their spouses (Daley 1992; Daley and Raskin 1991). The goal is to facilitate the addicted member's eventual entry into rehab. Thomas (1994) reported that two thirds of the addicted individuals in his three-and-a-half-year study (N = 26), whose spouses were involved in services, subsequently entered a rehab program for their alcohol abuse and stopped or reduced their drinking. Sessions involving this unilateral family therapy approach for spouses lasted four to six months and were designed to change aspects of the marital or family system that could support the addiction *and* the behavior of the uncooperative addicted potential client.

For example, targets for change within the family system included affection, sexual satisfaction, and level of life stress. Perhaps changes in these areas gave the cooperative spouses some control over their previously unmanageable situations and some hope that their significant others would accept rehab services. Such changes can provide a foundation for empowerment and a sense of competence for the spouses of addicts.

Community Support Approaches.   Community supports represent yet another strategy that has been studied related to chronic drug abusers whose family, social network, and community ties may have been severed by their addictions and lifestyles. Hawkins, Catalano, and Wells (1986) explored the effective use of social skills training on recovery outcomes. Their study involved adults in a long-term residential program who were trained in behavioral and problem-solving skills. An important component of this program, however, was the use of drug-free community partners who received training and worked supportively with clients in their natural communities. This effort to help clients create drug-free social networks in their communities was effective in the short term, but data on the impact upon long-term recovery had not been collected at the time the study was published.

Similarly, Budney and Higgins (1998) demonstrate the effective use of a community reinforcement and voucher model (services integration) with long-term cocaine abusers. Nowinski, Baker, and Carroll (1995) validate the effectiveness of outreach and consumer-centered supportive strategies for helping clients participate in AA, NA, CA, and other twelve-step programs in the community. Finally, Sisson and Azrin (1989) studied the use of systematic encouragement and community access procedures, including resource brokering, to increase clients' involvement in twelve-step groups. Community supports have often been associated with successful long-term recovery and self-efficacy in severely addicted clients. The studies presented in this section provide empirical documentation of the importance of such supports for effective interpersonal empowerment and recovery.

Lessons Learned from Empowerment Research

The lessons learned from the process and outcomes of empowerment research in the substance abuse field are useful for improving the quality of research, practice, and policy development. The principles listed here are derived from the general research literature that was reviewed in the previous section and from my own empowerment research.

Lessons from the Review of Research

The review of empowerment research was useful for documenting some important aspects of empowerment practice, including the process of empowerment, empowerment reciprocity, key service components and how they are organized, the role of consumers, and staff and organizational barriers to empowerment. Specific lessons learned are:

1. The process of empowerment often follows models such as Freire's (1989), which includes consciousness raising, education, planning, and political action; however, these parts of the process may occur simultaneously or overlap in actuality. A focus on youth leadership development in community action programs has facilitated empowerment outcomes related to political or large systems change (Wallerstein and Bernstein 1988).

2. Holistic community prevention/development programs focused on collective action, such as crime stoppers and drug hot lines, have been effective because they seem to mitigate against community members' loss of control and powerlessness (Rosenbaum, Lurigio, and Laurakas 1989; Eck and Spellman 1987; Fitzpatrick and Gerald 1993; Chavis and Wandersman 1990).

3. Consumer and community involvement in assessing needs and strengths and in implementing program evaluations leads to a sense of ownership and to improved service utilization rates (Wheller 1992).

4. Focusing only on factors that contribute to consumers' disempowerment and addiction can reinforce a staff emphasis on pathology and fails to help consumers, particularly women, clarify how they react to and cope with those experiences in recovery and prevention programs (Robinson 1984; Klee, Schmidt, and Ames 1991; Woodhouse 1990).

5. Including consumers, particularly dually diagnosed clients, on rehab programs' evaluation and research committees gives them a sense of empowerment and competence, thus improving their recovery, self-knowledge, and presentation skills (Pratt and Gill 1990).

6. A process of reciprocal empowerment results in prevention programs that use older youths to deliver services to younger teenagers when the needs of both populations are clearly identified and addressed (Porter, Lerch, and Lewis 1986).

7. Youth rehab programs can increase their clients' empowerment experiences by including components that help them to successfully manage developmental role conflicts with parents and ethnic identity and interpersonal conflicts (Freeman 1990).

8. Organizational and staff barriers to client empowerment include lack of specialized training for counselors to serve clients of color

effectively and negative staff attitudes about client-centered services (Gordon 1991).

9. For resistive severely addicted clients, who have often lost sources
of personal, interpersonal, and political power, effective recovery
involves training in personal coping and social skills for relapse
prevention, use of community supports involving drug-free social
networks and mentors, methadone maintenance, cognitive-
behavioral procedures, and participation in twelve-step self-help
groups.

Lessons from the Author's Research

My empowerment research has also been useful in identifying such lessons.
All clients who participated were able to identify one or more empowerment
and disempowerment experiences during their recovery or prevention services, and indicated that they had learned from both. Those experiences
often involved what seemed to be unpredictable combinations of forces and
conditions that were timely because they occurred during important transitions in rehab and often built upon previous experiences. The lessons from
these clients' experiences, in contrast to lessons from the literature, focus
more on key components of effective empowerment practice as well as contextual factors that contribute to or prevent empowerment.

1. Using data collection methods such as direct observation and qualitative interviews provides important subjective information about
the meaning of empowerment and disempowerment experiences
to consumers in terms of their recovery.
2. Some clients are able to spontaneously develop tools for mitigating
the effects of disempowerment and addiction experiences, such as
lessons learned from inoculation stories, to facilitate their recovery.
3. Experiential program components such as role reversal and naming ceremonies empower clients because they help to externalize
problems, identify important subjective reactions and feelings, ritualize growth and increased skill development, and help clients
apply tools and resources to prevent relapse.
4. Having an audience of peers, staff, or family members witness and
support a client's growth and transformation from empowerment

experiences provides greater validation of change and increased self-efficacy.

5. Collective brainstorming and resource pooling provides clients with insights about and evidence of their power to act, and a sense of competence in managing their issues.

6. The negative effects of disempowerment seem to be more severe and long lasting in situations where clients are unable to externalize and critically examine or deconstruct the stated or unstated negative messages. In those instances they accept the messages and implied blame without question and internalize them.

7. In other instances, clients are able to interpret negative messages from their disempowerment experiences as providing a different perspective about situations in which they have become stuck in recovery. They are able to internalize the critical messages in a way that reduces their avoidance and masking behaviors and releases them to involve themselves more actively in recovery.

8. Staff and program barriers to empowerment include staff misperceptions about services they believe are empowerment-oriented; lack of clarity about how to operationalize an empowerment approach; lack of training incentives for staff and direct feedback about their skills and successes; and lack of consumer involvement in developing and implementing the conceptual framework, service components, evaluation, and mechanisms for analyzing the effects of organizational and public policy on empowerment outcomes.

9. Staff and program supports for empowerment include ongoing staff training in empowerment practice and service components that encourage clients' reflection, deconstruction of negative media messages, collective education, and political action such as journaling, power analysis, stakeholder research or assets mapping, and skill development and application of political action strategies (legislative testimony, policy analysis and dissemination, and service on program policy-making committees).

10. Empowerment practice with people from oppressed groups, including people of color and women, is more effective when it integrates service components that ritualize cultural traditions and strengths with traditional recovery and prevention services.

Implications for Improving the Quality of Future Empowerment Research

A number of problems have been identified in the empowerment research literature. In order to improve the quality and methodological rigor of this research, additional strategies are needed for more effective conceptualization and implementation, including improved planning and prioritizing, more effective methods, and more research on disempowerment and resiliency.

Improved Planning and Prioritizing

The research literature is very sparse on both empowerment practice in general and substance abuse rehab and prevention services in particular. Of the latter, much is focused only on clients' substance abuse problems. This narrow view is not consistent with the complex and interrelated needs that problem drug users or addicted individuals experience on a daily basis, or with the more ecological definitions of empowerment discussed throughout this book. A few of the community action programs under study focus more holistically on the interrelated problems of individuals, families, and communities, including alcohol and drug abuse. However, other substance abuse prevention and rehab programs focus primarily on personal and interpersonal empowerment, excluding political empowerment or systems change. Community action research focused on youths is the exception, as the literature has documented how youths can effectively engage in political action to accomplish systems change (see, for example, Malekoff 1994; Wallerstein and Bernstein 1988; Freeman 1990).

 Therefore, researchers must increase the rate of research on empowerment practice in the substance abuse field and develop long-term plans for addressing over time the various issues and methods that should be the focus. Long-term developmental planning should include methods that encourage and reward researchers for using a more holistic and ecological lens in design, implementation, and analysis, and that include consumer involvement in all phases of the research and service delivery process (Fetterman 1995; Freeman 1996). Youth empowerment research can be used as a model for developing more ecologically focused consumer-centered services and research with other populations.

Revising Research Methods

Methodological problems in this research are numerous. With few exceptions, most studies do not include behavioral definitions of empowerment, detailed information on measurement strategies or procedures, or specific outcomes related to empowerment, even though that concept may be part of the study focus. When data on empowerment outcomes are included, they are not clearly reported, either descriptively or quantitatively. Exceptions include Gutiérrez and Ortega 1991; Gutiérrez, GlenMaye, and DeLois 1995; Chandler 1992; Lewis and Ford 1991; and Wallenstein 1992, with only the Wallenstein study specifically addressing outcomes in the area of substance abuse and empowerment practice.

Because many studies have not included process evaluations, aspects of empowerment practice that contribute to positive outcomes, including specific program factors and the processes of service implementation and consumer involvement, have seldom been documented. Primary components of the empowerment process and how they influence each other are also neglected. Often, researchers have failed to gather postrehab or prevention data in order to demonstrate whether long-term individual, community, or large systems changes are maintained over time. These methodological problems make replication of studies on empowerment practice difficult.

Empowerment research methodology can be improved by including process, impact, and outcome evaluations, along with clearer accounts of data collection processes and instruments. More clarity about empowerment outcomes is needed as well. Researchers should work toward helping program staff and consumers to describe empowerment processes and outcomes more behaviorally, and then, perhaps, collaborate in scaling or rating those outcomes when possible. Greater client involvement in identifying what outcomes are culturally meaningful to them and to community residents is an important step in improving this area of research and service delivery. More studies should include long-term follow-up data collection to determine if clients' empowerment outcomes, systems changes, and other prevention and recovery gains are maintained beyond a few months or one year.

Including More Research on the Effects of Resiliency on Disempowerment

Gaps in research include the failure to address and define disempowerment directly; often information about negative events and experiences is implied rather than stated explicitly, as noted in the discussion about research on women. Also, much of the existing research on disempowerment simply describes contributing factors without identifying clients' reactions or the effects on their substance abuse and other problems.

Research on disempowerment is important because it can explain how powerlessness affects the ways people cope, develop addictions, and react to rehab and prevention empowerment programs. Such research can also clarify how and under what individual and environmental conditions the effects of disempowerment can be mitigated. Clearly, more work is needed to clarify how consumers and community members use their strengths and resiliency to overcome disempowerment experiences. This research should clarify conditions that support drug abuse and community disorganization under which consumers are nevertheless able to mobilize themselves collectively and engage in political action and systems change. Research should explore how individual substance abusers and addicts overcome individual, family, community, or political barriers to recovery that disempower them. It should also identify factors that influence addiction development and disempowerment, as well as how disempowerment occurs and what factors help individuals develop resistance to or handle this process to enhance their growth and development.

Implications for Future Empowerment Practice and Policy

As noted in the previous section, research in this field needs to continue expanding its focus to explore individual and community resiliency and to use qualitative, client-centered methods. Countervailing forces in the larger sociopolitical environment emphasize maintaining a more narrow focus on rehab recidivism rates and drastically restricting clients' access to services through managed care policies. These influences will shape the future of empowerment practice and policies even under the best of circumstances, in which empowered stakeholders such as clients, staff, administrators, community residents and leaders, and other advocates work collaboratively toward systems and political changes.

Policy Development and Reforms

Research and practice experience have documented the importance of including political empowerment and systems changes as key rehab and prevention program outcomes. Discussions throughout this book also support the critical link between effective empowerment practice at the consumer level and supportive organizational and social policies. One implication is the need to strengthen the linkage between practice and policy. The roles of all stakeholders will need to be modified to require a more comprehensive and sophisticated set of politically focused intervention strategies. The goal should be to directly influence the multilevel policy-making process discussed in chapter 3 and in other chapters from the point at which problems and needs are being defined or redefined through the process of policy development, implementation, and reform. Chapin (1995) and other authors have clarified how policy makers' orientations (pathology versus strengths) directly influence funding patterns related to program resources, priorities, and desired outcomes. Therefore, many of the strategies identified from my empowerment research, including power analyses, deconstruction, collective consciousness raising, and political action such as dissemination of research findings and legislative testimony, will need to become a standard part of stakeholders' repertoires in the future.

Another implication is that certain essential program factors will have to be implemented to support the use of these intervention strategies. Such factors involve staff, peer, and staff-client collaborative procedures and include clients' participation in community service projects as part of rehab or prevention services (e.g., neighborhood cleanup projects); development of peer-directed political action activities (e.g., voter registration or marches to increase housing resources); and voluntary participation on staff-client evaluation committees using research outcomes to plan and implement improvements to the service program.

A third implication is the need for greater stakeholder awareness of changing external conditions that influence policy and large systems. This automatically requires the adoption of a proactive, rather than a reactive, approach to change, increasing empowerment through planning and action to counter powerlessness and immobility caused by community and policy changes.

Future Empowerment Practice

Changing external conditions will also affect the future of empowerment practice. An empowerment-oriented program philosophy and mission often underscore the importance of the context in which such practice occurs and clients' recovery and resistances to substances are strengthened. One research implication is that the context of empowerment practice will need to be addressed even more directly in the future. The educational component of such practice involves helping clients learn more about the sociopolitical environment as part of their recovery and prevention process and in turn, clients educating staff from their expert knowledge of the immediate and larger environments. Staff and administrators will need to become more sophisticated educators *and* learners in this reciprocal process. The change may also lead to increased and more effective use of peers, family members, and community resource people to strengthen the service team and its efforts to support client empowerment.

A related implication is the need for program administrators and staff to better understand the importance of organizational factors in clients' empowerment and disempowerment. Such understanding can encourage efforts to develop more integrated services models that provide a greater array of these factors at one site to address clients' needs more comprehensively and holistically (see chapter 5 for a discussion of these models and their benefits). For example, these models increase the likelihood of integrated, rather than categorical, funding and mandatory mechanisms for client involvement in organizational policy and programming decisions.

A final implication is that the current continuum of care, which perpetuates competition for demand reduction funding, will gradually encourage more fluid and integrated service provisionof intervention, prevention, and rehab services. Combining them in the same integrated services models or developing freestanding or comprehensive umbrella organizations that cover all three areas of the continuum should become more common. The result can be more client-centered service arrangements and more efficient and effective use of resources for individuals, families, and communities.

Conclusion

This epilogue foreshadows both an ending and a beginning. It summarizes and integrates important concepts about empowerment practice and policy addressed in previous chapters, providing final thoughts about the nature of empowerment practice and important interrelationships among research, policy, and practice in this area. The chapter documents the state of art in this field as an era of empowerment practice and research begins to shift and thus ends.

The chapter also looks ahead to the substance abuse prevention, intervention, and treatment field's future direction and focus, thus highlighting a new beginning. Programs will no longer be able to provide rehab or prevention services in isolation of the larger context, whether it involves peers, family, community, cultural groups, large social and political systems, policy, or combinations of those environmental components. Effective programs and services should be located in those parts of the environment where the roots of clients' needs and problems reside and where their strengths and resources can be built upon and mobilized. Most of all, for true empowerment to occur, program staff and policy makers will need to listen more creatively and actively to the voices of the people for whom the services were designed:

> Go to the people
> Work with them
> Learn from them
> Respect them
> Start with what they know
> Build with what they have
> And when the work is done
> The task completed
> The people will say,
> We have done this ourselves.
> —Lao Tsu, China, 700 B.C.

References

Ahlbrandt, R. S., J. Friedman, and A. Shabecoff. 1982. The private sector and neighborhood revitalization. *Journal of Community Action* 1 (1):9–13.

Albee, G. W. 1983. Psychopathology, prevention, and the just society. *Journal of Primary Prevention* 4:5–40.

American Psychiatric Association. 1994. *Diagnostic and Statistical Manual of Mental Disorders*, 4th ed. Washington, D.C.: American Psychiatric Association.

Amuleru-Marshall, O. 1991. African-Americans. In J. Kinney, ed., *Clinical Manual of Substance Abuse*. St. Louis, MO: Mosby Year Books.

Anderson, B. and R. A. Brown. 1980. Life history grid for adolescents. *Social Work* 25:321–22.

Anderson, H. and H. Goolishian. 1992. The client as expert: A not-knowing approach to therapy. In S. McNamee and K. J. Gergen, eds., *Therapy as Social Construction*, 25–39. Newbury Park, CA: Sage.

Anderson, S. C. and L. E. Wiemer. 1992. Administrators' beliefs about the relative competence of recovering and nonrecovering chemical dependency counselors. *Families in Society* 73:596–603.

Annis, H. M. 1993. The inventory of drug-taking situations. Unpublished assessment instrument. Toronto, Canada: Addiction Research Foundation.

————. 1986. A relapse prevention model for treatment of alcoholics. In W. R. Miller and N. Heather, eds., *Treating Addictive Behaviors*, 407–33. New York: Plenum.

Aquirre, L. M. 1995. California's efforts toward school-linked, integrated, comprehensive services. *Social Work in Education* 17:217–25.

Aquirre-Molina, M. and P. A. Parra. 1995. Latino youth and families as active participants in planning change: A community-university partnership. In

R. F. Zambrana, ed., *Understanding Latino Families: Scholarship, Policy and Practice*, 130–53. Thousand Oaks, CA: Sage.

Asante, M. 1990. *Afrocentricity and Knowledge*. Trenton, NJ: African World Press.

Auerbach, E. and M. Wallerstein. 1987. *ESL for Action: Problem-Posing at Work*. Reading, MA: Addison-Wesley.

Baker, M. R. and J. R. Steiner. 1995. Solution-focused social work: Meta messages to students in higher education opportunity programs. *Social Work* 40:225–32.

Bandura, A. 1989. Human agency in social cognitive theory. *American Psychologist* 44:1175–1184.

———. 1986. *Social Foundations of Thought and Action*. Englewood Cliffs, NJ: Prentice-Hall.

Barth, R. P. 1993. Shared family care: Child protection without parent-child separation. In R. Barth, J. Peitrzak, and M. Ramier, eds., *Families Living with Drugs and HIV: Intervention and Treatment Strategies*, 272–95. New York: Guilford.

———. 1986. *Social and Cognitive Treatment of Children and Adolescents: Practical Strategies for Problem Behaviors*. San Francisco: Jossey-Bass.

Bays, J. 1990. Substance abuse and child abuse: Impact of addiction on the child. *Pediatric Clinics of North America* 39 (4):881–904.

Behroozi, C. S. 1992. A model for social work with involuntary applicants in groups. *Social Work in Groups* 15:223–38.

Benard, B. 1992. Fostering resiliency in kids: Protective factors in the family, school, and community. *Prevention Forum* 12:1–16.

Berg, W. E. 1992. Evaluation of community-based drug abuse treatment programs: A review of the research literature. In E. M. Freeman, ed., *The Addiction Process: Effective Social Work Approaches*, 81–95. White Plains, NY: Longman.

Berger, P. L. and R. J. Neuhaus. 1980. *To Empower People: The Role of Mediating Structures on Public Policy*. Washington, D.C.: American Enterprise Institute.

Berger, R. L., J. T. McBreen, and M. J. Rifkin. 1996. *Human Behavior: A Perspective for the Helping Professions*. White Plains, NY: Longman.

Berlin, R. and R. Davis. 1989. Children from alcoholic families: Vulnerability and resilience. In T. Dugan and R. Coles, eds., *The Child in Our Time: Studies in the Development of Resiliency*, 81–105. New York: Brunner/Mazel.

Berman-Rossi, T. 1992. Empowering groups through understanding stages of group development. *Social Work with Groups* 15:239–55.

Blackmon, B. 1985. Assessment in inpatient and outpatient treatment programs. In E. M. Freeman, ed., *Social Work Practice with Clients Who Have Alcohol Problems*, 69–72. Springfield, IL: Thomas.

Blankertz, L. E. and R. A. Cnaan. 1994. Assessing the impact of two residential programs for dually diagnosed homeless individuals. *Social Service Review* 68:536–60.

———. 1992. Principles of care for dually diagnosed homeless: Findings from a demonstration project. *Research on Social Work Practice* 2:448–64.

Bloom, M. 1995. Primary prevention overview. In R. L. Edwards, ed., *Encyclopedia of Social Work*, 19th ed., 1:1895–1905. Washington, D.C.: National Association of Social Workers.

Blume, S. B. 1992. Alcohol and other drug problems in women. In J. H. Lowinson, P. Ruiz, R. Milliman, and J. G. Langrod, eds., *Substance Abuse: A Comprehensive Textbook*, 2nd ed., 794–807. Baltimore: Williams and Wilkins.

———. 1987. Public policy issues relevant to children of alcoholics. *Advances in Alcohol and Substance Abuse* 6:5–15.

Borden, W. 1992. Narrative perspective in psychosocial intervention following adverse life events. *Social Work* 37:135–41.

Bostwick, Jr., G. 1987. Where's Mary? A review of the group treatment dropout literature. *Social Work with Groups* 10:117–26.

Botvin, G. J. and S. Tortu. 1988. Preventing adolescent substance abuse through life skills training. In R. H. Price, E. L. Cowen, R. P. Lorion, and J. Ramos-McKay, eds., *14 Ounces of Prevention: A Casebook for Practitioners*, 98–110. Washington, D.C.: American Psychological Association.

Botvin, G. and T. Wills. 1985. Personal and social skills training: Cognitive-behavioral approaches to substance abuse prevention. In C. Bell and R. Battjes, eds., *Prevention Research: Deterring Drug Abuse Among Children and Adolescents*, 8–49. Washington, D.C.: U.S. Government Printing Office.

Bowlby, J. 1980. *Attachment and Loss: Vol. III*. New York: Basic.

Bracht, N. 1995. Prevention and wellness. In R. L. Edwards, ed., *Encyclopedia of Social Work*, 19th ed., 1:1895–1905. Washington, D.C.: National Association of Social Workers.

Brager, G. and S. Holloway. 1978. *Changing Human Service Organizations: Politics and Practice*. New York: Free Press.

Bricker-Jenkins, M. and N. R. Hooyman, eds. 1986. *Not for Women Only: Social Work Practice for a Feminist Future*. Silver Spring, MD: National Association of Social Workers.

Brill, M. and N. Nahmani. 1993. Clients' responses to separation from social work trainees. *Journal of Teaching in Social Work* 7:97–111.

Brody, J. E. 1989. Cocaine: Litany of fetal risks grows. *New York Times*, September 10, A1.

Brown, L. N. 1991. *Groups for Growth and Change*. New York: Longman.

Budney, A. J. and S. T. Higgins. 1990. *A Community Reinforcement Plus Voucher Approach: Treating Cocaine Addiction*. Rockville, MD: U.S. Department of Health and Human Services, National Institute of Health, National Institute on Drug Abuse.

Burman, S. and P. Allen-Meares. 1991. Criteria for selecting practice theories: Working with alcoholic women. *Families in Society* 72:387–93.

Burns, W. J. and K. A. Burns. 1988. Parenting dysfunction in chemically dependent women. In I. J. Chasnoff, ed., *Drugs, Alcohol, Pregnancy and Parenting*, 159–71. Boston: Kluwer.

Butler, S. M. 1981. The enterprise zone as an urban frontier. *Journal of Community Action* 1 (1):12–19.

Byron, W. J. 1992. Renewing community: When Congress does it right. *Commonweal* 119 (8):6–9.

Caplan, G. 1989. Recent developments in crisis intervention and the promotion of social support. *Journal of Primary Prevention* 10:3–25.

Caplan, M. Z. and R. P. Weissberg. 1989. Promoting social competence in early adolescence: Developmental considerations. In B. H. Schneider, G. Attili, J. Nadel, and R. P. Weissberg, eds., *Social Competence in Developmental Perspective*, 371–85. Boston: Kluwer.

Caplan, R. D., A. D. Vinokur, R. Price, and M. van Ryn. 1989. Job-seeking, reemployment and mental health: A randomized field experiment in coping with job loss. *Journal of Applied Psychology* 74:759–69.

Carley, G. 1997. The getting better phenomena: Videotape application of previously at-risk high school student narratives. *Social Work in Education* 19:115–20.

Carroll, K. 1998. *A Cognitive-Behavioral Approach: Treating Cocaine Addiction.* Rockville, MD: U.S. Department of Health and Human Services, National Institute of Health, National Institute on Drug Abuse.

Carroll, K. M., B. J. Rounsaville, and E. J. Garwin. 1991. A comparative trial of psychotherapies for ambulatory cocaine abusers: Relapse prevention and interpersonal psychotherapy. *American Journal of Drug and Alcohol Abuse* 17:221–47.

Cartwright, A. 1987. Group work with substance abusers: Basic issues and future research. *British Journal of Addictions* 82:951–53.

Catalano, R. and D. Dooley. 1980. Economic change in primary prevention. In R. H. Price, R. F. Ketterer, B. C. Bader, and J. Monahan, eds., *Prevention in Mental Health: Research, Policy, and Practice*, 21–40. Beverly Hills: Sage.

Chamberlain, R. 1995. Kansas mental health managed care: Enhancing client lives while controlling costs (Executive summary). Lawrence: University of Kansas, Office of Social Policy Analysis.

Chambers, D. 1993. *Social Policy and Social Programs*. 2nd ed. New York: Macmillan.

Chandler, G. 1992. The source and process of empowerment. *Nursing Administration Quarterly* 16:65–71.

Chang, V. N. 1993. Prevent and empower: A student-to-student strategy with alcohol abuse. *Social Work in Education* 15:207–13.

Chapin, R. K. 1995. Social policy development: The strengths perspective. *Social Work* 40:483–95.

————. 1993. Concepts for the analysis of methods of financing. In D. Chambers, ed., *Social Policy and Social Programs*, 217–44. New York: Macmillan.

Chau, K. L. 1990. Social work with groups in multicultural contexts. *Groupwork* 3:8–21.

Chavis, D. M. and A. Wandersman. 1990. Sense of community in the urban environment: A catalyst for participation and community development. *American Journal of Community Psychology* 18:55–61.

Checkoway, B. 1985. Neighborhood planning organizations: Perspectives and choices. *The Journal of Applied Behavioral Science* 21 (4):471–86.

Chestang, L. 1976. Environmental influences on social functioning: The black experience. In P. S. Cafferty and L. Chestang, eds., *The Diverse Society: Implications for Social Policy*, 59–74. New York: National Association of Social Workers.

Chiauzzi, E. J. and S. Liljegren. 1993. Taboo topics in addiction treatment. *Journal of Substance Abuse Treatment* 10:303–6.

Chidman, C. 1980. *Adolescence, Pregnancy and Childbearing: Findings from Research*. Washington, D.C.: U.S. Government Printing Office.

Chisum, G. M. 1986. Recognition and initial management of pregnant substance-abusing women. In I. Chasnoff, ed., *Drug Use in Pregnancy*, 17–22. Lancaster, England: Mother and Child MTP Press, Limited.

Clifford, P. R. and W. Jones. 1988. Alcohol abuse, prevention issues and the Black community. *Evaluation and the Health Professions* 11:272–77.

Cnaan, R. A., L. E. Blankertz, and J. R. Gardner. 1988. Psychosocial rehabilitation: Toward a definition. *Psychosocial Rehabilitation Journal* 11:61–77.

Cnaan, R. A., L. E. Blankertz, K. Messinger, and J. R. Gardner. 1989. Psychosocial rehabilitation: Toward a theoretical base. *Psychosocial Rehabilitation Journal* 13:33–56.

Cnaan, R. A. and J. Rothman. 1986. Conceptualizing community intervention: An empirical test of "Three Models" of community organization. *Administration in Social Work* 10 (3):41–55.

Coates, T. J. 1990. Strategies for modifying sexual behavior for primary and secondary prevention of HIV disease. *Journal of Consulting and Clinical Psychology* 58:57–69.

Cohen, B. E. and M. Burt. 1990. The homeless: Chemical dependency and mental health problems. *Social Work Research and Abstracts* 26:8–17.

Coleman, E. 1987. Child physical and sexual abuse among chemically dependent individuals. *Journal of Chemical Dependency Treatment* 1:27–38.

Cooney, N. L., R. M. Kadden, M. D. Litt, and H. Getter. 1991. Matching alcoholics to coping skills or interpersonal therapies: Two-year follow-up results. *Journal of Consulting and Clinical Psychotherapy* 59:598–601.

Creager, C. 1991. The treatment field meets the managed care challenge. *Professional Counselor* 5:42–49, 55.

Crowfoot, J., M. A. Chesler, and J. Boulet. 1993. Organizing for social justice. In E. Seidman, ed., *Handbook of Social Intervention*, 125–130. Beverly Hills: Sage.

Cunningham, M. S. 1993. Evaluating alcohol and other drug abuse programs. In E. M. Freeman, ed., *Substance Abuse Treatment: A Family Systems Approach*, 267–94. Newbury Park, CA: Sage.

Czarniawska-Joerges, B. 1992. *Exploring Complex Organizations: A Cultural Perspective*. Newbury Park, CA: Sage.

Daley, D. C. 1989. *Relapse Prevention: Treatment Alternatives and Counseling Aids*. Blue Ridge Summit, PA: TAB Books.

———. 1987. Relapse prevention with substance abusers: Clinical issues and myths. *Social Work* 32:138–42.

Daniels, S. 1986. Relationship of employment status to mental health and family variables in Black men from single parent families. *Journal of Applied Psychology* 71:386–91.

Dareisa Rehab Services. *Staff Manual 1995*. Washington, D.C.: Dareisa Rehab Services.

Dareisa Rehab Services. *Client Handbook 1994*. Washington, D.C.: Dareisa Rehab Services.

Dareisa Rehab Services. *Program Manual 1990*. Washington, D.C.: Dareisa Rehab Services.

Dareisa Rehab Services, Director. 1996. Interview by author. Washington, D.C., March.

Darvill, G. and G. Smale. 1990. *Pictures of Practice: Vol. 2. Partners in Empowerment: Networks of Innovation in Social Work*. London: National Institute for Social Work.

Davis, R. C., B. E. Smith, A. J. Lurigio, and W. G. Skogan. 1991. *Community Responses to Crack*. Washington, D.C.: National Institute of Justice.

DeJong, W. and J. A. Winsten. 1990. The use of mass media in substance abuse prevention. *Health Affairs* 9:30–46.

Delgado, M. 1995a. Community asset assessments by Latino youths. *Social Work in Education* 18:169–78.

———. 1995b. Hispanic natural support systems and alcohol and other drug services: Challenges and rewards for practice. *Alcoholism Treatment Quarterly* 12 (1):17–31.

Donohew, L., H. E. Sypher, and W. J. Bukoski, eds. 1991. *Persuasive Communication and Drug Abuse Prevention*. Hillsdale, NJ: Lawrence Erlbaum.

Dunst, C., C. Trivette, and A. Deal. 1989. *Enabling and Empowering Families: Principles and Guidelines for Practice*. Cambridge, MA: Brookline.

Dunst, C. J., C. M. Trivette, N. J. Gordon, and L. L. Pletcher. 1989. Building and mobilizing informal family support networks. In G. S. Singer and L. K. Irvin, eds., *Support for Caregiving Families: Enabling Positive Adaptation of Disability*, 121–42. Baltimore: Paul H. Brookes.

Dunst, C. J., C. M. Trivette, and N. LaPointe. 1992. Toward clarification of the meaning and key elements of empowerment. *Family Science Review* 5:111–30.

Eck, J. E. and W. Spelman. 1987. *Problem-Solving: Problem-Oriented Policing in Newport News*. Washington, D.C.: Police Executive Research Forum.

Elbow, M. 1987. The memory book: Facilitating terminations with children. *Social Casework* 68:180–83.

Ellis, A., J. F. McInerney, R. DiGiuseppe, and R. J. Yeager. 1988. *Rational-Emotive Therapy with Alcoholics and Substance Abusers*. New York: Pergamon.

Eng, E., M. E. Salmon, and F. Mullan. 1992. Community empowerment: The critical base for primary health care. *Family and Community Health* 15:1–12.

Etzioni, A. 1993. *The Spirit of Community: Rights, Responsibilities, and the Communitarian Agenda*. New York: Crown.

Evans, K. and J. M. Sullivan. 1990. *Dual Diagnosis: Counseling the Mentally Ill Substance Abuser*. New York: Guilford.

Farris-Kurtz, L. 1992. From natural helping to formal treatment to mutual aid. In E. M. Freeman, ed., *The Addiction Process: Effective Social Work Approaches*, 13–26. New York: Longman.

Favazza, A. and J. Thompson. 1984. Social networks of alcoholics: Some early findings. *Alcoholism: Clinical and Experimental Research* 8:9–15.

Ferris, P. A. and C. A. Marshall. 1987. A model project for families of the chronically mentally ill. *Social Work* 32:110–14.

Fetterman, D. M. 1994. Empowerment evaluation. *Evaluation Practice* 15 (1): 1–15.

Figueira-McDonough, J. 1993. Policy practice: The neglected side of social work intervention. *Social Work* 38:179–88.

Finkelstein, N. 1994. Treatment issues for alcohol and drug-dependent pregnant and parenting women. *Health and Social Work* 19:7–16.

———. 1993. Treatment programming for alcohol and drug-dependent pregnant women. *The International Journal of Addictions* 28:1275, 1309.

Fitzpatrick, J. L. and K. Gerard. 1993. Community attitudes toward drug use: The need to assess community norms. *International Journal of the Addictions* 28 (10):947–57.

Flanzer, J. P. and P. Delany. 1992. Multiple-member substance abuse: Exploring the initiative for change in addicted families. In E. M. Freeman, ed., *The Addiction Process: Effective Social Work Approaches*, 54–64. New York: Longman.

Florin, P. and A. Wandersman. 1990. An introduction to citizen participation, voluntary organizations, and community development: Insights for empowerment through research. *American Journal of Community Psychology* 18:41–54.

Fortune, A. E. 1995. Termination in direct practice. In R. L. Edwards, eds., *Encyclopedia of Social Work*, 19th ed., 3:2398–2404. Washington, D.C.: National Association of Social Workers.

Freeman, E. M. 1998. Addressing cultural diversity issues in substance abuse services through narrative approaches. Paper presented at the Mental Health Professional Development Series, July. Kansas City, MO: The Mental Health Consortium.

———. 1996a. Welfare reforms and services for children and families: Setting a new practice, research, and policy agenda. *Social Work* 41:421–32.

———. 1996b. Community practice and policy issues revisited (Editorial). *Social Work in Education* 18:3–6.

———. 1995. Multicultural and empowerment organizational assessment. Unpublished assessment inventory. Lawrence, KS: University of Kansas School of Social Welfare.

———. 1995. Multicultural and empowerment organizational assessment. Workshop presented at the Renaissance West Treatment Program, Kansas City, MO.

———. 1995. Conceptualizations of empowerment at micro, mezzo, and macro levels: Implications for substance abuse interventions. Unpublished paper. Lawrence, KS: University of Kansas School of Social Welfare.

———. 1995. Multicultural and empowerment organizational assessment. Unpublished assessment inventory. Lawrence, KS: University of Kansas School of Social Welfare.

———. 1994. Multicultural model for program evaluation. In J. U. Gordon, ed., *Managing Multiculturalism in Substance Abuse Services*, 199–215. Thousand Oaks, CA: Sage.

———. 1994. Developing alternative family structures for runaway, drug-addicted adolescents. In E. M. Freeman, ed., *Substance Abuse Treatment: A Family Systems Perspective*, 48–70. Newbury Park, CA: Sage.

———. 1994. African American women and the concept of cultural competence. *Journal of Multicultural Social Work* 4:120–25.

———. 1994. The impact of the socio-political environment and value issues on substance abuse policy and service delivery. Unpublished paper. Lawrence, KS: University of Kansas, School of Social Welfare.

———. 1993. Substance abuse treatment: Continuum of care in services to families. In E. M. Freeman, ed., *Substance Abuse Treatment: A Family Systems Perspective*, 1–20. Newbury Park, CA: Sage.

———. 1993. Final report: A retrospective evaluation of the Westside community's education planning process. Unpublished report. Kansas City, MO: The Kauffman Foundation.

———. 1992. Final report: A risk and protective factor approach to statewide substance abuse prevention, family involvement, and multilevel systems change.

Unpublished report. Lawrence, KS: The Institute for Urban Research and Development.

———. 1992a. Addicted mothers—addicted infants and children: Social work strategies for building support networks. In E. M. Freeman, ed., *The Addiction Process: Effective Social Work Approaches*, 108–12. New York: Longman.

———. 1992. Addictive behaviors: State-of-the-art issues in social work treatment. In E. M. Freeman, ed., *The Addictive Process: Effective Social Work Approaches*, 1–9. New York: Longman.

———. 1992. The use of storytelling techniques with African American males: Implications for substance abuse prevention. *Journal of Intergroup Relations* 29:53–72.

———. 1991. Social competence as a framework for addressing ethnicity and teenage alcohol problems. In A. R. Stiffman and L. E. Davis, eds., *Ethnic Issues in Adolescent Mental Health*, 247–66. Newbury Park, CA: Sage.

———. 1988. Role conflicts for supervisors in alcoholism treatment programs. *The Clinical Supervisor* 11:36–52.

———. 1985. Analyzing the organizational context of the school. *Social Work in Education* 7:151–64.

———. 1984. Multiple losses in the elderly: An ecological perspective. *Social Casework* 65:287–96.

———. 1984. Loss and grief in children: Implications for school social workers. *Social Work in Education* 6:241–58.

Freeman, E. M. and L. Dyer. 1993. High-risk children and adolescents: Family and community environments. *Families in Society* 74:422–33.

Freeman, E. M. and T. Landesman. 1992. Differential diagnosis and the least restrictive environment. In E. M. Freeman, ed., *The Addiction Process: Effective Social Work Approaches*, 27–42. New York: Longman.

Freeman, E. M., S. L. Logan, and E. A. Gowdy. 1992. Empowering single mothers. *Affilia* 7:123–41.

Freeman, E. M. and R. G. McRoy. 1986. Group counseling program for unemployed black teenagers. *Social Work with Groups* 9:73–90.

Freeman, E. M. and K. O'Dell. 1993. Helping communities redefine self-sufficiency from the person-in-environment perspective. *Journal of Intergroup Relations* 20:38–54.

Freeman, E. M. and M. Pennekamp. 1988. *Social Work Practice: Toward a Child, Family, School, Community Perspective*. Springfield, IL: Thomas.

Freedman, J. and G. Combs. 1996. *Narrative Therapy*. New York: Norton.

Freire, P. 1994. *Pedagogy of Hope*. New York: Continuum.

———. 1989. *Pedagogy of the Oppressed*. New York: Continuum.

Freire, P. and D. Macedo. 1987. *Literacy: Reading the Word and the World*. New York: Bergin and Garvey.

Friedman, E. G. 1993. Methadone maintenance in the treatment of addiction. In
    S.L.A. Straussner, ed., *Clinical Work with Substance-Abusing Clients*, 135–52.
    New York: Guilford.

Fusfeld, D. and T. Bates. 1984. *The Political Economy of the Urban Ghetto*. Car-
    bondale: Southern Illinois University Press.

Galanter, M., R. Castaneda, and H. Franco. 1991. Group therapy and self-help
    groups. In R. J. Frances and S. I. Miller, eds., *Clinical Textbook of Addictive
    Disorders*, 431–51. New York: Guilford.

Galanter, M., S. Egelko, G. DeLeon, and C. Rohrs. 1992. Crack/cocaine abusers in
    the general hospital: Combined professional and peer-led treatment. Unpub-
    lished paper. New York: New York University School of Medicine.

Galanter, M., H. Franco, A. Kim, E. J. Metzger, and G. DeLeon. 1993. Inpatient
    treatment for the dually diagnosed: A peer-led model for acute and intermediate
    care. In J. Solomon, S. Zimberg, and E. Schollar, eds., *Dual Diagnosis: Eval-
    uation, Treatment, Training, and Program Development*, 171–92. New York:
    Plenum.

Garvin, C. D. 1991. Barriers to effective social action by groups. *Social Work with
    Groups* 14:65–76.

Geiger, H. J. 1984. Community health centers: Health care as an instrument of
    social change. In V. W. Sidel and R. Sidel, eds., *Reforming Medicine: Lessons
    of the Last Quarter Century*, 210–17. New York: Pantheon.

Germain, C. B. and A. Gitterman. 1996. *The Life Model of Social Work Practice:
    Advances in Theory and Practice*. New York: Columbia University Press.

Gfroerer, J. 1987. Correlation between drug use by teenagers and drug use by older
    family members. *American Journal of Drug Alcohol Abuse* 13:95–108.

Gibson, C. M. 1993. Empowerment theory and practice with adolescents of color
    in the child welfare system. *Families in Society* 74:387–95.

Gitterman, A. 1994. Conversation with author. Columbia University School of So-
    cial Work, New York, NY.

Gitterman, A. and L. Shulman. 1994. *Mutual Aid Groups, Vulnerable Populations
    and the Life Cycle*. New York: Columbia University Press.

Golan, N. 1986. Crisis theory. In F. J. Turner, ed., *Social Work Treatment: Interlock-
    ing Theoretical Approaches*, 2nd ed., 499–534. New York: Free Press.

Goldner, V. 1985. Feminism and family therapy. *Family Process* 24:31–47.

Gomberg, E. 1988. Alcoholic women in treatment: The question of stigma and age.
    Alcohol and Alcoholism 23:507–14.

Gordon, A. and M. Zrull. 1991. Social networks and recovery: One year after in-
    patient treatment. *Journal of Substance Abuse Treatment* 8:143–52.

Gordon, J. U. 1994. African American perspective. In J. U. Gordon, ed., *Managing
    Multiculturalism in Substance Abuse Services*, 45–71. Thousand Oaks, CA:
    Sage.

————. 1993. A culturally specific approach to ethnic minority young adults. In
    E. M. Freeman, ed., *Substance Abuse Treatment: A Family Systems Perspective*,
    71–99. Newbury Park, CA: Sage.
Gorski, T. T. 1989. ACA recovery: How soon is too soon? *Alcoholism and Addiction*
    9:25–29.
Gottlieb, B. H. 1987. Using social support to protect and promote health. *Journal of*
    Primary Prevention 8:49–70.
Gowdy, E. A. and E. M. Freeman. 1993. Program supervision: Facilitating staff par-
    ticipation in program analysis, planning, and change. *Administration in Social*
    Work 17:39–58.
Granvold, D. K., ed. 1994. *Cognitive and Behavioral Treatment: Methods and Ap-*
    plications. Pacific Grove, CA: Brooks/Cole.
Gruber, J. and E. J. Trickett. 1987. Can we empower others? The paradox of em-
    powerment in an alternative public high school. *American Journal of Com-*
    munity Psychology 15:353–72.
Gulati, P. and G. Guess. 1990. The community-centered model: A garden-variety
    approach or a radical transformation of community practice? *Social Work*
    35:63–68.
Gullotta, T. P. 1987. Prevention's technology. *Journal of Primary Prevention*
    8:4–24.
Gunden, E. and S. Crisman. 1992. Leadership skills for empowerment. *Nursing*
    Administration Quarterly 16:6–10.
Gutheil, I. A. 1993. Rituals and termination procedures. *Smith College Studies in*
    Social Work 63:163–76.
Gutiérrez, L. 1990. Working with women of color: An empowerment perspective.
    Social Work 35:149–53.
Gutiérrez, L., L. GlenMaye, and K. DeLois. 1995. The organizational context of
    empowerment practice: Implications for social work administration. *Social*
    Work 40:249–58.
Gutiérrez, L. and P. Nurius. 1994. *Empowerment and Research for Empowerment*
    Practice. Seattle, WA: Center for Policy and Practice Research.
Gutiérrez, L. M. and R. Ortega. 1991. Developing methods to empower Latinos:
    The importance of groups. *Social Work with Groups* 14:23–43.
Hale, L. 1989. Interview by author. Hale House Foundation, New York, NY, 14 July.
————. 1994. Preserving and supporting black families. Paper presented at the Con-
    ference on Black Families, June 20. Kansas City, MO: Institute for the Study
    of Black Families.
Halim, M. 1992. Interview by author. Renaissance West Substance Abuse Treatment
    Center, Kansas City, MO, 2 September.
Hannan, M. T. and R. Freeman. 1989. *Organizational Ecology*. Cambridge, MA:
    Ballinger.

Hansen, W. 1988. Effective school-based approaches to drug abuse prevention. *Educational Leadership* 12:9–14.

Hanson, M. 1991. Alcoholism and other drug addictions. In A. Gitterman, ed., *Handbook of Social Work Practice with Vulnerable Populations*, 1–34. New York: Columbia University Press.

Hare-Mustin, R. T. 1987. The problem of gender in family therapy theory. *Family Process* 26:15–34.

Harper, F. D. 1991. Substance abuse and the black American family. *Urban Research Review* 13:1–5.

Harrison, W. D. 1995. Community development. In R. L. Edwards, ed., *Encyclopedia of Social Work*, 19th ed., 1:555–62. Washington, D.C.: National Association of Social Workers.

Hartman, A. 1995. Family therapy. In R. L. Edwards, ed., *Encyclopedia of Social Work*, 19th ed., 2:983–91. Washington, D.C.: National Association of Social Workers.

Hartman, A. and J. Laird. 1983. *Family-Centered Social Work Practice*. New York: Free Press.

Hawkins, J. D. and R. F. Catalano, Jr. 1992. *Communities That Care: Action for Drug Abuse Prevention*. San Francisco: Jossey-Bass.

Hawkins, J. D., R. F. Catalano, Jr., M. R. Gillmore, and E. A. Wells. 1989. Skills training for drug abusers: Generalization, maintenance, and effects on drug use. *Journal of Consulting and Clinical Psychology* 57:559–63.

Hawkins, J. D., R. F. Catalano, and E. A. Wells. 1986. Measuring effects of a skills training intervention for drug abusers. *Journal of Consulting and Clinical Psychology* 51:661–64.

Hayton, R. 1994. European American perspective: Some considerations. In J. U. Gordon, ed., *Managing Multiculturalism in Substance Abuse Services*, 99–116. Thousand Oaks, CA: Sage.

Heath, A. W. and M. D. Stanton. 1991. Family therapy. In R. J. Frances and S. I. Miller, eds., *Clinical Textbook of Addictive Disorders*, 406–30. New York: Guilford.

Hester, R. K. and W. R. Miller. 1989. Self-control training. In R. K. Hester and W. R. Miller, eds., *Handbook of Alcoholism Treatment Alternatives*, 141–49. New York: Pergamon.

Holcombe, S. 1995. *Managing to Empower: The Grameen Bank's Experience of Poverty Alleviation*. London: Zed Books.

Holland, T. P. 1995. Organizations: Context for social services delivery. In R. L. Edwards, ed., *Encyclopedia of Social Work*, 19th ed., 2:1787–1794. Washington, D.C.: National Association of Social Workers.

Horn, J. L., H. A. Skinner, K. Wanberg, and F. M. Foster. 1984. Alcohol Dependence Scale (ADS). Toronto, Canada: Addiction Research Foundation.

Hudson, W. 1982. *The Clinical Measurement Package: A Field Manual.* Chicago: Dorsey.

Hutchinson, J. R. and K. E. Nelson. 1985. How public agencies can provide family-centered services. *Social Casework* 66:367–72.

Ilgen, D. R. and H. J. Klein. 1988. Organizational behavior. *Annual Review of Psychology* 40:327–51.

Imbrogno, S. 1987. Group work practices in a policy system design. *Social Work with Groups* 10:25–31.

Indyk, D., R. Belville, S. Lachapelle, G. Gordon, and T. Dewart. 1993. A community-based approach to HIV case management: Systematizing the unmanageable. *Social Work* 38:380–87.

Innes, R. B. and C. A. Heflinger. 1989. An expanded model of community assessment: A case study. *Journal of Community Psychology* 17:225–35.

Israel, B. 1985. Social networks and social work: Implications for natural helper and community-level interventions. *Health Education Quarterly* 12:65–80.

Jackson, V. August 1995. A brief look at managed mental health care. Washington, D.C.: National Association of Social Workers, Office of Policy and Practice.

Jacobs, F. H. 1988. The state-of-the-art in family program evaluation. In H. Weiss and F. Jacobs, eds., *Final Report to the Mott Foundation: The Effectiveness and Evaluation of Family Support and Education Programs*, 64–98. Cambridge: Harvard Family Research Project.

Johnson, G. G. and M. Wahl. 1995. Families: Demographic shifts. In R. L. Edwards, ed., *Encyclopedia of Social Work*, 19th ed., 2:936–41. Washington, D.C.: National Association of Social Workers.

Johnson, V. E. 1986. *Intervention.* Minneapolis: Johnson Institute.

Joseph, H. 1992. Substance abuse and homelessness within inner cities. In J. H. Lowinson, P. Ruiz, R. Milliman, and J. G. Langrod, eds., *Substance Abuse: A Comprehensive Textbook*, 875–89. Baltimore: Williams and Wilkins.

Kahn, S. 1995. Community organization. In R. L. Edwards, ed., *Encyclopedia of Social Work*, 19th ed., 1:569–78. Washington, D.C.: National Association of Social Workers.

Kamerman, J. B. 1988. *Death in the Midst of Life.* Englewood Cliffs, NJ: Prentice Hall.

Kaminer, Y. 1991. Adolescent substance abuse. In R. J. Frances and S. I. Miller, eds., *Clinical Textbook of Addictive Disorders*, 320–46. New York: Guilford.

Katz, A. H. 1993. *Self-Help in America: A Social Movement Perspective.* New York: Twayne.

Kay, S. R., M. Kalathara, and A. E. Meinzer. 1989. Diagnosis and behavioral characteristics of psychiatric patients who abuse substances. *Hospital and Community Psychiatry* 40:1062–1064.

Keigher, S. M. 1994. The morning after deficit reduction: The poverty of U.S. maternal and child health policy (National Health Line). *Health and Social Work* 19:143–47.

Kerr, M. E. 1982. Application of family systems theory to a work system. In R. Sagar and K. Wiseman, eds., *Understanding Organizations*, 121–29. Washington, D.C.: Georgetown University Family Center.

Kimberly, J. R. 1980. The life cycle analogy and the study of organizations. In J. R. Kimberly, R. H. Miles, et al., eds., *The Organizational Life Cycle: Issues in the Creation, Transformation, and Decline of Organizations*, 119–27. San Francisco: Jossey-Bass.

Kleber, H. D. 1992. Federal role in substance abuse policy. Unpublished paper. Washington, D.C.: National Institute of Drug Abuse.

Klee, L., C. Schmidt, and G. Ames. 1991. Indicators of women's alcohol problems: What women themselves report. *The International Journal of the Addictions* 26:879–95.

Kolbe, L. J. 1986. Preventing drug abuse in the United States: Integrating the efforts of schools, communities, and science. *Journal of School Health* 56:357–63.

Kübler-Ross, E. 1969. *On Death and Dying*. New York: Macmillan.

Kunnes, R., R. Niven, T. Gustafson, M. Brooks, S. M. Levin, M. Edmunds, J. G. Trumble, and M. J. Coye. 1993. Financing and payment reform for primary health care and substance abuse treatment. *Journal of Addictive Disease* 12: 23–40.

Kurtz, L. F. 1997. Recovery, the 12 step movement, and politics. *Social Work* 42: 403–6.

Kurtz, L. F. and T. J. Powell. 1987. Three approaches to understanding self-help groups. *Social Work with Groups* 10:69–80.

Kurtz, P. D., S. V. Jarvis, and G. L. Kurtz. 1991. Problems of homeless youths: Empirical findings and human service issues. *Social Work* 36:309–14.

Lawson, A. W. 1989. Substance abuse problems of the elderly: Considerations for treatment and prevention. In G. W. Lawson and A. W. Lawson, eds., *Alcoholism and Substance Abuse in Special Populations*, 95–113. Rockville, MD: Aspen.

Lebow, J. A. 1985. Gender and sex role issues as family secrets. *Journal of Strategic and Systemic Therapies* 4:32–41.

Lee, J. M. 1994. Historical and theoretical considerations: Implications for multiculturalism in substance abuse services. In J. U. Gordon, ed., *Managing Multiculturalism in Substance Abuse Services*, 3–21. Thousand Oaks, CA: Sage.

LePantois, J. 1986. Group therapy for children of substance abusers. *Social Work with Groups* 9:39–51.

Lerner, M. 1979. Surplus powerlessness. *Social Policy* 9 (4):18–27.

Leukefeld, C. G. and R. J. Battjes. 1992. Intravenous drug use and AIDS: Community approaches to social work revisited. In E. M. Freeman, ed., *The Addiction Process: Effective Social Work Approaches*, 123–35. New York: Longman.

Levin, S. M., J. G. Trumble, M. Edmunds, J. M. Statman, and R. C. Petersen. 1993. Perspectives on linkage of primary health care and substance abuse treatment (Editorial). *Journal of Addictive Diseases* 12:1–8.

Lewis, E. 1991. Social change and citizen action: A philosophical exploration for modern social group work. *Social Work with Groups* 14:23–34.

Lewis, E. A. and B. Ford. 1990. The network utilization project: Incorporating traditional strengths of African American families into group work practice. *Social Work with Groups* 13:7–22.

Lewis, G. R. and S. M. Jordan. 1989. Treatment of the gay or lesbian alcoholic. In G. W. Lawson and A. W. Lawson, eds., *Alcoholism and Substance Abuse in Special Populations*, 165–203. Rockville, MD: Aspen.

Lex, B. W. 1991. Some gender differences in alcohol and polysubstance users. *Health Psychology* 10:121–32.

Linney, J. A. and A. Wandersman. 1991. Prevention plus III (Assessing alcohol and other drug prevention programs at the school and community level: A four-step guide to useful program assessment). Rockville, MD: Office of Substance Abuse Prevention, U.S. Department of Health and Human Services.

Logan, S. and E. M. Freeman. 1988. Adolescent pregnancy programs: Training manual and technical assistance for service providers. Lawrence: University of Kansas Institute for Black Leadership Development and Research.

Lovell, A. and J. Sokolovsky. 1990. Social networks and social supports. In J. P. Morrissey and D. L. Dennis, eds., *Homelessness and Mental Illness: Toward the Next Generation of Research Studies*, 28–35. Bethesda, MD: National Institute of Mental Health.

Lundy, C. 1987. Sex-role conflict in female alcoholics: A critical review of the literature. *Alcoholism Treatment Quarterly* 4 (1):69–78.

Lurigio, A. J. and R. Davis. 1992. Taking the war on drugs to the streets: The perceptual impact of four neighborhood drug programs. *Crime and Delinquency* 38:522–38.

Lynn, D. R. 1986. Things that work: Peer helpers—increasing positive student involvement in school. *School Counselor* 34:62–66.

McCann, O. T. 1995. Interview by author. Children's Mercy Hospital, Team for Infants Endangered by Substance Abuse, Kansas City, MO, 6 June.

McCarthy, M. 1993. The myth of the drunken Indian. *Anchorage Daily News. We Alaskans Supplement*, 21 March, G6–7.

McCrady, B. S. and S. Irvine. 1989. Self-help groups. In R. K. Hester and W. R. Miller, eds., *Handbook of Alcoholism Treatment Alternatives*, 153–69. New York: Pergamon.

Mackey, P. W., D. M. Donovan, and G. A. Marlatt. 1991. Cognitive and behavioral approaches to alcohol abuse. In R. J. Frances and S. I. Miller, eds., *Clinical Textbook of Addictive Disorders*, 452–81. New York: Guilford.

McKillip, J. 1987. *Need Analysis: Tools for the Human Services and Education.* Newbury Park, CA: Sage.

McLellan, A. T. and A. I. Alterman. 1991. Patient-treatment matching: A conceptual and methodological review with suggestions for future research. In R. W. Pickens, C. G. Leukefeld, and C. R. Schuster, eds., *Improving Drug Abuse Treatment,* 114–35 (NIDA Research Monograph 106). Rockville, MD: National Institute on Drug Abuse.

McLellen, A. T., L. Luborsky, and C. P. O'Brien. 1985. Improved diagnostic instrument for substance abuse patients: The Addiction Severity Index. *Journal of Nervous and Mental Disorders* 168:26–33.

McNeece, C. A. and D. M. DiNitto. 1994. *Chemical Dependency: A Systems Approach.* Englewood, NJ: Prentice-Hall.

McNeil, J. S. 1995. Bereavement and loss. In R. L. Edwards, ed., *Encyclopedia of Social Work,* 19th ed., 1:284–91. Washington, D.C.: National Association of Social Workers.

McRoy, R. G., C. T. Shorkey, and E. Garcia. 1985. Alcohol use and abuse among Mexican Americans. In E. M. Freeman, ed., *Social Work Practice with Clients Who Have Alcohol Problems,* 229–41. Springfield, IL: Thomas.

Malekoff, A. 1994. Action research: An approach to preventing substance abuse and promoting social competency. *Health and Social Work* 19:46–53.

Malloy, D. 1989. Peer intervention: An exploratory study. *Journal of Drug Issues* 19:319–36.

Marcenko, M. O., M. Spence, and C. Rohweder. 1994. Psychosocial characteristics of pregnant women with and without a history of substance abuse. *Health and Social Work* 19:17–22.

Marlatt, G. A. and W. H. George. 1984. Relapse prevention: Introduction and overview of the model. *British Journal of Addiction* 79:261–73.

Martinez-Brawley, E. E. 1995. Community. In R. L. Edwards, ed., *Encyclopedia of Social Work,* 19th ed., 1:539–48. Washington, D.C.: National Association of Social Workers.

Massey, R. and L. Neidigh. 1990. Evaluating and improving the functioning of peer-based alcohol abuse prevention organization. *Journal of Alcohol and Drug Education* 35:24–35.

May, P. A. 1982. Substance abuse and American Indians: Prevalence and susceptibility. *International Journal of the Addictions* 17:1185–1209.

Mbanuso, M. 1991. African Americans, public housing, and drug-related evictions: A structural analysis. *Urban Research Review* 13:6–9.

Meir, K. J. 1994. *The Politics of Sin: Drugs, Alcohol, and Public Policy.* Armonk, NY: M. E. Sharpe.

Milgram, D. and J. S. Rubin. 1992. Resisting resistance: Involuntary substance abuse group therapy. *Social Work with Groups* 15:95–110.

Miller, W. R. 1992. Motivational counseling and brief interventions in the addictive behaviors. Seminar conducted at the Research Institute on Addictions, Buffalo, New York.

———. 1983. Motivational interviewing with problem drinkers. *Behavioral Psychotherapy* 11:147–72.

Miller, W. R. and R. K. Hester, eds. 1989. *Handbook of Alcoholism Treatment Approaches: Effective Alternatives*. New York: Pergamon.

Minkoff, K. 1992. Program components of a comprehensive integrated care system for seriously mentally ill patients with substance disorders. In K. Minkoff and R. Drake, eds., *Dual Diagnosis of Major Mental Illness and Substance Disorders*, 13–27. San Francisco: Jossey-Bass.

———. 1989. An integrated treatment model for dual diagnosis of psychosis and addiction. *Hospital and Community Psychiatry* 40:1031–1036.

Molloy, J. P. 1990. Self-run, self-supported houses for more effective recovery from alcohol and drug addiction (DHHS Publication #ADM 90–1678). Washington, D.C.: U.S. Government Printing Office.

Mondros, J. B. and S. M. Wilson. 1994. *Organizing for Power and Empowerment*. New York: Columbia University Press.

Moreau, M. 1990. Empowerment through advocacy and consciousness raising: Implications of a structural approach to social work. *Journal of Sociology and Social Welfare* 17:53–67.

Morrell, C. 1996. Radicalizing recovery: Addiction, spirituality, and politics. *Social Work* 41:306–12.

Musto, D. E. 1987. *The American Disease: Origins of Narcotics Control*. New York: Oxford University Press.

National Association of Social Workers. 1996. Social workers urged to respond to governors' proposals on welfare and Medicaid (Government Relations Alert), 4 March. Washington, D.C.: National Association of Social Workers, Office of Government Relations.

———. 1996. *Highlights of Legislative and Executive Branch Issues*. Washington, D.C.: National Association of Social Workers, Office of Government Relations.

National Congress for Community Economic Development. 1991. *Human Investment—Community Profits* (Report and Recommendations of the Social Services and Economic Development Task Force). Washington, D.C.: National Congress for Community Economic Development.

National Institute on Drug Abuse. 1988. National household survey on drug abuse: Main findings 1985 (DHHS Publication No. ADM 88–1586). Rockville, MD: National Institute on Drug Abuse.

Nelson-Zlupo, P., E. Kauffman, and M. M. Dore. 1995. Gender differences in drug addiction and treatment: Implications for social work intervention with substance abusing women. *Social Work* 40:45–54.

New Alternatives Rehab Program. *Staff Handbook 1995*. Savannah, GA: New Alternatives Rehab Program.

New Alternatives Rehab Program, Clinical Director. 1996a. Interview by author. Savannah, GA, July.

New Alternatives Rehab Program, Staff. 1996b. Interview by author. Savannah, GA, July.

New Alternatives Rehab Program, Director. 1995a. Interview by author. Savannah, GA, August.

New Alternatives Rehab Program, Clinical Director. 1995b. Interview by author. Savannah, GA, August.

New Alternatives Rehab Program, Staff. 1995c. Interview by author. Savannah, GA, August.

New York Times. 1999. Crack mothers, crack babies and hope. 31 Dec., 17.

Nickerson, P. R. 1995. Solution-focused group therapy. *Social Work* 40:132–33.

Nowinski, J., S. Baker, and K. Carroll. 1995. Twelve-step facilitation therapy manual: A research guide for therapists treating individuals with alcohol abuse and dependence. Rockville, MD: U.S. Department of Health and Human Services, Public Health Service, National Institute of Health, National Institute on Alcohol Addiction and Abuse.

Nunes-Dinis, M. and R. P. Barth. 1993. Cocaine treatment and outcome. *Social Work* 38:611–17.

Nurius, P. S. and S. S. Berlin. 1994. Treatment of negative self-concept and depression. In D. K. Granvold, ed., *Cognitive and Behavioral Treatment: Methods and Applications*, 249–71. Pacific Grove, CA: Brooks/Cole.

O'Connor, G. G. and L. McCord. 1991. Networking among social service providers: An expanded and transformed practice. *The Journal of Applied Social Sciences* 15:7–29.

O'Dell, K. and E. M. Freeman. 1997. Ethnographic research methods for multicultural needs assessments: A systems change perspective. In J. Gordon, ed., *A Systems Change Perspective*, 315–20. New York: Mellen.

O'Donnell, S. 1993. Involving clients in welfare policy-making. *Social Work* 38:629–35.

O'Hare, T. 1995. Mental health problems and alcohol abuse: Co-occurrence and gender differences. *Social Work* 20:207–14.

Oliver, W. 1989. Black males and social problems: Prevention through Africentric socialization. *Journal of Black Studies* 20:15–39.

Palmer, J., E. Davis, A. Sher, and S. Hicks. 1989. High school senior athletes as peer educators and role models: An innovative approach to drug prevention. *Journal of Alcohol and Drug Abuse Education* 35:23–27.

Papp, P. 1983. *The Process of Change*. New York: Guilford.

Patton, M. Q. 1986. *Utilization Focused Evaluation*. 2nd ed. Beverly Hills: Sage.

Pelly-Effrat, M. P. 1974. Approaches to community: Conflicts and complementaries. In M. P. Effrat, ed., *The Community: Approaches and Applications*, 1–32. New York: Free Press.

Pennekamp, M. 1980. Merged funding alternatives: A base for integrated service delivery (Trends and Issues). *Social Work in Education* 1:66–73.

Perlmutter, F. D. 1995. Administering alternative social programs. In L. Ginsberg and P. R. Keys, eds., *New Management in Human Services*, 203–18. Washington, D.C.: National Association of Social Workers.

Pilat, J., and S. Boomhower-Kresser. 1992. Dynamics of alcoholism and child sexual abuse. In E. M. Freeman, ed., *The Addiction Process: Effective Social Work Approaches*, 65–78. White Plains, NY: Longman.

Pinderhughes, E. 1989. *Understanding Race, Ethnicity, and Power: The Key to Efficacy in Clinical Practice*. New York: Free Press.

———. 1983. Empowerment for our clients and ourselves. *Social Casework* 64:39–46.

Pinderhughes, E. B. and A. B. Pittman. 1985. A social cultural treatment model: Empowerment of worker and client. In M. W. Day, ed., *The Socio-Cultural Dimensions of Mental Health*, 82–111. New York: Vantage.

Plasse, B. R. 1995. Parenting groups for recovering addicts in a day treatment center. *Social Work* 40:65–74.

Poole, D. 1995. Beyond the rhetoric: Shared responsibility versus the Contract with America. *Health and Social Work* 20:83–86.

Porter, B. A., P. J. Lerch, and M. Lewis. 1986. Theory into practice: ORTF—A peer modeling program in Akron, Ohio. *Individual Psychology Journal of Adlerian Theory, Research, and Practice* 42:178–90.

Power, K. G., D. W. A. Jerrom, R. J. Simpson, M. J. Mitchell, and V. Swanson. 1989. A controlled comparison of cognitive-behavioral therapy, diazepam and placebo in the management of generalized anxiety. *Behavioral Psychotherapy* 17:1–14.

Pratt, C. W. and K. Gill. 1990. Sharing research knowledge to empower people who are chronically mentally ill. *Psychosocial Rehabilitation Journal* 13:75–79.

Price, R. H. and S. E. Smith. 1985. *A Guide to Evaluating Prevention Programs in Mental Health* (Publication No. [ADM] 85–1365). Washington, D.C.: U.S. Government Printing Office.

Primm, B. J. 1992. Future outlook: Treatment improvement. Unpublished paper. Washington, D.C.: National Institute of Drug Abuse.

Prochaska, J. O., C. C. DiClement, and J. C. Norcross. 1992. In search of how people change: Applications to addictive behaviors. *American Psychologist* 47:1102–1114.

Pulice, R. T., S. R. Lyman, and L. L. McCornick. 1994. A study of provider perceptions of individuals with dual disorders. *Journal of Mental Health Administration* 21:92–99.

Quintana, S. M. and W. Holahan. 1992. Termination in short-term counseling: Comparison of successful and unsuccessful cases. *Journal of Counseling Psychology* 39:299–305.

Rapp, C. A., W. Shera, and W. Kisthardt. 1993. Research strategies for consumer empowerment of people with severe mental illness. *Social Work* 38:727–35.

Rappaport, J. 1987. Terms of empowerment/exemplars of prevention: Toward a theory for community psychology. *American Journal of Community Psychology* 15:121–48.

———. 1984. Studies in empowerment: Introduction to the issues. In J. Rappaport and R. Hess, eds., *Studies in Empowerment: Steps Toward Understanding and Action*, 1–8. New York: Haworth.

———. 1981. In praise of paradox: A social policy of empowerment over prevention. *American Journal of Community Psychology* 9:1–25.

Rappaport, J., C. Swift, and R. Hess, eds. 1984. *Studies in Empowerment: Steps Toward Understanding and Action*. New York: Haworth.

Rasheed, J. M. 1996. Teaching Africentric practice with black males and families. Paper presented at the Annual Program Meeting of the Council on Social Work Education, Chicago, IL.

Read, M. R., E. C. Penick, and E. J. Nickel. 1993. Treatment for dually diagnosed clients. In E. M. Freeman, ed., *Substance Abuse Treatment: A Family Systems Perspective*, 123–56. Newbury Park, CA: Sage.

Reed, B. T. 1987. Developing women-sensitive drug dependence treatment services: Why so difficult? *Journal of Psychoactive Drugs* 19:151–64.

Recovery Works Dual Diagnosis Rehab Program. *Client Handbook 1994*. New York: Recovery Works Dual Diagnosis Rehab Program.

———. *Program Procedures Manual 1993*. New York: Recovery Works Dual Diagnosis Rehab Program.

———. *Staff Procedures Manual 1993*. New York: Recovery Works Dual Diagnosis Rehab Program.

Recovery Works Dual Diagnosis Rehab Program, Director. 1995. Interview by author. New York, NY.

Recovery Works Dual Diagnosis Rehab Program, Director and Staff. 1994. Interview by author. New York, NY.

Restore and Repair Perinatal Program for Women and Children. *Client Handbook 1995*. Los Angeles: Restore and Repair Perinatal Program for Women and Children.

———. *Program Procedures Manual 1995*. Los Angeles: Restore and Repair Perinatal Program for Women and Children.

———. *Staff Procedures Manual 1995*. Los Angeles, CA: Restore and Repair Perinatal Program for Women and Children.

Restore and Repair Perinatal Program for Women and Children, Director and Staff. 1996. Interview by author. Los Angeles, CA, June.

Restore and Repair Perinatal Program for Women and Children, Staff. 1995. Interview by author. Los Angeles, CA, December.

Restore and Repair Perinatal Program for Women and Children, Director. 1994. Interview by author. Los Angeles, CA, July.

Ridgely, S., H. H. Goldman, and M. Willenbring. 1990. Barriers to the care of persons with dual diagnoses: Organizational and financing issues. *Schizophrenia Bulletin* 16:123–32.

Robbins, M. L. 1994. Native American perspective. In J. U. Gordon, ed., *Managing Multiculturalism in Substance Abuse Services*, 148–76. Thousand Oaks, CA: Sage.

Robinson, S. D. 1984. Women and alcohol abuse—Factors involved in successful interventions. *The International Journal of the Addictions* 19:601–11.

Rogan, A. 1986. Recovery from alcoholism: Issues for black and Native-American alcoholics. *Alcohol Health and Research World* 2:42–44.

Rogers, R. L. and C. S. McMillan. 1989. *The Healing Bond: Treating Addictions in Groups*. New York: Norton.

Rooney, R. H. 1992. Work with involuntary clients in groups. In R. H. Rooney, ed., *Strategies for Work with Involuntary Clients*, 279–308. New York: Columbia University Press.

Rosenbaum, D. P., A. J. Lurigio, and P. J. Lavrakas. 1989. Enhancing citizen participation and solving serious crime: A national evaluation of crime stoppers programs. *Crime and Delinquency* 35:401–20.

Rounsaville, B. J. and K. M. Carroll. 1992. Individual psychotherapy for drug abusers. In J. H. Lowinson, P. Ruiz, R. Milliman, and J. G. Langrod, eds., *Substance Abuse: A Comprehensive Textbook*, 2nd ed., 496–507. Baltimore: Williams and Wilkins.

Rowe, D. and C. Grills. 1993. African-centered drug treatment: An alternative conceptual paradigm for drug counseling with African-American clients. *Journal of Psychoactive Drugs* 25:21–31.

Rubin, H. J. and I. Rubin. 1986. *Community Organizing and Development*. Columbus, OH: Bobbs-Merrill.

Rutter, T. 1987. Psychosocial resilience and protective mechanisms. *American Journal of Orthopsychiatry* 57:316–32.

Safer, D. 1987. Substance abuse by young adult chronic patients. *Hospital and Community Psychiatry* 38:511–14.

Sandmaier, M. 1980. Alcoholics invisible: The ordeal of the female alcoholic. *Public Policy* 5:25–30.

Saunders, D. N. 1995. Substance abuse: Federal, state, and local policies. In R. L. Edwards, ed., *Encyclopedia of Social Work*, 19th ed., 3:2338–2347. Washington, D.C.: National Association of Social Workers.

Schilit, R. and E. Gomberg. 1987. Social support structures of women in treatment for alcoholism. *Health and Social Work* 5:187–95.

Schinke, S. P., G. J. Botvin, and M. A. Orlandi. 1991. *Substance Abuse in Children and Adolescents: Evaluation and Intervention*. Newbury Park, CA: Sage.

Schleifer, S. J., B. R. Delaney, S. Tross, and S. E. Keller. 1991. AIDS and addictions. In R. J. Frances and S. I. Miller, eds., *Clinical Textbook of Addictive Disorders*, 299–319. New York: Guilford.

Schofield, R. 1980. Quality circles and educational systems change. Paper presented at the National School Social Work Conference. Denver: National Association of Social Workers.

Schonfeld, L. and L. W. Dupree. 1991. Antecedents of drinking for early- and late-onset elderly alcohol abusers. *Journal of Studies on Alcohol* 52:587–92.

Schopler, J. H. and M. J. Galinsky. 1995. Group practice overview. In R. L. Edwards, ed., *Encyclopedia of Social Work*, 19th ed., 2:1129–1142. Washington, D.C.: National Association of Social Workers.

Sciacca, K. 1991. An integrated treatment approach for severely mentally ill individuals and substance disorders. In K. Minkoff and R. Drake, eds., *Dual Diagnosis of Major Mental Illness and Substance Disorders*, 69–84. San Francisco: Jossey-Bass.

Segal, S. P., C. Silverman, and T. Temkin. 1993. Empowerment and self-help agency practice for people with mental disabilities. *Social Work* 38:705–12.

Selvini-Palazzoli, M., L. Boscolo, G. Cecchin, and G. Prata. 1978. *Paradox and Counter Paradox*. New York: Jason Aronson.

Selvini-Palazzoli, M., S. Cirillo, M. Selvini, and A. Sorrentino. 1989. *Family Games*. New York: Norton.

Shaffer, H. and J. Kauffman. 1985. The clinical assessment and diagnosis of addiction. In T. E. Bratter and G. G. Forrest, eds., *Alcoholism and Substance Abuse*, 225–51. New York: Free Press.

Shaffer, J. and M. D. Galinsky. 1989. *Models of Group Therapy*. 2nd ed. Englewood Cliffs, N.J.: Prentice-Hall.

Shapiro, B. Z. 1991. Social action, the group, and society. *Social Work with Groups* 14:7–21.

Sherraden, M. W. 1991. *Assets and the Poor: A New American Welfare Policy*. New York: M. E. Sharpe.

Shorkey, C. T. 1994. Use of behavioral methods with individuals recovering from substance dependence. In D. K. Granvold, ed., *Cognitive and Behavioral Treatment: Methods and Applications*, 135–58. Pacific Grove, CA: Brooks/Cole.

Shorkey, C. T. and W. Rosen. 1993. Alcohol addiction and codependency. In E. M. Freeman, ed., *Substance Abuse Treatment: A Family Systems Perspective*, 100–22. Newbury Park, CA: Sage.

Shulman, L. 1992. *The Skills of Helping: Individuals, Families, and Groups.* Itasca, IL: Peacock.

Shure, M. B. and G. Spivack. 1988. Interpersonal cognitive problem-solving. In R. Price, E. L. Cowen, R. P. Lorion, and J. Ramos-McKay, eds., *14 Ounces of Prevention: A Casebook for Practitioners*, 69–82. Washington, D.C.: American Psychological Association.

Siebold, C. 1992. Forced termination: Reconsidering the theory and techniques. *Smith College Studies in Social Work* 63:324–41.

Siegel, L. M., C. C. Attkisson, and L. G. Carson. 1995. Need identification and program planning in the community context. In J. E. Tropman, J. Erlich, and J. Rothman, eds., *Tactics and Techniques of Community Intervention*, 3rd ed., 10–34. Itasca, IL: Peacock.

Silver, R. L. and C. B. Wortman. 1980. Coping with undesirable life events. In J. Garber, eds., *Human Helplessness: Theory and Applications*, 279–340. New York: Basic.

Sisson, R. W. and N. H. Azrin. 1989. The community reinforcement approach. In R. K. Hester and W. R. Miller, eds., *Handbook of Alcoholism Treatment Alternatives*, 242–58. New York: Pergamon.

Skirrow, J. and E. Sawka. 1987. Alcohol and drug abuse prevention strategies—An overview. *Contemporary Drug Problems* 14:147–51.

Slaughter, D. T. 1988. Programs for racially and ethnically diverse American families: Some critical issues. In H. B. Weiss and F. H. Jacobs, eds., *Evaluating Family Programs*, 461–76. Hawthorne, NY: Aldine.

Smart, R. G. and E. M. Adlaf. 1998. Alcohol and drug use among the elderly: Trends in use and characteristics of users. *Canadian Journal of Public Health* 79:236–42.

Smyth, N. J. 1995. Substance abuse: Direct practice. In R. L. Edwards, ed., *Encyclopedia of Social Work*, 19th ed., 3:2328–2337. Washington, D.C.: National Association of Social Workers.

Solomon, B. 1987. Empowerment: Social work in oppressed communities. *Journal of Social Work Practice* 2:79–91.

Spaulding, J. and P. Balch. 1983. A brief history of primary prevention in the twentieth century: 1908–1980. *American Journal of Community Psychology* 11:59–80.

Straussner, S. L. 1993. Assessment and treatment of clients with alcohol and other drug problems: An overview. In S. L. Straussner, ed., *Clinical Work with Substance-Abusing Clients*, 3–30. New York: Guilford.

Strom, K. and W. J. Gingerich. 1993. Educating students for new market realities. *Journal of Social Work Education* 29:78–87.

Surls, R., Commissioner. 1994. Conversation with author. State Department of Mental Health, Albany, NY, November.

————. 1994. Interview by author. State Department of Mental Health, Albany, NY, 28 October.

Syme, S. 1986. Strategies for health promotion. *Preventive Medicine* 15:492–507.

Taber, M. A. 1988. A theory of accountability for the human services and the implications for social program design. *Social Work with Groups* 9:115–26.

Taylor, J. 1994. Rules on electronic transfers of money are being tightened by U.S. Treasury (Economy). *The Wall Street Journal* XCIV (26 September), A2.

Tebbitt, B. 1993. Demystifying organizational empowerment. *Journal of Nursing Administration* 23:18–23.

Thomas, E. J. 1994. Evaluation, advanced development, and the unilateral family therapy experiment. In J. Rothman and E. Thomas, eds., *Intervention Research: Design and Development for the Human Services*, 267–95. New York: Haworth.

Thomas, K. W. and B. A. Velthouse. 1990. Cognitive elements of empowerment: An "interpretive" model of intrinsic task motivation. *Academy of Management Review* 15:666–81.

Tobler, N. S. 1986. Meta-analysis of 143 adolescent drug prevention programs: Quantitative outcome results of program participants compared to a control or comparison group. *Journal of Drug Issues* 16:537–67.

Toseland, R. W. and M. Siporin. 1986. When to recommend group treatment: A review of the clinical and the research literature. *International Journal of Group Psychotherapy* 36:171–201.

Toumbourou, B. A. and M. Hamilton. 1993. Perceived client and program moderators of successful therapeutic community treatment for drug addiction. *International Journal of the Addictions* 28:1127–1146.

Treadway, D. C. 1989. *Before It's Too Late: Working with Substance Abusers in the Family*. New York: Norton.

Tropman, J. E. 1995. Community needs assessment. In R. L. Edwards, ed., *Encyclopedia of Social Work*, 19th ed., 1:563–69. Washington, D.C.: National Association of Social Workers.

Tropp, E. 1971. Social group work: The developmental approach. In R. Morris, ed., *Encyclopedia of Social Work*, 16th ed., 2:1246–1252. New York: National Association of Social Workers.

Tucker, M. B. 1985. U.S. ethnic minorities and drug use: An assessment of the science and practice. *International Journal of the Addictions* 20:1021–1047.

Turnbull, J. 1989. Treatment issues for alcoholic women. *Social Casework* 70:364–69.

Turner, F. J. 1996. *Social Work Treatment*. New York: Free Press.

U.S. Department of Health and Human Services. 1990. Report to Congress on the drug abuse prevention program for runaway and homeless youth, fiscal year 1990. Washington, D.C.: U.S. Government Printing Office.

Urbancic, J. 1992. Empowerment support with adult female survivors of childhood incest: Part I—Theories and research. *Archives of Psychiatric Nursing* 6:275–81.

Van Den Bergh, N. 1991. Having bitten the apple: A feminist perspective on addictions. In N. Van Den Bergh, ed., *Feminist Perspectives on Addictions*, 3–30. New York: Springer.

Van Wormer, K. 1987. Training social work students for practice with substance abusers: An ecological approach. *Journal of Social Work Education* 23:47–56.

Verity, C. W. 1982. The role of business in community service. *Journal of Community Action* 1 (1): 5–7.

Wallace, B. C. 1991. *Crack Cocaine: A Practical Treatment Approach for the Chemically Dependent.* New York: Brunner/Mazel.

Wallack, L. 1984. Practice issues, ethical concerns and future directions in the prevention of alcohol-related problems. *Journal of Primary Prevention* 4:199–224.

Wallerstein, N. 1992. Powerlessness, empowerment, and health: Implications for health promotion programs. *American Journal of Health Promotion* 6:197–205.

Wallerstein, N. and E. Bernstein. 1988. Empowerment education: Freire's ideas adapted to health education. *Health Education Quarterly* 15:379–94.

Walter, D. K. and R. W. Crocker. 1988. Measuring family system outcomes. In H. B. Weiss and F. H. Jacobs, eds., *Evaluating Family Programs*, 153–76. Hawthorne, NY: Aldine.

Walters, M., B. Carter, P. Papp, and O. Silverstein. 1988. *The Invisible Web: Gender Patterns in Family Relationships.* New York: Guilford.

Ward, P. M., ed. 1982. *Self-Help Housing: A Critique.* London: Manshell.

Wassermann, S. 1991. Louis E. Raths' theories of empowerment. *Childhood Education* 10:235–39.

Watson, M. 1990. The problem of drug addiction: Women, children, and families. Paper presented at the Black Women's Leadership Conference, Kansas City, MO, 25 February.

Weick, A. 1985. Overturning the medical model. *Social Work* 30:310–15.

Weick, A., C. Rapp, W. P. Sullivan, and W. Kisthardt. 1989. A strengths perspective for social work practice. *Social Work* 34:350–54.

Weil, M. O. and D. N. Gamble. 1995. Community practice models. In R. L. Edwards, ed., *Encyclopedia of Social Work*, 19th ed., 1:577–93. Washington, D.C.: National Association of Social Workers.

Weiss, C. H. 1983. The stakeholder approach to evaluation: Origins and promise. In A. S. Bryk, ed., *Stakeholder-Based Evaluation*, 3–14. San Francisco: Jossey-Bass.

Weiss, R. D., S. M. Mirin, and R. J. Frances. 1992. The myth of the typical dual diagnosis patient. *Hospital and Community Psychiatry* 43:107–108.

Westermeyer, J. and J. Neider. 1988. Social networks and psychopathology among substance abusers. *American Journal of Psychiatry* 145:1265–1269.

White, M. 1989. *Selected Papers.* Adelaide, South Australia: Dulwich Centre Publications.

White, M. and D. Epston. 1990. *Narrative Means to Therapeutic Ends.* New York: Norton.

Whitmore, E. and P. Kerans. 1988. Participation, empowerment, and welfare. *Canadian Review of Social Policy* 22:51–60.

Wilke, D. 1994. Women and alcoholism: How a male-as-norm bias affects research, assessment, and treatment. *Social Work* 19:29–35.

Wilson, W. J. 1987. *The Truly Disadvantaged: The Inner City, the Underclass, and Public Policy.* Chicago: University of Chicago Press.

Woodhouse, L. 1990. An exploratory study of the use of life history methods to determine treatment needs for female substance abusers. *Response* 13:12–15.

Wright, Jr., R., B. L. Kail, and R. F. Creecy. 1990. Culturally sensitive social work practice with black alcoholics. In S. M. L. Logan, E. M. Freeman, and R. G. McRoy, eds., *Social Work Practice with Black Families: A Culturally Specific Perspective*, 203–22. New York: Longman.

Yeich, S. and R. Levine. 1992. Participatory research's contribution to a conceptualization of empowerment. *Journal of Applied Social psychology* 22:1894–1908.

Young, T. 1987. Inhalant use among American Indian youth. *Child Psychiatry and Human Development* 18:37–46.

Zellman, G. L., P. D. Jacobson, H. DuPlessis, and M. R. DiMatteo. 1993. Detecting prenatal substance exposure: An exploratory analysis and policy discussion. *The Journal of Drug Issues* 23:375–87.

Zelvin, E. 1993. Treating the partners of substance abusers. In S. L. Straussner, ed., *Clinical Work with Substance-Abusing Clients*, 196–213. New York: Guilford.

Zimmerman, M. A. 1992. The measurement of psychological empowerment: Issues and strategies. Unpublished paper. Ann Arbor, MI: University of Michigan.

———. 1990. Toward a theory of learned hopelessness: A structural model analysis of participation and empowerment. *Journal of Research in Personality* 24:71–86.

Zimmerman, M. A. and J. Rappaport. 1988. Citizen participation, perceived control, and psychological empowerment. *American Journal of Community Psychology* 16:725–50.

Index

Adlaf, E. M., 64
African Americans. *See* Cultural diversity
Aguirre, L. M., 83, 98, 180, 191
Akabas, S., 50, 142, 148
Alanon, 215
Albee, G. W., 163, 164
Allen-Meares, P., 193
Alterman, A. I., 157
American Psychiatric Association, 197
Ames, G., 437, 442
Amuleru-Marshall, O., 397
Anderson, B., 185
Anderson, S. C., 192, 236, 297, 298
Annis, H. M., 187, 197, 296, 305
Asian and Pacific Islanders. *See* Cultural diversity
Assessment: barriers to an empowered process, 185; consumer roles related to, 188–189; empowerment evaluations related to, 194–195; empowerment tools—procedures for, 196 (figure 8.1), 199–200; purpose of, 184–185, 189–190; staff

roles for, 188–189; supports for an empowered process, 190–195; traditional tools for, 197–198; underlying empowerment philosophy, 186–188
Asante, M., 400, 403
Attkisson, C. C., 150, 154
Auerbach, E., 7
Azrin, N. H., 441

Baker, M. R., 145, 146, 147, 149, 201, 271
Baker, S., 440, 441
Balch, P., 164
Bandura, A., 10, 293, 305
Barth, R. P., 30, 63, 64, 145
Battjes, R. J., 53, 95
Bays, J., 97
Behroozi, C. S., 210, 211
Belville, R., 121
Berg, W. E., 437
Berger, R. L., 267
Berlin, R., 180
Berlin, S. S., 379, 388
Berman-Rossi, T., 211, 346